NEURODIVERSITY IN THE WORKPLACE

Neurodiversity in the Workplace presents a timely and needed perspective on the role and responsibility of employers and those working to increase the effectiveness of workplace practices to examine the many ways we preclude large segments of the population from employment; minimizing opportunities for building a truly inclusive work environment.

This collection provides an opportunity to look at how discrimination can occur across the employment process and what can be done to minimize the exclusionary practices that prevent neurodiverse individuals from getting into the workplace, advancing, thriving, and contributing as each of us desires to do. With expertise from leading professionals, this book provides a holistic look at the application of leadership theories in a neurodiverse context and how the workplace can be adapted to accommodate neurodiverse employees. This book also explores effective recruitment strategies by looking into applicant screening as well as interviewing and selection, adapting internal organizational resources to a neurodiverse workforce, and legal and regulatory environment considerations for autism hiring programs. Each chapter provides an overview of existing knowledge on effective workplace inclusion practices across the employment process, specific implications of research to date for a more neurodiversity-inclusive workplace, and what future research is needed to further inform these practices.

This volume is intended to increase awareness about the challenges and opportunities in making the workplace more neurodiversity-inclusive, making it instrumental for I/O and other psychologists. This book is also crucial for management and business consultants; employers; diversity, equity, and inclusion specialists; human resource professionals; and others interested in neurodiversity inclusion more broadly.

Susanne M. Bruyère, Ph.D., CRC, is professor of disability studies and director of the K. Lisa Yang and Hock E. Tan Institute on Employment and Disability, Cornell University ILR School, USA. The institute is a research, training, and technical assistance center focusing on disability inclusion in employment, education, and community.

Adrienne Colella, Ph.D., is the McFarland Distinguished Professor of Business at the A.B. Freeman School of Business, Tulane University, USA. She has published extensively in the area of disability and employment, as well as other human resource management topics.

SIOP Organizational Frontiers Series

The Organizational Frontiers Series is sponsored by the Society for Industrial and Organizational Psychology (SIOP). Launched in 1983 to make scientific contributions accessible to the field, the series publishes books addressing emerging theoretical developments, fundamental and translational research, and theory-driven practice in the field of Industrial-Organizational Psychology and related organizational science disciplines including organizational behavior, human resource management, and labor and industrial relations.

Books in this series aim to inform readers of significant advances in research; challenge the research and practice community to develop and adapt new ideas; and promote the use of scientific knowledge in the solution of public policy issues and increased organizational effectiveness.

The Series originated in the hope that it would facilitate continuous learning and spur research curiosity about organizational phenomena on the part of both scientists and practitioners.

The Society for Industrial and Organizational Psychology is an international professional association with an annual membership of more than 8,000 industrial-organizational (I-O) psychologists who study and apply scientific principles to the workplace. I-O psychologists serve as trusted partners to business, offering strategically focused and scientifically rigorous solutions for a number of workplace issues. SIOP's mission is to enhance human well-being and performance in organizational and work settings by promoting the science, practice, and teaching of I-O psychology. For more information about SIOP, please visit www.siop.org.

Neurodiversity in the Workplace
Interests, Issues, and Opportunities
Edited by Susanne M. Bruyère and Adrienne Colella

For more information about this series, please visit www.routledge.com/SIOP-Organizational-Frontiers-Series/book-series/SIOP

"This collection of chapters does what no other publication to date can claim: it integrates thoughtful and useful ideas and evidence on the incredibly important topic of neurodiversity. I'm so excited to see how this volume pushes the science and practice of I-O psychology forward!"

—**Eden King**, Ph.D. Rice University, Lynette S. Autrey Professor of Psychology
Co-Editor, *Journal of Business and Psychology*, Magister, Duncan College

"Susanne Bruyère and Adrienne Colella pose some challenging and thought-provoking questions to HR Professionals on creating an inclusive Neurodiverse Workforce."

—**Neil Barnett**, Director Inclusive Hiring People with Disabilities, Microsoft

"This book is a must read for organisations looking not only to establish a neurodiversity program, but sustain one. The book starts to discuss some of the more complex issues to sustain meaningful employment such as mental health, performance and career management. DXC Technology has been running a neurodiverse program since 2014; we wish we had this knowledge outlined in this book before we started!"

—**Michael Fieldhouse**, DXC Social Impact Practice Leader & Dandelion Program Executive

"Inclusive environments are the key for unlocking the power of human potential. This book provides a powerful perspective of how research around neurodiversity translates in the application to a work setting, and that ultimately creates exponential value for individuals, communities and business. The multifaceted approach the authors lay out, help us move from ideation to implementation. This is exactly what is needed for employers at the intersection of talent, diversity and to thrive in the future of work."

—**Hiren C. Shukla**, Global Neuro-Diverse Center of Excellence Leader, Executive Management, Ernst & Young LLP

"This volume provides a timely and critical contribution to the Organizational Frontiers Series. It explores diversity and inclusion within the workplace from a perspective often overlooked in our field – i.e., neurodiversity. The authors in this volume explore the challenges and opportunities involved in hiring and valuing an often talented but ignored segment of our population, applicants and employees whose behavior patterns and ways of seeing the world might deviate from more typical employees. Given increasing labor shortages, organizations face an increasing need to identify, select and promote employees who can contribute to their success, and as this volume shows, ways of effectively identifying neurodiverse applicants and employees who can make these contributions. The volume explores ways to maximize the integration and success of these workers by providing a work environment conducive to the success, sustainability and continued health of organizations and their members. In sum, this volume explores ways of enhancing an overlooked aspect of diversity by identifying creative practices that can also improve the quality of worklife for ALL organizational members."

—**Jeanette N Cleveland**, Ph.D., Professor Emeritus, Colorado State University

"Professors Colella and Bruyère have edited a timely and insightful book that explains what neurodiversity is and the employment law context around it. The various chapters of the book cover the entire employment process from an applicant's dilemma to disclose their neurodiversity to recruiting and selection, workplace accommodations, leadership, organizational diversity climate, performance management, well-being, and the overall experience of neurodiverse employees at work. This book answers many important and timely questions about neurodiversity at work, and it is helpful reading for anyone who wants to be an effective and inclusive coworker, supervisor, or leader in today's workforce."

—**María del Carmen Triana**, Ph.D., Professor and Cal Turner Chair in Moral Leadership at Vanderbilt University

"In the ground-breaking book *Neurodiversity in the Workplace*, authors from a variety of backgrounds and disciplines engage readers in discussing topics relevant to effectively managing organizations comprised of people with widely varying neurological functions. Readers will learn about the meaning and contested labeling of neurodiversity, the challenges and opportunities associated with workforce neurodiversity, as well as the many legal and social issues that neurodiversity poses for employers and employees alike. By including reviews of cutting-edge research and informative examples of supportive employment practices, Bruyère and Colella have produced a resource that is sure to promote more equitable workplace practices and stimulate new research aimed at understanding and improving the experiences of neurodivergent employees."

—**Susan E. Jackson**, PhD, Distinguished Professor Emerita, Rutgers University, Visiting Professor, University of Lucerne

NEURODIVERSITY IN THE WORKPLACE

Interests, Issues, and Opportunities

Edited by
Susanne M. Bruyère and Adrienne Colella

Routledge
Taylor & Francis Group
NEW YORK AND LONDON

SIOP
SOCIETY for INDUSTRIAL and ORGANIZATIONAL PSYCHOLOGY

Cover image: © Getty Images

First published 2022
by Routledge
605 Third Avenue, New York, NY 10158

and by Routledge
4 Park Square, Milton Park, Abingdon, Oxon, OX14 4RN

Routledge is an imprint of the Taylor & Francis Group, an informa business

Library of Congress Cataloging-in-Publication Data
Names: Bruyère, Susanne M., author. | Colella, Adrienne, 1961- editor.
Title: Neurodiversity in the workplace : interests, issues, and opportunities / Susanne M. Bruyère and Adrienne Colella.
Description: New York, NY : Routledge, 2022. | Series: New frontiers series
Identifiers: LCCN 2021061841 (print) | LCCN 2021061842 (ebook) | ISBN 9780367902971 (paperback) | ISBN 9780367902988 (hardback) | ISBN 9781003023616 (ebook)
Subjects: LCSH: Diversity in the workplace. | Neurodiversity.
Classification: LCC HF5549.5.M5 B78 2022 (print) | LCC HF5549.5.M5 (ebook) | DDC 658.30087/4—dc23/eng/20220103
LC record available at https://lccn.loc.gov/2021061841
LC ebook record available at https://lccn.loc.gov/2021061842

ISBN: 9780367902988 (hbk)
ISBN: 9780367902971 (pbk)
ISBN: 9781003023616 (ebk)

DOI: 10.4324/9781003023616

Typeset in Bembo
by Apex CoVantage, LLC

CONTENTS

SERIES FOREWORD

The world of work has traditionally offered few opportunities for individuals whose neurological functioning and behavior differ from the norm. In the last 20 years, there has been growing recognition that individuals exhibiting behaviors associated with autism, attention deficits, dyslexia, Tourette's syndrome, and the like often have much to offer to organizations. A recognition of this human variation in terms of neurodiversity rather than in terms of disorders that preclude participation in the workplace has important implications for workers and organizations.

Susanne M. Bruyère and Adrienne Colella have assembled an interdisciplinary team of authors to examine the challenges and opportunities organizations face as they develop programs and strategies for recruiting, selecting, training, and managing neurodiverse employees and to examine the impact of these strategies on the lives of individuals who have traditionally had limited opportunities for employment. A consistent theme running through many of these chapters is that traditional assumptions about who can or cannot contribute to organizations need to be re-examined, and that doing so is likely to bring important changes to organizations. These changes start with the processes used to recruit and screen job applicants, but in many ways, changing recruitment and selection systems represent the easy changes. Organizations that aspire to provide neurodiverse applicants with a fair chance to succeed and that hope to take advantage of what these applicants have to offer will face challenges in managing employees whose behaviors and capabilities do not conform with traditional assumptions, in providing a supportive climate and culture, and in accommodating the needs of a diverse set of employees. This volume examines the ways organizations can and should change to take advantage of what neurodiverse employees have to offer and also examines how they can take advantage of community partnerships and support from governmental agencies in rebuilding organizational systems to create conditions in which both diverse employees and organizations benefit from a recognition of neurodiversity. The volume describes programs that have been adopted by numerous organizations to attract and retain neurodiverse candidates and the lessons learned from these programs.

The goal of the *Organizational Frontiers* Series is to publish books that help to define and advance the frontiers of our knowledge about behavior in organizations and stimulate future research and applications. *Neurodiversity in the Workplace* not only meets this goal, it provides I-O psychologists with fresh perspectives and current thinking from a range of disciplines that will make an invaluable contribution to organizations and employees. We are proud to include this volume in the *Organizational Frontiers* Series.

Angelo DeNisi and Kevin Murphy
Series Co-Editors

1

NEURODIVERSITY IN THE WORKPLACE

An Overview of Interests, Issues and Opportunities

Susanne M. Bruyère and Adrienne Colella

Introduction

This volume is focused on neurodiversity in the workplace because the topic presents a timely and needed perspective on the role and responsibility of employers and those working to increase the effectiveness of workplace practices, such as I/O psychologists, to more fully examine the many ways in which we preclude large segments of the population from employment and thereby minimize opportunities for building a truly inclusive work environment. It has been over 30 years since the passage of the Americans with Disabilities Act, and yet working-age people with disabilities are less than half as likely to be employed in the United States as their nondisabled peers, 38% compared to 80% for those without disabilities (Erickson et al., 2021). The employment rate comparisons for those with autism provide an even starker employment gap, with young adults with autism having far lower rates of employment than other youth with disabilities (Roux et al., 2015). And for those who have been able to secure employment, many of these autistic young adults are in low-wage and part-time jobs (Roux et al., 2015), offering little opportunities for longer-term career growth and earning. In fact, even those with college educations and relevant training may have difficulty getting into the workplace, or when they do, they are underemployed; 46% of the autistic adults who are employed are over-educated or exceed the skill level needed for the roles they are in (Baldwin et al., 2014). Similar disparities are evidenced in other countries as well. In the United Kingdom, for example, the Office of National Statistics (ONS) reports that disabled people with autism are among those disabled people with the lowest employment rate, with just 22% of Autistic adults in any kind of employment (Office of National Statistics, 2021).

DOI: 10.4324/9781003023616-1

Individuals with autism certainly are not the only population in the United States (and globally, of course) who experience significant inequities in access to meaningful and remunerative employment. But the growing number of people diagnosed merits its focus in this volume, as does the response of select industry sectors in recognizing this group as a largely untapped and desired talent pool and the proactive response to see this as an opportunity. Approximately 1 in 44 children has been identified with autism, according to the Center for Disease Control (Maenner et al., 2021). This is up from 1 in 166 in 2005, or over a 300% growth in 15 years. So one of the compelling reasons to focus on this population is the increasing prevalence rate. The other is the stunning response from industry over the past 6 to 10 years to explore how to take the unique characteristics of a segment of this population, such as attention to detail, ability to focus and ability to see patterns in data, and capitalize on it to mutual advantage for both companies and the individual.

Yet hiring, including and promoting a neurodiverse workforce can present challenges that have not been addressed to any extent in the I/O literature. The purpose of this volume is to present what research has been done and to move the field forward into doing research and practice that promote a neurodiverse workforce. In this chapter, we discuss how the increased prevalence of this population, attention to the unique characteristics of Autistic people and the war for talent has led to a nexus of forces that have resulted in a potential revolution in appreciation of how difference can be an asset that should be valued and nurtured. We will talk about the evolution of affirmative hiring programs for people with disabilities in the context of the war on talent, provide some background information on neurodiversity with a focus on autism and provide an overview of the chapters that follow. The topics for this volume were selected because they provide an opportunity to look at how discrimination can occur across the employment process and what can be done to minimize the exclusionary practices that needlessly prevent Autistic individuals from getting into the workplace, advancing there and ultimately being able to thrive and contribute as each of us desires to do. The authors have been invited to contribute to this volume because of their unique expertise in addressing the topic, both from an organizational research perspective and from a diversity and inclusion perspective, particularly with a focus on neurodiversity. It is our hope that in the iterative story across these chapters about how to build a more neurodiversity-inclusive workplace, we will also learn lessons to take forward about how workplaces can be more welcoming to many other underrepresented groups.

The War for Talent and One Sector's Response

The term "war for talent" was coined by a group from McKinsey and Company in 1998 in a related publication by the same name (Chambers et al., 1998). The past two or three decades have shown a tremendous growth in the tech and tech-intensive corporate sectors, often far-outpacing the availability of qualified workers to fill the many new jobs created in response to the need. Almost a decade ago, McKinsey reported estimates suggesting that by 2020, employers in the world's richest nations will produce 18 million fewer college-educated workers than needed (Nielsen, 2012). More recently, Gartner (2019) reported that "today's organizations face a very dynamic talent landscape where it's increasingly hard to find and keep critical skills. Demand for talent is converging on the critical skills needed to meet business priorities, especially digitalization" (p. 3). Gartner TalentNeuron™ data reported that "49% of all job postings by S&P 100 companies in 2018 were for just 39 roles – all of which require in-demand skills such as data analysis, advanced coding and solution selling" (Gartner, 2019, p. 3). By 2030, it is estimated that the demand for skilled workers will outstrip supply, resulting in a global talent shortage of more than 85.2 million people (Korn, 2018).

One response to the need for talent has been an exploration by some companies to tap the talent of individuals with autism (Parmar, 2017; Szczerba, 2016). Employers in technology and tech-intensive sectors began to design and execute affirmative hiring programs for Autistic job candidates (Hedley et al., 2016; Hurley-Hanson & Giannantonio, 2017). An increasing number of companies are now following the early adopters, seeking to take advantage of what they see as a possible way to address needed talent for certain positions in which the distinct characteristics of Autistic individuals could be leveraged. This much more inclusive perspective takes the benefits of the perceived advantage of a diverse work team in creativity and productivity to a whole new level of what it means to be an inclusive workplace.

This trend has caught on in other large multinational software services and cybersecurity companies, as well as more recently in the finance and accounting sectors. SAP began its Autism at Work program in 2013 with an aspirational objective of having 1% of its workforce represented by employees with autism (Bort, 2013; Pisano & Austin, 2016). In Australia, DXC Technology, formerly Hewlett Packard Enterprise, initially building off of an approach used by Specialisterne, established The Dandelion Program in 2015 (Austin & Sonne, 2014) and added a contractual service offering for the company's government and later private-sector clients, drawing on the talents of people with autism. Microsoft's Autism Hiring Program began in 2015 and states that it is designed to identify and remove the barriers that would prevent those with autistic spectrum disorders from finding meaningful employment in the company, saying that "we built the Microsoft Neurodiversity Hiring Program on the belief that traditional recruiting does not allow individuals who are Neurodiverse to demonstrate their strengths and qualifications" (Microsoft, 2021). IBM has a long history of supporting people with disabilities and in 2015 initiated a neurodivergent recruitment program that by 2020 was in eight countries with plans to continue growing and expanding (IBM, 2020). With input from neurodivergent IBM employees, the company redesigned its hiring process to include more neurodivergent-friendly strategies with the intent of moving these approaches into the future mainstream of IBM hiring practices (IBM, 2020).

JPMorgan Chase launched Autism at Work in July 2015 as a four-person pilot. Since then, it has grown to include over 125 people in seven countries. People are hired into a variety of roles (reportedly now 40-plus roles in ten lines of business) in technology functions such as software engineering, app development, quality assurance, technology operations, and business analysis, with one employee reported to be a personal banker (JPMorgan Chase, 2019). In 2017, EY launched its second Center of Excellence (CoE) targeting Autistic employees in Dallas, where the team focuses on cybersecurity, robotic process automation, and complex analytics. The company also has been keeping comparative performance metrics on its CoE employees and reports that they perform a wide range of highly advanced tasks with remarkable quality and efficiency, with low error rates (EY, 2018), and continues to expand its programs to other parts of the United States (EY, 2021).

Despite the impact of the pandemic, the tech-sector economy continues to be strong, and companies are still looking for talent, suggesting that seeing what we can learn from these affirmative hiring programs for neurodiverse talent is timely, particularly given the drive to now learn more about improving employment equitably more broadly.

What Are Autism and Neurodiversity

Autism spectrum disorder (ASD) is a complex developmental condition that involves persistent challenges in social interaction, speech and nonverbal communication and restricted/repetitive behaviors. The effects of ASD and the severity of symptoms are different in each person (American Psychiatric Association, 2019). Autism differs greatly from person to person. Individuals with ASD demonstrate a wide range of abilities and characteristics, and it is important to understand that people with the same diagnosis may present themselves quite differently. While many people with autism have normal intelligence or above, others have mild or significant intellectual delays. In addition, people with ASD are at greater risk for some medical conditions such as sleep problems, seizures and mental illnesses (American Psychiatric Association, 2019).

Neurodiversity is the diversity of ways in which human brains think, learn, relate to others and interpret the world (Honeybourne, 2020). The term "neurodiversity" is credited to Judy Singer, who, in her book *Neurodiversity: The Birth of an Idea*, talks about how autism has risen from a medicalized diagnosis to become a social movement (2016). "Neurodiversity is a concept where neurological differences are to be recognized and respected as any other human variation. These differences can include those labeled with Dyspraxia, Dyslexia, Attention Deficit Hyperactivity Disorder, Dyscalculia, Autistic Spectrum, Tourette's Syndrome and others" (National Symposium on Neurodiversity at Syracuse University, 2011; Sumner & Brown, 2015).

The current interest in affirmative hiring of neurodiverse individuals, starting with a focus on Autistic individuals, is helping, however, to change the thinking about neurodiversity from something that has been labeled a "disorder" toward an appreciation of these differences as a natural part of human diversity and as having potential assets to be valued. In this volume, you will see a wide variety of language used describing the population of focus, based on the literature that our authors are drawing from, their own disciplinary backgrounds and familiarity with the changing thinking around how we talk about autism and Autistic people. Among autism advocates, the word "condition" is preferred to "disorder," which connotes something that is wrong. Some leaders in the autism self-advocacy movement prefer the terms "neurominority" or "neurodivergent," and you will see these and other terminology differences reflected in select chapters in this volume. The terminology is continually shifting and under discussion, reflecting a conceptual evolution as different societies and stakeholders progress their understanding of the meaning of variances in cognition and the implications for employment and the workplaces of the future (Doyle & McDowell, 2021).

In addition, some individuals with autism see their characteristics as a valued part of their identity, which they embrace. The following explanation from the Autistic Self Advocacy Society (ASAN) provides a fuller explanation of the conversation around language regarding autism and Autistic individuals:

> In the autism community, many self-advocates and their allies prefer terminology such as "Autistic," "Autistic person," or "Autistic individual" because we understand autism as an inherent part of an individual's identity – the same way one refers to "Muslims," "African-Americans," "Lesbian/Gay/Bisexual/Transgender/Queer," "Chinese," "gifted," "athletic," or "Jewish." On the other hand, many parents of Autistic people and professionals who work with Autistic people prefer terminology such as "person with autism," "people with autism," or "individual with ASD" because they do not consider autism to be part of an individual's identity and do not want their children to be identified or referred to as "Autistic." They want "person-first language," that puts "person" before any identifier such as "autism," in order to emphasize the humanity of their children.
>
> (ASAN, 2021)

In this volume, we want to acknowledge the growing preference of the autism advocacy community while staying true to the terminology in the literature that chapter authors are drawing from and respecting authors' language preferences and understanding of these current dialogues about identity-first versus person-first language that is occurring. Consistent with identity-first language, we capitalize the word "Autistic" when referring to an individual and use lowercase references to autism as a condition or diagnosis.

An Overview of This Neurodiversity SIOP Frontiers Research Volume

With this background about the interest in neurodiversity hiring and autism in particular, we proceed with an overview of the material in this volume, providing a brief overview of each chapter, highlighting why the chapter has been included in this volume and what it offers to the overall picture of understanding the initiatives, the challenges and the solutions being explored currently by companies, and that I/O psychologists can contribute to, in working to increase employment and workplace inclusion of neurodiverse individuals, especially those who are Autistic.

To begin, Chapter 2 explores how organizations can bolster their workplace inclusion in ways that consider the natural variation in human neurocognitive functioning to provide altered workplace environments that leverage the strengths of all employees. In a chapter entitled "Shaping Organizational Climates to Develop and Leverage Workforce Neurodiversity," by Sabrina Volpone, Derek Avery and Julie Wayne, the authors ask why "instead of placing the unnecessary burden on neurodivergent individuals, what if workplaces altered their environments so that all employees – including those who are neurodivergent – could easily apply their strengths at work?" Throughout the chapter, the authors discuss how neurotypical norms have dominated human resource management practices for so long that there is a crucial need to critically analyze these norms and establish new norms if we are going to be able to support neurodivergent applicants and employees. The response offered by these authors is to closely examine all facets of the employment process in light of the role of climate in considering neurodiversity in the workplace. This is accomplished by an initial discussion of the role of psychological climates and their role in supporting neurodiversity in organizations. Specifically, the authors identify diversity, inclusion and ethical climates as crucial to focus on as organizations make changes in their workplaces to be more supportive of neurodiversity. They next review the literature surrounding organizational efforts thus far to discuss what practices have been successful as companies have implemented neurodiversity programs. This discussion is tightly tied to specific ways to bolster diversity, inclusion and ethical climates across each of the eight primary functions of human resource management (HRM) (i.e., selection, compensation/benefits, employee relations, occupational health/safety, training/development, talent management, job design, and retention).

Following the steps in the employment process, Chapter 3, "Recruitment Strategies: Generating a Neurodiverse Workforce," by Cristina Giannantonio and Amy Hurley-Hanson, examines the role that recruitment strategies might play in generating a neurodiverse workforce for the benefit of organizations, neurodivergent individuals and members of Generation A, the half million Autistic individuals who are expected to enter the workforce in the current decade. While there has been extensive research conducted on recruitment activities from the organization's perspective more broadly, far less empirical work has been conducted to date that is research examining the efficacy of recruitment strategies for promoting an effective pipeline development of candidates for a more neurodiverse workforce. In this chapter, research on recruitment strategies is reviewed from both an organizational and an individual perspective. A process view of recruitment, with particular attention on the signaling hypothesis, is presented to understand how recruitment may operate to influence the attitudes, reactions and behaviors of neurodiverse applicants. The benefits of and the barriers to recruiting neurodivergent candidates are discussed, focusing on both the external environment and the perspective of the (neurodiverse) individual who is in job search. The authors point out that the external environment focus has historically been the emphasis but that an examination of strategies that motivate applicants to apply for job openings and accept job offers is also critical for this population. They make the point that signaling theory has been offered as one explanation for recruitment effects – applicants are likely to use elements of recruitment activities as signals about unknown organizational and job characteristics. Among these signals can be interaction with recruiters, which can be used as a signal of the likelihood of the candidate being considered a viable applicant. The authors close with offering suggestions for improving recruitment strategies, issues specific to the recruitment interview and alternatives to the traditional recruitment interview process.

Getting in the front door of an organization is the first step toward employment. This includes several critical steps, from getting into the applicant pool by applying, making it through any prescreening mechanisms and having your resume and application selected to navigating and succeeding in the interview process. Prior related research has provided guidance regarding effective hiring strategies that promote job success; however, this research has, again, overwhelmingly focused on neurotypical employee populations and fails to incorporate neurodiverse populations. The content in Chapter 4 is integrally tied to the prior chapter, focusing on the role of organizations' human resource practices and function for ensuring equity and the development of neurodiverse talent pools, addressing what happens when neurodiverse applicants make it to the interview process. In "Neurodiverse Applicant Screening, Interviewing, and Selection," authors Matthew Saleh, Hsiao-Ying (Vicki) Chang, Susanne M. Bruyère and Timothy Vogus point out that there are a range of modifications to screening and application procedures (e.g., the job interview) that can help ensure hiring practices avoid implicit biases and are more equitable for Autistic individuals. This especially includes factors that affect hiring decisions (e.g., nonverbal and verbal cues, self-presentation and promotion), which may not actually be meaningfully related to future job performance. In exploring how to effectively address potentially problematic processes for neurodiverse populations, Saleh et al. provide a brief overview of traditional and emerging screening and selection methods and summarize what is known about affirmative screening/selection approaches from other underrepresented labor force populations that may be relevant for Autistic candidates. They finally discuss the disparate impact (for neurodivergent applicants) and other risks stemming from relying on selection criteria (e.g., social behavior) that does not predict job performance and share recommendations for approaches that will promote fairer processes not only for neurodiverse job candidates but also for more diverse talent pools generally.

While workplaces are adopting the label "neurodiversity" to acknowledge variation in cognitive abilities among workers, continued effort is needed to advance workplace practices and social environments that reflect a fully inclusive approach to neurodiversity. The focus in Chapter 5 interjects into the broader conversation of employment opportunities for neurodiverse individuals, a critical discussion on disclosure and its impact on employment opportunities and inclusion. Alecia Santuzzi and Robert Keating's chapter, "Neurodiversity and the Disclosure Dilemma," addresses the problem presented to neurodiverse individuals, especially for those whose condition is not evident, about whether to disclose their neurodiverse identity. Current workplace practices for recruiting and integrating workers with neurodivergent features are often congruent with approaches to disability, with an emphasis on protections against discrimination and providing accommodations for workers to perform in the neurotypical work environment. Similar to disabilities in general, workers with neurodivergent features might need to disclose in order to determine if the features qualify as a disability and subsequently benefit from protections against discrimination and receive accommodations to perform work tasks that were designed with the neurotypical worker in mind. However, the decision to disclose either formally to organization leadership or informally to coworkers involves careful consideration of the costs and benefits of doing so. In this chapter, the authors discuss the potential gains and losses of disclosing neurodivergent features in the workplace and the role that workplace environments and neurodivergent features play in those consequences. Although neurodiversity is a relatively new framework for discussing disclosure and other workplace social challenges, the authors borrow lessons from existing literature on how workers manage concealable stigmatized identities (CSIs) – devalued attributes or social identities that can be hidden from others at work – with literature on concealable or invisible disabilities providing the most relevant insights. The authors end with a discussion on how research endeavors and organizational practices might adapt as workplace environments embrace a neurodiversity perspective.

Leadership is a robust and well-researched area in the field of management. However, diversity in organizations is increasing, and the generalizability of many leadership concepts may be placed into question. This is particularly true when considering increasing neurodiversity in organizations. The center of Chapter 6 is the acknowledgement of the critical role that management, particularly organizational leadership, plays in building inclusive workplaces of all kinds and how leadership theories may apply to this neurodiverse population of focus. In Stephanie Seitz's chapter, "Do Traditional Leadership Theories Work in a Neurodiverse Context?" the author discusses how traditional leadership theories have generally been developed and tested in neurotypical environments, and the assumption that they are applicable to neurodivergent employees comes from the perspective of the "abled" organization. Seitz questions whether traditional leadership theories apply in neurodiverse work contexts. To do so, the most prominent traditional and contemporary leadership theories are analyzed for their applicability to neurodivergent employees, including: group-oriented leadership, which may be either targeted at a group or arise within a group; development-based leadership approaches, which are characterized by helping and encouraging followers to achieve goals and engage in self-development; individual-based leadership theories that focus on how leaders use individual-based leadership approaches to view and treat their followers as individuals; vision-based leadership approaches, which rely on the ability of the leader to tap into followers' sense of a big picture and overarching shared goal and includes charismatic and transformational leadership styles; outcomes-based leadership, which focuses on task and goal completion (i.e., outcomes), with leaders providing followers the tools and resources needed for desired outcomes; and several other contemporary leadership theories. Seitz concludes that in order to engage in the kind of leadership that is tailored and individualized for neurodivergent employees, it is important to understand how generalizations and biases about disability can hinder the leadership process and the successful needed nurturing of neurodiverse talent.

Leaders and managers are not alone in their ability to impact the experience of inclusion (or lack thereof) for neurodiverse individuals; employee coworkers/colleagues also can have a significant impact. Relationships with coworkers can play a formative role in shaping an employee's work experience, both for better and for worse. In Chapter 7, Longmire and Taylor focus on "The Role of Colleagues in Work Experiences of Employees with Autism," operating on the belief that relationships with coworkers may be even more consequential for workers with autism. Workplaces are often highly formalized contexts, creating a set of social expectations that might be difficult for Autistic individuals, who might find the verbal and nonverbal nuances of every workplace conversation difficult to decipher. Because the characteristics of an Autistic person may include social and interpersonal difficulties, the authors include among their points in this chapter the importance of proactively identifying ways to help avoid or minimize interpersonal friction among coworkers in an effort to enable organizations to harness the full potential of neurodiverse employees. To accomplish this intended purpose of the chapter, the authors summarize the literature on the impact of coworkers on employees' experiences generally then delve into the literature around disability and coworkers, ending with a focus on autism specifically. The authors point out the criticality of having good relationships across coworkers, which can contribute to more positive job attitudes and overall effectiveness at work, as well as contributing to workplace adjustment, especially for newcomers to the workplace (like neurodiverse recruits to Autism at Work affirmative hiring programs). In contrast, negative experiences with colleagues can result in feelings of social exclusion and loneliness and, consequently, in lowered job performance and resulting job turnover. The authors conclude with recommendations for future research that extends theory beyond these initial stages to better understand the role of coworkers in the ongoing work experiences of neurodiverse employees.

Workplace policies and practices often originate from legally defined parameters to which organizational legal, human resource and employee and labor relations representatives are responding. This is no less true for policies and practices that are designed to protect the interests of individuals with disabilities, including those who identify as being neurodiverse. Several chapters in this volume recognize and discuss the legal context that governs disability protections, particularly those provided in the U.S. context, such as workplace accommodations. While laws in the United States and many other countries require employers to provide accommodations for workers with autism, many Autistic individuals and employers struggle to request and implement accommodations. Chapter 8, by author Eric Patton, focuses on "Workplace Accommodations for a Neurodiverse Workforce." The manifestations of the condition, the spectrum nature of autism that requires different supports for nominally the same condition, general stigmas around mental health issues and perceptions of coworkers and supervisors create a situation in which legal requirements are not sufficient to ensure individuals with autism get the supports they need. Patton's chapter, while recognizing the legal context within workplace policies and practices often reside, discusses the importance demonstrated by Autism at Work initiatives in moving beyond the regulatory requirements to address effective workplace inclusion. The author provides a holistic overview of accommodations and autism, with an emphasis on legal issues, specific accommodations that individuals and employers should consider and the need to develop an organizational culture that embraces neurodiversity.

Individuals with autism face a number of barriers to entry in the workplace. Once hired, moreover, challenges for this neurodiverse population do not stop. In Chapter 9, authors Samuel Hunter and Melissa Hunter consider how to support individuals once they cross recruitment and hiring barriers to actually securing employment and the challenges posed in staying in the workplace and advancing. Entitled "Performance Management and Career Development for Employees with Autism: Uncovering Hidden Requirements," the authors combine a thorough examination of related literature with a disciplinary perspective beyond management and business literature, with concrete and well-organized descriptions of how to put the ideas discussed in the literature into practice. To do so, they utilize literature from the education and school psychology research and the field of applied behavior analysis. Supplementing lessons from outside of I-O psychology, they also consider what industry is doing to successfully manage

Autistic employees. Specifically, they consider approaches to performance management and career development that were developed for neurotypical employees and discuss ways in which such approaches must be adjusted for employees with autism. In addition, they attempt to uncover ways that supervisors can uncover hidden requirements that serve as barriers to Autistic employees. The authors discuss how individuals with autism may not be successful in employment settings because they are not aware of or find it difficult to understand the unspoken and unwritten rules and expectations regarding social behaviors, attitudes and values and procedures and norms within the setting. Very specific recommendations for supervisors are offered to assist in the performance management and career advancement processes such as: defining performance goals, providing feedback in alternative formats, considering breaking performance up into smaller goals that allow rewards to be earned more frequently, assigning peer mentors, providing exposure to growth opportunities on a trial basis and allowing shadowing of others in possible new roles.

Mental health challenges are common in people with an autism diagnosis but have, to date, been largely overlooked within current autism employment programs and interventions. The authors of Chapter 10, Simon Bury, Jennifer Spoor, Susan Hayward and Darren Hedley, take on this information gap in their chapter entitled "Supporting the Mental Health and Well-Being of Autistic and Other Neurodiverse Employees in the Work Environment." While workplace initiatives to help support individuals in the workplace with autistic characteristics are relatively successful, the authors contend that the complexities of mental health in autism present as potential risk factors for the sustainability of autism employment programs. In this chapter, they first detail common co-occurring psychiatric conditions in autism. They then investigate the complex interaction between mental health and well-being, autism characteristics and the workplace through the lens of job demand-resource theory and to argue the importance of developing specific mental health supports in autism employment programs and initiatives. The authors address the potential utility of established mental health initiatives for the general population, and their limitations in supporting the mental health and well-being of Autistic employees are then explored. Employee assistance programs (EAPs) are employer-sponsored programs designed to help employees identify and resolve acute personal and behavioral issues that may actually or potentially impact work performance. Mental health first aid follows a physical first aid model, whereby members of the public are trained to provide initial support to someone developing a mental health issue or experiencing a mental health crisis until appropriate professional help is available. Finally, Bury et al. present two new autism-specific mental health initiatives that may help fill the resource gap in this area that are being employed in a company-sponsored autism hiring program in Australia. One is similar to the mental health first aid model, but tailored to people with autism. The other is a mobile platform which provides general behavior supports that can be beneficial to many employees.

In Chapter 11, we go back to a broader organization context perspective as author Nancy Doyle provides an overview of the considerations in "Adapting Other Internal Organizational Resources to a Neurodiverse Workforce." The author sets the context for this chapter in the framing of the distinctions between the "medical model" of disability, which has focused on the physical impairment at the individual level, and the "social model" of disability. This framing is currently imbedded in the United Nations Convention on the Rights of People with Disabilities of 2006. The social model of disability says that disability is caused by the way society and the environment are organized and the barriers that this poses in limiting the choices that the individual has and their ability to fully function in the world. Neurodiversity researchers, like the author herself, advocate a paradigm that treats neurodiversity more from the social model, seeing it not as a deficit but rather as a natural variation in strengths and weaknesses that bestows talents as well as struggle. The author then details some approaches to facilitate building work environments and workplace resources that will be more inclusive of neurodiverse individuals, consistent with the premise of the social model of disability. The first is the framework provided by the seven principles of universal design (UD), which is a design approach that has at its core creating an environment that can be accessed, understood and used to the greatest extent possible by all people regardless of their physical or intellectual characteristics. The author provides us with a related workplace universal design for neurominorities framework that specifically addresses the workplace and environmental design considerations that will minimize barriers and maximize effective supports for this population. The author concludes the chapter with an overview of how three common workplace well-being resources can be better tailored to the needs of neurodiverse individuals, including employee assistance programs (EAPs), occupational health (OH) resources and medical health benefits.

We return to a more concerted focus on the legislative framework that supports employment disability nondiscrimination in Chapter 12, by authors Matthew Saleh and Michael Bernick. The chapter does not cover all of the potential federal and state law that might apply to employers and their employees who are Autistic. The authors focus on the federal requirements related to employment nondiscrimination in the workplace, particularly around hiring, accommodating, advancing and equal access to the benefits and privileges of employment. Specifically, the relationship of the federal legislative and regulatory requirements (e.g., under the Americans with Disabilities Act and Section 503 of the Rehabilitation Act) to autism hiring initiatives and programs, including: (a) compliance with disability disclosure and medical inquiry requirements; (b) provision of reasonable accommodations; (c) structuring autism and, more broadly, neurodiversity hiring processes; (d) integrating job coaches, mentorship opportunities and other support staff in an equitable fashion; and (e) ensuring equality across the employment process, including performance management, advancement, discipline and termination and benefits eligibility. The objective of this chapter is to set out for the reader processes by which employers can meet their goals of increasing neurodiverse talent pools and employees while also satisfying federal legal requirements for nondiscrimination in opportunity across the work experience (including hiring, advancement and what are termed the "benefits and privileges" of employment) and even possibly further applying what they have learned to more traditional hiring practices within the organization so as to increase organizational adherence to nondiscrimination requirements for other previously underrepresented segments of the labor force. A key theme throughout this chapter involves the importance of ensuring that neurodiversity programs do not disproportionately prioritize the "front end" of the employment experience (e.g., recruiting, hiring and on-board training) at the expense of treating employees, once integrated into the organization, as equal participants in the workforce entitled to the accommodations, job development opportunities and workplace climate that will allow them to carry out fulfilling work on an equal basis with others.

In the concluding Chapter 13, we close this volume by noting and discussing some fertile avenues for future research and important questions for I/O psychologists that are woven throughout the chapters in this volume, as well as those emerging from current issues posed by the pandemic and the increased emphasis on social justice issues. Thus, rather than provide a summary of the chapters in this volume, as is done in the current chapter, the volume finishes with observations about how work on neurodiversity can push the frontiers of the science and practice of I/O psychology. These key themes include the wisdom of generalizing from research on other disadvantaged groups; the overreliance on the evaluation of social skills in applicant and employee assessment; the need to consider the social skills and behavior on the part of coworkers and supervisors; the need to rethink some theories popular in the I/O literature from a neurodiversity perspective; the need to take a multidisciplinary perspective on the issue of neurodiversity and learn from other disciplines; and the need to take a long-term perspective on the disclosure question.

We also briefly discuss how the effects of economic downturns are usually disproportionately felt by working-age people with disabilities (Livermore & Honeycutt, 2015), and these historical trends have been no less true in the economic downturn that started in March 2020 imposed by the pandemic. In addition, those with intersectional identities (e.g., disability, gender, race and ethnicity) are more significantly impacted, highlighting social justice issues. Yet during the pandemic some companies with affirmative hiring programs for persons with autism not only maintained their programs but pivoted to a virtual environment and describe the longer-term benefit in so doing for both the company and their Autistic job candidates. We conclude by observing that more can be learned for the future workplace from these companies' creative responses in addressing the needs of historically underrepresented populations during these challenging times.

We hope that this summarizing chapter, and the volume as a whole, will spur needed further interest for I/O psychologists to apply their many skills to identify and facilitate the practices needed across the employment process that will build more neurodiversity-inclusive future workplaces.

References

American Psychiatric Association. (2019). *What is autism spectrum disorder?* Retrieved from http://bit.ly/2Mf38JV

Austin, R. D., & Sonne, T. (2014, May 19). The Dandelion principle: Redesigning work for the innovation economy. *MIT Sloan Management Review*. Retrieved from http://bit.ly/2Mog8gq

Autistic Self Advocacy Network. (2021). *Identity-first language*. Retrieved from https://autisticadvocacy.org/about-asan/identity-first-language/

Baldwin, S., Costley, D., & Warren, A. (2014). Employment activities and experiences of adults with high-functioning autism and Asperger's disorder. *Journal of Autism and Developmental Disorders, 44*, 2440–2449. https://doi.org/10.1007/s10803-0142112-z

Bort, J. (2013, May 31). SAP just vowed to hire a whole bunch of people with autism. *Business Insider*. Retrieved from http://bit.ly/2Wv84OG

Chambers, E. G., Foulon, M., Handfield-Jones, H., Hankin, S. M., & Michaels, E.G., III. (1998). The war for talent. *The McKinsey Quarterly, 3*, 44–57.

Doyle, N., & McDowell, A. (2021). Diamond in the rough? An "empty review" of research into "neurodiversity" and a road map for developing an inclusion agenda. *Equality, Diversity, and Inclusion*. https://doi.org/10.1108/EDI-06-2020-0172/full/html

Erickson, W., Lee, C., & von Schrader, S. (2021). *Disability Statistics from the 2018 American Community Survey (ACS)*. Ithaca, NY: Cornell University Yang-Tan Institute (YTI). Retrieved from Cornell University Disability Statistics website www.disabilitystatistics.org

EY. (2018). *Neurodiversity: Driving innovation from unexpected places*. Retrieved from https://go.ey.com/2M9Ivyr

EY. (2021). *EY US launches first Neuordiverse Center of Excellent in Boston*. Retrieved from www.ey.com/en_us/news/2021/04/ey-us-launches-first-neuro-diverse-center-of-excellence-in-boston

Gartner TalentNeuron™ (2019). *Who is winning the war on talent? How leading companies are making the right talent decisions*. Retrieved from Gartner.com at https://emtemp.gcom.cloud/ngw/globalassets/en/human-resources/documents/trends/winning-the-talent-war.pdf

Hedley, D., Uljarevic, M., Cameron, L., Halder, S., Richdale, A., & Dissanayake, C. (2016). Employment programmes and interventions targeting adults with autism spectrum disorder: A systematic review of the literature. *Autism, 21*(8), 929–941. https://doi.org/10.1177/1362361316661855

Honeybourne, V. (2020). *The neurodiverse workplace: An employer's guide to managing and working with neurodivergent employees, clients, and customers*. London: Jessica Kingsley Publishers.

Hurley-Hanson, A. E., & Giannantonio, C. M. (eds.). (2017). Special issue: Autism in the workplace. *Journal of Business and Management, 22*(1), 5–152.

IBM. (2020). *Neurodiversity@IBM – Nothing about us, without us*. Retrieved from www.youtube.com/watch?v=2noTl6ThDRg&list=PLOpaMLFA3D1MAZYFzAtgSQpAtqDRvtC4u&index=8

JP Morgan Chase. (2019). *Neurodiverse hiring brings social and business benefits*. Retrieved from www.jpmorganchase.com/corporate/news/stories/neurodiverse-hiring-brings-social-and-business-benefits.htm

Korn, F. (2018). *Future of work: The global talent crunch*. Retrieved from http://bit.ly/2MfSYbX

Livermore, G. A., & Honeycutt, T. C. (2015). Employment and economic well-being of people with and without disabilities before and after the Great Recession. *Journal of Disability Policy Studies, 26*(2), 70–79. http://doi.org/10.1177/1044207315583875

Maenner, M. J., Shaw, K. A., Bakian, A.V., et al. (2021). Prevalence of autism spectrum disorder among children aged 8 years – Autism and developmental disabilities monitoring network, 11 Sites, United States, 2018. *Morbidity and Mortality Weekly Reports Surveillance Summaries, 70*(SS–11), 1–16. http://dx.doi.org/10.15585/mmwr.ss7011a1

Microsoft. (2021). *Microsoft neurodiversity hiring program & FAQ*. Retrieved from www.microsoft.com/en-us/diversity/inside-microsoft/cross-disability/neurodiversityhiring

National Symposium on Neurodiversity at Syracuse University. (2011). Syracuse, NY. Retrieved from http://bit.ly/2WtesWC

Nielsen, M. (2012, November 21). McKinsey predicts that the war for talent will go nuts by 2020. *Business Insider*. Retrieved from www.businessinsider.com/rich-countries-producing-too-few-grads-2012-11?IR=T

Office for National Statistics (2021). *Outcomes for disabled people in the UK: 2020*. Retrieved from file:///C:/Users/smb23/Downloads/Outcomes%20for%20disabled%20people%20in%20the%20UK%202020.pdf

Parmar, N. (2017, October 25). Why Microsoft, chase and others are hiring more people with autism. *Entrepreneur*. Retrieved from https://www.chron.com/news/article/Why-Microsoft-Chase-and-Others-Are-Hiring-More-12304814.php

Pisano, G., & Austin, R. (2016). SAP SE: Autism at work. *Harvard Business School*, Case 616–042.

Roux, A. M., Shattuck, P.T., Rast, J. E., Rava, J. A., & Anderson, K. A. (2015). *National autism indicators report: Transition into young adulthood*. Philadelphia, PA: Life Course Outcomes Research Program, A.J. Drexel Autism Institute, Drexel University, 2015.

Singer, J. (2016). *Neurodiversity: The Birth of an Idea*. Published as a Kindle e-book in 2016; published in print in 2017.

Sumner, K., & Brown, T. (2015). Neurodiversity and human resource management: Employer challenges for applicants and employees with learning disabilities. *The Psychologist-Manager Journal, 18*(2), 77–85.

Szczerba, R. (2016, January 19). This visionary may completely disrupt the tech industry as we know it. *Forbes*. Retrieved from http://bit.ly/2WwuvTv

2

SHAPING ORGANIZATIONAL CLIMATES TO DEVELOP AND LEVERAGE WORKFORCE NEURODIVERSITY

Sabrina D. Volpone, Derek R. Avery, and Julie H. Wayne

> I have high-functioning autism, and this means that I usually look normal on the outside . . . If I was standing next to you waiting for an elevator, I would make small talk and smile and you wouldn't know I'm autistic. This is purposeful and requires significant intellectual investment . . . I wish I could shout from the rooftops: You have no idea how hard I have to work to appear this way! . . . Then imagine that, under this assault, you concentrate on maintaining an elaborate performance to relate to those around you while suppressing your natural mode of speaking and acting . . . I have tried being myself, plenty of times, and the universally negative feedback I received from early childhood through college taught me that that self is not welcome in a neurotypical world.
>
> – Christine Condo in the *Washington Post* (Condo, 2020)

As this quote illustrates, our world is set up with neurotypical people in mind, and this can place a considerable number of barriers into daily interactions for individuals that are neurodivergent. By neurotypical, we mean having cognitive functioning within the bounds of what society dictates as 'normal' (CIPD, 2018), whereas neurodivergent or neurodiverse means that cognitive functioning is different from what society dictates as 'normal' (CIPD, 2018). Conditions that have been considered under the umbrella of the term 'neurodiversity' include attention deficit hyperactivity disorders (ADHD), autism (including Asperger's syndrome), depression, dyscalculia, dysgraphia, dyslexia, dyspraxia, learning disabilities, and Tourette syndrome (Armstrong, 2010; Babineau, 2010; Burnett & Trerise, 2019; Hendrickx, 2010; Richards et al., 2019; Rogers, 2017; Rothstein, 2012; Sumner & Brown, 2015). Instead of placing the unnecessary burden on neurodivergent individuals, what if workplaces altered their environments so that all employees – including those who are neurodivergent – could easily apply

DOI: 10.4324/9781003023616-2

their strengths at work? That is, instead of having applicants and employees spend significant intellectual resources trying to fit into a world that is not designed to embrace neurodiversity, what if organizations bolstered their climates in ways that take into account the natural variation in human neurocognitive functioning and, in doing so, positioned themselves to reap benefits that contribute directly to the bottom line?

At first glance, one might ask why it is important to examine the role of climate in considering neurodiversity in the workplace. For many readers, exposure to neurodiversity comes from media portrayals that often oppose the experience described in the opening quote by depicting that workplaces are inclusive of, and value, the skills and abilities of neurodivergent individuals. That is, through the use of characters in books, TV shows, and movies that have savant-like abilities, storylines are built around these characters' sought-after skills and abilities. For example, in crime dramas, viewers are often presented with a detective or investigator that solves crimes others cannot (e.g., Sherlock Holmes, Monk in *Monk*, Carrie in *Homeland*, Dr. Brennan in *Bones*; Faragher, 2018; Loftis, 2014; McHugh, 2018). Similar portrayals are also seen in medical dramas, such as Dr. Shaun Murphy in *The Good Doctor* and in academic contexts such as Dr. Sheldon Cooper in *The Big Bang Theory*. Based on such media portrayals, it seems that workplace climates accept and welcome neurodivergent employees and, in fact, that their skills and abilities are sought-after while the 'realities' of the neurodivergent condition often are brought into the storyline in ways that enhance the entertainment value (e.g., awkward social interactions with others providing a moment of comic relief).

In contrast to these many media portrayals, the idea of organizations supporting or even seeking out neurodiversity for their workforces is not a typical experience for many neurodivergent employees; there is evidence for the unemployment, underemployment, and exclusion of neurodivergent individuals from workforces (Eden, 2019; Carter et al., 2012; National Autistic Society, 2016; Richards, 2012; Snowling et al., 2000). In fact, research shows that most organizations at this point have failed to consider the benefits that a neurodiverse workforce can bring to their employees and the organization overall. However, this gap that exists between the lived reality of many neurodivergent employees (one marked by unemployment, underemployment, and exclusion) and the limited portrayals of neurodiversity through books, TV, and movies (one marked by employment and inclusion) presents an opportunity for researchers and practitioners looking to change the way organizations operate so that they are more supportive of neurodiversity. To elaborate, the addition of these characters to mainstream media is increasing society's understanding of the strengths that neurodivergent employees can bring to their jobs as detectives, investigators, doctors, and scientists through the use of the limited savant stereotype (Dale, 2013; Woods, 2014). This growth in neurodiversity as a social movement (Armstrong, 2010; Krcek, 2013; Haney, 2018; Orsini & Smith, 2010) presents an opportunity for researchers and practitioners to present evidence that counters narratives built on limited stereotypes that focuses on genius (McHugh, 2018)[1] while also providing a platform to discuss how organizations can support a neurodiverse workforce through strategic changes that will bolster the climates in their workplaces.

Through this chapter, we discuss how neurotypical norms have dominated our human resource management practices for so long that organizations need to establish new norms if we are going to be able to support neurodivergent applicants and employees. Then, we suggest that developing and maintaining diversity, inclusion, and ethical climates in a way that supports neurodiversity can provide a foundation for organizations to be able to support all employees while also leveraging the strengths of their employees to increase the organization's bottom line. Because the neurodiversity movement is still in its infancy (den Houting, 2019) but gaining traction, now is the perfect time for researchers and practitioners to explore ways to include and support individuals in the neurominority, or those who are neurodivergent.

The remainder of this chapter is structured as follows: First, we discuss the role of psychological climates and their role in supporting neurodiversity in organizations. Psychological climates are defined in this chapter as an employee's "cognitive appraisals of environmental attributes in terms of their acquired meaning and significance to the individual" (James & Ashe, 1990, p. 54). Specifically, we identify diversity, inclusion, and ethical climates as crucial to focus on as organizations make changes in their workplaces to be more supportive of neurodiversity. Second, we review the literature surrounding organizational efforts thus far to discuss what practices have been successful as companies have implemented neurodiversity programs. To make this discussion as useful as possible, we discuss ways to bolster diversity, inclusion, and ethical climates across each of the eight primary functions of human resource management (HRM; i.e., selection, compensation/benefits, employee relations, occupational health/safety, training/development, talent management, job design, and retention). Third, we present directions for future research to offer research questions and topics that scholars should explore to contribute to the conversation about how changes in organizations' climates can increase support of neurodiverse workforces. Overall, this chapter aims to explore how organizations can bolster their climates in ways that take into account the natural variation in human neurocognitive functioning to provide altered workplace environments that leverage the strengths of all employees.

Organizational Climates – A Review of the Relevant Literature

We begin with an overview of three types of psychological climate and describe why these three facets in particular are essential for organizations to consider when bolstering their climates to support neurodiversity. Researchers have demonstrated previously that multiple facets of climate can exist concurrently in the work context (Ostroff et al., 2003). Though there is not always scholarly agreement about the specific dimensions that comprise the construct of psychological climate (Martin et al., 2005; Parker et al., 2003), and different people can and do perceive different psychological climates when observing the same workplace environments (James et al., 2008), we believe that diversity, inclusion, and ethical climates have extensive research behind them such that considering these three facets in our exploration of how organizations can alter existing climates to better embrace neurodiversity will be fruitful. Specifically, in this chapter, we focus on three dimensions of psychological climate: (a) perceived diversity climate and (b) perceived inclusion climate and (c) perceived ethical climate.

Diversity Climates

First, diversity climate, or "the degree to which a firm advocates fair human resource policies and socially integrates underrepresented employees" (McKay et al., 2008, p. 350), is a type of psychological climate (Martin et al., 2005; Parker et al., 2003) that is a natural consideration for organizations to consider when building policies and procedures that are supportive of neurodiversity. The underlying idea behind building and maintaining strong diversity climates is that the organization focuses on equality of treatment across employees through the use of fair policies and the absence of discrimination (e.g., Larkey, 1996), as well as integration of all personnel. This focus could certainly benefit applicants and employees who are neurodivergent.

Previous research shows that the factors that make up employees' perceptions of an organization's diversity climate are the organization's demographic makeup, the presence of diversity across structures, leaders' commitment to diversity, and the employees' personal experiences with diversity (e.g., Hurtado et al., 1998; Mayhew et al., 2006). Organizations with strong diversity climates typically have demographic diversity in their workforce (Avery & McKay, 2010; Hyde & Hopkins, 2004) that is found throughout ranks of the organization (Kossek & Zonia, 1993).

Investing in a strong diversity climate has been shown to be advantageous for employees and organizations by providing a competitive advantage for organizations (Cox, 1994; Hicks-Clarke & Iles, 2000; Holmes et al., 2021). For example, diversity climate is related to how employees feel about their job and employer, job/career satisfaction, job involvement, organizational identification (Hicks-Clarke & Iles, 2000), sales performance (McKay et al., 2008), organizational effectiveness (Hicks-Clarke & Iles, 2000; McKay et al., 2008), and lower levels of turnover (e.g., McKay & Avery, 2005; McKay et al., 2007; Stewart et al., 2011). However, it is unknown how well these relationships apply to neurodiverse workforces, as many organizations have not considered this form of difference as a type of diversity. It may be that the type of accommodations required to support neurodivergent employees are unique from those of other potentially marginalized groups. Given that organizations invest a significant amount of money in their diversity climate efforts (the median annual investment by organizations to improve diversity climate is $1.2 million; Catalyst, 2005) and that a majority of organizations will either maintain (i.e., 62%) or increase (i.e., 35%) their investments in diversity initiatives (Talley, 2017), it is imperative that researchers and practitioners begin to expand their definition of diversity to include neurodiversity. Only then can these investments build an infrastructure that supports neurodivergent stakeholders in addition to other types of diversities traditionally considered by organizations.

The need to expand current definitions to incorporate neurodiversity has true implications in an organization's ability to support neurodiversity. To elaborate, how society understands neurodiversity in many ways stems from the *medical model* (Haney, 2018; Waltz, 2013). This model promotes neurodiverse conditions as disabilities and disorders (Krcek, 2013) characterized by inabilities and impairments (Jaarsma & Welin, 2012) that need a cure (Haney, 2018). On the surface, the medical model supports organizations' efforts to strengthen diversity climates for neurodivergent employees because diversity-supportive organizations have an infrastructure in place around disabilities; and thinking about neurodiversity as a disability allows organizations to account for this new type of diversity without making too many changes in workplace practices.

However, thinking about neurodiversity within an existing diversity climate paradigm that includes neurodiversity as a type of disability[2] has been damaging to the neurodiversity community and is not truly supportive of neurodivergent stakeholders. Specifically, a line of thinking along the medical model has led the U.S. Equal Employment Opportunity Commission to state that neurodivergent conditions such as autism should be almost always covered under the Americans with Disabilities Act given the limitations to brain function involved that often restrict major life activities (Hensel, 2017; c.f., Patton, 2019) when the applicant or employee is qualified to perform the essential functions of the job. The medical model is reinforced as the media continues to discuss neurodivergent conditions like autism using terms like 'autism epidemics' (Baker, 2011). This medical model has impacted research on neurodiversity, as well. For instance, the research on neurodiversity that has been produced so far has stemmed largely from perspectives that subscribe to the medical model (e.g., psychiatrists, psychologists, neuroscientists). This is demonstrated by the theoretical models (e.g., weak central coherence from Frith & Happé, 1994; executive dysfunction from Ozonoff et al., 1991) that are based on the cognitive deficits of neurodivergent individuals (O'Dell et al., 2016). While some individuals who are neurodivergent do have disabilities (Baron-Cohen, 2019), being labeled in terms specific to the medical model (e.g., as disabled, as someone with a disorder) has been limiting and even offensive for some individuals who may even develop a sense of pride regarding their neurodivergent identity. As such, using existing HR practices that follow laws and EEOC mandates around disability may help organizations begin to develop their diversity climates to incorporate neurodivergent individuals into workplaces, but doing so without further consideration (e.g., redefining diversity to think of neurodiversity and disability as two types of diversity or considering the role of other types of climates to support efforts around building workplaces that are supportive of neurodiversity) will not produce the changes that are needed for organizations to be truly supportive of neurodiversity.

Indeed, creating strong climates in organizations that support neurodiversity will need to go beyond having diversity climates that implement equitable HRM practices focused on increasing the representation of employees with more varied types of disabilities. Others have realized the limitations of a medical model, birthing the *social model* as a way to view neurodiversity as a difference rather than as a disease, dysfunction, or disorder (Muskat, 2017; Paletta, 2013). The social model coincides with the *neurodiversity movement* (Baron-Cohen, 2019) that promotes inclusion, self-determination, and recognition of diverse cognitive styles as part of one's identity (Haney, 2018).[3] As such, to have climates in organizations that are supportive of neurodiversity, organizations have to broaden their reliance on a strong diversity climate and disabilities to explain the differences that employees are bringing into the workplace (Bruyère, 2016; Bruyère, 2019; von Schrader et al., 2014). To accomplish the incorporation of the social model and the neurodiversity movement into organizations' efforts to bolster their climates to support neurodiversity, we explore the role that a strong inclusion climate can have when paired with a strong diversity climate. Research supports the idea of multiple facets of climate working together to present consistent messages to stakeholders (e.g., Stewart et al., 2011). Moreover, given that stakeholders typically react positively to diversity climates that have strong inclusion elements (e.g., those that encourage employees to maintain their identity and include minorities through the formation of affinity groups and institutional commitments to diversity that are public; Berry, 1990; Chen et al., 2012; LaFromboise et al., 1993; Stewart et al., 2011) and promote synergies that help to leverage differences (Richard et al., 2019), we believe that the full effects of supportive climates for neurodiversity cannot be realized fully without also examining the effects of other facets of climate such as inclusion climate, as we will discuss next.

Inclusion Climates

Next, we explore inclusion climate as a form of psychological climate important for employers to consider – in addition to diversity climate – to strengthen support for neurodiversity within their organizations. This idea aligns with current research from inclusion researchers that suggests that organizations need to create inclusive environments to be able to leverage diversity's benefits (Hayes et al., 2002; Holvino et al., 2004). Overall, an inclusive climate is characterized as a feeling or sense of belonging (Shore et al., 2009, 2011). As such, inclusion climate is broader in scope than diversity climate, and this broad focus could be beneficial as applicants redesign procedures to be more supportive of applicants and employees who are neurodivergent.

In inclusive workplace environments, the goal is that employees of all backgrounds are fairly treated, valued for who they are, and included in core decision-making (Nishii, 2013). That is, there are three dimensions of inclusion climate (Nishii, 2013). The first dimension of inclusion climate focusses on *fairly implemented employment practices*. This dimension closely resembles the principles of diversity climate but is more expansive, as creating inclusive climates requires more than increasing diverse representation and implementing equitable HRM practices; it requires a change in interaction patterns. The second dimension of inclusion climate focuses on the *integration of differences*, within the workplace that depicts the comfort employees feel when bringing their identities to work (Nishii, 2013). The third dimension of inclusion climate focuses on *inclusion in decision-making* within the workplace that captures the extent to which the diverse perspectives of employees are voiced and used (Nishii, 2013).

To provide an example of how organizations can strengthen their inclusion climates along each of the three dimensions to support neurodiversity, let's consider the topic of employee accommodations. It is often the case that organizations are familiar with implementing accommodations that are associated with physical disabilities. Indeed, installing ramps or elevators are common prototypes of accommodations. In an organization with a strong diversity and strong inclusion climate, leaders and managers would have broadened accommodation prototypes beyond a disability paradigm to embrace accommodations that are more typical for neurodivergent stakeholders (e.g., quiet workspaces, the use of noise-canceling headphones; see chapters by Patton and Doyle in this volume for more comprehensive discussion of accommodations). These efforts fairly implement accommodations across different types of employees, integrate the different needs of employees whose accommodation needs fall outside of traditional accommodations associated with physical disabilities, and also represent inclusion in decision-making, because if neurodivergent employees are comfortable requesting accommodations (many may have to, as neurodiverse conditions are not visibly detected, though this is not always the case), they are able to participate in designing their workplace to better leverage their strengths. Research suggests organizations are less ready to consider what accommodations look like for employees whose differences are not visibly seen and understood (e.g., those applicants and employees who are neurodivergent; Krcek, 2013). Hence, diversity and inclusion climates need to be considered simultaneously during efforts to strengthen organizational support for employee neurodiversity.

It is worth noting that accommodations may be mistaken for preferential treatment and, therefore, precipitate negative reactions among coworkers who may be unaware that the recipient is neurodivergent or what such status entails. It may also be difficult for the organization to be completely transparent about the need for the accommodation given the legal restrictions against the organization disclosing sensitive health information about any of its employees. Nevertheless, a core component of diversity climate is the provision of equal employment opportunity (McKay et al., 2007), which entails creating and maintaining a level playing field through accommodations (Cox, 1994). Accordingly, employees can be informed (a priori) and reassured (ad hoc) that any observed differences in treatment are aimed at eliminating disadvantages as opposed to creating or enhancing advantages – even if the organization is not at liberty to discuss specific accommodations for neurodivergent forms of difference (unless the employee discloses it publicly).

Though diversity and inclusion climates are clearly important, to further the discussion on bolstering climates to support neurodiversity within organizations, we believe that considering ethical climate is necessary, as well. As Haney (2018) points out, neurodiversity is not as simple as applying diversity and inclusion principles to individuals with neurological differences, mostly because there are complex ethical considerations concerning neurodiversity. For instance, if all other employees are assigned to a highly concentrated common (and potentially noisy) workspace, a neurominority employee requiring a distraction-free environment could violate the principle of consistency (i.e., treating all employees the same). Therefore, we suggest that creating strong climates that support neurodiversity should consider diversity, inclusion, *and* ethical climates.

Ethical Climates

Next, we explore ethical climate, perceptions concerning the organization's rules, policies, values, and practices (Schwepker, 2001), as a form of psychological climate that provides a distinct and important lens to consider for organizations building and maintaining workplaces that support neurodiversity. Ethical climates are crucial to consider because to gain a full understanding of the neurodiversity movement, it is necessary to engage in conversations related to moral, social, legal, and medical topics that are strongly related to ethics (Eden, 2019; Herrera, 2013; Richards et al., 2019). In short, it is unethical to exclude any group of prospective employees based on a characteristic that is not indicative of performance capability, and many neurodivergent individuals are indeed capable if provided with accommodations where required. Overall, an ethical climate can be described as focusing on establishing and maintaining an ethical code through organizational communication and policies (Jaramillo et al., 2006; Mulki et al., 2008; Schwepker, 2001; Weeks et al., 2006) with elements related to instrumental, caring, independence, rules, and law (Martin & Cullen, 2006).

Investing in a strong ethical climate has been shown to be advantageous for employees and organizations (Mulki et al., 2008; Schwepker, 2001; Tsai & Huang, 2008), as ethical climates are linked positively with job attitudes such as organizational commitment and job satisfaction (Martin & Cullen, 2006) and negatively with turnover intentions (Coldwell et al., 2008; Martin & Cullen, 2006; Mulki et al., 2008; Pettijohn & Taylor, 2008; Tsai & Huang, 2008). However, it is not yet clear whether neurodivergent employees exhibit these positive outcomes to a similar extent in response to ethical climates. Because the neurodiversity movement has a lens of positivity through its focus on an individual's strengths, how neurodivergent employees experience their workplaces is a big determinant of an organization's support for neurodiversity. As Constantino (2018) put it, "If quality of life is improved and neurodiversity helps people find meaning and joy in their experiences, then it is helpful. If the movement discourages neurodivergent individuals from seeking help and, therefore, it lessens their quality of life, then it is harmful." This means that in organizations, embracing neurodiversity as a type of diversity and including neurodivergent employees in the workforce may not be enough to support neurodiversity, as these diversity and inclusion efforts may not have positive effects for employees without considering social justice elements such as the distribution of wealth, opportunities, and privileges within a society that are often barriers for neurodivergent individuals.

Organizations are well positioned to promote social justice and ethical initiatives to support all employees, including those who are in the neurominority. Organizations have natural platforms to promote knowledge (e.g., through trainings) and their ways of doing business (e.g., through their cultures, norms) that can communicate the organization's support of neurodiversity while also emphasizing the organization's stance that supporting neurodiversity is a part of its efforts to maintain ethical practices and a strong ethical climate. Though research suggests everyone stands to benefit from an organizational emphasis on social justice and ethics (Martin & Cullen, 2006), a failure to do so disproportionately impacts those who differ from the prototypical employee in any meaningful way such as being neurodivergent. It may seem easier to avoid making any accommodations, thereby excluding neurodivergent employees. Doing what is easy, however, is not always synonymous with doing what is right (providing equal employment opportunity) and what is smart (hiring highly capable employees).

Considering Diversity, Inclusion, and Ethics Climates Simultaneously

To capture the spirit of the neurodiversity movement that focuses on leveraging the strengths of employees rather than viewing neurodiverse conditions as disabilities or diseases, we believe that diversity, inclusion, and ethical climates within organizations have to be considered simultaneously. To provide an example of these three climates interacting to create a workplace that is supportive for neurodiversity, we present an example from Ernst and Young (EY), a company that has been a pioneer in this area through the establishment and growth of its neurodiversity program (Cohn, 2017). Here is how Lori Golden, EY's abilities strategy leader, describes the company's efforts around neurodiversity:

> We've been a leader in this space. We have a very strong commitment to both fostering a culture that's what we refer to as 'abilities inclusive,' a

> culture that feels welcoming and productive for people of all physical, cognitive or socioemotional abilities, meaning mental health abilities. We have real proactive efforts and innovative efforts to reach out to candidates with disabilities . . . With the neurodiversity program, for example, we currently have 14 individuals with autism employed at two of what we call Neurodiverse Centers of Excellence . . . We have plans to open two more Centers of Excellence a year for the next three years, with an average number of 10 individuals per center.

From her description of its neurodiversity program (c.f. Cohn, 2017), it is evident that its efforts are rooted in a strong diversity climate that strives to promote diversity efforts (i.e., a neurodiversity program) with considerable demographic diversity in this area compared to other organizations in this industry (i.e., 14 employees with plans for 10 employees per center). Then, there is evidence of an emphasis on inclusion climate, as these employees are valued for who they are through the company's development of a culture that is abilities inclusive. Moreover, it is evident that a strong ethics climate is at the foundation of these considerations, as the changes the company has made in the HRM practices speak to caring, law, and other elements of ethics climates (Martin & Cullen, 2006) that are the foundation of how they have approached these changes to become a leader in creating a work environment with a strong commitment to maintaining a culture that is productive for employees that fall anywhere on the neurodiversity spectrum (i.e., all employees).

Strengthening Diversity, Inclusion, and Ethics Climates Around Neurodiversity Initiatives: What Organizations Can Do

To this point in the chapter, we have discussed how climates generally are important to consider for organizations in their efforts to create and maintain workplaces that are supportive of neurodiversity. In the remainder of this section, we describe key concerns that practitioners should consider when building diversity, inclusion, and ethical climates. Given neurodiversity practices are likely to be at an embryonic stage of development in most organizations, we include examples of the best HRM practices available in our effort to focus on the knowledge and skills that will be most useful in organizations' efforts to change their policies and practices to be more supportive of neurodiversity. To achieve this, we review the efforts of organizational thought leaders in this area, a title gained through their creation and development of successful neurodiversity programs in their organizations. Specifically, we will discuss the best practices reported by companies like Ernst & Young (EY), SAP, Microsoft, Hewlett Packard Enterprise (HPE; now known as DXC Technology), Ford, Deloitte, IBM, Dell Technologies, Hasbro, Walgreens, JPMorgan Chase, Caterpillar, Willis Towers Watson, the Australian Defense Department, and the Israeli defense force (Austin & Pisano, 2017; Eden, 2019; Faragher, 2018; Patton, 2019), as they have transformed their HRM processes to be more supportive of neurodiversity.

We place the spotlight on these organizations to show both progress and the difficulty associated with making it. For instance, we note that EY has a Neurodiversity Center of Excellence that was launched in 2015 that has been noted for its initiatives' efficacy in moving the needle (Association for Talent Development, 2018; Ovaska-Few, 2018). Conversely, SAP's Autism at Work program was launched in 2013 and has proven quite slow in producing change such that their organization has a goal to have 1% of its workforce made up of neurodivergent employees by this year (i.e., Faragher, 2018). Other interesting success stories come from governments, like the Israeli defense force that created a division focused on analyzing satellite images that is made up of employees who all identify as neurodivergent (Austin & Pisano, 2017; Faragher, 2018). We also acknowledge that we draw on the suggestions of well-known consulting companies (e.g., Specialisterne) that have worked with some of these organizations in establishing their successful neurodiversity programs.

Overall, we discuss how organizations should consider specific changes to their HRM procedures as a way to bolster their diversity, inclusion, and ethical climates to be more supportive of neurodiversity. The suggestions overall adhere to two guiding principles of tenets derived from the neurodiversity movement. First, the suggestions follow the idea that organizations should focus on the strengths that applicants and employees bring to the organization. Every employee has areas that are strengths and areas that present difficulties (Baron-Cohen, 2017; Faragher, 2018). What organizations with more successful neurodiversity programs have realized is that the benefits provided by having neurodivergent employees fill an important gap in their workplaces. For example, employees from the neurominority are typically committed and loyal workers (Association for Talent Development, 2018). Employees with dyslexia often have strengths around pattern recognition (Rothstein, 2012) and above-average presentation abilities (Burnett & Trerise, 2019; Rothstein, 2012). Moreover, employees with autism sometimes (though this too can be an overgeneralization) have strengths related to repetitive work, an ability to focus and develop an expertise in systems and their parts (Austin & Pisano, 2017; Elliott, 2018; Wright, 2016). Other examples are the strengths of employees with ADHD around their problem-solving abilities and predisposition toward entrepreneurial mindsets (Moore et al., 2021) and the strengths of employees with mental illnesses to tap into deep reserves of creative talent and exhibit unparalleled levels of warmth (Nyhan, 2018). Though these are only a few examples of the strengths that organizations have reaped, the overall point is that by focusing on employees' strengths, organizations can build and maintain climates that support neurodiversity. Importantly, we recognize that generalizations, whether positive or negative, inherently run the risk of stereotyping employees (or prospective ones). Our point here is to identify some of the potentially overlooked characteristics often possessed by neurominorities that might make these employees particularly well suited to enhance organizational functioning. This should not, however, be taken as suggesting that all members of this diverse group are in any way uniform in their strengths, weaknesses, or characteristics.

Second, our suggestions in this section follow the idea that organizations should eliminate unnecessary barriers in the environment that would present obstacles to employees leveraging their strengths and bringing those to their work. By starting with the notion that each employee thinks differently rather than following the typical way of implementing HRM practices that are developed around neurotypical preferences, organizations eliminate many of the barriers that present challenges to applicants and employees in the neurominority (Faragher, 2018; Manning, 2018) – and applicants and employees in general.

Next, we present our suggestions for organizational practices that follow both principles (i.e., focus on strengths, eliminate unnecessary barriers) and do so for each of the eight major HRM functions while showing the impact of each set of suggestions for diversity, inclusion, and ethical climates. Moreover, we provide additional specific practical suggestions not covered in the text as a part of Table 2.1. This table is also organized across the HRM life cycle.

TABLE 2.1 Suggestions for Human Resource Management Practices That May Strengthen Diversity, Inclusion, and Ethics Climates to Be More Supportive of Neurodiversity

Selection
▪ Engage in target recruiting with community partners (Erickson et al., 2014) such as Landmark College, in Vermont, which exclusively enrolls students who learn differently (Nyhan, 2018) ▪ Avoid jargon in recruitment ads, as EY has success with this practice (Association for Talent Development, 2018) ▪ Review preemployment screenings to evaluate if applicants' strengths are being assessed (Erickson et al., 2014) ▪ Consider replacing traditional interviews, like EY does, with applied tasks that assess problem-solving abilities (e.g., using Legos to build robots) (Ovaska-Few, 2018)
Compensation and Benefits
▪ Ensure that opportunities to work full-time match the desires of the employee (Austin & Pisano, 2017) ▪ Do not assume the credentials of applicants with neurodivergent conditions (Ali et al., 2011)
Employee Relations
▪ Have leaders openly support accommodations (Austin & Pisano, 2017; Patton, 2019; Wright, 2016) ▪ Authentic leadership styles are often more supportive than transformational leadership styles for employees with many neurodivergent conditions (Wright, 2016) ▪ Encourage leaders and managers to play an active role in supporting neurodiversity (Patton, 2019)

(Continued)

TABLE 2.1 (Continued)

Occupational Health and Safety
▪ Acknowledge the lack of understanding the general public has about neurodivergent conditions (Rothstein, 2012) ▪ Address negative stereotypes and discrimination that employees with neurodivergent conditions often encounter in the workplace (Atherton et al., 2019; Gray, 2001; Hinshaw & Stier, 2008; Johnson & Joshi, 2016; Mawson et al., 1985)
Training and Development
▪ Have managers who have taken formal training in neurodiversity conduct onboarding trainings, as EY has success with this practice (Association for Talent Development, 2018) ▪ Provide opportunities for employees to acclimate themselves to the workforce and workplace before starting in their positions (Nyhan, 2018) ▪ Provide opportunities for employees to socialize with employees who are neurodivergent (Nyhan, 2018) ▪ Allow for alternative types of training (e.g., self-paced tutorials) (Sumner & Brown, 2015)
Talent Management and Performance
▪ Engage office champions as mentors or coaches (Ovaska-Few, 2018) ▪ Have external coaches consults by phone to help them navigate interpersonal and life-management issues (Association for Talent Development, 2018)
Job Design
▪ Listen to new hires about what they need in their work environment (Ovaska-Few, 2018; Patton, 2019) ▪ Dedicate workspaces as quiet areas, as EY has success with this practice (Ovaska-Few, 2018) ▪ Dedicate workspaces as low-traffic areas, as EY has success with this practice (Ovaska-Few, 2018) ▪ Create different working zones, such as a zone for 'creative' group work and another for 'quiet' project work (Burnett & Trerise, 2019) ▪ Support flexible working patterns for employees with ADD/ADHD (Adamou et al., 2013; Painter et al., 2008) ▪ Support flexible start times based on employees' preferred routines (Johnson & Joshi, 2016) ▪ Allow headphones to block out environmental noise and prevent auditory overstimulation (Austin & Pisano, 2017) ▪ Allow lighting changes to block out visual distractions (Hensel, 2017)
Retention
▪ Create supportive 'ecosystems' for employees. SAP has had success creating support circles, while HPE has had success uses a 'pod' system (Austin & Pisano, 2017) ▪ Support employees' interactions with online communities as a source of support for neurodivergent individuals (Haney, 2018; Jaarsma & Welin, 2012; Runswick-Cole, 2014) ▪ Encourage employees to celebrate in their neurodivergent identity(ies) (Bagatell, 2010; Baker, 2011; Jaarsma & Welin, 2012; Jordan, 2010; Ortega, 2009; Strauss, 2013)

Note. Not every suggestion is appropriate for each type of neurodiversity.

Selection

Recruitment

In this volume, Giannantonio and Hurley-Hanson provide a comprehensive review of recruiting neurodivergent job seekers. But recruiting is where workplace (neurodiversity) inclusion begins, so for the sake of completeness, we briefly review extant research that may be useful in providing ways to strengthen diversity, inclusion, and ethical climates to support neurodiversity. First, diversity recruitment research shows that applicants have stronger intentions to accept an employment offer from organizations that are supportive of diversity (Avery et al., 2013), contributing to a stronger diversity climate as the organization gains more employees who are neurodivergent. This research is replicated in applicants with health conditions, especially if the organization has a history of committing to actions such as recruiting individuals from similar populations (von Schrader, Xu, et al., 2014; von Schrader, Malzer, et al., 2014). Overall, this effect is explained by organizations' efforts to be inclusive by affirming applicants' valued identities. This strengthens the inclusion climate of the organization, as their work environment is then one that is supportive of employees and their social identities. Moreover, it may make the organization more attractive to people who are more likely to accept the identities of dissimilar others (Avery et al., 2013).

Organizations have used a number of altered recruitment strategies to reach talent that is neurodivergent (Patton, 2019). Specific strategies are described in Table 2.1, but these can be summarized as reconceptualizing where targeted recruitment efforts take place (e.g., colleges that only admit students who are in the neurominority) and how that recruitment is taking place (e.g., changing the language traditionally used in job ads). Targeted strategies at the recruitment stage are necessary, as research in tangential literatures shows that only 11% of employers have recruiting strategy specific to attracting people with disabilities,[4] despite repeated statements about their desire to hire more people from this group (Dixon et al., 2003; c.f. Erickson et al., 2014). Such reconceptualized efforts around recruitment will help bolster diversity and inclusion climates in ways that better support applicants, including those who are neurodivergent.

A key consideration during recruitment around the organization's ethical climate concerns *disclosure*. Based on prevalence rates of neurodiverse conditions, we know that there are plenty of potential applicants for organizations to recruit that would achieve the goal of diversifying their workforce along the neurodiversity spectrum. For instance, approximately 1 in every 54 children in the United States (and 1 in every 160 worldwide) has autism (Baker, 2011; CDC, 2020; WHO, 2019). To give another example, between 5% and 20% of children in school (11% in college) have dyslexia (Rogers, 2017; Rothstein, 2012). Though we present some estimates here, the numbers are likely higher, but fear and stigma around neurodivergent conditions can prevent individuals from reporting or disclosing that they are part of the neurominority (Elliott, 2018), especially in a workplace context as opposed to a school context. Even considering the possibility of low estimates, we know that approximately half a million individuals with autism in the U.S. are estimated to become adults and potentially join the workforce this decade (Chu, 2015; Demer, 2018). Therefore, there are plenty of potential applicants to recruit. But we have also started to uncover that not all individuals disclose their neurodivergent conditions. This could present a barrier for organizations wanting to recruit from this population.

Research supports the idea that employees with autism actively avoid discussing their condition at work and specifically point to concerns about stigma (Johnson & Joshi, 2016). This is echoed by other research that shows many who are dyslexic do not see many benefits that would come from disclosure (Morris & Turnbull, 2007). Moreover, we have to consider that some individuals do not disclose because they do not identify with the labels that would be assigned to them if they did so (Brown & Leigh, 2018). Because disclosure is associated with disabilities and medical conditions, these types of labels are increasingly rejected by those with neurodivergent conditions that support the social movement around neurodiversity (Brown & Leigh, 2018).

Considering that disclosure is a barrier that impacts the recruitment of neurodivergent applicants (or prospective applicants), organizations will find that common strategies for targeted recruitment efforts, such as working with universities to establish pipelines of talented recruits, may not be fruitful. This is because records about students' personal information are likely confidential and not made available to organizations outside of the university. Moreover, most universities do not have systems in place that account for if a student is neurodivergent as separate from having a documented disability and therefore may not even be able to give that information (if a graduating student belonged to the neurominority) to potential employers, even if it was not considered personal information (Austin & Pisano, 2017). Overall, the consideration of disclosure further promotes the need for organizations to have climates that support neurodiversity – so that employees feel comfortable disclosing their neurodivergent status. Researchers have shown the importance of trust with managers in research done with dyslexic employees (Brown & Leigh, 2018); perhaps this translates to trust with recruiters as well. As such, stronger diversity, inclusion, and ethics climates that are supportive of neurodiversity will aid not only recruitment efforts but also other HRM functions that we will discuss next.

Hiring

Saleh, Chang, Bruyère, and Vogus (this volume) describe the role of interviewing in selecting neurodiverse job candidates. But since we see this as a critical part of a broader workplace neurodiversity-inclusive culture, we here briefly discuss several ways that hiring practices can be improved to strengthen diversity, inclusion, and ethics climates to support neurodiversity. To improve the organization's diversity climate, strategic changes can result in more neurodivergent applicants passing hurdles during selection. For example, many organizations include tests in their hiring process that heavily depend on reading and math. For applicants with learning disabilities, this can present a number of obstacles that have nothing to do with the strengths (e.g., intelligence or abilities in comprehension or mathematics) that they are going to contribute to the organization (Goldstein et al., 2011; Sumner & Brown, 2015). In short, these selection batteries often confound cognitive speed with power. A general approach recommended for organizations trying to enhance the supportiveness of their diversity climate concerning neurodiversity is to approach hiring with the idea that "Different isn't just good or bad. It isn't a qualifier. It just is" (Carmichael, 2013). Along these lines, it is the case that traditional hiring processes rely on strong communication skills that include timely verbal responses and expected eye contact (Goldstein et al., 2011; Sumner & Brown, 2015). At this point in the chapter, it should be clear that organizations supportive of neurodiversity should embrace people who express themselves in different ways (Rogers, 2017). This spirit towards neurodiversity is not captured in traditional interviews that are often constructed around structured question sets that assess behavioral responses as a way to eliminate bias. This is especially true as more and more companies are utilizing panel interviews or group interviews – both of which may require applicants to do some things not required by the job itself and therefore might unfairly screen out diverse employees. For neurodivergent applicants, Burnett and Trerise (2019) suggest altering these traditional hiring processes and let the applicant have space and time to analyze the questions, even being able to return their response on another day. This may support their strengths (e.g., the ability to focus on specific details) without needing to address the bigger picture or bigger issue that interview questions often target.

To improve inclusion climate, organizations can use the interview to support neurodiversity by asking questions designed to learn about the applicant's strengths. After gathering this information, the hiring manager can then move forward with the hiring process by "then try[ing] to match those skills up with a job that might be opening" (Lancaster, 2017; a strategy that Butler, a construction and development company, uses). Alternatively, organizations can assess applicants in ways that do not require interviews (Austin & Pisano, 2017). For instance, the Armed Services use more general assessments to ascertain which jobs align with a candidate's abilities rather than assessing how well the candidate fits with a specific job. These types of changes are truly inclusive of neurodiversity, as companies are redesigning hiring practices to go beyond measuring math and communication skills while aiming to focus on applicants' strengths that may lie outside of those particular skills (Faragher, 2018).

To improve the organization's ethical climate in ways that are more supportive of neurodiversity, we suggest adjusting the goal that is inherent in adopting traditional hiring practices. Most organizations rely on hiring practices that capture generalizable skills and abilities for most of applicants they have in their system. This goal of scalability is cost efficient, but it is not ethical from the perspective of a neurodivergent applicant. This is because these traditional hiring practices commonly are not oriented toward capturing the unique strengths of many neurodivergent applicants (Austin & Pisano, 2017). Overall, to improve diversity, inclusion, and ethical climates through changes to selection processes, it is necessary to focus on applicants' strengths instead of applying the philosophy that the hiring process is to weed out people by testing them in ways that aren't relevant to their job or the tasks they will be focusing on while employed at the organization.

Compensation and Benefits

For incumbent employees, there are a number of considerations around compensation and benefits procedures that can be restructured to strengthen diversity, inclusion, and ethics climates in a way that better supports neurodiversity. For instance, neurodivergent individuals have high rates of unemployment and underemployment (estimates ranging from 80% [Eden, 2019] to as high as 90% [Autism Speaks, 2017]). Specifically, reports show that individuals with Asperger's (the highest level of functioning autism) have an unemployment rate of 80% to 85% (Richards, 2012; National Autistic Society, 2016). These statistics show a need for organizations to build diversity climates that support the employment of neurodivergent individuals.

To build inclusive climates that are supportive of neurodiversity, organizations should be aware of conflict that may arise when neurodivergent employees work in part-time, as opposed to full-time, positions. Research shows that differences in employment status can have effects on inclusion that lead to withdrawal (Avery et al., 2012). Though part-time positions can be a wonderful consideration of a neurodivergent employee's possible stress in the work environment (Austin & Pisano, 2017), full-time employees can find this problematic if project deadlines fall outside of a key team member's work schedule. This conflict can erode the gains that organizations are making in the inclusiveness of their climate around neurodiversity if not addressed.

Moreover, when neurodivergent employees are hired, it is important that the organization has a strong ethical climate that addresses the underemployment of neurodivergent employees. It is a common experience for those who are neurodivergent to be underemployed (placed in low-level, unskilled jobs beneath their qualification level; Bjelland et al., 2010). Organizations that are trailblazers in this area have reported that the applicants to their neurodiversity programs often have college degrees, master's degrees, dual degrees, and even patents (Ali et al., 2011; Austin & Pisano, 2017). Both of these points – about unemployment and underemployment – suggest that when neurodivergent employees are hired, organizations have an ethical consideration to deploy and pay them fairly, as the educated and skilled workers that they are. It is unethical to let standard compensation and promotion practices of rewarding political skill (Munyon et al., 2015) continue if (a) political skill is not a job requirement and (b) such a practice adversely impacts many neurodivergent employees. Again, the point is that neurodivergent employees have unique strengths that are useful for the organization; these should be compensated as such. This approach will improve diversity, inclusion, and ethical climates by strengthening the association between rewards and performance.

Employee Relations

A third HRM area concerns the number of changes around traditional employee relations practices that can be restructured to strengthen diversity, inclusion, and ethics climates to support neurodiversity. Though there are numerous elements important to the topic of employee relations, we will focus on the role of managers and leaders, as they play a key role in how employees view their relationship with their organization. A key aspect of a strong diversity climate is that there is support for diversity throughout levels of the organization; and top management support is crucial. With neurodiversity, this is also true. Research on autism shows that having supportive senior managers and direct supervisors is related to having a work environment that is accepting of accommodations (Austin & Pisano, 2017; Patton, 2019; Wright, 2016). This support can be communicated in a number of ways. One example provided by Faragher (2018) describes how a director at an organization signed his emails with the following statement: 'excuse the typos, I'm dyslexic.'

Beyond management and leader support, certain types of leadership can aid neurodiversity-related efforts to be more inclusive. That is, transformational leadership often is not an effective leadership style for employees who are neurodivergent because the visionary aspects to transformational leadership are too abstract to provide guidance to employees that think in more specific ways (Hurley-Hanson & Giannantonio, 2017; Parr et al., 2013). However, a number of researchers have suggested that authentic leadership (Boekhorst, 2015; Dwertmann & Boehm, 2016; Hurley-Hanson & Giannantonio, 2017; Parr & Hunter, 2014; Walumbwa et al., 2008) is a leadership style that is inclusive of neurodiversity. This is also a truly inclusive approach, as authentic leadership will likely have a strong impact on how others in the organization embrace changes made to support neurodiversity (Patton, 2019). Further elaboration on leadership styles and their possible impact on maximizing workplace neurodiversity inclusion are addressed in the chapter by Seitz in this volume.

To maintain ethical climates that are supportive of neurodiversity, organizations can approach employee relations with the knowledge that strong management and leadership can exert a substantial impact on the experiences of neurodivergent employees (if their experiences are riddled with stigma, for example). Due to communication barriers and social deficits, employees with some neurodivergent conditions may not be especially proficient at discussing their condition, advocating for themselves or for neurodiversity in general, and overall may not be skilled at conveying to others the strengths and values they bring to the workgroup or organization overall. As such, managers and supervisors have a role in creating strong diversity and inclusion climates – but also a strong ethics climate – in the organization to help ensure that the environments they are creating actively involve neurodivergent workers by eliminating negative attitudes and behaviors (e.g., stigmatization, stereotyping, ostracism, or discrimination) directed at any employees, but especially those who may find it difficult to communicate their strengths for themselves. Managers and leaders can play a huge role in these types of changes and should, from an ethical perspective (Patton, 2019).

Occupational Health and Safety

A fourth set of considerations involves the roles of diversity, inclusion, and ethics climates in facilitating occupational health and safety. For the purposes of this chapter, we look at stigma and discrimination as important aspects of occupational health and safety. Regarding diversity climate, neurodivergent applicants and employees often report that diversity climates in their organizations are weak regarding occupational health and safety for employees in the neurominority. Research supports this, as employees with neurodivergent conditions are shown to face discrimination in the workplace around hiring practices, treatment on the job, and others' resistance to their workplace accommodations (Richards, 2012). Giving attention to building a diversity climate that reduces and eliminates these experiences for all employees will make diversity climates in organizations more supportive of neurodiversity (and all employees).

Training and Development

Changes in organizational talent enhancement procedures also can help produce diversity, inclusion, and ethics climates that are more supportive of neurodiversity. To strengthen diversity climates in this regard, organizations should consider alternative types of learning (other than traditional classroom-type trainings) if they want training and development to be effective for all employees. Companies have had success with self-paced tutorials or on-the-job training as compared to classroom training or training that takes place on a computer (Patton, 2019; Sumner & Brown, 2015). It is easy to see how traditional classroom-type trainings may be ineffective for employees with dyslexia, for example, as they are expected to process large amounts of reading or text through training exercises, the training presentations, after-training quizzes, etc. (Sumner & Brown, 2015).

To strengthen their inclusion climates, some organizations have developed creative alternatives to traditional training and development procedures. For example, at the College of William and Mary, the Bridge Program provides the opportunity for new students to arrive on campus early to meet other students who are neurodivergent and become familiar with the campus overall (Nyhan, 2018). Similar programs could be adapted easily to the organizational environment. Inclusion climates are also strengthened when managers meet directly with employees to demonstrate performance expectations during training initiatives and provide the level of detail needed during development efforts (Lancaster, 2017).

Concerning ethical climate initiatives, it is important that neurodivergent employees are considered for training and development opportunities. Research shows that neurodivergent employees are often overlooked and not selected for important career-building trainings (Patton, 2019; Sumner & Brown, 2015). Across the board, employees say that they want more training and development opportunities (O'Connor et al., 2007). As such, reconceptualizing how we prioritize and deliver training and development to reach more employees can only have positive implications for organizations along their diversity, inclusion, and ethical climates.

Talent Management and Performance

A comprehensive treatment of performance management of autistic employees by Hunter and Hunter is included later in this volume. Here, we want to include a brief set of considerations around how organizations can adapt their talent management and performance procedures to strengthen diversity, inclusion, and ethics climates in a way that supports neurodiversity. For example, good mentoring is a cornerstone of a strong diversity climate. For neurodivergent employees, experienced practitioners suggest that existing employees who are champions of diversity – or are even specifically neurodiversity champions – may make great mentors for employees who are in the neurominority. Given the prevalence of many neurodivergent conditions (e.g., autism, dyslexia), it would not be surprising to find that some current employees have family members who are neurodivergent and, therefore, possess experience in communicating across this form of difference (being aware of and using language associated with the social model rather than the medical model of neurodiversity) in addition to having a personal motivation to see employees who are neurodivergent succeed (Ovaska-Few, 2018).

Efforts that include others (champions as mentors) in the workplace also strengthen inclusion climates for neurodiversity. That is, by engaging employees as mentors, it spreads acceptance that this is the way that the organization chooses to conduct business. Some organizations have gone beyond mentoring systems to enhance diversity and inclusion climates to enhance their talent management practices. Some companies (i.e., SAP, Freddie Mac, and Hewlett Packard; Austin & Pisano, 2017; Wright, 2016) have had success with support circles made up of coworkers that act in different capacities to ensure that employees who are neurodivergent feel included and have access to advice and feedback from multiple perspectives within the organization (in both formal and informal ways). Overall, performance feedback can morph from an environment of correcting errors to one of learning from mistakes and gaining skills (Rebora, 2017) or focusing on strengths (Kluger & Nir, 2010) to strengthen inclusion climates to be more supportive of neurodiversity.

To strengthen ethical climates to be more supportive of neurodiversity, performance management systems need to recognize that many neurodivergent employees possess above-average intelligence and ensure that this is mirrored in positive performance evaluations (Austin & Pisano, 2017; Patton, 2019; Parr et al., 2013). In the case of giving performance feedback to an employee who is neurodivergent, it is important to consider how the working environment may have contributed to his or her performance (or lack thereof). For example, if an employee with dyslexia received excellent performance ratings but was reprimanded during their annual evaluation and then marked down for failure to complete trainings required by HR, it may in fact be unfair that such a demand was expected of them (Sumner & Brown, 2015). Taking a step back and understanding the true spirit of the neurodiversity paradigm means that cultures understand that neurodivergent employees have faced numerous barriers in school and in employment settings, along with many challenges in society overall. Organizations have a role in righting these wrongs by creating work environments that help individuals in the neurominority (and other employees and stakeholders) understand that there is an appreciation for the strengths and that their strengths are appreciated and supported by the organization (Eden, 2019). Importantly, this is not about lowering expectations or standards. Rather, it is about developing the requisite environmental infrastructure to ensure that neurodivergent employees are equally enabled to achieve the same performance standards used to assess those in the neuromajority. An expanded discussion on considerations in performance management and career development of a neurodiverse workforce are provided in the chapter by Hunter and Hunter in this volume.

Job Design

There are numerous ways organizations can approach job design differently to produce diversity, inclusion, and ethics climates that support neurodiversity. To strengthen diversity climates in this regard, job design needs to rely heavily on the accommodation process. So many researchers and practitioners have emphasized that accommodations are not as expensive or disruptive as many organizational decision-makers assume them to be (Ovaska-Few, 2018). For example, finding quiet workspaces or low-traffic locations for employees who are neurodivergent are accommodations that researchers (Association for Talent Development, 2018; Austin & Pisano, 2017; Hensel, 2017; Johnson & Joshi, 2016; Wright, 2016) and organizations such as EY suggests as impactful accommodations that do not cost anything (Schur et al., 2014; von Schrader, Xu, et al., 2014). Table 2.1 also lists similar accommodations such as allowing the use of headphones and flexible start times that cost little, if anything at all (Patton, 2019 and see also Patton and Doyle in this volume). It should be noted that many employees who are in the neurominority have attended schools, especially universities, where accommodations are part of the climate (Sumner & Brown, 2015). As such, they may be accustomed to certain provisions and even expect them (and be entitled to them). Thus, considering the role of accommodations in maintaining a strong diversity climate for the workforce, including employees in the neurominority, is imperative.

Organizations should follow these practices related to accommodation, as they also bolster inclusion climates in addition to diversity climates. Specifically, providing accommodations is truly inclusive of neurodiversity overall. Von Schrader and colleagues have done research that show how accommodations can become part of a culture that helps everyone – it does not have to create a situation wherein those not receiving accommodations are resentful or those requesting accommodations are scared to do so (von Schrader, Malzer, et al., 2014; von Schrader, Xu, et al., 2014). If anyone in the workforce can request accommodations around scheduling, policy changes, lighting, workspace, and other environmental factors (within reason), it bolsters an inclusion climate for everyone (Patton, 2019; Schur et al., 2014). Everyone can thrive through strong inclusion climates that are accepting of those that request simple environment modifications (Armstrong, 2010), including employees who belong to the neurominority.

The neurodiversity paradigm states that societal institutions such as schools and organizations should be set up to have accommodations as part of their operating procedures. On an ethical level, employees should be allowed to deviate from established practices to follow these principles from the neurodiversity paradigm. Acknowledging that society (including most organizations) is organized for neurotypical people strengthens an organization's ethical climate, especially when they establish norms in policies and procedures that accommodate neurodivergence. A different way of thinking about this is captured in the following quote by human–computer interaction specialist Steve Krug (2014, p. 163):

> The one argument for accessibility that doesn't get made nearly enough is how extraordinarily better it makes some people's lives. How many opportunities do we have to dramatically improve people's lives just by doing our job a little better?

This is truly an ethical approach to accommodations and to job design overall that fully embraces the neurodiversity paradigm. Overall, reconceptualizing how we approach accommodations to improve job design can have positive implications for organizations by strengthening their diversity, inclusion, and ethical climates so that they are more friendly for all employees.

Retention

Finally, there are considerations around retention procedures that can be restructured to enhance climates. To make diversity climates more supportive of neurodivergent employees, organizations should work to eliminate tokenism (only employing a small number of employees from the neurominority) around neurodiversity. Much of the stigma and stereotypes that neurodivergent employees experience in the workplace comes from neurotypical employees. Indeed, social interactions between neurotypical and neurodivergent individuals can be a source of stress due to the social demands that neurotypical employees may unknowingly place on colleagues who are neurodivergent (Chown, 2014; Dekker, 1999; Heasman & Gillespie, 2019). The more neurodivergent employees that are employed in the organization, the more that employees who are neurodivergent can have resources from others that understand their experience as someone in the neurominority (i.e., a critical mass). Moreover, a greater presence of neurodivergent employees could help facilitate better understanding of neurodiversity among those in the neuromajority.

You may be thinking, if neurodivergent individuals sometimes have trouble with social interactions, why would having additional neurodivergent employees to interact with help? As an example, Kapp et al. (2019) point out that autistic adults may understand one another better than nonautistic people understand a person with autism (Gernsbacher et al., 2017; Gillespie-Lynch et al., 2017; Komeda, 2015; Milton, 2014). In a study of autistic boys, researchers noted that the boys bonded with each other and recognized the similarities that existed amongst them (i.e., their similar experiences and traits) (Muskat, 2017). Moving beyond tokenism can mean that employees who are neurodivergent can have others they can share their experiences with, in a social context that does not place social demands on them, such as those found in most social spaces in workplaces (Runswick-Cole, 2014).

Next, to strengthen inclusion climates to be more supportive of neurodivergent employees around retention, many organizations have found success creating inclusive and supportive 'ecosystems' for employees. Companies like SAP have created support circles that include people in the workplace (i.e., a manager, a team buddy, a job coach, a mentor, and someone from HR) and also people in the employee's nonwork life (Austin & Pisano, 2017). HPE uses a 'pod' system in which neurodivergent employees work with four other employees overseen by a manager and neurodiversity consultant (Austin & Pisano, 2017; materials available online at https://digitalcommons.ilr.cornell.edu/dandelionprogram/). Moreover, supportive systems can come from outside the organization as well. A number of communities exist online as a source of support for neurodivergent individuals, especially those that prefer nonverbal communication (Haney, 2018; Jaarsma & Welin, 2012; Runswick-Cole, 2014). Perhaps companies could be inclusive of the need for that support and allow outside websites to be accessed at work. This could also be inclusive for other groups of employees (e.g., employees who are breastfeeding) who do not want to discuss their experiences with their colleagues due to stigma around the topic but can easily find the support they need online.

To strengthen ethics climates to be more supportive of neurodivergent employees around retention, it is suggested that organizations encourage neurodivergent employees to claim, feel pride in, and celebrate their identity(ies). This is central to the neurodiversity paradigm (Bagatell, 2010; Baker, 2011; Jaarsma & Welin, 2012; Jordan, 2010; Kapp et al., 2012, 2013; Ortega, 2009; Strauss, 2013), and it is ethical to support employees bringing their full selves to work. In practice, this entails organizations supporting employees as they participate in identity and community-building events (e.g., Autistic Pride Day), join identity and community-building organizations (e.g., Autism Network International), sport identity and community-building artifacts (T-shirts, stimming toys,), and use vocabulary that is identity and community- building (e.g., Aspie) (Angulo-Jiménez & DeThorne, 2019; Bagatell, 2010; Davidson, 2008; Donaldson et al., 2017). Ethical climates not only tolerate the existence or even inclusion of neurodivergent employees but also embrace neurodivergent culture; this has been compared to the celebration of Deaf culture within the Deaf community (Bagatell, 2010; Kermit, 2010; Sparrow, 2005). It is tempting to assume that organizations that accept neurodivergent employees would also allow the pride related to their neurodivergent culture to be a part of what they bring into the workplace. However, that is not always true. As a case in point, we recently saw that organizations that claimed to support the Black Lives Matter (BLM) movement banned BLM shirts (artifacts) (Segran, 2020). Accepting the employee and accepting the pride related to that identity are different conversations that require an ethical lens to understand the difference and be accepting of both.

We note that the seemingly opposing set-ups suggested in the diversity and inclusion climate sections of this discussion on retention (i.e., surround employees who are neurodivergent with more employees that are neurodivergent; surround employees who are neurodivergent with more employees that are neurotypical) further highlights the need for multiple climates to work together simultaneously for organizations to be able to truly embrace and support neurodiversity. Indeed, employees who are neurodivergent should have access to *both* employees who are neurodivergent and employees who are neurotypical to have successful careers that leverage their strengths in organizations. These climates (and suggestions associated with each) work together to provide a full experience that supports employees in the workplace in multiple ways, leading to their overall success if diversity, inclusion, and ethical climates simultaneously support neurodiversity.

Suggestions for Future Research

Next, we suggest future directions to guide scholars in addressing the many important issues, gaps, and challenges around ways to optimize organizational climates in ways that better support neurodiversity. Because the topic of neurodiversity is emergent, it is understandably understudied in academic scholarship (Haney, 2018); this is the case within the management literature as well. Promoting future research on the topic of neurodiversity is necessary, as the current lack of research on neurodiversity follows a trend in management research to study visible conditions as compared to nonvisible types of diversity (Santuzzi et al., 2014). As the topic of neurodiversity continues to gain attention, several areas of management research will benefit from the many available opportunities (Richards et al., 2019). Nevertheless, given our focus on the importance of strong climates for organizations, in this section of the chapter, we focus on climate-related topics that are in particular need of further research inquiry given the current state of the literature on neurodiversity in the management field.

Construct Definitions

As organizations create and strengthen climates to be more supportive of neurodiversity, it is important that researchers work to better understand the implications of defining neurodiversity in certain ways on their diversity, inclusion, and ethical climates. For example, as mentioned earlier in this chapter, organizations need definitions of diversity that include neurodiversity as separate from disability. Doing so should enhance the diversity climate in the organization, but future research should confirm this notion. However, we elaborate on this idea here in an effort to discuss some of the barriers to investigating definitions of diversity. Overall, becoming aware – as scholars and practitioners – of the terms we are using (e.g., neurodiversity, neurodivergent, disability) and making sure we are applying them correctly will guide diversity climate efforts in all areas of HRM. The goal is that organizations can reconceptualize what is normal rather than adding neurodiversity to a long list of other diversities (e.g., sex, race, age) that the organization claims to support and accept.

When considering how defining diversity would strengthen the diversity climate in an organization, it is important to consider that many applicants and employees who identify as neurodivergent also may have identities that are considered disabilities (Baron-Cohen, 2019; den Houting, 2019). As an example of this, more than 95% of autistic children have at least one condition in addition to autism; some of these conditions may be considered disabilities, while others are not disabilities (Baron-Cohen, 2019; den Houting, 2019). For disability compliance purposes, organizations need working definitions that identify what is a disability and what is not. Yet, this can get in the way of inclusion efforts, because the language and connotation around the term 'disability' brings the medical model and related language into the conversation (Baron-Cohen, 2017). Overall, disability and neurodiversity have different connotations (Brown & Leigh, 2018), so when both terms are applicable, it can produce confusion for practitioners and employees' perceptions of the sincerity of organizations' diversity and inclusion efforts. Future research on the use of the terms 'disability' and 'neurodiversity' would be useful, especially in cases where employees have both a disability (or disabilities) and belong to the neurominority.[5]

Then, to improve the inclusiveness of organizational climates, future research should attempt to study all of the neurodivergent conditions under the neurodiversity umbrella. The current state of research on neurodiversity is that most research has focused on a single condition: autism (and by extension, Asperger's). Similarly, most corporate programs around neurodiversity also have focused on hiring and retaining people with autism (Austin & Pisano, 2017). Due to the range of types of conditions that fall under the neurodiversity umbrella, it would be useless to try and generalize the impact on organizational climate that one type of condition has to other types of neurodiversity. In an effort to have work in this area be generalizable and more useful to practitioners as well, future research should attempt to study autism but also the other neurodivergent conditions covered by the term 'neurodiversity.'

Further, scholars would benefit from studying the implications of how neurodiversity definitions adopted by organizations impact the ethical climates of those companies by researching how opportunities afforded to employees who are neurodivergent may range as a function of where they fall on the spectrums within their condition(s). Specifically, most conditions that fall within the neurodiversity umbrella (e.g., autism, ADHD, dyslexia, depression) exist on a spectrum (Chu, 2015; Patton, 2019; Rothstein, 2012). To present this more realistically with an example, even if employees are at the same place on a spectrum of ADHD, one employee's ADHD can present as inattention while another employee's ADHD presents as hyperactivity (Hendrickx, 2010; Rothstein, 2012). In an effort to simplify the possibility of ranges and presentations of many neurodivergent conditions, many simplify the descriptions of neurodiverse conditions using the classifications of 'high functioning' and 'low functioning' (Lorenz et al., 2017).

These simplistic dichotomies contribute to stereotypes, stigma, and misinformation about neurodiversity. If organizations are not accounting for the nuances of employees' experiences across the spectrum or ignoring the 'low-functioning' end of the spectrum altogether, their ethical climate could weaken. For instance, organizations with good intentions around strengthening their diversity and inclusion climates may applaud themselves for hiring employees who are neurodivergent and making their HRM procedures more inclusive. But if the efforts are only targeted at those they consider 'high functioning,' how ethical is that? To have strong climates that support neurodiversity, organizations need definitions of neurodiversity that support all ranges of behavior associated with neurodivergent conditions, even if some may term certain behaviors low-functioning. Overall, future research aimed at finding construct definitions precise enough to include a wide range of neurodiverse conditions yet inclusive of the range of behaviors we expect in neurodivergent applicants and employees will contribute to research on neurodiversity in a way that strengthens diversity, inclusion, and ethics climates simultaneously.

New Theoretical Perspectives

As we mentioned previously, much research in this area started from a medical model. Thus, outside of management, theories (from psychiatrists and psychologists) on neurodivergent conditions have focused on neurobiological perspectives. Due to this medical model approach that focuses on individuals' deficiencies, theories since the 1980s to explain neurodiversity have tended to focus on cognitive deficits (e.g., weak central coherence; Frith & Happé, 1994).

As management scholars have started to apply our own theories to the topic of neurodiversity, scholars have most commonly applied stigma, disability-related, or person–environment fit theories (e.g., Johnson & Joshi, 2016; Santuzzi et al., 2014). We have already discussed the limitations (but also some strengths) stemming from taking a disability focus when researching the topic of neurodiversity. The neurodiversity literature that applies person–environment fit theories suggests there are industries and organizational environments that are particularly conducive to those who think differently. On the one hand, some have gone as far to say that Silicon Valley was built by individuals that are neurodivergent (Faragher, 2018). Creating cultures in which people can be themselves, even if their behavior is typically thought of as odd or nerdy (Austin & Pisano, 2017), can mean that employees who are neurodivergent will find better fit in these more diverse, inclusive, and ethical organizations. On the other hand, fit theories are somewhat limited, because organizations can apply the idea of 'fit' incorrectly in that they try and 'fix' deficits (e.g., communication differences or workstyle preferences) by having the person who is neurodivergent fit the organizational environment (assimilation) instead of changing the organizational climates so that they can leverage employees' strengths (accommodation). This suggests that future research in this area would benefit from novel theories and frameworks to understand the experiences of employees that are neurodivergent and the experiences of neurotypical employees around having increased support for neurodiversity in their workplaces. We present some ideas for future research that explores employee experiences around neurodiversity next.

Identity Theories

Incorporating theories that bring in an identity perspective to the study of neurodiversity will be fruitful for future research. Examining identity theories would be in line with a neurodiversity paradigm because self-advocates for neurodiversity often claim and celebrate their neurodivergent condition as something that is inseparable from their identity (Baker, 2011; Bagatell, 2010; Jaarsma & Welin, 2012; Jordan, 2010; Kapp et al., 2013; Ortega, 2009; Strauss, 2013). That is, to an employee who identifies as neurodivergent, identity is a key part of how they view themselves. This is behind statements such as "If I could snap my fingers and become non-autistic I would not do so. Autism is part of who I am" (Grandin, 1996, p. 16). As such, research would benefit from exploring how the identities of employees who are neurodivergent play a role in their experiences at work. These findings can help organizations understand how to build climates that are more supportive of neurodiversity.

Just as it is important to have future research explore the role of identity for those that do identify as neurodivergent, it is also important to have future research that explores the experiences of employees who do not claim an identity consistent with the neurodiversity paradigm. Some individuals may reject any category, as more and more employees find that existing categories of identities (e.g., male and female for sex) are limited and, instead, embrace a fluid approach in thinking about their identities (Clair et al., 2019). Moreover, some employees with diagnoses of autism, Asperger's, or other neurological conditions that fall under the neurodiversity umbrella may not identify with the label of neurodiversity (Baron-Cohen, 2019; Mitchell, 2015). For example, some employees may identify their neurodivergent condition as a disability and not a type of neurodiversity (O'Dell et al., 2016). Research has described how some people view their neurodivergent condition as synonymous with loneliness, stigma, being different, and exclusion (e.g., Humphrey & Lewis, 2008; Huws & Jones, 2008; Portway & Johnson, 2005; Ruiz Calzada et al., 2012). As such, they may find a sense of community with groups that support employees who identify as disabled. Along these lines, the employee may be focused on treatments and cures rather than embracing and celebrating their identities as defined by the neurodiversity movement (Bagatell, 2010; Ortega, 2009; Punshon et al., 2009).

To further advocate for identity theories in future scholarship that explores ways to enhance organizational climates to support neurodiversity, it is important to consider how identity-related statements were expressed recently by those in the neurominority when the new version of the DSM came out. In the DSM-V, definitions of autism, for example, were drastically changed as compared to previous versions of the published manual. Because categories of autism are being removed in the new version (e.g., terms like 'Asperger syndrome' that have been used for decades), some found the elimination of terms they identified with as confusing and hurtful to their identities (Krcek, 2013).

Intersectional Frameworks

As scholars move to advance work on neurodiversity, there is a pressing need to consider intersectional frameworks. Future research that includes intersectional frameworks can help scholars in discovering new ways to strengthen diversity, inclusion, and ethics climates so that they are more supportive of neurodiversity. Though a focus on intersectionality represents in general a recent push across diversity and identity research to incorporate this framework into management theory and research (Creary et al., 2015; Hall et al., 2019; Rosette et al., 2018; Rosette et al., 2016), there is a true need to consider intersectional frameworks due to the nature of many neurodivergent conditions.

First, we will consider the example of how neurodivergent conditions can be understood differently when considering an employee's sex as well. To elaborate, with autism, in the U.S., the prevalence rates vary widely by gender (diagnoses are 1 in 42 among boys as compared to 1 in 189 among girls; Fombonne, 2005; Krcek, 2013), meaning that some neurodivergent conditions exist within other identities (in this case, sex). Second, we will consider the example of gender identity. The term 'double helix rainbow kids' is used by researchers (Ehrensaft, 2018) to describe the high rates (eight times as high; DeVries et al., 2010) of individuals with autism that simultaneously exist along the gender spectrum (i.e., are gender nonconforming in their gender identities and/or gender expressions) and the autism spectrum. That is, research has demonstrated a significant correlation between autism and gender nonconformity, at least in children (Jacobs et al., 2014; Janssen et al., 2016; Shumer et al., 2015; Strang et al., 2014). These findings reinforce the application of an intersectional framework to better understand this type of diversity, as it demonstrates how an individual who is neurodiverse has a lived experience of existing differently – even outside of highly structured social norms around established identities like sex (Ehrensaft, 2018; Strang et al., 2018).

Third, we can also consider the example of race to establish the importance of future research using an intersectional framework to better understand the experiences of employees who are neurodivergent. Recent evidence suggests that additional research on the intersection of race and neurodiversity may be fruitful, as researchers are starting to establish differences in prevalence among different racial groups in key neurodivergent conditions (e.g., autism). Historically, the prototypical representation of autism was a depiction of a White child with a high socioeconomic background. However, the most recent research has indicated an increase (i.e., at 1.8%) in Black individuals having the highest rates among any racial or ethnic group (CU Boulder Today, 2020).

Other Climates

Though we highlighted that organizations should strengthen their diversity, inclusion, and ethics climates to be more supportive of neurodiversity, subsequent scholarship should examine elements of other types of climates within the organization that could influence employees' perceptions that the organization is supportive of neurodiversity. For example, justice climate may be pertinent to account for in future research on the topic of climate and neurodiversity. Previous research shows that organizational justice climate has a relationship with indicators of diversity, inclusion, and ethics, as it has been shown to deter sexual harassment (Rubino et al., 2018). Understandably, justice concerns could develop and may need to be addressed when making changes in the workplace to support neurodiversity. Consider the following example: An employee receives noise-cancelling headphones while stationed with colleagues in cubicles in an open space (example adapted from Sumner and Brown, 2015). The headphones are a reasonable accommodation for an employee that works better when overstimulation from noise makes work impossible. However, if accommodations are being given to some employees and not everyone, justice concerns could develop. Luckily, there are simple solutions around open communication (that respect employee rights to privacy) with all employees about the organization's values, priorities, and explanations for their decisions that can balance these concerns. Nevertheless, it could be argued that a strong justice climate needs to be supported by strong diversity, inclusion, and ethics climates for organizations to support neurodiversity in their workplaces. Therefore, future research should examine the role of justice climate, and perhaps other types of climates, in addition to diversity, inclusion, and ethics climates as they investigate the role of organizational climate in supporting neurodiversity in workplaces.

Research That Includes Neurotypicals

To improve climates, multiple stakeholders need to buy in to the way the organization is doing business for a climate to be diverse and feel truly inclusive and ethical. As such, it is necessary that future research on neurodiversity incorporates the role that others (other than the neurodivergent employee) have in creating and maintaining organizational climates supportive of neurodiversity (Jepsen et al., 2012).[6] For instance, individuals that are influential in an employee's life may see their neurodivergent condition(s) differently than the organization and/or the employee does. Research shows that families – in particular caretakers – often have viewpoints that focus on cures, treatments, and other medical-model lenses and that this focus can differ from the viewpoint of the neurodivergent individual (Baker, 2011; Haney, 2018). In addition to families and caretakers, job coaches are another example of individuals who are important stakeholders in the workplace experiences of many employees with neurodivergent conditions. How do organizations work with these stakeholders if their viewpoints on neurodiversity are different from the employees and their own? This is a research question that would be fruitful as organizations build and maintain climates to be more supportive of neurodiversity.

Moreover, knowing more about the experiences of neurotypicals as they interact with neurodivergent employees may help identify barriers in enhancing climates – areas where managers could intervene with training, for example. This is similar to any groups of employees who may be coming to the organization with different backgrounds and life experiences – they may not understand the other's experiences and perspectives, thus not listening or understanding, dampening communication and acceptance (Awbrey, 2007; Haney, 2018). Both parties (neurotypicals and neurodivergent employees) should have expectations to grow in this area. Training can help strengthen inclusion, as neurotypicals can understand the experiences of neurodivergent employees, some common barriers, their role as neurotypical employees in leveraging and breaking down those barriers (Ovaska-Few, 2018).

Research suggests that nonautistic people often misunderstand the behavior of employees from the neurominority (Faso et al., 2015; Sheppard et al., 2016). An example of something that could be covered in this training are common behaviors that might be experienced that some have not been exposed to before. Specifically, many neurodivergent conditions can exhibit behaviorally with stimming, "repetitive, usually rhythmic behavior that was commonly expressed through body movements (variously described as hand flapping, finger flicking, hair pulling or pinching, feet flexing, spinning, necklace playing) but also vocalizations (e.g. muttering, grunting, stuttering, whistling, singing)" (Kapp et al., 2019, p. 1785). Kapp et al. (2019) suggest that understanding these as a soothing coping mechanism can help others be supportive and points to research suggesting that all humans use these types of behaviors as coping behaviors (e.g. Jaswal & Akhtar, 2018; Lindsmith, 2014). Training that highlights these similarities enhances climates around neurodiversity while increasing understanding and providing skills to enhance interactions in the workplace, therefore strengthening organizational climates. It should be noted that for training to be truly impactful, it has to be more than awareness training (Kalev et al., 2006), should include real-life examples (Patton, 2019), and should be inclusive of neurodivergent voices rather than being based on stereotypes or definitions of conditions provided by medical professionals.

Discussion

In this chapter, we aimed to show the role that psychological climates have in supporting neurodiversity in organizations. Through a focus on diversity, inclusion, and ethical climates, we demonstrated ways to bolster climates across each of the eight primary functions of HRM in an effort to highlight ways that organizations make changes in their workplaces to be more supportive of neurodiversity. We also presented future research directions to guide management scholars as they continue their exploration of neurodiversity as a type of diversity important to organizations. Our hope is that presenting research focused on the importance of studying organizational climates from both practical and research lenses to support neurodiversity in workplaces will contribute to workplaces with altered environments so that all employees – including those who are neurodivergent – could easily apply their strengths at work.

Overall, we showed that creating and maintaining climates that support neurodiversity involves recreating policies and practices, and that can be complex. As Golden from EY noted:

> [A] lot of investment goes into setting these programs up because we are sourcing differently . . . We are screening and interviewing differently outside of our usual recruitment process, training and assessment process, and then we make offers. Then they go through a customized onboarding process, and they're managed by hiring managers that are specifically trained, and they have office buddies who support them and they have coaches who support them. It's a fairly intensive endeavor.
>
> (Cohn, 2017)

However, the investment is worth it in so many ways. As one woman with ADHD described,

> Having ADHD has been an advantage. I work well to deadlines and can get a lot done in a short time, so a two-hour visit to a potential customer's home is perfect. I can produce plans in a few minutes, while it can take my colleagues all day . . . I can't work with distractions, so would rather be in a cupboard than an open-plan office, but my sales conversion rate is 40% higher than the rest of my team, so it's worth them making allowances.
>
> (Faragher, 2018)

In the remainder of the discussion, we will summarize why the investment in strengthening climates to be more supportive of neurodiversity can truly pay off for organizations.

The business case for neurodiversity has been established. Research has shown that neurodiverse workforces bring new perspectives to their companies and approach complex issues in different (creative) ways (Austin & Pisano, 2017; Eden, 2019; Nyhan, 2018; Ovaska-Few, 2018). Further, research demonstrated that more neurodiverse software testing teams were 30% more productive than less neurodiverse testing teams (Austin & Pisano, 2017). To provide additional examples, both SAP and HPE report that by having neurodiverse employees on teams, those teams generated significant innovations (at SAP, one of these innovations helped the company develop a technical fix worth an estimated $40 million in savings; Austin & Pisano, 2017). Indeed, employees in the neurominority have broken stereotypes and exceeded expectations in many instances. As such, some companies started neurodiversity programs with limitations on the types of roles (quality-testing roles, work with repetitive tasks), but they are now expanding those self-imposed limitations (Austin & Pisano, 2017; Faragher, 2018).

Given these expected and unexpected business benefits for employees and organizations, we would like to state that strengthening diversity, inclusion, and ethical climates to be more supportive of neurodiversity not only has benefits for organizations and for employees in the neurominority – but it actually strengthens workplace climates for *all* employees. For example, many of the accommodations made for neurodivergent employees, such as clearer communication, enhanced task structure for projects, and an enhanced working environment (such as augmenting the climates discussed in this chapter), can be of benefit to all employees (Burnett & Trerise, 2019; Faragher, 2018). As an example, Austin and Pisano (2017) in their *Harvard Business Review* article about neurodiversity spoke with an executive who explained how efforts to make corporate communications more direct improved communication across the organization. Others have commented "accommodations we made for individuals for the spectrum actually helped the whole team" (Association for Talent Development, 2018).

Overall, SAP, Hewlett Packard Enterprise, Microsoft, Willis Towers Watson, and EY have discussed publicly how reforming HR practices to capitalize on the talents of neurodiverse people have unlocked their ability to better leverage the skills of *all* workers (Austin & Pisano, 2017). These improvements across the workforce have motivated many organizations with neurodiversity programs to make broader changes to mainstream their neurodiversity programs. Specifically, SAP and Microsoft have goals to make their talent processes so mainstream that they can close the neurodiversity programs (Austin & Pisano, 2017).

Further evidence of how strengthening climates to support neurodiversity improves the workplace for *all* employees comes from the gains in skill sets of neurotypical employees. Research has shown that when neurotypical employees are taught about neurodiversity, they do not see 'ability' and 'disability' as distinct terms that are mutually exclusive (Robertson, 2010). Moreover, managers involved in neurodiversity programs gain skills relating to their team members as individuals, and these skills make them better managers overall (Faragher, 2018); some have stated that after being involved in neurodiversity programs, they are more compassionate (Austin & Pisano, 2017; Elliott, 2018). Moreover, neurotypical employees also report gains in their workplace when they work with employees that are neurodivergent; these gains include an increased appreciation of different perspectives, the ability to challenge groupthink tendencies, experiencing higher morale, and viewing their work as more meaningful (Austin & Pisano, 2017; Faragher, 2018).

The logic that strengthening climates to support neurodiversity supports organizations in their overall business efforts extends even further. Given the prevalence of neurodivergence in the general population (Appiah, 2018) and the assumption that there are a lot of people who are misdiagnosed or undiagnosed (Butterworth & Kovas, 2013), the likelihood is high that many organizations are already encountering inefficiencies in their existing HRM practices. This is because the likelihood is high that leaders and managers are already involved with managing applicants and employees that are in the neurominority. Given this high likelihood, organizations should embrace the idea of strengthening their climates to support neurodiversity, as the need already exists. Indeed, it is estimated that around 10% of the population is neurodivergent, so employers that do not adapt their climates to support neurodiversity by changing their HRM practices to strengthen their diversity, inclusion, and ethics climates are missing out on the talent that research shows increases the creativity, innovation, productivity, and resilience of their workforce (Austin & Pisano, 2017; Faragher, 2018).

Notes

1. Admittedly, some character portrayals in the media are beginning to explore neurodiversity beyond the savant stereotype (e.g., the film *Neurotypical,* the Netflix show *Atypical*), though many of these portrayals do not specifically speak to the role of neurodiversity for employees or organizations.
2. Disability in this chapter is defined as when a person falls below an average level of functioning in one or more psychological or physical functions (Baron-Cohen, 2019).
3. The neurodiversity movement is defined in this chapter as a perspective that supports the notion that there is no one 'normal' brain type; this is in contrast to the medical model that views neurodivergent conditions as disorders (Baron-Cohen, 2019).
4. We note that employees with disabilities are not the same population as neurodivergent (though they can, and often do, overlap; Baron-Cohen, 2019), hence our pull on a tangential literature for inspiration, as research on neurodiversity specifically is not as developed yet.
5. To complicate the practicality of this, the medical community and other authorities that have traditionally defined terms adapted in society around neurodiversity-related topics are currently reconceptualizing how they define individual conditions that fall under the neurodiversity umbrella. For example, in the fourth edition of the *Diagnostic and Statistical Manual of Mental Disorders* (DSM), autism was defined with details about subcategories. But then, in the fifth edition of the DSM, this approach changed in favor of a more concise definition without subcategories (Hensel, 2017). While these changes can signal more inclusion if organizations choose similar changes in their definitions, they can also signal less inclusion to others who identify with the terms used in the previous, more detailed definition.
6. We suggest this focus on neurotypical individuals while acknowledging fully that the neurodiversity movement would not exist without the voice of individuals with neurodivergent conditions themselves discussing their own experiences of using their strengths to benefit their work (den Houting, 2019; Haney, 2018). Our suggestion to focus on the role of neurotypicals does not imply a shift in focus from the voices and perspectives of employees who have neurodivergent conditions.

References

Adamou, M., Arif, M., Asherson, P., Aw, T. C., Bolea, B., Coghill, D., Guðjónsson, G., Halmøy, A., Hodgkins, P., Müller, U., Pitts, M., Trakoli, A., Williams, N., & Young, S. (2013). Occupational issues of adults with ADHD. *BMC Psychiatry, 13*, 59. https://doi.org/10.1186/1471-244X-13-59

Ali, M., Schur, L., & Blanck, P. (2011). What types of jobs do people with disabilities want? *Journal of Occupational Rehabilitation, 21*, 199–210. https://doi.org/10.1007/s10926-010-9266-0

Angulo-Jiménez, H., & DeThorne, L. (2019). Narratives about autism: An analysis of YouTube videos by individuals who self-identify as autistic. *American Journal of Speech-Language Pathology, 28*, 569–590. https://doi.org/10.1044/2018_AJSLP-18-0045

Appiah, K. A. (2018, January). Can autism make me a diversity hire? *The New York Times Magazine*, 20.

Armstrong, T. (2010). *Neurodiversity: Discovering the extraordinary gifts of autism, ADHD, dyslexia, and other brain differences.* Boston, MA: Da Capo Lifelong Books.

Association for Talent Development. (2018). Embracing neurodiversity. *Talent Development at Work.* Retrieved from www.td.org/magazines/td-magazine/embracing-neurodiversity

Atherton, G., Lummis, B., Day, S. X., & Cross, L. (2019). What am I thinking? Perspective-taking from the perspective of adolescents with autism. *Autism, 23*, 1186–1200. https://doi.org/10.1177/1362361318793409

Austin, R. D., & Pisano, G. P. (2017, May). Neurodiversity as a competitive advantage. *Harvard Business Review.* Retrieved from https://hbr.org/2017/05/neurodiversity-as-a-competitive-advantage

Autism Speaks. (2017). *Facts about autism.* Retrieved from www.autismspeaks.org/what-autism/facts-about-autism

Avery, D. R., & McKay, P. F. (2010). Doing diversity right: An empirically based approach to effective diversity management. In G. Hodgkinson & J. K. Ford (Eds.), *International review of industrial and organizational psychology* (Vol. 25, pp. 227–252). West Sussex: Wiley.

Avery, D. R., Volpone, S. D., McKay, P. F., King, E., & Wilson, D. C. (2012). Is relational demography relative? How employment status influences effects of supervisor – Subordinate demographic similarity. *Journal of Business and Psychology, 27*, 83–98. https://doi.org/10.1007/s10869-011-9230-9

Avery, D. R., Volpone, S. D., Stewart, R., Luksyte, A., Hernandez, M., McKay, P. F., & Hebl, M. R. (2013). Examining the draw of diversity: How diversity climate perceptions affect job pursuit intentions. *Human Resource Management, 52*, 175–193. https://doi.org/10.1002/hrm.21524

Awbrey, S. M. (2007). The dynamics of vertical and horizontal diversity in organization and society. *Human Resource Development Review, 6*, 7–32. https://doi.org/10.1177/1534484306295638

Babineau, S. (2010). *Neuro-diversity works: A study of employees with ADHD, Asperger's syndrome and PTSD.* North Charleston, SC: CreativeSpace.

Bagatell, N. (2010). From cure to community: Transforming notions of autism. *Ethos, 38*, 34–58. https://doi.org/10.1111/j.1548-1352.2009.01080.x

Baker, D. L. (2011). *The politics of neurodiversity: Why public policy matters.* Boulder, CO: Lynne Rienner.

Baron-Cohen, S. (2017). Editorial perspective: Neurodiversity – a revolutionary concept for autism and psychiatry. *Journal of Child Psychology and Psychiatry, 58*, 744–747. https://doi.org/10.1111/jcpp.12703

Baron-Cohen, S. (2019). The concept of neurodiversity is dividing the autism community. *Scientific American Mind.* Retrieved from https://blogs.scientificamerican.com/observations/the-concept-of-neurodiversity-is-dividing-the-autism-community/

Berry, J. W. (1990). The role of psychology in ethnic studies. *Canadian Ethnic Studies, 22*, 8–21.

Bjelland, M. J., Bruyère, S. M., von Schrader, S., Houtenville, A. J., Ruiz-Quintanilla, A., & Webber, D. A. (2010). Age and disability employment discrimination: Occupational rehabilitation implications. *Journal of Occupational Rehabilitation, 20*, 456–471. https://doi.org/10.1007/s10926-009-9194-z

Boekhorst, J. A. (2015). The role of authentic leadership in fostering workplace inclusion: A social information processing perspective. *Human Resource Management, 54*, 241–264. https://doi.org/10.1002/hrm.21669

Brown, N., & Leigh, J. (2018). Ableism in academia: Where are the disabled and ill academics? *Disability & Society, 33*(6), 985–989, doi: 10.1080/09687599.2018.1455627

Brown, S. P., & Leigh, T. W. (1996). A new look at psychological climate and its relationship to job involvement, effort, and performance. *Journal of Applied Psychology, 81*, 358–368. https://doi.org/10.1037/0021-9010.81.4.358

Bruyère, S. M. (2016). *Disability and employer practices: Research across the disciplines*. Ithaca, NY: Cornell University Press.

Bruyère, S. M. (2019). *Employment and disabilities: Issues, innovations and opportunities*. Champaign, IL: Labor and Employment Relations Association.

Burnett, K., & Trerise, M. (2019, March). Embracing neurodiversity in the workplace. *Training Journal*. Retrieved from www.trainingjournal.com/articles/features/tj-magazine-embracing-neurodiversity-workplace

Butterworth, B., & Kovas, Y. (2013). Understanding neurocognitive disorders can improve educational for all. *Science, 340*, 300–305. https://doi.org/10.1126/science.1231022

Carmichael, J. (2013). Retrieved from http://writingandotherlifelessons.blogspot.com/2014/04/shout-out-to-chapters-st-vital.html

Carter, E. W., Austin, D., & Trainor, A. A. (2012). Predictors of postschool employment outcomes for young adults with severe disabilities. *Journal of Disability Policy Studies, 23*, 50–63. https://doi.org/10.1177/1044207311414680

Catalyst. (2005). *Catalyst member benchmarking report 2005*. New York: Catalyst.

Centers for Disease Control and Prevention. (2020). *Data & statistics on autism spectrum disorder*. Retrieved from www.cdc.gov/ncbddd/autism/data.html

Chen, X.-P., Liu, D., & Portnoy, R. (2012). A multilevel investigation of motivational cultural intelligence, organizational diversity climate, and cultural sales: Evidence from U.S. real estate firms. *Journal of Applied Psychology, 97*, 93–106. https://doi.org/10.1037/a0024697

Chown, N. (2014). More on the ontological status of autism and double empathy. *Disability and Society, 29*, 1672–1676. https://doi.org/10.1080/09687599.2014.949625

Chu, F. (2015). Making it work. *Inc. Magazine, 37*, 34–45.

CIPD. (2018). *Neurodiversity at work*. Retrieved from www.cipd.co.uk/Images/neurodiversity-at-work_2018_tcm18-37852.pdf

Clair, J. A., Humberd, B. K., Rouse, E. D., & Jones, E. B. (2019). Loosening categorical thinking: Extending the terrain of theory and research on demographic identities in organizations. *The Academy of Management Review, 44*(3), 592–617. https://doi.org/10.5465/amr.2017.0054

Cohn, M. (2017). EY reaches out: The firm steps up recruitment of disabled and autistic employees. *Accounting Today*. Retrieved from www.accountingtoday.com/news/ey-steps-up-recruitment-of-disabled-and-autism-spectrum-employees

Coldwell, D. A., Billsberry, J., van Meurs, N., & Marsh, P. J. G. (2008). The effects of person organization ethical fit on employee attraction and retention: Towards a testable explanatory model. *Journal of Business Ethics, 78*, 611–622. https://doi.org/10.1007/s10551-007-9371-y

Constantino, C. D. (2018). What can stutterers learn from the neurodiversity movement? *Seminars in Speech and Language, 39*, 382–396. https://doi.org/10.1055/s-0038-1667166

Cox Jr., T. H. (1994). *Cultural diversity in organizations: Theory, research, & practice*. San Francisco, CA: Berrett-Koehler.

Creary, S. J., Caza, B. B., & Roberts, L. M. (2015). Out of the box? How managing a subordinate's multiple identities affects the quality of a manager-subordinate relationship. *Academy of Management Review, 40*, 538–562. https://doi.org/10.5465/amr.2013.0101

CU BoulderToday. (2020). Retrieved from https://www.colorado.edu/today/2020/03/19/autism-rates-declining-among-wealthy-whites-escalating-among-poor

Dale, D. (2013, July 28). Honest to goodness. *The Sydney Morning Herald*. Retrieved from www.smh.com.au/entertainment/honest-to-goodness-20130726-2qny9.html

Davidson, J. (2008). Autistic culture online: Virtual communication and cultural expression on the spectrum. *Social & Cultural Geography, 9*, 791–806. https://doi.org/10.1080/14649360802382586

Dekker, M. (1999). *On our own terms: Emerging autistic culture*. Retrieved from www. autscape.org/2015/programme/handouts/Autistic-Culture- 07-Oct-1999.pdf

Demer, L. L. (2018). The autism spectrum: Human rights perspectives. *Pediatrics, 141*, eS369. https://doi.org/10.1542/peds.2016-4300O

den Houting, J. (2019). Neurodiversity: An insider's perspective. *Autism, 23*(2), 271–273. https://doi.org/10.1177/1362361318820762

DeVries, A. L., Noens, I. L., Xohen-Kettenis, P.T., van Berckalaer-Onnes, I. A., & Doreleijers, T. A. (2010). Autism spectrum disorder in gender dysphoric children and adolescents. *Journal of Autism and Developmental Disorders, 40*, 930–936. https://doi.org/10.1007/s10803-010-0935-9

Dixon, K. A., Kruse, D., & Van Horn, C. E. (2003). *Restricted access: A survey of employers about people with disabilities and lowering barriers to work, Rutgers University*. New Brunswick, NJ: Heldrich Center for Workforce Development.

Donaldson, A., Krejcha, K., & McMillin, A. (2017). A strengths-based approach to autism: Neurodiversity and partnering with the autism community. *Perspectives of the ASHA Special Interest Groups, 2*, 56–68. https://doi.org/10.1044/PERSP2.SIG1.56

Dwertmann, D. J. G., & Boehm, S. A. (2016). Status matters: The asymmetric effects of supervisor – Subordinate disability incongruence and climate for inclusion. *Academy of Management Journal, 59*, 44–64. https://doi.org/10.5465/amj.2014.0093

Eden, P. (2019, January/February). Corporate America must invest in neurodiversity. *University Business*, 48–48.

Ehrensaft, D. (2018). Double helix rainbow kids. *Journal of Autism and Developmental Disorders, 48*, 4079–4081. https://doi.org/10.1007/s10803-018-3716-5

Elliott, N. (2018, June). Neurodiversity: The next frontier in social justice. *Diverse*, 32.

Erickson, W. A., von Schrader, S., Bruyère, S. M., VanLooy, S. A., & Matteson, D. S. (2014). Disability-inclusive employer practices and hiring of individuals with disabilities. *Rehabilitation Research, Policy, and Education, 28*, 309–327. https://doi.org/10.1891/2168-6653.28.4.309

Faragher, J. (2018). Thinking differently has made us winners at work. *People Management*, 32–36.

Faso, D. J., Sasson, N. J., & Pinkham, A. E. (2015). Evaluating posed and evoked facial expressions of emotion from adults with autism spectrum disorder. *Journal of Autism and Developmental Disorders, 45*, 75–89. https://doi.org/10.1007/s10803-014-2194-7

Fombonne, E. (2005). Epidemiology of autistic disorder and other pervasive developmental disorders. *Journal of Clinical Psychiatry, 66*, 3–8.

Frith, U., & Happé, F. (1994). Autism: Beyond 'theory of mind'. *Cognition, 50*, 115–132.

Gernsbacher, M. A., Stevenson, J. L., & Dern, S. (2017). Specificity, contexts, and reference groups matter when assessing autistic traits. *PLoS ONE, 12*, e0171931. https://doi.org/10.1371/journal.pone.0171931

Gillespie-Lynch, K., Kapp, S., Brooks, P., Pickens, J. & Schwartzman, B. (2017). Whose expertise is it? Evidence for autistic adults as critical autism experts. *Frontiers in Psychology, 8*, 438. https://doi.org/10.3389/fpsyg.2017.00438

Goldstein, S., Naglieri, J. A., & DeVries, M. (2011). *Learning and attention disorders in adolescence and adulthood* (2nd ed.). Hoboken, NJ: Wiley.

Grandin, T. (1996). *Thinking in pictures: And other reports from my life with autism*. New York: First Vintage Books.

Gray, J. R. (2001). Emotional modulation of cognitive control: Approach-withdrawal states double-dissociate spatial from verbal two-back task performance. *Journal of Experimental Psychology: General, 130*, 436–452. https://doi.org/10.1037//0096-3445.130.3.436

Hall, E., Hall, A., Galinski, A., & Phillips, K. (2019). MOSAIC: A model of stereotyping through associated and intersectional categories. *Academy of Management Review, 44*, 643–672. https://doi.org/10.5465/amr.2017.0109

Haney, J. L. (2018). Reconceptualizing autism: An alternative paradigm for social work practice. *Journal of Progressive Human Services, 29*, 61–80, https://doi.org/10.1080/10428232.2017.1394689

Hayes, B. C., Bartle, S. A., & Major, D. A. (2002). Climate for opportunity: A conceptual model. *Human Resource Management Review, 12*, 445–468. https://doi.org/10.1016/S1053-4822(02)00050-5

Heasman, B., & Gillespie, A. (2019). Neurodivergent intersubjectivity: Distinctive features of how autistic people create shared understanding. *Autism, 23*, 910–921. https://doi.org/10.1177/1362361318785172

Hendrickx, S. (2010). *The adolescent and adult neuro-diversity handbook: Asperger Syndrome, ADHD, dyslexia and dyspraxia and related conditions*. London: JKP Gateshead.

Hensel, W. F. (2017). People with Autism spectrum disorder in the workplace: An expanding legal frontier. *Harvard Civil Rights-Civil Liberties Law Review, 52*, 73–102.

Herrera, C. (2013). What's the difference? In C. Herrera & A. Perry (Eds.), *Ethics and neurodiversity* (pp. 1–17). Newcastle upon Tyne: Cambridge Scholars.

Hicks-Clarke, D., & Iles, P. (2000). Climate for diversity and its effects on career and organizational attitudes and perceptions. *Personnel Review, 29*, 324–346. https://doi.org/10.1108/00483480010324689

Hinshaw, S. P., & Stier, A. (2008). Stigma as related to mental disorders. *Annual Review of Clinical Psychology, 4*, 367–393. https://doi.org/10.1146/annurev.clinpsy.4.022007.141245

Holmes, O., Jiang, K., Avery, D. R., McKay, P. F., Oh, I-S., & Tillman, C. J. (2021). A meta-analysis integrating 25 years of diversity climate research. *Journal of Management, 47*(6), 1357–1382. doi: 10.1177/0149206320934547

Holvino, E. H., Ferdman, B. M., & Merrill-Sands, D. (2004). Creating and sustaining diversity and inclusion in organizations: Strategies and approaches. In M. S. Stockdale & F. J. Cosby (Eds.), *The psychology and management of workplace diversity* (pp. 245–276). Malden, MA: Blackwell.

Humphrey, N., & Lewis, S. (2008). "Make me normal": The views and experiences of pupils on the autistic spectrum in mainstream secondary schools. *Autism, 12*, 23–46. https://doi.org/10.1177/1362361307085267

Hurley-Hanson, A. E., & Giannantonio, C. M. (2017). LMX and autism: Effective working relationships. In T. A. Scandura & E. Mouriño-Ruiz (Eds.), *Leading diversity in the 21st century* (pp. 281–302). Charlotte, NC: IAP Information Age Publishing.

Hurtado, S., Milem, J. F., Clayton-Pedersen, A. R., & Allen, W. R. (1998). Enhancing campus climates for racial/ethnic diversity through educational policy and practice. *The Review of Higher Education, 21*, 279–302. https://doi.org/10.1353/rhe.1998.0003

Huws, J. C., & Jones, R. S. P. (2008). Diagnosis, disclosure, and having autism: An interpretative phenomenological analysis of the perceptions of young people with autism. *Journal of Intellectual and Developmental Disability, 33*, 99–107. https://doi.org/10.1080/13668250802010394

Hyde, C. A., & Hopkins, K. (2004). Diversity climates in human service agencies: An exploratory assessment. *Journal of Ethnic and Cultural Diversity in Social Work, 13*, 25–43. https://doi.org/10.1300/J051v13n02_02

Jaarsma, P., & Welin, S. (2012). Autism as natural human variation: Reflections on claims of the neurodiversity movement. *Health Care Analysis, 20*, 20–30. https://doi.org/10.1007/510728-011-0169-9

Jacobs, L. A., Rachlin, K., Erickson-Schroth, L., & Janssen, A. (2014). Gender dysphoria and co-occurring autism spectrum disorders: Review, case examples, and treatment considerations. *LGBT Health, 1*, 277–282. https://doi.org/10.1089/lgbt.2013.0045

James, L. R., Choi, C. C., Ko, C.-H. E., McNeil, P. K., Minton, M. K., Wright, M. A., & Kim, K.-i. (2008). Organizational and psychological climate: A review of theory and research. *European Journal of Work and Organizational Psychology, 17*(1), 5–32. https://doi.org/10.1080/13594320701662550

James, L. R., James, L. A., & Ashe, D. K. (1990). The meaning of organizations: The role of cognition and values. In B. Schneider (Ed.), *Organizational climate and culture* (pp. 40–84). San Francisco, CA: Jossey-Bass.

Janssen, A., Huang, H., & Duncan, C. (2016). Gender variance among youth with autism spectrum disorders: A retrospective chart review. *Transgender Health, 1*, 63–68.

Jaramillo, F., Mulki, J. P., & Solomon, P. (2006). The role of ethical climate on salesperson's role stress, job attitudes, turnover intention, and job performance. *Journal of Personal Selling & Sales Management, 26*, 271–282. https://doi.org/10.2753/PSS0885-3134260302

Jaswal, V. K., & Akhtar, N. (2018). Being vs. appearing socially uninterested: Challenging assumptions about social motivation in autism. *Behavioral and Brain Sciences, 2018*, 1–84. https://doi.org/10.1017/S0140525X18001826

Jepsen, M. I., Gray, K. M., & Taffe, J. R. (2012). Agreement in multi-informant assessment of behaviour and emotional problems and social functioning in adolescents with autistic and Asperger's disorder. *Research in Autism Spectrum Disorders, 6*, 1091–1098. https://doi.org/10.1016/j.rasd.2012.02.008

Johnson, T. D., & Joshi, A. (2016). Dark clouds or silver linings? A stigma threat perspective on the implications of an autism diagnosis for workplace well-being. *Journal of Applied Psychology, 101*, 430–449. https://doi.org/10.1037/apl0000058

Jordan, C. J. (2010). Evolution of autism support and understanding via the World Wide Web. *Intellectual and Developmental Disabilities, 48*, 220–227. https://doi.org/10.1352/1934-9556-48.3.220

Kalev, A., Dobbin, F., & Kelly, E. (2006). Best practices or best guesses? Assessing the efficacy of corporate affirmative action and diversity policies. *American Sociological Review, 71*, 589–617. https://doi.org/10.1177/000312240607100404

Kapp, S. K., Gillespie-Lynch, K., Sherman, L. E., & Hutman, T. (2013). Deficit, difference, or both? Autism and neurodiversity. *Developmental Psychology, 49*, 59–71. https://doi.org/10.1037/a0028353

Kapp, S. K., Steward, R., Crane, L., Elliott, D., Elphick, C., Pellicano, E., & Russell, G. (2019). 'People should be allowed to do what they like': Autistic adults' views and experiences of stimming. *Autism, 23*, 1782–1792. https://doi.org/10.1177/1362361319829628

Kermit, P. (2010). 'Hearing' or 'Deaf'? Discussing epistemological and methodological issues related to the bioethical discourse on paediatric cochlear implantation. *Scandinavian Journal of Disability Research, 12*, 91–107. https://doi.org/10.1080/15017410903338838

Kluger, A. N., & Nir, D. (2010). The feedforward interview. *Human Resource Management Review, 20*, 235–246. https://doi.org/10.1016/j.hrmr.2009.08.002

Komeda, H. (2015). Similarity hypothesis: Understanding of others with autism spectrum disorders by individuals with autism spectrum disorders. *Frontiers in Human Neuroscience, 9*, 124. https://doi.org/10.3389/fnhum.2015.00124

Kossek, E. E., & Zonia, S. C. (1993). Assessing diversity climate: A field study of reactions to employer efforts to promote diversity. *Journal of Organizational Behavior, 14*, 61–81. https://doi.org/10.1002/job.4030140107

Krcek, T. E. (2013). Deconstructing disability and neurodiversity: Controversial issues for autism and implications for social work. *Journal of Progressive Human Services, 24*, 4–22. https://doi.org/10.1080/10428232.2013.740406

Krug, S. (2014). *Don't make me think revisited – A common sense approach to web and mobile usability* (3rd ed.). San Francisco, CA: Pearson Education.

LaFromboise, T., Coleman, H. L. K., & Gerton, J. (1993). Psychological impact of biculturalism: Evidence and theory. *Psychological Bulletin, 114*, 395–412. https://doi.org/10.1037/0033-2909.114.3.395

Lancaster, A. (2017). Hiring for neurodiversity. *Food Service Director*. Retrieved from www.foodservicedirector.com/workforce/how-foodservice-operators-are-hiring-neuro diversity

Larkey, L. K. (1996). The development and validation of the workforce diversity questionnaire: An instrument to assess interactions in diverse workgroups. *Management Communication Quarterly, 9*, 296–337. https://doi.org/10.1177/0893318996009003002

Lindsmith, K. (2014, May 16). *Stimming 101, or: How I learned to stop worrying and love the stim*. Retrieved from https://kirstenlindsmith.wordpress.com/2014/05/16/stimming-101-or-how-i-learned-to-stop-worrying-and-love-the-stim/

Loftis, S. F. (2014). The autistic detective: Sherlock Holmes and his legacy. *Disability Studies Quarterly, 34*. Retrieved from http://dsq-sds.org/article/view/3728/3791#top

Lorenz, T., Reznik, N., & Heinitz, K. (2017). A different point of view: The neurodiversity approach to autism and work. In M. Fitzgerald & J. Yip (Eds.), *Autism: Paradigms, recent research and clinical applications* (pp. 3–13). Berlin: Intech Open. https://doi.org/10.5772/65409

Manning, E. (2018). Me lo dijo un pajarito: Neurodiversity, Black life, and the university as we know it. *Social Text, 36*, 1–24. https://doi.org/10.1215/01642472-S6o9c17ia7412

Martin, A. J., Jones, E. S., & Callan, V. J. (2005). The role of psychological climate in facilitating employee adjustment during organizational change. *European Journal of Work and Organizational Psychology, 14*, 263–328. https://doi.org/10.1080/13594320500141228

Martin, K. D., & Cullen, J. B. (2006). Continuities and extensions of ethical climate theory: A meta-analytic review. *Journal of Business Ethics, 69*, 175–194. https://doi.org/10.1007/s10551-006-9084-7

Mawson, D., Grounds, A., & Tantam, D. (1985). Violence and Asperger's syndrome: A case study. *The British Journal of Psychiatry, 147*, 566–569. https://doi.org/10.1192/bjp.147.5.566

Mayhew, M., Grunwald, H., & Dey, E. (2006). Breaking the silence: Achieving a positive campus climate for diversity from the staff perspective. *Research in Higher Education, 47*, 63–88. https://doi.org/10.1007/s11162-004-8152-z

McHugh, K. (2018). The female detective, neurodiversity, and felt knowledge in engrenages and bron/broen. *Television & New Media, 19*, 535–552.

McKay, P. F., & Avery, D. R. (2005). Warning! Diversity recruitment could backfire. *Journal of Management Inquiry, 14*, 330–336. https://doi.org/10.1177/1056492605280239

McKay, P. F., Avery, D. R., & Morris, M. A. (2008). Mean racial-ethnic differences in employee sales performance: The moderating role of diversity climate. *Personnel Psychology, 61*, 349–374. https://doi.org/10.1111/j.1744-6570.2008.00116.x

McKay, P. F., Avery, D. R., Tonidandel, S., Morris, M.A., Hernandez, M., & Hebl, M. R. (2007). Racial differences in employee retention: Are diversity climate perceptions the key? *Personnel Psychology, 60*, 35–62. https://doi.org/10.1111/j.1744-6570.2007.00064.x

Milton, D. E. (2014). Autistic expertise: A critical reflection on the production of knowledge in autism studies. *Autism, 18*, 794–802. https://doi.org/10.1177/1362361314525281

Mitchell, J. (2015, March 16). What autism means to me. *Autism Daily Newscast*. Retrieved from www.autismdailynewscast.com/neurodiversity-means/24193/guest/

Moore, C. B., McIntyre, N. H., & Lanivich, S. E. (2021). ADHD-related neurodiversity and the entrepreneurial mindset. *Entrepreneurship Theory and Practice, 45*(1), 64–91. https://doi.org/10.1177/1042258719890986

Morris, D., & Turnbull, P. (2007). A survey-based exploration of the impact of dyslexia on the career progression of UK registered nurses. *Journal of Nursing Management, 15*, 97–106. https://doi.org/10.1111/j.1365-2934.2006.00649.x

Munyon, T. P., Summers, J. K., Thompson, K. M., & Ferris, G. R. (2015). Political skill and work outcomes: A theoretical extension, meta-analytic investigation, and agenda for the future. *Personnel psychology, 68*, 143–184. https://doi.org/10.1111/peps.12066

Mulki, J., Jaramillo, J., & Locander, W. (2008). Effect of ethical climate on turnover intention: Linking attitudinal and stress theory. *Journal of Business Ethics, 78*, 559–574. https://doi.org/10.1007/s10551-007-9368-6

Muskat, B. (2017). Celebrating neurodiversity: An often-overlooked difference in group work. *Social Work with Groups, 40*, 81–84. https://doi.org/10.1080/01609513.2015.1067131

National Autistic Society. (2016). *Autism facts and history*. Retrieved from www.autism.org.uk/about/what-is/myths-facts-stats.aspx

Nishii, L. H. (2013). The benefits of climate for inclusion for gender-diverse groups. *Academy of Management Journal, 56*, 1754–1774. https://doi.org/10.5465/amj.2009.0823

Nyhan, S. (2018). Disability or divergent characteristic? Inside the neurodiversity movement. *The Journal of College Admission*, 50–53.

O'Connor, B., Bronner, C., & Delaney, M. (2007). *Learning at work*. Amherst, MA: HRD Press.

O'Dell, L., Rosqvist, H. B., Ortega, F., Brownlow, C., & Orsini, M. (2016). Critical autism studies: Exploring epistemic dialogues and intersections, challenging dominant understandings of autism. *Disability & Society, 31*, 166–179. https://doi.org/10.1080/09687599.2016.1164026

Orsini, M., & Smith, M. (2010). Social movements, knowledge and public policy: The case of autism activism in Canada and the US. *Critical Policy Studies, 4*, 38–57. https://doi.org/10.1080/19460171003714989

Ortega, F. (2009). The cerebral subject and the challenge of neurodiversity. *BioSocieties, 4*, 425–445. https://doi.org/10.1017/S1745855209990287

Ostroff, C., Kinicki, A. J., & Tamkins, M. M. (2003). Organizational climate and culture. In W. C. Borman, D. R. Ilgen, & R. J. Klimoski (Eds.), *Comprehensive handbook of psychology* (pp. 365–402). Mahwah, NJ: Erlbaum.

Ovaska-Few, S. (2018). Promoting neurodiversity: A pilot program at EY recruits workers with autism. *Journal of Accountancy*. Retrieved from www.journalofaccountancy.com/issues/2018/jan/ey-pilot-program-workers-with-autism.html

Ozonoff, S., Pennington, B. F., & Rogers, S. J. (1991). Executive function deficits in high-functioning autistic individuals: Relationship to theory of mind. *Journal of Child Psychology and Psychiatry, 32*, 1081–1105. https://doi.org/10.1111/j.1469-7610.1991.tb00351.x

Painter, C. A., Prevatt, F., & Welles, T. (2008). Career beliefs and job satisfaction in adults with symptoms of attention deficit/hyperactivity disorder. *Journal of Employment Counseling, 45*(4), 178–188. https://doi.org/10.1002/j.2161-1920.2008.tb00057.x

Paletta, D. (2013). Equality, capability and neurodiversity. In C. Herrera & A. Perry (Eds.), *Ethics and neurodiversity* (pp. 39–51), Newcastle upon Tyne: Cambridge Scholars.

Parker, C. P., Baltes, B. B., Young, S. A., Huff, J. W., Altmann, R. A., Lacost, H. A., & Roberts, J. E. (2003). Relationships between psychological climate perceptions and work outcomes: A meta-analytic review. *Journal of Organizational Behavior, 24*, 389–416. https://doi.org/10.1002/job.198

Parr, A. D., & Hunter, S. T. (2014). Enhancing work outcomes of employees with autism spectrum disorder through leadership. *Autism, 18*, 545–554. https://doi.org/10.1177/1362361313483020

Parr, A. D., Hunter, S. T., & Ligon, G. S. (2013). Questioning universal applicability of transformational leadership: Examining employees with autism spectrum disorder. *The Leadership Quarterly, 24*, 608–622. https://doi.org/10.1016/j.leaqua.2013.04.003

Patton, E. (2019). Autism, attributions and accommodations: Overcoming barriers and integrating a neurodiverse workforce. *Personnel Review, 48*, 915–934. https://doi.org/10.1108/PR-04-2018-0116

Pettijohn, C., Pettijohn, L., & Taylor, A. (2008). Salesperson perceptions of ethical behaviors: Their influence on job satisfaction and turnover intentions. *Journal of Business Ethics, 78*, 547–557. https://doi.org/10.1007/s10551-007-9367-7

Portway, S. M., & Johnson, B. (2005). Do you know I have Asperger's syndrome? Risks of a non-obvious disability. *Health, Risk & Society, 7*, 73–83. https://doi.org/10.1080/09500830500042086

Punshon, C., Skirrow, P., & Murphy, G. (2009). The not guilty verdict: Psychological reactions to a diagnosis of Asperger syndrome in adulthood. *Autism, 13*, 265–283. https://doi.org/10.1177/1362361309103795

Rebora, A. (2017). Making space for learning differences. *Perspectives*. Retrieved from www.ascd.org/publications/educational-leadership/apr17/vol74/num07/Making-Space-for-Learning-Differences.aspx

Richard, O. C., Avery, D. R., Luksyte, A., Boncoeur, O. D., & Spitzmueller, C. (2019). Improving organizational newcomers' creative job performance through creative process engagement: The moderating role of a synergy diversity climate. *Personnel Psychology, 72*, 421–444. https://doi.org/10.1111/peps.12316

Richards, J. (2012). Examining the exclusion of employees with Asperger syndrome from the workplace. *Personnel Review, 5*, 630–646. https://doi.org/10.1108/00483481211249148

Richards, J., Sang, K., Marks, A., & Gill, S. E. (2019). I've found it extremely draining: Emotional labour and the lived experience of line managing neurodiversity. *Personnel Review, 48*, 1903–1923. https://doi.org/10.1108/PR-08-2018-0289

Robertson, S. M. (2010). Neurodiversity, quality of life, and autistic adults: Shifting research and professional focus onto real-life challenges. *Disability Studies Quarterly, 30*. Retrieved from http://dsq-sds.org/article/view/1069/1234

Rogers, C. (2017). How to hire neurodiverse people. *Marketing Week*. Retrieved from www.marketingweek.com/brand-benefits-neurodiversity/

Rosette, A. S., de Leon, R. P., Koval, C., & Harrison, D. (2018). Intersectionality: Connecting experiences of gender with race at work. *Research in Organizational Behavior, 38*, 1–22. https://doi.org/10.1016/j.riob.2018.12.002

Rosette, A. S., Koval, C., Ma, A., & Livingston, R. (2016). Race matters for women leaders: Intersectional effects on agentic deficiencies and penalties. *The Leadership Quarterly, 27*, 429–445. https://doi.org/10.1016/j.leaqua.2016.01.008

Rothstein, A. (2012). Mental disorder or neurodiversity? *The New Atlantis*, *36*, 99–115.

Rubino, C., Avery, D. R., McKay, P. F., Moore, B. L., Wilson, D. C., Van Driel, M. S., Witt, L. A., & McDonald, D. P. (2018). And justice for all: How organizational justice climate deters sexual harassment. *Personnel Psychology*, *71*, 519–544. https://doi.org/10.1111/peps.12274

Ruiz Calzada, L., Pistrang, N., & Mandy, W. P. (2012). High- functioning autism and Asperger's disorder: Utility and meaning for families. *Journal of Autism and Developmental Disorders*, *42*, 230–243. https://doi.org/10.1007/s10803-011-1238-5

Runswick-Cole, K. (2014). 'Us' and 'them': The limits and possibilities of a 'politics of neurodiversity' in neoliberal times. *Disability & Society*, *29*, 1117–1129. https://doi.org/10.1080/09687599.2014.910107

Santuzzi, A. M., Waltz, P. R., Finkelstein, L. M., & Rupp, D. E. (2014). Invisible disabilities: Unique challenges for employees and organizations. *Industrial and Organizational Psychology: Perspectives on Science and Practice*, 7, 204–219. https://doi.org/10.1111/iops.12134

Schur, L., Nishii, L., Adya, M., Kruse, D., Bruyère, S., & Blanck, P. (2014). Accommodating employees with and without disabilities. *Human Resource Management*, *53*, 593–621. https://doi.org/10.1002/hrm.21607

Schwepker, C. H. J. (2001). Ethical climate's relationship to job satisfaction, organizational commitment and turnover in the sales force. *Journal of Business Research*, *54*, 39–52. https://doi.org/10.1016/S0148-2963(00)00125-9

Segran, E. (2020). Starbucks banned employees from wearing BLM T-shirts. Now it's making its own. *Fast Company*. Retrieved from www.fastcompany.com/90516865/starbucks-banned-employees-from-wearing-blm-t-shirts-now-its-designing-its-own

Sheppard, E., Pillai, D., Wong, G. T.-L., Ropar, D., & Mitchell, P. (2016). How easy is it to read the minds of people with autism spectrum disorder? *Journal of Autism and Developmental Disorders*, *46*, 1247–1254. https://doi.org/10.1007/s10803-015-2662-8

Shore, L. M., Chung-Herrera, B. G., Dean, M. A., Holcombe Ehrhart, K., Jung, D. I., Randel, A. E., & Singh, G. (2009). Diversity in organizations: Where are we now and where are we going? *Human Resource Management Review*, *19*, 117–133. https://doi.org/10.1016/j.hrmr.2008.10.004

Shore, L. M., Randel, A. E., Chung, B. G., Dean, M. A., Ehrhart, K. H., & Singh, G. (2011). Inclusion and diversity in work groups: A review and model for future research. *Journal of Management*, *37*, 1262–1289. https://doi.org/10.1177/0149206310385943

Shumer, D., Reisner, S., Edwards-Leeper, L., & Tishelman, A. (2015). Evaluation of Asperger syndrome in youth presenting to a gender dysphoria clinic. *LGBT Health*, *3*, 387–390. https://doi.org/10.1089/lgbt.2015.0070

Snowling, M. J., Adams, J. W., Bowyer-Crane, C., & Tobin, V. A. (2000). Levels of literacy among juvenile offenders: The incidence of specific reading difficulties. *Criminal Behaviour and Mental Health*, *10*, 229–241. https://doi.org/10.1002/cbm.362

Sparrow, R. (2005). Defending deaf culture: The case of cochlear implants. *The Journal of Political Philosophy*, *13*, 135–152. https://doi.org/10.1111/jopp.2005.13.issue-2

Stewart, R. W., Volpone, S. D., & Avery, D. R. (2011). You support diversity, but are you ethical? Examining the interactive effects of diversity and ethical climate perceptions on turnover intentions. *Journal of Business Ethics*, *100*, 581–593. https://doi.org/10.1007/s10551-010-0697-5

Strang, J. F., Kenworthy, L., Dominska, A., Sokoloff, J., Kenealy, L. E., Berl, M., . . . Wallace, G. L. (2014). Increased gender variance in autism spectrum disorders and attention deficit hyperactivity disorder. *Archives of Sexual Behavior, 43*, 1525–1533. https://doi.org/10.1007/s1050 8-014-0285-3

Strang, J. F., Meagher, H., Kenworthy, L., de Vries, A. L. C., Menvielle, M., Leibowitz, S., . . . Anthony, L. G. (2018). Initial clinical guidelines for co-occurring autism spectrum disorder and gender dysphoria or incongruence in adolescents. *Journal of Clinical Child & Adolescent Psychology, 47*, 105–115. https://doi.org/10.1080/15374416.2016.1228462

Strauss, J. (2013). *Autism as culture* (4th ed., pp. 460–484). New York: Routledge.

Sumner, K. E., & Brown, T. J. (2015). Neurodiversity and human resource management: Employer challenges for applicants and employees with learning disabilities. *The Psychologist-Manager Journal, 18*, 77–85. https://doi.org/10.1037/mgr0000031

Talley, K. (2017). Companies to spend more to achieve greater diversity, inclusion. *FierceCEO*. Retrieved from www.fierceceo.com/human-capital/spending-diversity-moving-up

Tsai, M. T., & Huang, C. C. (2008). The relationship among ethical climate types, facets of job satisfaction, and the three components of organizational commitment: A study of nurses in Taiwan. *Journal of Business Ethics, 80*, 565–581. https://doi.org/10.1007/s10551-007-9455-8

von Schrader, S., Malzer, V., & Bruyère, S. M. (2014). Perspectives on disability disclosure: The importance of employer practices and workplace climate. *Employee Responsibilities & Rights Journal, 26*, 237–255. https://doi.org/10.1007/s10672-013-9227-9

von Schrader, S., Xu, X., & Bruyère, S. M. (2014). Accommodation requests: Who is asking for what? *Rehabilitation Research, Policy, and Education, 28*, 329–344.

Waltz, M. (2013). *Autism: A social and medical history*. New York: Palgrave Macmillan.

Walumbwa, F. O., Avolio, B. J., Gardner, W. L., Wernsing, T. S., & Peterson, S. J. (2008). Authentic leadership: Development and validation of a theory-based measure. *Journal of Management, 34*, 89–126. https://doi.org/10.1177/0149206307308913

Weeks, W. A., Loe, T. W., Chonko, L. B., Martinez, C. R., & Wakefield, K. (2006). Cognitive moral development and the impact of perceived organizational ethical climate on the search for sales force excellence: A cross-cultural study. *Journal of Personal Selling & Sales Management, 26*, 205–217. https://doi.org/10.2753/PSS0885-3134260207

Woods, J. (2014). From Sherlock to the bridge, it's mind over matter. *Telegraph*. Retrieved from www.telegraph.co.uk/culture/tvandradio/10584397/From-Sherlock-to-The-Bridge-its-mind-over-matter.html

World Health Organization (2019). *Autism spectrum disorders*. Retrieved from www.who.int/news-room/fact-sheets/detail/autism-spectrum-disorders

Wright, A. D. (2016). Autism speaks, and employers listen. *HR Magazine, 61*, 60–64.

3

RECRUITMENT STRATEGIES

Generating a Neurodiverse Workforce

Cristina M. Giannantonio and Amy E. Hurley-Hanson

Researchers have identified several potential skill sets and common characteristics of neurodivergent individuals that may benefit organizations. Much of this research has focused on the skill sets of individuals with ASD. These skills include visual acuity, more deliberative decision-making, increased attentional focus, logical thinking, and affinity for technology, as well as professional and occupational interests in science, technology, engineering, and math (STEM) fields (Crespi, 2016). STEM fields are of particular interest, as there is a growing need for a skilled workforce in these areas (U.S. Bureau of Labor Statistics, 2018). While there is a lot of emphasis on hiring neurodivergent individuals in technology and software fields, it is important to remember that neurodivergent individuals may have interests and talents in all fields (Ovaska-Few, 2018). While neurodivergent individuals may appear to be an ideal fit for this segment of the labor market, it should be recognized that some individuals may experience challenges with other aspects of employment, such as job-required social interaction. While most neurodivergent individuals will be successful at work, organizations must be cognizant of the challenges and barriers they face and acknowledge the possibility that some individuals and programs may not be successful. This chapter considers organizational and job practices that may mitigate many of these challenges. Relatively little is known about the job search and choice experiences of neurodivergent individuals. While Austin and Pisano (2017) note that the traditional interview process may screen out neurodivergent applicants, thereby creating obstacles to being hired, the effects of other recruitment strategies have received limited research attention.

Despite the potential advantages of hiring neurodivergent applicants, their unemployment and underemployment rates, as compared to those of the general population, remains staggeringly high (Baldwin et al., 2014; Krieger et al., 2012;

DOI: 10.4324/9781003023616-3

Nord et al., 2016; Richards, 2012; Roux et al., 2013; Scott et al., 2015; Shattuck et al., 2012). Recent unemployment statistics for adults with ASD reveal that 85% are unemployed and that 69% of them want to work (National Autistic Society, 2016). Additional research has shown that many individuals with ASD have never been members of the labor force (Cidav et al., 2012).

Shattuck et al. (2012) found that 35% of young adults with ASD have never held a job, been members of the labor force, or attended educational programs after high school (Shattuck et al., 2012; Cidav et al., 2012). A study of 200 transition-age young adults with ASD found that 81% were unemployed (Gerhardt & Lainer, 2011). A small study of young adults with ASD and IQs above 50 found that only 11.76% were employed (Howlin et al., 2004). Other studies have found that approximately half of young adults with ASD have worked for pay after high school (Roux et al., 2013). The same study also found that the odds of ever having a paid job were higher for those who were older, from higher-income households, or had better conversational or functional skills (Roux et al., 2013).

The statistics for young adults are particularly troubling, as it is estimated that half a million individuals with autism spectrum disorder (ASD) will reach adulthood in the current decade and will be poised to enter the workplace in unprecedented numbers. These numbers are staggering and suggest the need to examine the long-term employment, career, and life outcomes for this generational cohort. Hurley-Hanson et al. (2020) introduced the term *Generation A* to refer to this generational cohort of young adults with ASD. According to Autism Speaks (2019a), "Autism Spectrum Disorder (ASD) and autism are both general terms for a group of complex disorders of brain development. These disorders are characterized, in varying degrees, by difficulties in social interaction, verbal and nonverbal communication, and repetitive behaviors." The World Health Organization (2013) describes ASD as "neurodevelopmental impairments in communication and social interaction and unusual ways of perceiving and processing information" (p. 7). As such, individuals with ASD often have difficulty in understanding the thoughts, intentions, and emotions of others (Bruggink et al., 2016). Some individuals with ASD may have difficulty regulating their own emotions. These challenges may create transition and employment issues for young adults with ASD (Samson et al., 2012), not only as they enter the workplace but potentially throughout their work lives as their careers unfold.

According to the Centers for Disease Control and Prevention, 1 in 54 children are on the autism spectrum, and the presence of ASD is 4.3 times more common in boys (1 in 34) than in girls (1 in 144) (CDC, 2020). Autism Speaks (2019b) estimates that there are 3.5 million people with ASD in the United States. The number of people affected by ASD is estimated to be in the tens of millions worldwide. Although it is difficult to get exact numbers, it is estimated that 1% of the world's population has autism (CDC, 2018; Malcolm-Smith et al., 2013; Wallace et al., 2012; Grønborg et al., 2013).

The United Nations annually hosts World Autism Awareness Day. The theme in 2015 was employment (The Autism Advantage, 2015). The theme highlighted the potential for persons with autism to make significant contributions in the workplace given their unique individual strengths. It noted the widespread discrimination in the workplace against people with autism and the limited vocational training and job opportunities available for those with autism. The number of individuals with ASD both in the United States and throughout the world represents an untapped and, at times, overlooked segment of the labor force for organizations seeking to fill job vacancies and meet current and projected skills gaps (Braddock & Bachelder, 1994).

It is within this context that this chapter focuses on the role that recruitment strategies may play in generating a neurodiverse workforce for the benefit of both organizations and individuals with ASD. The first section of this chapter reviews previous research on recruitment strategies from both the organization's perspective and the individual's perspective. Rynes's (1991) process view of recruitment and the signaling hypothesis are presented to gain an understanding of how recruitment is hypothesized to influence applicants' reactions and behaviors. The second section of the chapter briefly discusses research on disabilities in the workplace before discussing the benefits of recruiting and hiring neurodiverse candidates. The third section of the chapter specifically focuses on the recruitment of neurodiverse candidates, examining barriers in the traditional recruitment process, suggestions for improving the process, issues specific to the recruitment interview, and alternatives to the recruitment interview. The chapter concludes with suggestions for future research and implications for organizational best practices, policies, and strategies for generating a neurodiverse workforce.

Recruitment Strategies

Recruitment strategies comprise an important element of an organization's human resource management activities (Osman & Thunborg, 2019). This importance is reflected in the attention that recruitment research has received in the academy (Breaugh, 2008). Thirty years ago, Rynes (1991, p. 429) defined recruitment as "encompassing all organizational activities and decisions that affect either the number, or types, of individuals who are willing to apply for, or to accept, a vacancy." The bulk of recruitment research has focused on external recruitment, which Breaugh (2008, pp. 103–104) defines "as encompassing an employer's actions that are intended to: (a) bring a job opening to the attention of potential job candidates who do not currently work for the organization, (b) influence whether these individuals apply for the opening, (c) affect whether they maintain interest in the position until a job offer is extended, and (d) influence whether a job offer is accepted."

Central to both Breaugh and Rynes's definitions of recruitment is recognition of the dual functions of recruiting activities. Recruitment includes motivating applicants to apply for job openings *and* encouraging them to accept job offers. In order to understand how recruitment strategies may help organizations generate a neurodiverse workforce, it is important to examine these dual recruitment functions from the perspective of both organizations and applicants. The pattern of previous recruitment research reveals both perspectives, starting with scholars' interest in understanding recruitment from the organization's perspective and moving to a shift in understanding recruitment from the applicant's perspective. Viewing recruitment as a *process* (Rynes, 1991) shifted the focus of recruitment research onto an understanding of how recruitment activities affect applicant attitudes and behaviors, as well as organizational goals and outcomes. It should be noted that this chapter will focus on *external* recruitment and will consider the effect of organizational recruitment strategies on the reactions, behavioral intentions, and job choice outcomes of neurodivergent applicants, with a particular emphasis on individuals with ASD. In the future, as more organizations generate neurodiverse workforces and as their employees seek opportunities for internal mobility, it is expected that recruitment research will expand its focus to include internal recruitment strategies and their effects.

Recruitment From the Organization's Perspective

Early recruitment research focused on recruitment strategies from the organization's perspective, where the primary focus of recruitment activities was to generate a pool of qualified applicants (Barber, 1998). Recruitment strategies focused on making applicants aware of job openings and motivating them to apply for posted positions – the traditional "selling" approach of recruitment. Thus, the focus of much early recruitment strategies and research was on crafting the recruitment message and the effectiveness of various print and visual media for reaching job candidates through job advertisement postings. An unintended consequence of selling strategies was that new employees experienced reality shock once they were on the job as the unrealistic expectations formed while being recruited failed to materialize. Rising turnover rates by newly hired employees led to research examining the advantages of providing applicants with realistic job previews (RJPs) during recruitment instead of relying on traditional selling messages (Baur et al., 2014).

Organizationally focused recruitment research also examined the issue of who should be recruited. This involved identifying and targeting candidates most likely to meet the job qualifications and specifications of job vacancies. During periods of labor market shortages, organizations were encouraged to expand their recruitment efforts to include nontraditional and underrepresented segments of the labor market and to use a variety of internal and external recruitment sources to fill job vacancies. Internal sources of recruitment include filling job vacancies with existing, retired, and former employees through transfers, promotions, demotions, and interim appointments. There are a myriad number of external sources of recruitment for reaching new and previous applicants. These include company websites, career sites, job portals, and social networking platforms. External sources also include the use of placement agencies, search firms, job fairs, campus placements, professional associations, service provider agencies, local and state government agencies, university offices for students with disabilities, and career placement offices. The recruitment strategies discussed above focus on recruitment from the organization's perspective, with little attention directed toward gaining an understanding of recruitment from the applicant's perspective.

Recruitment From the Applicant's Perspective

In order to gain a more complete understanding of the recruitment process, it is also necessary to consider recruitment from the applicant's perspective. One reason that recruitment has an effect on applicants is related to the uncertainty that individuals experience during recruitment and job search activities. Three areas of uncertainty may be experienced by applicants. These include uncertainty due to incomplete and potentially inaccurate information about the availability of employment opportunities in general, the job and organizational attributes associated with specific employment opportunities, and the applicant's perceived probability of receiving a job offer from a company. It is important to recognize that without uncertainty, recruitment strategies would be less likely to influence applicants' reactions, behaviors, and decisions during job search and job choice.

As noted by Dipboye (1992), the absence of complete information about a job or a company often causes applicants to rely on the recruiter to form impressions of the organization. Recruiters and recruitment interviews may have a large effect on an organization's ability to attract and hire qualified applicants, as organizations are concerned with motivating applicants to apply for and to actually accept a job offer (Harold & Ployhart, 2008). Recruiter effects have traditionally been researched from the perspective of the applicant and within the context of the recruitment interview. There are many factors that may affect applicants' perceptions of the recruiter, which may, in turn, influence applicants' perceptions of the organization and the job itself. Characteristics of recruiters and recruitment interviews that have been studied include demographic characteristics of the recruiter (e.g., age and gender), the recruiter's personality (e.g., recruiter friendliness and empathy), the recruitment messages (e.g., the amount and type of information about the job and the organization provided by the recruiter), and the recruiter's screening behaviors (e.g., the way that they speak and whether they show interest in the applicant).

Previous research suggests that applicants prefer and are more attracted to recruiters with pleasant personalities (Anderson, 2003; Chapman et al., 2005; Ryan & Ployhart, 2000; Wiles & Spiro, 2004). Recruiter personableness (Chapman et al., 2005) and recruiter personality in general (Turban et al., 1995) have influenced applicants' perceptions of organizational attractiveness and willingness to pursue or accept a job offer. Recruiter personality has also influenced applicants' perceptions of receiving a job offer (Saks & Uggerslev, 2010).

Applicants have expressed preferences with respect to how recruiters conduct the interview, how they speak, and the recruiter's level of preparation (Carless, 2006). Applicants have complained about the types of information that recruiters provide about job and organizational characteristics and report that recruiters do not tell them as much information about these factors as they would like to know (Wiles & Spiro, 2004). Applicants do not usually perceive recruiters as credible sources of job information, although organizational representatives who were job incumbents and not formal recruiters have been perceived as more credible sources of job information (Breaugh, 2017).

This stream of recruitment research from the applicant's perspective supports the important role that recruiters play in affecting applicants' decisions to apply for and to accept a job offer. However, the role of employment inducements in applicants' decisions must also be taken into account. Research examining the effects of recruitment activities and employment inducements on applicant reactions have yielded mixed results. Whereas some studies suggest that recruitment activities may influence applicant reactions (Breaugh, 2017; Uggerslev et al., 2012), other studies have found that recruitment effects are usually overshadowed by employment inducements which can be "deal breakers" (Osborn, 1990). Some researchers posit that applicants use rational economic models and only apply to jobs that meet minimum requirements or a "reservation wage" (Anderson et al., 2001; Chapman et al., 2005). These results suggest a need to study the effects of recruitment activities and employment inducements on applicant reactions, ideally by examining their effects simultaneously (Goltz & Giannantonio, 1995; Giannantonio et al., 2019).

Recruitment as a Process

Recruitment research has more recently focused on the *process* of recruitment, with the goal of gaining an understanding of *how* recruitment influences applicants' reactions and behaviors. Rynes's (1991) process view of recruitment has driven much of the empirical research on recruitment effects and provides a framework for gaining a better understanding of how recruitment strategies may be utilized to generate a neurodiverse workforce. As illustrated in her model, Rynes's (1991) identifies four components of the recruitment process: recruiting activities and decisions, recruitment processes, recruiting outcomes, and the context of recruitment. Consideration of each element in the four components of her model is beyond the scope of this chapter. The focus in this section will be to introduce those elements and components of the model that may be most salient to and critical for generating a neurodiverse workforce. In subsequent sections of the chapter, these issues will be discussed in more detail.

The first component of the model, recruiting activities and decisions, includes the choice of recruiter, recruiting sources, characteristics of the vacancy, selection standards, and administrative procedures. As noted, much research on recruitment effects has focused on the characteristics and behaviors of recruiters. The recruiter is often the applicant's first "human" contact with the organization, and for certain jobs, is the only source of information about an employment opportunity. This suggests that organizations prefer that recruiters are well perceived since one goal of recruitment is to present a favorable image of the organization to applicants (Breaugh, 2017; Ehrhart & Ziegert, 2005).

While much is known about recruiter effects on neurotypical applicants, little is known about the influence of recruiters' characteristics and behaviors on neurodivergent applicants' perceptions of recruiters and subsequent attraction to the job and impression of the organization. A recruiter's ability to interact with and fairly evaluate applicants who may express themselves differently during the recruitment interview may be favorably perceived by neurodivergent job applicants, potentially influencing an applicant's attraction to and willingness to accept a job offer from that company. The second component of Rynes's model, recruitment processes, includes self-selection processes, time-related processes, information related processes, interactive processes, posthire adjustment processes, and individual differences. Self-selection processes examine the reasons why individuals choose to apply for some jobs but not for other employment opportunities. Self-selection processes also examine individuals' decisions to apply for jobs with some organizations but not others. Little is known about the self-selection processes of neurodivergent individuals and the reasoning behind their decision to apply for certain jobs and to certain organizations.

Research suggests that job listings are a large factor in determining applicant pools. Many job advertisements are written very generally or include more skills and experience than are actually needed for the position. These types of miscommunications in job postings may result in an organization inadvertently causing qualified candidates to self-select out of the applicant pool. If talented, qualified neurodivergent applicants do not perceive themselves to possess all of the specific or general skills listed in job postings, this may result in them not applying for positions that they would, in fact, be qualified to perform (Baxter & Heys, 2019).

Another variable that might affect self-selection is whether a company mentions diversity and inclusion in its job postings and advertisements. Research suggests that ads that mention diversity are more attractive to many applicants (Avery et al., 2013; Avery & McKay, 2006; Bopp et al., 2014; Walker et al., 2012). Neurodivergent individuals may be looking for evidence that a company is willing to hire neurodivergent applicants. Neurodivergent applicants may not apply to job postings that refer to inclusivity if they do not also include words such as "neurodiverse" or "autism" (Davis, 2017). Organizations should also take into account that their recruitment of neurodivergent employees will have an effect on their applicant pool as a whole. The information a company relays to all participants regarding their employment policies about inclusivity and their inclusion of a neurodivergent population in their applicant pool and hired employees may affect other applicants' attitudes toward the organization and their willingness to work for the organization (Ray et al., 2018). Organizations should periodically do postrecruitment surveys to evaluate their recruiting process (Ciampi, 2019).

The third component of the model, recruiting outcomes, includes both prehire and posthire outcomes. Prehire outcomes include perceptions, intentions, and behaviors; posthire outcomes include attitudes, behaviors, and effects on insiders. Organizations that wish to generate a neurodiverse workforce need to establish both prehire and posthire employment goals. A model for implementing such a plan was presented by Hurley-Hanson et al. (2020) and offers guidelines for organizations seeking to hire and retain neurodivergent individuals. The model presented in their book has seven steps: Appraise, Assess, Network (Resources), Formulate Strategy or Plan, Implementation, Continuous Monitoring, and Continuous Improvement. The goal of the model is to help organizations strategically implement programs to hire individuals with ASD. Recruiting strategies can play a role in several steps of this model as organizations develop initiatives to increase their commitment to hiring and retaining neurodivergent individuals, particularly individuals with ASD.

Finally, the fourth component of Rynes's model, the context of recruitment, includes external environments, organizational characteristics, and institutional norms. Interest in recruitment strategies in the academic and popular press has waxed and waned as a function of fluctuations in labor market supply and demand. The demand for and supply of qualified applicants to meet current and future skills gaps would typically be expected to drive organizations' interests in generating a neurodiverse workforce. However, it is difficult to make long-term predictions regarding organizations' interest in and ability to focus on generating a neurodiverse workforce in the face of the global pandemic arising from COVID-19. While it is clear that the manner in which we work, the places where we work, and the nature of the work we do have all changed dramatically, it is too early to predict the coronavirus's impact on organizations' abilities to reopen, to recover, and ultimately to stay in business. Moreover, the long-term impact of the pandemic on the demand for and supply of labor across various occupations and industries may not be felt for several months or years. While these effects are currently unknown, it may be hypothesized that the pandemic will result in increased recruiting by some organizations and not others, reconsideration of the amount of financial resources devoted to recruiting activities, and evaluation of the manner in which recruiting practices are affected by social distancing. Such challenges are a reminder that the impact of the external environment on organizational recruitment strategies cannot be minimized. Adopting a process view of recruitment may help organizations to gain a better understanding of how recruitment strategies may be used to generate a neurodiverse workforce in the "new normal" of the future.

The Signaling Hypothesis in Recruitment

Signaling theory has been offered as one explanation for recruitment effects. Given the uncertainty inherent in job search and choice, applicants are likely to use elements of recruitment activities as signals about unknown organizational and job characteristics. This phenomenon is referred to as the signaling hypothesis in recruitment and is based on Spence's (1974, 1973) signaling theory. Spence developed signaling theory in economics to focus on situations in which incomplete or ambiguous information exists and where intentional efforts are made to persuade others. Signaling theory identifies signals as specific behaviors that transmit information about individuals' abilities and intentions to the marketplace. Signaling promotes attentional focus by increasing the salience of stimuli, or informational signals, in the work environment (Taylor & Fiske, 1978).

Characteristics of individuals, organizations, and jobs can all serve as signals transmitted to the marketplace and may serve to reduce the uncertainty experienced by stakeholders. Information about job characteristics (e.g., salary) or the work environment (e.g., organizational culture) during recruitment may serve as signals about unknown job and organizational characteristics associated with a specific employment opportunity (Ferris & Judge, 1991). The effective presentation of information about jobs and organizations serves to distinguish specific features of that context in the eyes of recruits, which promotes attentional focus, thus rendering this information more salient and increasing interest and attraction of job candidates being recruited (Treadway et al., 2014).

Research has demonstrated that recruiters, in their role as organizational representatives and the "face" of the organization, may also serve as signals to applicants influencing applicants' perceptions about unknown job and organizational characteristics, as well as perceptions about their performance in the interview and the likelihood of receiving a job offer. Demonstrating a pleasantly favorable interpersonal style, friendly recruiters can make salient and transmit critical contextual qualities and information to others (Fiske & Taylor, 1984). Research suggests that an applicant's experiences during recruitment may be used as a signal of the organization's likelihood of extending a job offer (Lievens et al., 2005). A number of recruiting activities may influence applicants' perceptions of the likelihood of receiving a job offer (Rynes & Cable, 2003; Lievens et al., 2005; Danko, 2015; Goltz & Giannantonio, 1995; Rynes, 1991; Singh, 2011; Giannantonio et al., 2019). Additional research suggests that an applicant's experiences during recruitment may be used as a signal of the likelihood of an employment opportunity providing desired job attributes (Saks & Uggerslev, 2010), as signals of unknown organizational characteristics (Rynes et al., 1980; Rynes, 1991), and as the basis for inferences about unknown job and organizational characteristics when limited information is available (Rynes et al., 1980; Rynes, 1991; Goltz & Giannantonio, 1995; Giannantonio et al., 2019).

Despite the importance of signaling theory in understanding recruitment effects with neurotypical applicants, little is known about the process by which neurodivergent applicants may be influenced by signaling effects during recruitment activities. It would be important to understand whether and to what extent recruiter characteristics such as personableness and friendliness serve as signals about unknown job and organizational characteristics, perceptions of organizational fit, and the decision to self-select out of an employment opportunity. Similarly, research is needed to determine the role that different job (e.g., salary) and organizational (e.g., organizational culture) variables serve as signals about unknown characteristics associated with an employment opportunity and the influence of these variables on neurodivergent applicants' attitudes and behaviors during job search and choice. As described earlier, research suggests that perceptions of an organization's diversity climate have an effect on applicants' job pursuit intentions (Avery et al., 2013). Research is needed to assess the long-term effectiveness of neurodiversity hiring programs from both the organizational and the individual perspective.

In summary, much is known about the effects of recruitment strategies on the reactions, behavioral intentions, and job choice outcomes of neurotypical applicants. A growing body of research has begun to examine the effects of recruitment strategies on neurodivergent candidates and the benefits of recruiting and hiring neurodivergent individuals. The next section of this chapter examines these benefits, previous research on disabilities in the workforce, and research focused on answering the questions of what happens when neurodivergent candidates go through the regular hiring processes? How may traditional recruitment strategies overlook or discourage neurodivergent candidates? What approaches have been used to date by companies with Autism at Work initiatives to source qualified candidates? What seems to be working and not working and why?

Disabilities in the Workplace

Research on the workplace experiences of individuals with disabilities may provide insight into the employment experiences of individuals with ASD. Previous research suggests that individuals with disabilities have been found to have lower employment rates and to be overemployed in low-paying jobs (Bowe, 1992; Stone, 1996). In addition, past research on individuals with disabilities has revealed high levels of job performance and low levels of turnover (Greenwood & Johnson, 1987). Research on the recruitment and employment of individuals with disabilities has found that although many employers say they are willing to hire those with disabilities, their actual hiring practices do not show efforts in this area (Hernandez et al., 2003). Respondents cited fears about hiring individuals with disabilities, including the belief that it would take too much time and effort to supervise and train employees with disabilities. In addition, some respondents expressed safety concerns (Morgan & Alexander, 2005), the prohibitive cost of accommodations, and the belief that they would never be able to terminate a disabled employee once hired (Hernandez et al., 2003; Loprest & Maag, 2003; Peck & Kirkbride, 2001). Despite these fears, most employers report positive experiences when hiring individuals with a disability (Cooper, 1991) and say that they would hire more individuals with disabilities in the future (Morgan & Alexander, 2005). Related research found that 57% of employers reported no additional costs from hiring an individual with ASD and did not require assistance from tax incentives in order to hire them (Job Accommodation Network, 2018).

Several interesting parallels have been observed when examining the employment experiences of American veterans. There are some significant similarities between individuals with disabilities, neurodivergent individuals, and veterans. As of 2019, approximately 25% (0.7 million) of veterans have disabilities related to their service in the military (U.S. Bureau of Labor Statistics, 2020). For veterans who served after 2001, the percentage with disabilities is 41% (1.8 million people (U.S. Bureau of Labor Statistics, 2020). This is a much higher percentage than in the general population of the United States, where in 2019, the percentage of people with a disability was 12.7% (40.7 million people) (Census Bureau QuickFacts, 2018). Veterans also have low employment rates (Prudential, 2012). In 2019, the employment rate for veterans with a disability was 4.9%. The rate was 5.5% for those serving since 2001 (Census.gov, 2019). In contrast, the employment rate for the general population was 3.6% (5.9 million people) in 2019 (Census.gov, 2019).

Stone and Stone (2015) explored how veterans are treated in the employment process based upon Stone and Colella's 1996 model of the factors that influence the treatment of disabled individuals in work organizations. Stereotypes attributed to individuals with disabilities have also been applied to veterans, negatively affecting their employment opportunities (Stone & Colella, 1996). A study by Bordieri and Drehmer (1984) found that raters viewed Vietnam veterans as more likely to have psychological problems and viewed them as less suitable for jobs than nonveterans. Research suggests that veterans who return with invisible disabilities also have negative attributes applied to them (Harrell & Berglass, 2012). Another factor affecting the recruitment of veterans was whether their disability was long term or short term. Research on disabilities revealed that when an applicant had a long-term disability, the person was rated more negatively than when he or she had a temporary disability (Stone & Colella, 1996). ASD is likely to be viewed as a long-term disability; this may result in recruiters perceiving individuals with ASD as not being qualified for the job or suitable for their organization.

Stone and Colella (1996) developed a model exploring the factors that affect the treatment of individuals with disabilities in organizations. They propose that both person and environmental factors influence how individuals with disabilities are treated. Their model covers all aspects of the interactions between individuals with disabilities and organizations. This includes an initial interest in applying to an organization, the recruitment and hiring process, and being employed with an organization. Their model examines how the attributes of the person with a disability and the attributes of the observer affect how individuals with disabilities are perceived. They contend that observers, such as recruiters and interviewers, use stereotypes to categorize individuals with disabilities and make inferences about individuals with disabilities regarding their traits and abilities (Stone & Colella, 1996). These inferences have important implications for how applicants with disabilities are viewed and evaluated during the recruitment process, influencing perceptions of person–job and person–organization fit and whether a job offer is extended. When recruiters and interviewers are uncertain about all details of an applicant's job experiences and skills, they may use these stereotypes and personal experiences to make judgments about an applicant's fit with the job (Heilman, 1983). This is an important point. Recruiters who have incomplete and possibly biased information about the skills and abilities of applicants with disabilities may be more likely to screen those applicants out of employment opportunities.

Research has consistently revealed that more undesirable traits are attributed to individuals with disabilities than to individuals without disabilities (Fichten & Amsel, 1986). Research suggests that individuals with intellectual disabilities are viewed more negatively than those with physical disabilities (Goldstein & Blackman, 1975; Harasymiw et al., 1976; Jones, 1974; Tringo, 1970). Sixty years ago, Richardson et al. (1961) found that individuals reacted more negatively to those who were former mental patients than to those who had physical disabilities. These stereotypes create beliefs about the suitability of individuals with disabilities for employment. Research on individuals with disabilities revealed that applicants in a wheelchair were offered fewer interviews than their able-bodied counterparts (Johnson & Heal, 1976). In addition, organizational attributes such as technology, norms, and values lead to images about what job specifications are required and how a job should be performed. Observers compare these images to their beliefs about the abilities of the individual with disabilities to perform the job. If neurodivergent individuals are not believed to fit these images, they may not be considered suitable for the job.

Additionally, their model found that some human resource practices such as job analysis, recruitment, and selection led to individuals with disabilities not being hired (Stone & Colella, 1996). They note, for example, that job analyses often describe the ideal profile of job-holders rather than essential or minimal job requirements (e.g., Cascio, 1993). Consequently, many individuals with disabilities may be denied employment or promotion because they do not match these ideal characteristics or do not match the observer's image of a person in that job (Stone & Colella, 1996). They recommend that job analyses identify essential job requirements rather than ideal job requirements and that recruiters and interviewers are trained to distinguish essential from marginal job requirements (Stone & Colella, 1996). All of these factors need to be taken into account if organizations wish to develop diversity initiatives to increase the recruitment and retention of underrepresented groups in the workplace.

The Benefits of Recruiting and Hiring Neurodivergent Candidates

Organizational diversity initiatives have traditionally focused on protected characteristics covered by federal employment laws including sex, color, race, religion, national origin, age, and handicapped status. Over time, diversity initiatives expanded to include protected characteristics covered by various state, city, and local employment laws including sexual orientation, gender identity, and gender expression. Recently, organizations' diversity initiatives have expanded to include the recruitment of neurodivergent individuals (Austin & Pisano, 2017). These diversity initiatives usually stem from altruism, legal compliance with employment laws, and local and community pressure from parents and support agencies. In addition to responding to these influences, there are numerous benefits that organizations can reap from recruiting neurodivergent individuals. These benefits include expanding the talent pool of applicants, gaining a workforce with desirable knowledge, skills, and abilities, improving productivity, decreasing turnover, increasing intellectual capital associated with a more diverse workforce, decreasing legal action, obtaining financial incentives, and enhancing a company's reputation and social capital. Each of these benefits are discussed in more detail in what follows.

Expanding the Talent Pool of Applicants

Diversity initiatives allow companies to expand the talent pool for recruiting qualified applicants and building a workforce that is reflective of local labor markets. Austin and Pisano (2017) suggest that neurodivergent applicants represent an enormous pool of untapped talent that could increase companies' productivity. One estimate suggests that the talent pool of neurodivergent individuals represents 10 million people (Accenture, 2018). Another benefit of neurodiversity initiatives is the potential to overcome the shortage of qualified applicants in many fields. The STEM field receives the most attention, as many firms have developed initiatives to hire neurodivergent individuals to fill the skills gaps in these areas.

Recruiters grapple with how to widen the pool of qualified applicants in a number of fields. For example, prejudice against the military makes it difficult to attract and recruit a diverse pool of potential candidates. The military has begun to realize the limitations of screening out neurodivergent applicants during the recruitment process. In the United States, the number of eligible recruits for the U.S. Army continues to dwindle due to declining health, declining education, and increasing criminal history (Christeson et al., 2018). The army has stringent standards for entrance into military service. As such, a person who does not meet the prescribed criteria is disqualified for service. There have been many proposals to allow the army to expand its pool of recruits to reflect the population. The army has successfully increased its applicant pool to reflect society in terms of race and ethnicity (CNA, 2018). With the large population of neurodivergent individuals who take medications for diagnoses such as ADHD, the army should consider including neurodiversity as a societal category that should be reflected in its applicant pool (Gorgas et al., 2018). There are 6.1 million children with ADHD, most of whom are ineligible to be in the army's applicant pool (Census Bureau QuickFacts, 2018). These individuals may be able to successfully serve in the military with modifications to training programs (e.g., boot camp) and the military's organizational culture.

The Israeli Defense Force and the Australian Army currently recruit neurodivergent individuals into their applicant pool. The Israeli Defense Force has developed a recruitment process for individuals on the autism spectrum. They find that 86% of applicants on the autism spectrum that they recruit are able to be placed in the force (Kushner, 2019). The Australian Defense Organization has also put in place a recruitment process for applicants on the autism spectrum. A recent Harvard Business School case described their process for recruiting cyber analysts on the autism spectrum (Austin et al., 2017).

Gaining a Workforce with Desirable Knowledge, Skills, and Abilities

Several studies have reported the knowledge, skills, and abilities that neurodivergent individuals bring to the workplace (Austin & Pisano, 2017). These include the ability to maintain a high level of concentration when the subject is of interest to them, interest in and passion about certain subjects and topic areas, the ability to see patterns and understand systems that are difficult for neurotypical individuals to discern, and a willingness to work at jobs that are repetitive and which require attention to detail. The latter point may reduce the need for job enrichment and job enlargement programs that organizations utilize to motivate employees who perform routine jobs. Research also suggests that adults with ASD may be highly skilled at visual and technical tasks (Baldwin et al., 2014). The ability to become very focused on a topic or work process may lead to expertise in specific job areas, which can then be shared with coworkers to help them understand the task or process (Smith et al., 1995). The ability to see patterns, solve problems, and understand systems may lead to greater innovation, improved problem solving, and long-term productivity gains (Austin & Pisano, 2017).

Improving Productivity

Workforce diversity can increase a company's intellectual capital by bringing different perspectives to the decision-making process and providing a better understanding of a more diverse customer base. Recruiting individuals with these skills and abilities may result in productivity gains for organizations. For example, being detail-oriented can lead to increased accuracy, reduced error rates, and increased productivity in certain jobs. Performing tasks that are repetitive or that involve limited skill variety may not be perceived as boring by some individuals with ASD, resulting in higher productivity (Smith et al., 1995). JP Morgan & Chase Company has employed more than 70 individuals with ASD over the past three years (Eng, 2018). Representatives of JP Morgan Chase & Company report that their employees with ASD are 48% to 140% more productive than their neurotypical colleagues (Eng, 2018). They also anticipate hiring hundreds more individuals with ASD globally in the coming years (Mahoney, 2017). EY (Ernst & Young) reported the findings of their hiring initiative for people with ASD. They found that those with ASD were able to identify process improvements that cut training time in half. They also found that their quality of work, efficiency, and productivity was equal to that of their other employees (Twaronite, 2019). A few studies have compared the job performance ratings of employees with and without ASD. Managers tended to rate the job performance of the employee with ASD as average or above average (Hagner & Cooney, 2005; Hillier et al., 2007; Unger, 2002). Jacob et al. (2015) found that when neurodivergent employees are in an organization that supports and encourages them, they are very successful in their jobs committed and conscientious, very loyal, and very productive.

Decreasing Turnover

Research also suggests that adults with ASD have positive qualities such as "honesty, efficiency, precision, consistency, low absenteeism, and a disinterest in 'office politics'" (Baldwin et al., 2014, p. 2440; Richards, 2012). Organizations may benefit from the reduced absenteeism rates and tardiness levels of employees with ASD. Employees with ASD have been found to have fewer absences and are more likely to arrive at work on time than other employees (Hendricks, 2010; Hillier et al., 2007; Howlin et al., 2005). Research suggests that employees with disabilities are more reliable (Jacob et al., 2015) and have fewer absences than their nondisabled colleagues (Graffam et al., 2002).

Research suggests that employees with ASD have dramatically lower turnover rates than neurotypical employees (Pisano, 2016). Turnover is a significant expense for organizations. In some industries such as software, the turnover rate is close to 15% nationally. Employees with autism have a 7% turnover rate. The costs of replacing a worker earning less than $50,000 are estimated to be 20% of their annual salary (Boushey & Glynn, 2012). As salaries rise, so do the costs of replacing those employees. Lower turnover rates by individuals with ASD should not be assumed to mean that all individuals with ASD wish to remain employed in the same job and at the same level throughout their career. Research is needed to understand the work experiences of neurodivergent individuals across their careers. Research on career patterns would be extremely helpful in determining whether traditional stage models of careers are representative of the career experiences of neurodivergent individuals (Super, 1957). Driver's (1988) linear, steady state, spiral, and transitory career patterns may offer insights into the career experiences of neurodivergent individuals, as may Mervis and Hall's construct of the boundaryless career (1994).

Decreasing Legal Action and Costs

Organizations have faced lawsuits over their recruitment strategies of neurodivergent prospective employees. These lawsuits have looked at recruitment practices and accommodations in these practices for neurodivergent individuals. A 2017 British case was filed because an individual with Asperger's was required to take a multiple-choice test (*Government Legal Service v Brookes* [2017]). The Employment Tribunal and the Appeal Tribunal not only found that the organization had placed an unjustified requirement on the applicant and that this was unlawful, indirect disability discrimination but that the organization should have provided an accommodation for the applicant and altered the format of the test. Not only did the employer have to pay compensation to the applicant, but they were ordered to review their recruitment processes and especially look into providing greater flexibility when doing psychometric testing (Baxter & Heys, 2019).

There have been other cases regarding discrimination against neurodiverse applicants and employees. These have usually centered on not making reasonable accommodations (*Sherbourne v Npower Ltd* [2019]), workplace bullying (*Morris v J.B. Fix Ltd* [2018]), failure to adjust company policies (*Wells v Governing Body of Great Yarmouth High School* [2017]); companies' lack of understanding of how the employee's disability might affect their job (*A v Z Ltd* [2019]), perceiving a negative effect on the employee's performance due to their disability with no actual data to support this (*X v East Cheshire NHS Trust* [2019]); and finally termination of an employee based on beliefs regarding the disability (*Hobbs v Senator Security South Ltd* [2019]). Training and education about neurodiversity in the workplace may help organizations to avoid these types of lawsuits. In addition, organizations may be losing qualified candidates during the recruitment process because of a lack of understanding and training about neurodiversity (Baxter & Heys, 2019). Saleh and Bernick will cover legal issues associated with neurodiversity in the workplace in more depth in a later chapter of this book.

Financial Incentives

Research suggests that organizations that recruit individuals with disabilities may also receive financial benefits. A study by Accenture in 2018 found that companies committed to disability inclusion outperformed their peers and were twice as likely to have higher shareholder returns. The Accenture study identified 45 companies that are leading disability employment and inclusion efforts. These "Champions" represent 32% of the 140 United States companies in their study. They found that Champions were 2 times more likely to outperform peers in shareholder returns. Companies with improved Disability Equality Index (DEI) scores were 4 times more likely to have total shareholder returns that outperform their peers. Accenture developed the DEI as a benchmark tool that gives businesses an objective score on their disability inclusion policies and practices (Accenture, 2018). Some organizations are motivated to recruit neurodivergent individuals because of the financial incentives and federal and state tax breaks provided to companies that hire individuals with ASD. For example, the Disabled Access Credit (I.R.C. § 44.) applies to small businesses with revenues less than $1,000,000 or 30 or fewer full-time employees. A tax credit of up to $5,000 is available to provide accommodations for neurodivergent employees. The Work Opportunity Tax Credit (I.R.C. § 51.) provides $2,400 in direct federal tax credit for any individual with a disability who is referred from vocational rehabilitation or is a Supplemental Security Income (SSI) recipient. There are also numerous financial incentives for hiring veterans including tax credits (www.whitehouse.gov, 2011), and some organizations have developed veteran hiring initiatives (Stone & Stone, 2015).

Increasing Firm Reputation

Recruiting individuals with ASD may enhance a company's reputation and social capital. This is an area in which organizations can enhance their firms' reputations by hiring individuals with ASD and developing diversity and inclusion initiatives. Companies need to be aware of the effects of consumers and coworkers' positive attitudes towards organizations that hire people with disabilities (Morgan & Alexander, 2005; Siperstein et al., 2006). A study of employers with employees who were disabled found that they felt they could increase their public image and reputation by hiring people with disabilities (Olson et al., 2001). A study of people who had worked with a colleague with a disability felt that their colleague's performance was good or very good. A majority of those who had received service from an employee with a disability felt the service was satisfactory or very satisfactory (Siperstein et al., 2006). A 2006 study found that most people preferred companies that hired individuals with disabilities. Ninety-two percent of the people surveyed rated companies that hire people with disabilities higher than those that do not (Siperstein et al., 2006). This result was stronger for female respondents than for males. Eighty-seven percent of people felt that by hiring these individuals, the companies were helping employees with disabilities to lead more productive lives (Siperstein et al., 2006).

The Recruitment of Neurodiverse Candidates

Osman and Thunborg (2019) suggest that there is no perfect recruitment process for selecting underrepresented groups. They interviewed HR experts for their perspectives on the efficacy of four different types of recruitment practices for increasing diversity. These types are the informal, the pragmatic, the standardized, and the strategic recruitment practice. Two of their classifications do not appear to be relevant to the recruitment of neurodivergent individuals: informal recruitment practices refer primarily to internal recruitment (which is not the focus of this chapter) and standardized recruitment practices, which refer to relying on utilizing outside hiring agencies (which are rarely used for entry-level positions). They found that while standardized recruitment practices may guard against discrimination, they may not necessarily enhance diversity. The authors report that according to the HR experts queried, "the pragmatic recruitment practices creates a dilemma of balancing between recruiting someone to fit the organizational culture or recruiting for diversifying the organization." Finally, the experts note that several difficulties may arise even when recruiting strategically for diversity. Interestingly, the authors conclude

> that there seems to be a paradox between counteracting discrimination and enhancing diversity; recruitment practices that counteract discrimination do not necessarily enhance diversity, and recruitment practices that work to increase diversity could be seen as discriminatory. One might well ask if there exists an effective recruitment practice for the recruitment of under-represented groups in the labor market; from this study, the answer is no.
>
> (Osman & Thunborg, 2019, p. 15)

Austin and Pisano (2017) note that one of the obstacles to hiring more neurodivergent individuals in general and individuals with ASD specifically is that the traditional interview process may screen out neurodivergent applicants. One suggestion to overcome this issue is for recruiters to focus on the technical skills and job-related abilities of a person with ASD rather than their interviewing and communication skills (Sanchez, 2018). Interviewing skills will be covered in more depth in the chapter by Saleh, Chang, Bruyère, and Vogus. To realize the benefits discussed earlier, organizations need to change their human resource practices, including recruitment strategies (Austin & Pisano, 2017). This section of the chapter will discuss barriers in the recruitment process and will offer recommendations for modifying recruitment strategies in ways that may have positive effects on neurodiverse candidates.

Barriers in the Traditional Recruitment Process

There are many barriers to obtaining employment that neurodivergent individuals may face during the recruitment process (Hedley et al., 2017; Smith et al., 2014; Vogus & Lounds-Taylor, 2018). These include finding out where to look for job vacancies, finding help with the recruitment process, developing a realistic awareness of careers and the work environment, anxiety, lack of confidence in job search abilities, diminished motivation to persist in job search, and logistical challenges such as having access to transportation (Ciampi, 2019). Neurodivergent candidates may be unsuccessful with typical recruitment practices regardless of their qualifications and abilities (Baxter & Heys, 2019). Ciampi (2019) provides a list of barriers specific to the recruitment process. The list is long and includes barriers that neurotypical recruiters may not be aware of. These barriers include uncertainty about how much detail to provide in a resume; interpreting a job description literally and disqualifying oneself from applying for a job; being discouraged by descriptors such as *self-starter, good communication skills, works well on a team*, or *multitasking;* inferring that education, experience, and skill sets must be an exact match to the job description in order to qualify to apply for the job; not knowing the reason behind multiple job losses; interpreting job posting language literally without understanding business jargon and idioms (*learn the ropes, team player, the bottom line*); narrowing down what experience to mention; uncertainty regarding what to share and what not to share; conveying an accurate picture of aptitudes and expanding on positive traits; differentiating between marketing one's skills and bragging, exaggerating, or lying; answering hypothetical questions that project into the future; speaking in a monotone voice and sounding bored or unmotivated; and coming across as overly enthusiastic, overly confident, or struggling to scrape by.

Suggestions for Improvement

In order to attract, select, and retain qualified applicants with ASD, companies must examine their recruitment and selection processes, policies, and practices, especially the recruitment interview. In order to successfully implement strategic neurodiversity initiatives, HR must develop a framework to build an inclusive workplace (Sumner & Brown, 2015). Rao and Polepeddi (2019) view inclusive employment as an HR strategy. Their proposed framework takes a top-down approach. Top management needs to establish the neurodiversity strategy for the firm after considering the resources and needs of the organization. This plan would be communicated to middle managers along with the goals, resources, and limitations of the initiative. Middle management would then work with HR and the managers of the organization to implement the strategy. Job analyses of positions in the organization need to be developed. Human resources may then look to partners in the local area, including schools and nonprofit support agencies. These partners may not only offer possible applicants, but they may provide skills training to the applicants. Human resource departments and the agencies they partner with can perform job mapping utilizing the established job descriptions to identify possible applicants. This process is one way to ensure that person–job fit is achieved (Rao & Polepeddi, 2019).

Organizations may make a deliberate decision to expand their talent pool to include neurodivergent individuals. They may start a neurodiversity initiative or hiring program. One of the first decisions the organization will need to make is whether they will do the hiring and training of neurodivergent individuals on their own or whether they will engage in supported work, where they receive help from an outside agency. Supported work is a collaborative effort between the business community and a social service delivery system (Harbor Regional Center, 2017). Supported work usually includes providing individuals with job coaches at no cost to the organization. Job coaches can be instrumental in the successful employment of individuals with ASD. Supported work organizations have the goal of helping people with autism get jobs that complement their abilities while helping organizations achieve maximum productivity and cost-effectiveness.

Companies should look to outside agencies that serve the needs of neurodivergent people to help recruit and integrate these employees into the company. Integration may include training for new as well as current employees. Best practices for communicating with new hires would also be useful. Organizations reaching out to local resource programs may be able to find a fit between the needs of the organization and the career interests of individuals. For example, Coding Autism is a social enterprise that trains people with ASD for jobs in the technology industry. Coding Autism offers both technical and soft skills training (Codingautism.com, 2019). The organization Daivergence works to build a recruiting pipeline between companies and the neurodiverse population (Schein, 2020). Rangam Consultants, Inc. has created a website for Autism Speaks on which organizations can advertise for applicants on the autism spectrum (Ovaska-Few, 2018).

Organizations need to set goals for their neurodiversity recruitment initiative. Hiring goals need to be SMART (specific, measurable, attainable, relevant, and timely) (Barcelos, 2017). Specific goals are well defined and focused and will inform the firm's hiring intentions. Organizations are encouraged to set specific goals such as "Our company will hire two neurodivergent employees" instead of "We want to hire neurodivergent people." Including numbers in goals makes them measurable. A goal to make 10% of a company's workforce neurodiverse is measurable and allows the organization to track its progress towards the goal. It is also important to set attainable goals, as setting expectations too high may lead to disappointment if the initiative is not successful. Expecting to hire 100 neurodivergent people would not be attainable for a small or medium-sized company. The goal must be attainable so that people in the organization can work towards the goal. Relevant goals should be set that are realistic and based on current conditions, including the general employment environment, local employment assistance, and the condition of the firm itself. For example, a firm that is struggling to avoid bankruptcy would not set a goal to start an inclusion initiative, knowing that the program would require extensive resources that are not currently available. Finally, goals should include timelines. "Hiring two neurodivergent employees in the next year" would be a smart goal for a small company. Well-thought-out goals will help organizations develop successful plans for recruiting neurodivergent workers. They will also provide a blueprint for examining whether existing human resource management programs need to be modified or redesigned. In addition to these general strategic recruiting suggestions, several suggestions for recruiting policies and best practices are described in what follows.

Implications for Organizations

As discussed earlier in the chapter, the importance of the recruitment interview to applicants' attitudes, reactions, and behaviors cannot be underestimated. Current recruitment interview processes have been found to not provide adequate accommodations for neurodivergent individuals (Demer, 2018; Hensel, 2017). It is important to note that this chapter focuses on the recruitment interview, which typically occurs in the early stages of hiring as a preliminary means of screening job applicants and determining whether they will advance into the next stage of the selection process. The following chapter by Chang, Saleh, Bruyère, and Vogus will delve more deeply into the selection interview and neurodiversity. This section of the chapter will discuss several implications for companies interested in increasing neurodiversity in their organizations.

Issues With the Recruitment Interview

The process of determining who will be considered further in the recruitment process is a potential area in which discrimination against neurodivergent applicants may occur. Some neurodivergent applicants may have nonlinear employment or educational histories. This may be due to nonsupportive environments, medical issues, or the inability to be successful at interviewing (CIPD, 2018). Austin and Pisano (2017) and Vogus and Lounds-Taylor (2018) found that the recruitment interview may pose a unique barrier for individuals with ASD. Their research found that it is difficult for individuals with ASD to navigate the social cues present during an interview. Research has found that individuals with ASD experience high anxiety levels during interviews (Baldwin et al., 2014; Hara & Bigham, 2017). A study of adults with high-functioning ASD participating in an interview process reported that 100% of the participants found that their high levels of anxiety negatively influenced their experience with the interview process. The participants also reported that anxiety negatively affected their communication and performance in the interview (Megrew, 2019). This is an important finding given that anxiety is often comorbid with ASD (Spain et al., 2018; Vogus & Lounds-Taylor, 2018). The study also found that all participants viewed the interview as a negative experience due to issues of verbal and nonverbal communication, the process of the interview, and anxiety. Neurodivergent applicants may engage in tangential topic conversations or overstate their weaknesses in an attempt to be honest. Previous negative experiences with interviews often lead to low self-confidence during the interview (Austin & Pisano, 2017). In a case study of SAP's hiring process, Austin and Pisano (2017) found that many of the highly qualified candidates in the program would not have made it through a traditional recruitment process and/or would not have applied for the job because they believed they would not get hired (Holland, 2016).

Recruiters play an important role in the hiring process, and the effects of recruiters on applicants' reactions are well documented (Giannantonio et al., 2019). Research suggests that recruiters give higher ratings to applicants that are similar to them and with whom they identify (Turban et al., 1998). Since recruiters serve as gatekeepers into later stages of the hiring process, companies need to train recruiters to avoid both implicit and explicit discrimination against applicants with ASD. Neurodivergent candidates have been found to earn lower scores in interviews than neurotypical candidates (Austin & Pisano, 2017).

Types of Accommodations for Neurodivergent Applicants

It is essential that organizations provide accommodations to prospective neurodivergent employees throughout the recruitment process. The interview provides an opportunity for organizations to not only provide accommodations but also show their commitment to inclusivity. Accommodations may include adjusting time limits or sending the applicant the questions before the interview (Baxter & Heys, 2019).

Organizations using traditional recruiting interviews should provide applicants adequate notice to allow them to prepare for their interview. It is suggested that candidates are provided with the start and end times of the interview, the interview setting, and relevant sensory information. Details about the interview should be provided, including information about the location of the building and the office where the interview will take place, directions, parking, and even dress code expectations. Companies should consider sending the interview questions to the candidates in advance of the interview. It is recommended that concrete questions be asked instead of ambiguous hypothetical questions and that practical assessments are used rather than strict question-and-answer situations (Fraser.org, 2016).

Before conducting any type of interview, recruiters need to anticipate any sensory issues or distractions that may negatively affect neurodivergent applicants. This might include asking the candidate if there are things in the room that they find distracting or if any environmental changes are required. For example, individuals with sensory differences such as acute hearing may be distracted by a ticking clock, while individuals with sensitivity to smells may find scented candles to be irritating (DMA Talent, 2019). DXC Technology has developed recruitment workshops in which applicants participate in training exercises and group projects. The workshops are designed to address sensory issues. There is no music, minimal décor, and natural lighting (Carrero et al., 2019).

Recruiters need to consider situations that might be going on in or around the building on the day of the interview that could increase anxiety or act as a distraction for neurodivergent candidates. These situations may include scheduled fire alarms, construction and repair work to the building, or special events involving large crowds and excessive stimuli. Providing this information to candidates may be extremely helpful in eliminating situations that could induce anxiety in neurodivergent applicants (DMA Talent, 2019).

During the interview itself, managers need to be aware that individuals with ASD may not demonstrate the types of nonverbal behaviors that neurotypical individuals are coached to display in interviews and other social interactions, such as maintaining direct eye contact and conveying interest through body language (Spezio et al., 2007). It may be necessary to modify the recruitment interview so that recruiters do not negatively evaluate candidates who exhibit this type of nonverbal behavior. Recruiters need training on how to interact with and fairly evaluate individuals who may not exhibit status quo social conventions. Interviewers are likely to need training to recognize the verbal and nonverbal response patterns of individuals with ASD who may struggle with the informal portions of an interview such as making small talk before the interview formally commences. Laura Williams, a British cat-rescue worker with Asperger's, recalls that in past interviews, she found it hard to know when to shake hands and what to say when greeting the interviewer. When meeting new people, she sometimes creates scripts to ease her nerves, working out in advance when to say things like "hello" and "thank you" (The Economist, 2016).

Additionally, as some individuals with ASD often speak bluntly, interviewers need training to help them understand these response patterns and avoid penalizing candidates whose verbal behaviors may violate conversational social norms. For example, when asked what he thought of team meetings, one neurodivergent candidate replied, "They don't work. Before digging into the problem at hand, people waste time talking about their weekends. Great, but I don't care." While many neurotypical people would wholeheartedly agree with this statement, few would say so openly in a job interview (The Economist, 2016).

While neurotypical people may routinely exaggerate their abilities in the interview, some individuals with ASD may find it difficult to engage in impression management and may be more likely to answer questions with the literal truth. Kurt Schöffer of Auticon, a German IT consultancy that hires people with ASD, spoke with a candidate whom he knew to be a brilliant Java coder. When asked if he was an expert programmer, the candidate said no. Only when pressed did he explain that he did not consider himself an expert because he had not fully mastered all the other computer languages (The Economist, 2016). Interviewers need to be trained to ask probing questions that will allow the candidate to accurately convey their knowledge, skills, and abilities. Finally, companies may wish to allow a "supporter" to accompany the neurodivergent candidate. The supporter will not answer questions for the candidate, but they may help to ensure that the candidate understands the questions (DMA Talent, 2019).

Provide a Recruitment Process Document

Neurodivergent applicants, particularly individuals with ASD, are more successful when there is certainty about what is going to happen (Ciampi, 2019). To alleviate stressors, businesses should establish clear parameters for hiring, including the length of assessment periods and when hiring decisions will be made. It is important to explain every step of the recruitment process to the applicant, to meet established deadlines, and to communicate delays. Organizations may consider creating a recruitment process document that provides both an overview and specific details to be given to all potential applicants. This document would explain each step in the process, how long each step will take, when the applicant will hear from the organization, as well as who to contact with questions (Ciampi, 2019). A recruitment process document is a good recruiting practice for both neurotypical and neurodivergent individuals and would appear to be particularly helpful in expanding the range of neurodivergent individuals recruited.

Alternative Ways for Candidates to Demonstrate Their Skills

It is often suggested that alternatives to traditional interviews be used when evaluating neurodivergent job applicants to allow them to demonstrate their skills. These may involve not emphasizing the applicants' paper resumes (Davis, 2017) and instead using video resumes (Ovaska-Few, 2018). Organizations should consider the emphasis that is placed on communication skills to determine the required level of competency for various jobs. Depending on the employment opportunity, these could include using online questionnaires or phone interviews or having them develop a website or video showing their skills (Ciampi, 2019).

The Autism@Work roundtable was created by a group of industry leaders including EY, JP Morgan Chase & Co., Microsoft, SAP, Ford, IBM, Travelers Insurance, Fidelity Investments, Freddie Mac, and Cintas. The group was developed to help organizations hire people on the autism spectrum. It also has created the Autism@Work Playbook which includes alternative methods for organizations to help neurodivergent applicants demonstrate their skills. The Playbook also provides specific suggestions and techniques for organizations creating a diversity initiative. The Playbook helps prospective employers with recruiting, interviewing, training, and maintaining employment of neurodivergent individuals (ASHA Leader, 2019).

Specialisterne has developed "hangouts" for organizational recruitment that prospective employees are invited to join (Austin & Pisano, 2017). At the hangout, neurodivergent individuals can demonstrate their abilities to company representatives from a variety of different firms in a casual atmosphere. Some applicants are then selected for two more weeks of assessment. DXC Technology viewed hiring neurodivergent employees as an opportunity to improve its talent pool.

The company designed a program to recruit employees with high functioning autism (Carrero et al., 2019). It partnered with local universities in Australia and New Zealand to establish Neurodiversity Hubs. These Hubs help students obtain work experience and internships in information technology. The students that are selected to apply to DXC from the Hub next go through a three-week recruitment and selection workshop.

As candidates advance into the next stage of the hiring process, various selection assessments have been utilized to provide neurodivergent applicants with opportunities to demonstrate their knowledge, skills, and abilities. Large companies with hiring initiatives to create a more diverse workforce see positive results with these types of programs along with using skills-based group screening processes and specific assessment measures used for hiring employees with ASD.

Internet Recruitment

The increased use of the internet for recruitment allows organizations to reach a wider breadth of potential candidates including neurodivergent applicants. Internet recruitment allows organizations to shape the recruiting message and, relatedly, the organizational image they wish to portray. Despite its benefits, there are many issues regarding internet recruitment that organizations need to address when developing job postings, particularly when implementing a neurodiversity hiring initiative. If they hope to include neurodivergent applicants in their hiring pool, they need to make sure that their recruiting efforts are both reaching neurodivergent individuals and not inadvertently screening them out. Outreach may be done by working with local, state, and federal agencies. Organizations can also post job openings on neurodiversity-related websites such as Autism Speaks, SpectrumCareers.com, and Autism@Work's online Job Marketplace (ASHA Leader, 2019). There are also online recruiting events for neurodivergent individuals, such as the Autism at Work Virtual Career Fair. Participating companies include Bloomberg, Deloitte, EY, Ford, IBM, JP Morgan Chase & Co, Microsoft, SAP, and DXC Technology (Parker, 2019). It should also be noted that outside agencies, both for-profit and not-for-profit, exist that help neurodivergent individuals navigate the recruitment process. One example is Mentra, a software application that matches neurodivergent individuals with mentors to help them navigate the recruiting process (Albertson, 2020).

Job Postings

Central to internet recruitment is the issue of developing appropriately written job postings. Establishing the job specifications of job openings is an essential first step in this process. Organizations need to identify the knowledge, skills, and abilities that are genuinely needed for job vacancies. This helps to ensure that neurodivergent candidates are not inadvertently screened out from positions they are qualified for (Härtel et al., 2013). Job postings should include the specific skills necessary for the position. Job postings should use precise, literal language. It is essential to be precise because applicants with ASD may interpret words and phrases literally. For example, do not advertise for a self-driven employee. Advertise for a person who can work with little direct supervision. Job postings with vague language, figures of speech, or acronyms can be confusing for all candidates. Many job advertisements are written very generally and often include more skills and experience than are actually needed for the position. Many businesses list similar criteria for all of their vacancies, but hiring managers should think critically about each position and only list what the job truly requires. Organizations should consider whether positions actually require teamwork skills or exceptional communication skills. Saying that every position requires excellent teamwork skills may prevent individuals with ASD from applying for jobs. This may result in companies missing out on hiring individuals who are technically qualified for the job but who do not consider themselves to be good at teamwork. In a related manner, organizations should scrutinize their use of software matching programs when screening applicants. These programs may exclude individuals the firm may want to interview if the applicant does not use the exact language in their resume that the software program is searching for.

Online job postings often list attributes that neurodivergent candidates may not identify with. The language used in the posting may deter certain groups of candidates from applying for the job (Collier & Zhang, 2016). Job descriptions are often written in a general manner with a long wish list of skills, which may deter neurodivergent candidates from applying if they believe they do not possess all of the skills listed in the posting (HRD Connect, 2018). Studies show that people usually do not want to waste time and energy applying for a position if they do not possess the required skills and experience outlined in the job qualifications (Mohr, 2015).

Regarding job postings, the EEOC (2015) suggests using inclusive language and stating the company's commitment to equal hiring practices (e.g., "This company is an Equal Opportunity Employer. We encourage qualified applicants from diverse backgrounds and experiences, including those with ASD, to apply. Accommodations are available."). Businesses need to be clear in their job postings that they have neurodiversity policies in place and communicate that the organizational environment is supportive and inclusive. Employers may wish to ensure that potential applicants see neurodiversity as part of the corporate brand (CIPD, 2018). They should also state that applicants should request accommodations for the interview if needed. A diversity and inclusion statement should be included in the job posting stating willingness to discuss and provide accommodations (CIPD, 2018). Barnhart (2016) suggests that organizations may want to use the term "neurodiversity" when recruiting applicants with autism. Potential neurodivergent applicants may be more likely to apply to a job posting that includes the word "neurodiverse" (Davis, 2017).

Internal Recruiting and Employee Resource Groups

An organization's current employees may serve as internal recruiting sources when filling job vacancies. Current employees may know neurodivergent individuals who would be qualified for positions, ideally leading to greater person–job and person–organization fit. Research has found that personal contact may enhance attitudes toward people with disabilities, especially when the contact reveals non-stereotypical behavior (Frith & Mitchell, 1981; Stone & Stone, 2015). Current employees who recommend individuals for positions typically are invested in seeing those individuals succeed and may become supporters, allies, and mentors to neurodiverse employees. In SAP's neurodiversity program, new hires with ASD are assigned a mentor within the company (Eng, 2018). Often, these mentors are current employees who are a parent, a relative, or a friend of an individual with ASD. Research has not examined the prevalence of and the effects of internal recruiting on hiring a neurodiverse workforce. One interesting aspect of internal recruiting is involving current neurodivergent employees in the recruitment process. This could include seeking suggestions from them or having them sit in on interviews (Ciampi, 2019). This may lead to more successful outcomes for both the organization and the applicant.

Some organizations have created employee resource groups (ERGs) that focus on neurodiversity. ERGs are "voluntary, employee-led groups made up of individuals who join together based on common interests, background or demographic factors such as gender, race, or ethnicity" (SHRM.org). Information about an organization's ERG that focuses on neurodiversity may send important signals about the organization's commitment to neurodiversity and inclusion and may help to recruit neurodivergent applicants. Listing these ERGs on a company's website may help the organization to recruit neurodivergent candidates (Goode & Dixon, 2016).

Issues Surrounding Disclosure

In order to successfully generate a neurodiverse workforce, the effects of disclosure must be recognized by both organizations and individuals. Disclosure of neurodiversity in the workplace is a complex issue with personal, professional, and legal ramifications (Megrew, 2019). Hedley et al. (2017) found that 100% of their participants struggled with the decision whether to disclose their disability. All applicants should be asked if they will need reasonable accommodations during the recruitment process. If they disclose early in the process, an organization may be able to help them with alternative recruitment methods. If a candidate does disclose a disability to a recruiter, the recruiter should not ask further questions about the disability (CIPD, 2018). The disclosure of a disability by an applicant may put the prospective employer at an increased risk of legal liabilities as a result of becoming aware of the disability (von Schrader et al., 2014).

Neurodivergent individuals may be concerned that potential employers may misunderstand their diagnosis or may discriminate against them because of it. Megrew (2019) found that 75% of the applicants in the study did not disclose their disability. One problem with concealment strategies is that subsequent disclosure of a health condition or disability may violate others' expectations and result in negative reactions (Ragins, 2008; Stone et al., 1986; Tagalakis et al., 1988). The research on concealment strategies indicates that their effectiveness may depend on the nature of the disability and the degree to which the disclosure is seen as voluntary (Stone, 1986; Stone et al., 1986; Tagalakis et al., 1988).

Future Research

As this chapter has illustrated, there is a need for additional research on the topic of how recruitment strategies may best be designed for generating neurodiverse workforces for the benefit of both organizations and neurodivergent individuals. Following the trajectory of previous recruitment research, future research is suggested along three rich lines of inquiry. First, research is needed to understand the efficacy of organizational recruitment strategies for motivating neurodivergent applicants to apply for job openings *and* encouraging them to accept job offers. Research examining the effects of realistic job previews (RJPs) on neurodivergent applicants' willingness to accept a job, as well as their subsequent attitudes (e.g., job satisfaction) and behaviors (e.g., turnover) would be an important extension of understanding the effects of RJPs. Research is needed to understand which external sources of recruitment generate positive yield ratios for organizations seeking to recruit neurodivergent job applicants.

Second, it is critical that future research is conducted from the perspective of neurodivergent applicants. It is important to understand the role that uncertainty plays in the recruitment and job search process for neurodivergent individuals. Previous research suggests that some individuals with ASD possess limited information about the availability of employment opportunities in general, as well as the job and organizational attributes associated with specific employment opportunities. Additionally, little is known about neurodivergent applicants' perceptions of their job search skills, self-efficacy, and self-esteem and how these perceptions influence self-evaluations of their chances of receiving a job offer or cause them to self-select out of certain employment opportunities.

Recruiter effects have been well documented with neurotypical applicants. Research is needed to determine if these effects generalize to neurodivergent individuals. To what extent is the recruiter an important influence on perceptions of the job, organizational attractiveness, willingness to pursue or accept a job offer, and perceptions of receiving a job offer? Recruiter effects need to be examined in the context of employment inducements to better understand neurodivergent applicants' job choice decisions.

Third, it is critical that future research employs a process perspective of recruitment in order to understand *how* recruitment influences neurodivergent applicants' reactions and behaviors. Additional research is needed to understand if and how the signaling hypothesis may operate with neurodivergent individuals. Research may investigate which characteristics of individuals, organizations, and jobs serve as signals and whether these signals serve to reduce the uncertainty experienced by neurodivergent applicants. Of particular interest would be research focused on the inferences that neurodivergent individuals form about unknown job and organizational characteristics when limited information is available. Finally, future research will no doubt focus on the impact of the coronavirus pandemic on the demand for and supply of labor across various occupations and industries and its effects on the level and amount of recruiting activities undertaken by organizations. Adopting a process view of recruitment may help organizations to gain a better understanding of how recruitment strategies may be used to generate a neurodiverse workforce in the "new normal."

In summary, much is known about the effects of recruitment strategies on the reactions, behavioral intentions, and job choice outcomes of neurotypical applicants. A growing body of research has begun to examine the effects of recruitment strategies on neurodivergent candidates and the benefits of recruiting and hiring neurodivergent individuals. Future research along these three lines of inquiry has practical implications for organizational best practices, policies, and strategies and the potential to improve work and life outcomes for Generation A, the half million individuals with autism spectrum disorder (ASD) who will reach adulthood in the current decade and who will be poised to enter the workplace in unprecedented numbers.

References

Accenture. (2018). *Getting to equal: The disability inclusion advantage.* Retrieved from www.accenture.com/_acnmedia/pdf-89/accenture-disability-inclusion-research-report.pdf

Albertson, K. (2020). Solutions in practice: Case study Georgia Tech duo creates app to link people with autism to jobs. *ISE Magazine*, 480–490.

Anderson, N. (2003). Applicant and recruiter reactions to new technology in selection: A critical review and agenda for future research. *International Journal of Selection & Assessment, 11*(2/3), 121–136.

Anderson, N., Born, M., & Cunningham-Snell, N. (2001). Recruitment and selection: Applicant perspectives and outcomes. In N. Anderson, D. Ones, H. Kepir Sinangil, & C. Viswesvaran (Eds.), *Handbook of industrial, work and organizational psychology* (Vol. 1, pp. 200–218). London: SAGE.

ASHA Leader. (2019). Playbook helps companies hire people with ASD. *ASHA Leader, 24*(5), 13. https://doi.org/10.1044/leader.NIB4.24052019.13

Austin, R. D., Fieldhouse, M., Mohan, A., & Quinn, P. (2017, December 7). Why the Australian Defence Organization is recruiting cyber analysts on the autism spectrum. *Harvard Business Review.* Retrieved from https://hbr.org/2017/12/why-the-australian-defence-organization-is-recruiting-cyber-analysts-on-the-autism-spectrum

Austin, R. D., & Pisano, G. (2017, May-June). Neurodiversity as a competitive advantage. *Harvard Business Review*, 98–104.

Autism Speaks. (2019a). Retrieved from www.autismspeaks.org/what-autism

Autism Speaks. (2019b). Retrieved from www.autism-society.org/what-is/facts-and-statistics/

A v Z Ltd. (2019). *A v Z Ltd & anor* [2019] ET case no S/4102808/16.

Avery, D. R., & McKay, P. F. (2006). Target practice: An organizational impression management approach to attracting minority and female job applicants. *Personnel Psychology, 59*(1), 157–187.

Avery, D. R., Volpone, S. D., Stewart, R. W., Luksyte, A., Hernandez, M., McKay, P. F., & Hebl, M. R. (2013). Examining the draw of diversity: How diversity climate perceptions affect job-pursuit intentions. *Human Resource Management, 52*(2), 175–193.

Baldwin, S., Costley, D., & Warren, A. (2014). Employment activities and experiences of adults with high-functioning Autism and Asperger's disorder. *Journal of Autism and Developmental Disorders, 44*(10), 2440–2449. https://doi.org/10.1007/s10803-014-2112-z

Barber, A. E. (1998). *Recruitment employees.* Thousand Oaks, CA: SAGE.

Barcelos, K. (2017). *How to set SMART hiring goals in 2018–2019.* Retrieved from www.jobsoid.com/set-smart-hiring-goals-2018/

Barnhart, G. S. (2016). Clinician perspectives of adult high-functioning autism support groups' use of neurodiversity concept. *Dissertation Abstracts International: Section B: The Sciences and Engineering,* 77(7-B)(E),2017.UMI Order Number:AAI10025737.Retrieved from http://gateway.proquest.com.libproxy.chapman.edu/openurl?url_ver=Z39.88-2004&rft_val_fmt=info:ofi/fmt:kev:mtx:dissertation&res_dat=xri:pqm&rft_dat=xri:pqdiss:10025737

Baur, J. E., Buckley, M. R., Bagdasarov, Z., & Dharmasiri, A. S. (2014). A historical approach to realistic job previews. *Journal of Management History, 2020*(2), 200–223. https://doi.org/10.1108/JMH-06-2012-0046

Baxter, K., & Heys, T. (2019). Neurodiversity and the workplace. *Employment Law Journal* 12–14.

Bordieri, J. E., & Drehmer, D. E. (1984). Vietnam veterans: Fighting the employment war. *Journal of Applied Social Psychology, 4*, 341–347.

Bopp, T., Goldsmith, A., & Walker, M. B. (2014). Commitment to diversity. The impact of diversity and inclusiveness on athletic department organizational attractiveness and job pursuit intentions. *Journal of Applied Sport Management, 6*(4), 1–26.

Boushey, H., & Glynn, S. J. (2012). *There are significant business costs to replacing employees.* Retrieved from www.americanprogress.org/issues/economy/reports/2012/11/16/44464/there-are-significant-business-costs-to-replacing-employees/

Bowe, F. (1992). *Adults with disabilities: A portrait.* Washington, DC: President's Committee on Employment of People with Disabilities.

Braddock, D., & Bachelder, L. (1994). *The glass ceiling and persons with disabilities.* Washington, DC: Glass Ceiling Commission, U.S. Department of Labor.

Breaugh, J. A. (2008). Employee recruitment: Current knowledge and important areas for future research. *Human Resource Management Review, 18*, 103–118.

Breaugh, J. A. (2017). The contribution of job analysis to recruitment. In H. W. Goldstein, E. D. Pulakos, J. Passmore, & C. Semedo (Eds.), *The Wiley Blackwell handbook of the psychology of recruitment, selection and employee retention* (pp. 12–28). Wiley Blackwell. https://doi.org/10.1002/9781118972472.ch2

Bruggink, A., Huisman, S., Vuijk, R., Kraaij, V., & Garnefski, N. (2016). Cognitive emotion regulation, anxiety and depression in adults with autism spectrum disorder. *Research in Autism Spectrum Disorders, 22*, 34–44.

Carless, S. A. (2006). Applicant reactions to multiple selection procedures for the police force. *Applied Psychology: An International Review, 55*(2), 145–167.

Carrero, J., Krzeminska, A., & Härtel, C. (2019). The DXC technology work experience program: Disability-inclusive recruitment and selection in action. *Journal of Management & Organization, 25*(4), 535–542. https://doi.org/10.1017/jmo.2019.23

Cascio, W. F. (1993). International human resource management issues for the 1990s. *Asia Pacific Journal of Human Resources, 30*(4), 1–18. https://doi.org/10.1177/103841119303000401

Census.gov. (2019). Retrieved from www.census.gov/newsroom/facts-for-features/2019/disabilities-act.html#:~:text=40.7%20million%20or%2012.7%25,disability%20in%20the%20United%20States

Census Bureau Quick Facts. (2018). *U.S. and world population clock*. Retrieved September 9, 2018, from www.census.gov/popclock/

Chapman, D. S., Uggerslev, K. L., Carroll, S. A., Piasentin, K. A., & Jones, D. A. (2005). Applicant attraction to organizations and job choice: A meta-analytic review of the correlates of recruiting outcomes. *Journal of Applied Psychology, 90*, 928–944.

Christeson, W., Taggart, A. D., & Messner-Zidell, S. (2018). Ready, willing, and unable to serve, mission readiness. *Mission Readiness*. Retrieved June 26, 2018, from http://cdn.missionreadiness.org/NATEE1109.pdf

Ciampi, M. (2019). Workplace challenges for women with autism. *Spectrumly Speaking* episode 68. Retrieved from www.differentbrains.org/workplace-challenges-for-women-with-autism-with-marcie-ciampi-m-ed-samantha-craft-spectrumly-speaking-ep-68/

Cidav, Z., Marcus, S. C., & Mandell, D. S. (2012). Implications of childhood autism for parental employment and earnings. *Pediatrics, 129*(4), 617–623. https://doi.org/10.1542/peds.2011-2700

CDC. (2018). *Centers for Disease Control and Prevention*. Retrieved from www.cdc.gov/ncbddd/autism/data.html

CDC. (2020). *Centers for Disease Control and Prevention*. Retrieved from www.cdc.gov/ncbddd/autism/data.html

CIPD. (2018). *Neurodiversity at work*. Retrieved from www.cipd.co.uk/Images/neurodiversity-at-work_2018_tcm18-37852.pdf

CNA. (2016). *Population representation in the military services*. Accessed September 1, 2018, from www.cna.org/pop-rep/2016/summary/summary.pdf

Codingautism.com. (2019). Retrieved from www.codingautism.com/about-us

Collier, D., & Zhang, C. (2016). *Can we reduce bias in the recruiting process and broaden/diversify pools of candidates by using different types of words/styles in job descriptions?* Retrieved July 6, 2020, from http://digitalcommons.ilr.cornell.edu/student/140 Cornell University ILR School

Cooper, B. (1991). Employment potential of persons with mild intellectual impairments. *Canadian Journal of Rehabilitation, 5*, 81–92.

Crespi, B. J. (2016). Autism as a disorder of high intelligence. *Frontiers in Neuroscience, 10*, 300. https://doi.org/10.3389/fnins.2016.00300

Danko, K. S. (2015). *The role of generational differences on perception of employer reputation to job applicants: A phenomenological study* (Doctoral dissertation). Capella University.

Davis, G. P. (2017, March 17). Diversity is not enough. Inclusion is the key. *Higher Education Today.com*. Retrieved from www.higheredtoday.org/2017/03/17/diversity-not-enough-inclusion-key/

Demer, L. (2018). The autism spectrum: Human rights perspectives. *Pediatrics, 141*(4), 369–374. https://doi.org/10.1542/peds.2016-4300O

Dipboye, R. L. (1992). *Selection interviews: Process perspectives*. Cincinnati, OH: South-Western Pub.

DMA Talent. (2019). *Autism employer guide*. Retrieved from https://dma.org.uk/uploads/misc/dma-talent-autism-employer-guide-final.pdf

Driver, M. J. (1988). Careers: A review of personal and organizational research. In C. L. Cooper and I. Robertson (Eds.), *International review of industrial and organizational psychology* (pp. 79–139). New York: Wiley.

EEOC. (2015, February 3). *Recruiting, hiring, retaining, and promoting people with disabilities: A resource guide for employers*. Retrieved from www.eeoc.gov/eeoc/interagency/upload/employing_people_with_disabilities_toolkit_february_3_2015_v4-2.pdf.

Ehrhart, K. H., & Ziegert, J. C. (2005). Why are individuals attracted to organizations? *Journal of Management, 31*, 901–919.

Eng, D. (2018). Retrieved from https://fortune.com/2018/06/24/where-autistic-workers-thrive/

Ferris, G. R., & Judge, T. A. (1991). Personnel/human resources management: A political influence perspective. *Journal of Management, 17*, 447–488.

Fichten, C. S., & Amsel, R. (1986). Trait attributions about college students with a physical disability: Circumplex analyses and methodological issues. *Journal of Applied Social Psychology, 16*, 410–427.

Fiske, S. T., & Taylor, S. E. (1984). *Social cognition*. Reading, MA: Addison-Wesley.

Fraser.org. (2016). *Autism's hidden strengths*. Retrieved from http://fraser-www.s3.amazonaws.com/a/for-employers-tip-sheet.pdf

Frith, G. H., & Mitchell, J. W. (1981). The attitudes of nonhandicapped students toward the mildly retarded: A consideration in placement decisions. *Education and Training of the Mentally Retarded, 16*, 79–83.

Gerhardt, P. F., & Lainer, I. (2011). Addressing the needs of adolescents and adults with autism: A crisis on the horizon. *Journal of Contemporary Psychotherapy, 41*(1), 37–45.

Giannantonio, C. M., Hurley-Hanson, A. E., Segrest, S. L., Perrewé, P. L., & Ferris, G. R. (2019). Effects of recruiter friendliness on applicant reactions. *Personnel Review, 48*(6), 1491–1506.

Goldstein, K. M., & Blackman, S. (1975). Generalizations regarding deviant groups. *Psychological Reports, 37*, 278.

Goltz, S. M., & Giannantonio, C. M. (1995). Recruiter friendliness and attraction to the job: The mediating role of inferences about the organization. *Journal of Vocational Behavior, 46*, 109–118.

Goode, S., & Dixon, I. (2016). Are employee resource groups good for business? *SHRM.org*. Retrieved from www.shrm.org/hr-today/news/hr-magazine/0916/pages/are-employee-resource-groups-good-for-business.aspx

Gorgas, M. J., Nelson, M. D., & Rader, S. (2018). *Attention Deficit Hyperactivity Disorder (ADHD) and the U.S. Army: Recruiting and readiness implications*. Calhoun: The NPS Institutional Archive Space Repository Theses and Dissertations. Retrieved from https://calhoun.nps.edu/bitstream/handle/10945/61251/18Dec_Rader_Nelson_Gorgas.pdf?sequence=1&isAllowed=y

Government Legal Service v Brookes (2017). UKEAT 0302/16/RN.

Graffam, J., Shinkfield, A., Smith, K., & Polzin, U. (2002). Factors that influence employer decisions in hiring and retaining an employee with a disability. *Journal of Vocational Rehabilitation, 17*, 175–181.

Greenwood, R., & Johnson, V. A. (1987). Employer perspectives on workers with disabilities. *Journal of Rehabilitation, 53*, 37–45.

Grønborg, T. K., Schendel, D. E., & Parner, E. T. (2013). Recurrence of autism spectrum disorders in full- and half-siblings and trends over time: A population-based cohort study *JAMA Pediatrics, 167*(10), 947–953. https://doi.org/10.1001/jamapediatrics.2013.2259

Hagner, D., & Cooney, B. F. (2005). "I Do That for Everybody": Supervising employees with autism. *Focus on Autism and Other Developmental Disabilities, 20*(2), 91–97. https://doi.org/10.1177/10883576050200020501

Hara, K., & Bigham, J. (2017, October 20–November 1). Introducing people with ASD to crowd work. ASSETS'17. In *Proceedings of the 19th International ACM SIGACCESS Conference on Computers and Accessibility, Baltimore, MD* (pp. 42–51). Research Collection School of Information Systems. Retrieved from https://ink.library.smu.edu.sg/sis_research/4016

Harasymiw, S. J., Horne, M. D., & Lewis, S. C. (1976). A longitudinal study of disability group acceptance. *Rehabilitation Literature, 37*, 98–102.

Harbor Regional Center, (2017). Retrieved from www.harborrc.org/files/uploads/Employment_Session_2_Packet__Presentation.pdf

Harold, C. M., & Ployhart, R. E. (2008). What do applicants want? Examining changes in attribute judgments over time. *Journal of Occupational and Organizational Psychology, 81*(2), 191–218.

Harrell, M. C., & Berglass, N. (2012). *Employing America's veterans*. Washington, DC: Center for a New American Security.

Härtel, H., Härtel, G. F., & Trumble, R. (2013). IDADA: The individual difference approach to assessing and developing diversity awareness. *Journal of Management & Organization, 19*(1), 60–74. https://doi.org/10.1017/jmo.2013.4

Hedley, D. H., Uljarevic, M., Cameron, L., Dissanayake, C., Halder, S., & Richdale, A. (2017). Employment programs and interventions targeting adults with autism spectrum disorder: A systematic review of the literature. *Autism, 21*(8). https://doi.org/10.1177/1362361316661855

Heilman, M. (1983). Sex bias in work settings: The lack of fit model. In B. M. Staw & L. L. Cummings (Eds.), *Research in organizational behavior* (Vol. 5, pp. 269–298). Greenwich, CT: JAI Press.

Hendricks, D. (2010). Employment and adults with autism spectrum disorders: Challenges and strategies for success. *Journal of Vocational Rehabilitation, 32*, 125–134. https://doi.org/10.3233/JVR-2010–0502

Hensel, W. F. (2017). People with autism spectrum disorder in the workplace: An expanding legal frontier. *Harvard Civil Rights-Civil Liberties Law Review, 52*, 74–103.

Hernandez, B., Keys, C. B., & Balcazar, F. E. (2003). Disability rights: Attitudes of private and public sector representatives. *Journal of Rehabilitation, 70*(1), 28–37.

Hillier, A., Campbell, H., Mastriani, K., Izzo, M. V., Kool-Tucker, A. K., Cherry, L., & Beversdorf, D. Q. (2007). Two-year evaluation of a vocational support program for adults on the autism spectrum. *Career Development for Exceptional Individuals, 30*(1), 35–47. https://doi.org/10.1177/08857288070300010501

Hobbs v Senator Security South Ltd (2019). *ET case no 1400267/2017*. Retrieved from www.gov.uk/employment-tribunal-decisions/mr-s-hobbs-v-senator-security-south-ltd-1400267–2017

Holland, R. (2016, July 11). The benefits of recruiting employees with autism spectrum disorder. *Forbes*. Retrieved from www.forbes.com/sites/hbsworkingknowledge/2016/07/11/the-benefits-of-recruiting-employees-with-autism-spectrum-disorder/#368dc83840a2

Howlin, P., Alcock, J., & Burkin, C. (2005). An 8 year follow-up of a specialist supported employment service for high-ability adults with autism or Asperger syndrome. *Autism, 9*, 533–549. https://doi.org/10.1177/1362361305057871

Howlin, P., Goode, S., Hutton, J., & Rutter, M. (2004). Adult outcome for children with autism. *Journal of Child Psychology and Psychiatry, 45*(2), 212–229.

HRD Connect. (2018). Retrieved from www.hrdconnect.com/2018/02/28/untapping-neurodiverse-talent-pools-interview-dr-jill-miller/

Hurley-Hanson, A. E., Giannantonio, C. M., & Griffiths, A. J. (2020). *Autism in the workplace. Creating positive outcomes for generation A. Palgrave explorations in workplace stigma*. Cham: Palgrave Macmillan.

I.R.C. § 44. Expenditures to provide access to disabled individuals.

I.R.C. § 51. Amount of Work Opportunity Tax credit.

Jacob, A., Scott, M., Falkmer, M., & Falkmer, T. (2015). The costs and benefits of employing an adult with autism spectrum disorder: A systematic review. *PLoS One, 10*(10), e0139896. https://doi.org/10.1371/journal.pone.0139896

Job Accommodation Network. (2018). *Workplace accommodations: Low cost, high impact*. Retrieved February 9, 2018, from https://askjan.org/topics/costs.cfm

Johnson, R., & Heal, L. W. (1976). Private employment agency responses to the physically handicapped applicant in a wheelchair. *Journal of Applied Rehabilitation Counseling,* 7(1), 12–21.

Jones, R. L. (1974). The hierarchical structure of attitudes toward the exceptional. *Exceptional Children, 40*, 430–435.

Krieger, B., Kinebanian, A., Prodinger, B., & Heigl, F. (2012). Becoming a member of the workforce: Perceptions of adults with Asperger syndrome. *Work, 43*(2), 141–157.

Kushner, D. (2019, April). Neuroforce. *Esquire*, 91–105.

Lievens, F., Van Hoye, G., & Schreurs, B. (2005). Examining the relationship between employer knowledge dimensions and organizational attractiveness: An application in a military context. *Journal of Occupational and Organizational Psychology*, *78*, 553–572.

Loprest, P., & Maag, E. (2003). Issues in job search and work, accommodation. *Research in Social Science and Disability, 3*, 87–108.

Mahoney, J. (2017). *How JPMorgan Chase's autism at work program is helping to win top tech talent*. Retrieved from www.forbes.com/sites/jpmorganchase/2017/06/05/how-jpmorgan-chases-autism-at-work-program-is-helping-to-win-top-tech-talent/#660a965830bb

Malcolm-Smith, H. M. Ing, N., De Vries, P. J., & Thomas, K. G. F. (2013). Autism spectrum disorders – Global challenges and local opportunities *Journal of Child and Adolescent Mental Health, 25*(1). https://doi.org/10.2989/17280583.2013.767804

Manpower Group. (2021). *Solving the talent shortage* (Q3 2021). Retrieved from https://go.manpowergroup.com/talent-shortage

Megrew, L. E. (2019). *Neurodiversity and the organizational interview process: A phenomenological study of adult high-functioning autistics (Order No. 27542600)*. Dissertations & Theses Global (2321034834). Retrieved from https://login.libproxy.chapman.edu/login?url=https://search-proquest-com.libproxy.chapman.edu/docview/2321034834?accountid=10051

Mervis, P. H., & Hall, D.T. (1994). Psychological success and the boundaryless career. *Journal of Organizational Behavior, 15*(4), 365–380. https://doi.org/10.1002/job.4030150406

Mohr, T.S. (2015). Why women don't apply for jobs unless they're 100% qualified. *Harvard Business Review*, 20. Retrieved from https://hbr.org/2014/08/why-women-dont-apply-for-jobs-unless-theyre-100-qualified

Morgan, R. L., & Alexander, M. (2005). The employer's perception: Employment of individuals with developmental disabilities. *Journal of Vocational Rehabilitation, 23*(1), 39–49.

Morris v J. B. Fix Ltd (2018). *Morris v JB Fix Ltd* [2018] ET case no 3201483/2017. Retrieved from www.gov.uk/employment-tribunal-decisions/mr-c-morris-v-jb-fix-ltd-3201483-2017

National Autistic Society. (2016). Retrieved April 2016, from www.autism.org.u.k

Nord, D. K., Stancliffe, R. J., Nye-Legerman, K., & Hewitt, A. S. (2016). Employment in the community for people with and without autism: A comparative analysis. *Research in Autism Spectrum Disorders, 24*, 11–16.

Olson, D., Cioffi, A., Yovanoff, P. D., & Mank, D. (2001). Employers' perceptions of employees with mental retardation. *Journal of Vocational Rehabilitation, 16*(2), 125–133.

Osborn, D. P. (1990). A reexamination of the organizational choice process. *Journal of Vocational Behavior, 36*(1), 45–60.

Osman, A., & Thunborg, C. (2019). The challenge of recruiting underrepresented groups – Exploring organizational recruitment practices in Sweden. *Nordic Journal of Working Life Studies, 9*(1). https://doi.org/10.18291/njwls.v9i1.113085

Ovaska-Few, S. (2018). Promoting neurodiversity: A pilot program at EY recruits workers with autism. *Journal of Accountancy,* 46–49.

Parker, K. (2019). Autism @ Work career fair. *AccessibleCareer.com*. Retrieved from https://accessiblecareer.com/2019/04/02/autism-work-virtual-career-fair/

Peck, B., & Kirkbride, L. T. (2001). Why businesses don't employ people with disabilities. *Journal of Vocational Rehabilitation, 16*(2), 71–75.

Pisano, G. (2016). Towards a prescriptive theory of dynamic capabilities: Connecting strategic choice, learning, and competition (Working Paper 16-146).

Prudential. (2012). *Veteran employment challenges: Perceptions and experiences of transitioning from military to civilian life*. Newark, NJ: Prudential Financial Inc.

Ragins, B. R. (2008). Disclosure disconnect: Antecedents and consequences of disclosing invisible stigmas across life domains. *Academy of Management Review, 33*, 194–215.

Rao, B., & Polepeddi, J. (2019). Neurodiversity workforce: Inclusive Employment as an HR Strategy. *Strategic HR Review, 18*(5), 204–209.

Ray, K. L., DePriest, T. K., Rogers, T. D., & Frame, M. C. (2018). *The role of ADA inclusive policies in the recruiting of applicants with Autism Spectrum Disorders*. 14th Annual river cities industrial and organizational psychology conference. https://scholar.utc.edu/rcio/2018/sessions/10/

Richards, J. (2012). Examining the exclusion of employees with Asperger syndrome from the workplace. *Personnel Review, 41*(5), 630–646.

Richardson, S. A., Goodman, N., Hastorf, A. H., & Dornbusch, S. M. (1961). Cultural uniformity in reaction to physical disabilities. *American Sociological Review, 26*(2), 241–247.

Roux, A. M., Shattuck, P. T., Cooper, B. P., Anderson, K. A., Wagner, M., & Narendorf, S. C. (2013). Postsecondary employment experiences among young adults with an Autism Spectrum Disorder RH: Employment in young adults with autism. *Journal of the American Academy of Child & Adolescent Psychiatry, 52*(9), 931–939.

Ryan, A. M., & Ployhart, R. E. (2000). Applicants' perceptions of selection procedures and decisions: A critical review and agenda for the future. *Journal of Management, 26*, 565–606.

Rynes, S. L. (1991). Recruitment, job choice, and post-hire consequences: A call for new research directions. In M. D. Dunnette & L. M. Hough (Eds.), *Handbook of industrial and organizational psychology* (Vol. 2, pp. 399–444). Palo Alto, CA: Consulting Psychologists Press, Inc.

Rynes, S. L., & Cable, D. M. (2003). Recruitment research in the twenty-first century. In W. C. Borman & D. R. Ilgen (Eds.), *Handbook of psychology: Industrial and organizational psychology* (2nd ed., Vol. 12, pp. 55–76). New York: John Wiley & Sons.

Rynes, S. L., Heneman, H. G., III, & Schwab, D. P. (1980). Individual reactions to organizational recruiting: A review. *Personnel Psychology, 33*, 529–542.

Saks, A. M., & Uggerslev, K. L. (2010). Sequential and combined effects of recruitment information on applicant reactions. *Journal of Business and Psychology, 25*(3), 351–365.

Samson, A. C., Huber, O., & Gross, J. J. (2012). Emotional reactivity and regulation in adults with autism spectrum disorders. *Emotion, 12*, 659–665. https://doi.org/10.1037/a0027975

Sanchez, D. A. (2018). *Neurodiversity in the workplace*. SHRM Member2Member Solutions. Retrieved from https://www.dashrconsulting.com/inclusion-revolution-neurodiversity-in-the-workplace/

Scott, M., Falkmer, M., Girdler, S., & Falkmer, T. (2015). Viewpoints on factors for successful employment for adults with autism spectrum disorder. *PloS One, 10*(10), e0139281.

Sexton-Brown, E. (2018, February 18). Untapping neurodiverse talent pools: Interview with Dr Jill Miller. Retrieved from https://www.hrdconnect.com/2018/02/28/untapping-neurodiverse-talent-pools-interview-dr-jill-miller/

Shattuck, P. T., Narendorf, S. C., Cooper, B., Sterzing, P. R., Wagner, M., & Taylor, J. L. (2012). Postsecondary education and employment among youth with an autism spectrum disorder. *Pediatrics, 129*(6), 1042–1049.

Schein, E. (2020). Hiring from the autism spectrum. *Communications of the Association for Computing Machinery, Inc., 63*(6), 17–30.

Sherbourne v Npower Ltd [2019] *Sherbourne v Npower Ltd [2019] ET case no 1811601/2018*. Retrieved from www.gov.uk/employment-tribunal-decisions/mr-t-sherbourne-v-n-power-ltd-1811601-2018

Singh, A. (2011). Signaling theory and applicant attraction outcomes. *Personnel Review, 40*(2), 222–238.

Siperstein, G., Romano, N., Mohler, A., & Parker, R. (2006). A national survey of consumer attitudes towards companies that hire people with disabilities. *Journal of Vocational Rehabilitation, 24*, 3–9.

Smith, M., Belcher, R. G., & Juhrs, P. D. (1995). *A guide to successful employment for individuals with autism*. Baltimore, MD: Paul H. Brookes Publishing.

Smith, M. J., Ginger, E. J., Wright, K., Wright, M. A., Taylor, J. L., Humm, L. B., Olsen, D. E., Bell, M. B., & Fleming, M. F. (2014). Virtual reality job interview training in adults with autism spectrum disorder. *Journal of Autism and Developmental Disorders, 44*, 2450–2463. https://doi.org/10.1007/s10803-014-2113-y

Spain, D., Sin, J., Linder, K., McMahon, J., & Happe, F. (2018). Social anxiety in autism spectrum disorder: A systematic review. *Research in Autism spectrum disorders, 52*, 51–68. https://doi.org/10.1016/j.rasd.2018.04.007

Spence, A. M. (1973). Job market signaling. *Quarterly Journal of Economics, 87*, 845–856.

Spence, A. M. (1974). *Market signaling: Informational transfer in hiring and related screening processes*. Cambridge, MA: Harvard University Press.

Spezio, M. L., Adolphs, R., Hurley, R., & Piven, J. (2007). Analysis of face gaze in autism using "Bubbles." *Neuropsychologia, 45*(1), 144–151.

Stone, C., & Stone, D. L. (2015). Factors affecting hiring decisions about veterans. *Human Resource Management Review, 25*(1), 68–79.

Stone, D. L. (1996). *The effects of nondisclosure of physical handicaps on personnel selection decisions*. Paper presented at the annual meeting of the Academy of Management, Chicago, IL.

Stone, D. L., & Colella, A. (1996). A model of factors affecting the treatment of disabled individuals in organizations. *Academy of Management Review, 21*(2), 352–401.

Stone, E. F., Shetzer, L., & Eggleston, S. (1986). *Effect of handicap type, handicap revelation mode, and interviewee ratings of applicant suitability*. Paper presented at the annual meeting of the Academy of Management, Chicago, IL.

Sumner, K. E., & Brown, T. J. (2015). Neurodiversity and human resource management: Employer challenges for applicants and employees with learning disabilities. *The Psychologist-Manager Journal, 18*(2), 77–85. https://doi.org/10.1037/mgr0000031

Super, D. E. (1957). *Psychology of careers*. New York: Harper & Row.

Tagalakis, V., Amsel, R., & Fichten, C. S. (1988). Job interview strategies for people with a visible disability. *Journal of Applied Psychology, 18*, 520–532.

Taylor, S. E., & Fiske, S. T. (1978). Salience, attention, and attribution: Top of the head phenomena. In L. Berkowitz (Ed.), *Advances in experimental social psychology* (Vol. 11, pp. 249–288). New York: Academic Press.

The Autism Advantage. (2015). Retrieved from http://webtv.un.org/watch/2015-world-autism-awareness-day-employment-the-autism-advantage/4149043523001

The Economist. (2016). *The Rise of Autism: SPectrum Shift*. Retrieved from www.economist.com/briefing/2016/04/16/spectrum-shift

Treadway, D. C., Adams, G., Hanes, T. J., Perrewé, P. L., Magnusen, M. J., & Ferris, G. R. (2014). The roles of recruiter political skill and performance resource leveraging in NCAA football recruitment effectiveness. *Journal of Management, 40*, 1607–1626.

Tringo, J. L. (1970). The hierarchy of preference toward disability groups. *The Journal of Special Education, 4*, 295–306.

Turban, D. B., Campion, J. E., & Eyring, A. R. (1995). Factors related to job acceptance decisions of college recruits. *Journal of Vocational Behavior, 47*, 193–213.

Turban, D. B., Forret, M. L., & Hendrickson, C. L. (1998). Applicant attraction to firms: Influences of organization reputation, job and organizational attributes, and recruiter behaviors. *Journal of Vocational Behavior*, 24–44.

Twaronite, K. (2019). How neurodiversity is driving innovation from unexpected places. *EY.com*. Retrieved from www.ey.com/en_us/diversity-inclusiveness/how-neurodiversity-is-driving-innovation-from-unexpected-places

Uggerslev, K. L., Fassina, N. E., & Kraichy, D. (2012). Recruiting through the stages: A meta-analytic test of predictors of applicant attraction at different stages of the recruiting process. *Personnel Psychology, 65*(3), 597–660.

Unger, D. (2002). Employers' attitudes toward persons with disabilities in the workforce: Myths or realities? *Focus on Autism and Other Developmental Disabilities, 17*(1), 2–10. https://doi.org/10.1177/108835760201700101

U.S. Bureau of Labor Statistics. (2018). Retrieved from www.bls.gov/opub/mlr/2018/home.htm

U.S. Bureau of Labor Statistics. (2020). *Employment situation of veterans*. Retrieved from www.bls.gov/news.release/pdf/vet.pdf

Vogus, T., & Lounds-Taylor, J. (2018). Flipping the script: Bringing an organizational perspective to the study of autism at work. *Autism, 22*(5), 514–516.

von Schrader, S., Malzer, V., & Bruyère, S. (2014). Perspectives on disability disclosure: The importance of employer practices and workplace climate. *Employee Responsibilities and Rights Journal, 26*, 237–255. https://doi.org/10.1007/s10672-013-9227-9

Walker, H. J., Feild, H. S., Bernerth, J. B., & Becton, J. B. (2012). Diversity cues on recruitment websites: Investigating the effects on jobseekers' information processing. *Journal of Applied Psychology, 97*(1), 214–224.

Wallace, S., Fein, D., Rosanoff, M., Dawson, G., Hossain, S., Brennan, L., Como, A., & Shih, A. (2012). A global public health strategy for autism spectrum disorders. *Autism Research, 5*(3), 211–217. https://doi.org/10.1002/aur.1236

Wells v Governing Body of Great Yarmouth High School (2017). ET case no 3401100/2015. Retrieved from www.gov.uk/employment-tribunal-decisions/mr-i-wells-v-the-governing-body-of-great-yarmouth-high-school-3401100–2015.

Wiles, M. A., & Spiro, R. L. (2004). Attracting graduates to sales positions and the role of recruiter knowledge: A re-examination. *Journal of Personal Selling and Sales Management, 24*, 39–48.

World Health Organization. (2013). *Autism spectrum disorders and other developmental disorders: From raising awareness to building capacity* (p. 7). Geneva: Author.

www.whitehouse.gov. (2011). Retrieved from https://obamawhitehouse.archives.gov/joiningforces/resources.

X v East Cheshire NHS Trust (2019). ET case no 2404031/2018. Retrieved from www.gov.uk/employment-tribunal-decisions/x-v-east-cheshire-nhs-trust-2404031-2018

4

NEURODIVERSE APPLICANT SCREENING, INTERVIEWING, AND SELECTION

Matthew C. Saleh, Hsiao-Ying Chang, Susanne M. Bruyère, and Timothy J. Vogus

Employment Selection Methods and Individuals with Autism Spectrum Disorder

Getting in the front door of an organization is the first step toward employment. This includes several critical steps, including getting into the applicant pool by submitting an application, making it through any prescreening mechanisms, having your résumé and application selected, and navigating and succeeding in the interview process. At many organizations, these steps consist of a blend of traditional assessment strategies (e.g., interviews by multiple or groups of people, employment tests, and work samples) and newer technology-based approaches, such as the use of "back-end" human resources management software that helps manage key administrative tasks, asynchronous video interviews, or the use of social platforms such as LinkedIn for recruitment. Many of these steps contain potential pitfalls for individuals with autism spectrum disorder (ASD) that can prevent them from getting hired.

Unemployment rates for individuals with ASD in the United States are disproportionately high compared to the general population – and even compared to other disability categories – with unemployment estimates approaching or exceeding 80% (Taylor & Seltzer, 2011; Hendricks, 2010; Autism Speaks, n.d.). A review of employer practices during the screening, interview, and selection process can help illustrate some of the barriers that lead to these poor employment outcomes and can help identify strategies and alternatives for making these processes more equitable. The barriers discussed may include practices and processes among employers who are affirmatively aiming to recruit neurodiverse applicants, as well as those by employers who do not yet have a specific focus on inclusive hiring. That said, there is an increasing focus, especially among larger

DOI: 10.4324/9781003023616-4

companies, on acknowledging the "business case" for developing neurodiverse talent pools (Austin & Pisano, 2017). The business case for hiring neurodiverse individuals is that (1) when provided with an enabling environment, neurodiverse individuals represent a qualified but undertapped source of productivity in terms of task performance and organizational improvement (direct productivity) and (2) a neurodiverse workforce also enhances organizational culture and reputation in ways that potentially broaden and diversify the customer base (indirect productivity) (Saleh & Bruyère, 2018). We take a holistic view of the interview process that includes its antecedents (i.e., screening processes) and consequences (i.e., selection processes). An inclusive interview process and methodology may be ineffective if the screening processes do not result in enough neurodiverse candidates making it to the interview stage. Similarly, affirmative recruitment efforts and interview practices may be of little value if the final selection criteria ultimately diverge from inclusive organizational intentions (Rivera, 2012).

Prior research provides guidance regarding effective hiring strategies that promote job success. Specifically, there is robust research regarding (1) the validity of selection methods for determining future job performance (Schmidt & Hunter, 1998), (2) procedures for correcting potential adverse impact for marginalized populations of job applicants (Bobko & Roth, 2013), and (3) the effect of "applicant reactions" to different selection criteria on decisions to pursue or abandon the application process (McCarthy et al., 2017; Konradt et al., 2017). However, this research has overwhelmingly focused on neurotypical employee populations and fails to incorporate neurodiverse populations (Whelpley et al., 2020). This is important because oftentimes, interviewer ratings of how candidates present themselves in an interview (e.g., appearance, impression management, and verbal/nonverbal behavior) are often influential but are not always predictive of actual job performance (Barrick et al., 2009). Thus, normative assumptions about appropriate or desirable self-presentation may constitute one barrier to neurodiverse hiring practices. Developing neurodiverse talent pools requires an employer to acknowledge potential implicit (or even explicit) biases in the hiring process and (re)examine and broaden the concept of what might be valid predictors of future job performance, as well as recognize that there may be a variety of ways to demonstrate effective work performance. As we will see in the discussion of the literature throughout this chapter, there is a range of modifications to screening and application procedures (e.g., the job interview) that can help ensure hiring practices avoid implicit biases and are more equitable for people with ASD. These modifications consider factors that affect hiring decisions, such as acknowledging how people with ASD present themselves during interviews may not be meaningfully related to their ability to perform the job. It is important to note the importance of these characteristics and their relevance to job performance is likely to depend on the type of work and job sector: for instance, "customer-facing" service work may require different behavioral displays and expectations than information technology jobs like computer programming. Although we caution against generalizations about the diverse experiences and skills of individuals with ASD (Bury et al., 2019), some empirical findings indicate that specific challenges faced by job-seeking individuals with ASD could include: understanding complex job application materials and demonstrating job fit through résumés and materials; acclimatizing and reacting quickly to unpredictable or open-ended interview conditions, procedures, and questions; and managing sensory sensitivities during the interview (Baldwin et al., 2014; Robertson, 2010; Hurlbutt & Chalmers, 2004).

There is also a growing body of research on the employer perspective on hiring neurodiverse talent that complements vocational rehabilitation literature on improving disability outcomes in the workplace (e.g., Baldwin et al., 2014; Krzeminska et al., 2019; Whelpley et al., 2020). Studies on hiring innovations in this literature have direct relevance to improving job application outcomes, especially interview performance. Emerging research on targeted supported employment programs can help circumvent barriers in traditional hiring processes and are otherwise more inclusive of neurodiverse populations (Flower et al., 2019). For instance, early-stage research on customized and supported employment for individuals with ASD who receive services from employment support organizations shows higher success rates in obtaining competitive employment and a greater likelihood of retaining these positions with lower levels of support over time (Brooke et al., 2018). On a more micro level, there is growing evidence that technological interventions also enhance specific skills related to job acquisition and performance, including (a) covert audio coaching to supplement job skills and social interactions (Bennett et al., 2013; Gilson & Carter, 2016); (b) prompting delivered via mobile devices to teach vocational skills and promote independence in employment processes (Van Laarhoven et al., 2018); and (c) video-modeling, virtual reality, and prompting to teach various employment and interview skills (Burke et al., 2013; Hayes et al., 2015). This research points to possibilities but also highlights limitations; prior work has focused on using vocational rehabilitation professionals and job coaches to provide the employer perspective; the actual employer perspective remains underrepresented (e.g., Wehman et al., 2016; Wehman et al., 2017; Chappel & Somers, 2010; Hendricks, 2010).

Therefore, we focus on the role of organizations' human resource practices and functions for ensuring equity and the development of neurodiverse talent pools (Markel & Elia, 2016). In this chapter, we specifically concentrate on elements of the hiring process that influence the inputs and outcomes of the interview process for neurodiverse candidates. We discuss research related to interview screening and selection, including the types of interview modalities (virtual or in-person) and selection criteria that employers can consider, as well as potential alternative approaches and alterations to these processes. In looking forward, we highlight the dilemma of the interview process as a potential barrier to employment for individuals with ASD and offer an alternative approach that incorporates research and practice, indicating how to create the conditions for increasing the successful hiring of individuals with ASD.

First, we provide a brief overview of traditional and emerging screening and selection methods. Second, we summarize what is known about affirmative screening/selection approaches from other underrepresented labor force populations that may be relevant for Autistic candidates. Third, we also discuss the disparate impact (for neurodiverse applicants) and other risks stemming from relying on selection criteria (e.g., social behavior) that does not predict job performance. We pair this with recommendations for approaches that will promote fairer processes and more diverse talent pools. Our review is informed by prior published research, preliminary results from a qualitative study that the authors conducted for a funded research project on the use of artificial intelligence (AI) tools to support improving employment outcomes for individuals with ASD, and lessons learned from an annual internship in neurodiversity hiring programs for students at Cornell University's Industrial and Labor Relations (ILR) School. We combine these sources of information in an effort to enhance understanding of the need for an alternative screening, interviewing, and selection process, incorporating stakeholder perspectives from employers with affirmative neurodiversity hiring programs, community employment service providers, university career counselors working with neurodiverse students, and individuals with ASD. The comments from these stakeholder groups illustrate real-world experiences, barriers, and potential alternative approaches that might be helpful in maximizing success for people with ASD in the interview process. We close by suggesting a research and practice agenda for industrial and organizational (I/O) psychologists in designing and implementing more neurodiversity-inclusive interview processes.

Selection Criteria and the Interview Process

The employment interview is often the place where the employment process is halted for Autistic applicants (Krzeminska et al., 2019; Whelpley et al., 2020). There are several reasons the employment interview has represented a barrier to employment for Autistic individuals, ranging from normative assumptions regarding the background, behaviors, and nonverbal social cues and self-presentation strategies exhibited by "ideal" candidates (Austin & Pisano, 2017) to disadvantageous aspects of the interview environment (e.g., high sensory stimulus load) and design (e.g., daylong-multi-person interview process) itself (Booth, 2016).

The unique social, communication and behavioral characteristics associated with Autistic individuals raise specific concerns about the appropriateness and relevance of "traditional" interview processes and selection criteria (Hendricks, 2010). Companies successfully executing affirmative hiring initiatives are incorporating accommodations and modifications in the interview process for Autistic candidates. Such accommodations are in place to address the biases and overemphasis on social and communication deficits (Crespi, 2016), which can often override the candidate's strengths and job-related abilities (Bury et al., 2019) and preclude obtaining a job. These adjustments may present a challenge for I/O psychologists to develop valid and appropriate selection methods. In addition, Autistic individuals typically have a more limited job and even interview experience based on workplace environments lacking the appropriate supports (Booth, 2016). The traditional neurotypical-driven hiring processes may exacerbate these challenges by focusing on in-person serial interviews and/or panel interviews (i.e., with multiple questioners simultaneously). As we discuss in the next section, the traditional interview processes and selection criteria that inform those processes can place Autistic people at a disadvantage. In addition, the physical environment of interviews (e.g., lights, sounds, or noise), the intensity of social interaction (e.g., number of interviewers), and the ambiguous and uncertain nature (e.g., no foreknowledge of questions, ambiguous questions often using idioms) are just some of the potentially systematically disadvantageous factors for Autistic people. Teasing out the factors within this process that create employment-process barriers and identifying alternative ways to approach the interview process and heightening the likelihood of success for applicants who might need these alternatives is a critical first step in making change.

Commonly Used Screening, Interview, and Selection Methods

This section discusses screening strategies and tools that are commonly used by organizations. We first focus on how organizations create candidate interest (preapplication), then we detail approaches that reduce the applicant pool (e.g., employment tests and other forms of résumé/credential screening). We then describe research on approaches to interviewing.

Features of Online Recruiting Sites That Heighten Candidate Interest

Corporate advertising, recruitment, and general reputation all influence decisions to apply and have direct effects on applicant pool quantity and quality (Collins & Han, 2004). These efforts signal what it means to "fit" with the organization (Chen et al., 2012). More broadly, there is growing awareness of the extent to which initial impressions of workplace culture fit and opportunities for career growth affect job seeker decisions to apply for and accept jobs (Gallup, 2020). One of the first strategies to attract candidates is by crafting an effective job advertisement that lists organization values, employment benefits, and job descriptions. Research has shown that word choice and the language used in job advertisements have contributed to job seekers' decision to apply for the job (Born & Taris, 2010; Gaucher et al., 2011). Word choice can also discourage applications, especially for underrepresented groups. For example, including more feminine language in job descriptions for STEM-related positions attracts more female applicants (Krome, 2016), and using words with less lexical ambiguity can better support neurodiverse applicants to process and understand job requirements (Dow et al., 2020) as well as their qualifications for the job. These initial impressions of fit with the organization and the job influence decisions to apply or not (Dow et al., 2020; Gaucher et al., 2011). Auditing career pages for the inclusiveness of their content and messaging can be a direct, cost-effective way to reach applicants and engender positive first impressions of organizational attractiveness and fit (Saleh, 2020). However, an analysis of the career pages for forty randomly selected Fortune 500 companies found that few companies (20%) included references to existing targeted hiring and recruitment initiatives (e.g., neurodiversity, autism at work, disability hiring plans) (Erickson et al., 2020). Using direct and inclusive language in career page can help message to individuals with Autistic applicants that the company values inclusion and is actively interested in hiring a neurodiverse workforce.

Screening Processes Leading to Candidate Selection

Once applicants apply, organizations increasingly use a mix of traditional methods (e.g., in-person interviews) and technology (e.g., online application and talent management/acquisition technologies) to evaluate the candidate pool (Chapman & Webster, 2003). Talent acquisition and management systems/software typically allow employers to perform a host of common functions: sorting and organizing applicants using keyword scans, highlighting top candidates, setting up video interviews and online preemployment tests, documenting follow-up, and developing reports or third-party background checks (Partnership on Employment & Accessible Technology (PEAT), 2015). Social platforms, such as LinkedIn or Facebook, have become an increasingly popular tool that recruiters and companies use to advertise job openings and screen, select, and recruit qualified candidates (Morgan, 2016). Talent acquisition and management technologies, such as commercial applications (e.g., Boolean search) that screen résumés for keywords, offer a range of opportunities to reduce cost while also increasing applicant talent pools. However, it has been noted that the difficulties in managing, filtering, and sorting incoming applications may increase as talent pools expand (Chapman & Webster, 2003). Early on, some researchers and stakeholders highlighted the potential promise of information technology in screening/selection to reduce employer bias toward marginalized and underrepresented populations through more valid measures of applicant fit and reducing human bias and error (Gallois et al., 1992).

Although ostensibly less biased, evidence from the past two decades indicates that screening and selection technologies have the unintended consequence of creating a range of disadvantages and barriers for applicants with disabilities. One way this occurs is through the gradual incorporation of "real world" bias into algorithmic filtering tools. For example, these tools rely on potentially arbitrary keywords or criteria (e.g., job posting keywords, formatting criteria), or résumé filters (e.g., past work or educational metrics; Booth, 2016; Trewin, 2018), which disadvantage groups who have historically experienced educational and workplace discrimination. The rapid ascension of this online visibility (e.g., professional social media like LinkedIn) offers another avenue for employers to evaluate job candidates during the personnel selection process, yet also another source of career capital that may be differentially available to people with disabilities (Berkelaar & Buzzanell, 2015). To provide a simple example, groups that experience more barriers to the labor market will have less digital career capital to convey on, for instance, social networking sites, and technological access gaps may also contribute to differences in the ability to leverage the potential advantages of online networking and skill competency demonstrations. The term *digital career capital* refers to using multiple digital platforms to demonstrate skill competencies and leverage networks to find work, brought on by the new age of mass proliferation and visibility of personal online information (Berkelaar & Buzzanell, 2015). There is evidence that people with disabilities have less access to technology than people without disabilities, including access to and use of social media (see, e.g., Jaeger, 2011; Kochhar, 2020). Research has further shown that use of social media and online networking platforms is lower among individuals with ASD than other developmental disabilities even with equivalent access to technology (Mazurek et al., 2011).

The issue of digital career capital and differential levels of it becomes more pressing as some organizations now use data-mining algorithms (e.g., sentiment analyses from scraping existing online data) to source candidates. These algorithms can help HR departments with the costly and time-consuming process of filtering a good-fit "shortlist" of candidates from increasingly large and unruly initial applicant pools (Hmoud & Laszlo, 2019). It is important to note that the use of these types of algorithmic tools is likely to be common in certain sectors (e.g., technology) and among companies with larger applicant pools that are inherently more difficult to sort and manage (see Chien & Chen, 2008). This trend can be especially problematic for young Autistic adults, who may have digital or social capital deficits as they enter the competitive labor market and seek visibility in candidate talent pools and may need guidance and support to overcome these barriers (Ditchman et al., 2018).

We next discuss how differences in underlying experience and digital career capital are amplified by algorithmic identity profiling tools (as well as more ad hoc strategies like having a hiring professional perform search engine or social media searches) that accentuate social biases against groups who are traditionally more likely to be excluded from employment, like neurodiverse individuals (Ciston, 2019).

Algorithmic Screening and Filtering Tools

One persistent challenge for employers seeking to develop diverse and robust talent pipelines through online recruitment is the generation of unsuitable applicants through improperly calibrated filtering mechanisms (Sharma, 2014). Research also suggests that employers sometimes have difficulty integrating online and offline processes in developing these pipelines. Employers tend to focus only on the "front end" of the recruitment process (e.g., application selection and moving candidates to the interview stage) rather than the full recruitment cycle, which would include discussion of candidates and final selection (Sharma, 2014). The disproportionate focus on the front end of the recruitment cycle could entail a tendency for employers to focus on equity in soliciting applications but not in making final decision-making and without adequately considering barriers to employment occurring after the initial recruitment phase (Sharma, 2014). Achieving fairness in AI applications might present unique challenges to support groups that have experienced discrimination in society due to the extreme diversity in the ways that disability manifests and the wide range of ways that individuals adapt to disabling social and environmental conditions (O'Neil, 2016; Trewin, 2018). Research on machine learning has indicated that biases in algorithms are often the result of biased data. Some research already highlights the capacity for machine learning models – in specific instances but not necessarily across all AI applications – to amplify discrimination by integrating, encoding, and ultimately reinforcing existing systemic and human biases (e.g., Angwin et al., 2016; Buolamwini & Gebru, 2018). An example of how this could affect neurodiverse candidates is with hiring systems that in part rely on AI-driven facial movement and eye contact tracing in virtual interviews to generate an "employability score" (Harwell, 2019). The bias is potentially higher where the information of interest cannot be directly measured, and other data is used as a proxy – as is often the case in AI-driven selection tools trying to ascertain valid measures for future employment performance (Trewin, 2018). Another example of this could be using verbal and social cues as a proxy for teamwork and collaboration in a manner that might disproportionately exclude candidates based on facial features or gestures that do not conform with neurotypical or able-bodied normative standards. The heterogeneity of disability as a broad category – and ASD in particular – presents challenges both in making online applications accessible and fair in selecting or filtering so as not to exclude people with disabilities at early stages. While AI researchers have begun to examine whether the application of these technologies reflects the awareness of intersectional contexts and identity politics (Ciston, 2019), more research is needed as current AI, such as screening tools, are still limited in their capacity to overcome these biases and challenges.

These limitations of AI heighten the risk of excluding candidates based on disability attributes rather than predictors of job performance. Specifically, machine-learning applications often rely on finding patterns, forming groups, and assigning favorable outcomes but may not be able to account for heterogeneity in the manifestation of disability characteristics. Because disclosure of a disability is a complicated issue, and many job seekers choose not to disclose their disability during the job application process, there is a risk of filtering on criteria that have the systematic effect of excluding disability types (e.g., question response time for applicants using screen-reader technology). There is reason to believe that early-stage reactions to disability messaging by a company can influence employee decisions to disclose their disability to the employer (von Schrader et al., 2014).

Disclosure can improve employer and employee outcomes by mitigating bias. Research on disability disclosure during the interview process indicates that it can improve interviewers' perceptions of interviewee performance (Macan & Hayes, 1995) by appropriately modifying the interviewer's reliance on normative social and physical characteristics and by moderating the effect of preinterview impressions on postinterview evaluations. AI researchers have advocated "fairness through awareness" and efforts to adjust screening algorithms and models to mitigate bias in their tools (Dwork et al., 2012). Efforts to address these potential biases within the organizational algorithmic screening and filtering tools should be multilens and multipronged support efforts, which must include an organization's leadership, human resource and equal employment opportunity professionals, and those who are involved in procurement for the organization (EARN/PEAT, 2020). Since these tools are increasingly ubiquitous throughout all hiring efforts, a concerted effort to identify where bias and needless screening out of potential new talent is imperative. These individuals may present quite differently than the traditional candidates, and companies must make efforts to identify areas where changes may successfully mitigate the loss of this potential expanded labor pool. The research on how larger organizations that are using these applications to manage large applicant pools is not well developed, necessitating commitment from leadership and human resources professionals to carefully select systems and third-party vendors that incorporate efforts to reduce bias in screening and selection tools. Again, it is important to qualify that not all employers are using these tools at present, so these research focal areas may necessarily focus on employers in technology as well as other industries with large applicant pools to manage.

Employment Tests and Skill Demonstration

Another common strategy to assess and evaluate job seekers is administering employment tests ranging from personality tests to specific skill demonstrations. Previous research has suggested that the use of a variety of psychometric assessments, such as personality and cognitive ability tests, may be a more objective means of assessing applicants, as compared to interviews and other processes that might rely more on subjective social cues (Whelpley et al., 2020). That is, employment tests demonstrate criterion validity (link to performance and actual fit for a job) fit rather than measuring disability characteristics and applicant ability to conform to (unstated) employer expectations (Griffith & McDaniel, 2006). This line of reasoning focuses on the fact that employment tests (e.g., personality employment test or situational judgment tests) can offer more valid and reliable measures of an employee's ability to perform actual job functions – thereby mitigating discrimination in the selection process – although more research evidence is needed to deepen the understanding of fairness and performance on such tests for Autistic individuals (Whelpley et al., 2020).

However, even personality and employment skills assessments are not a panacea for evaluating a person's appropriateness for a position. Because these assessments may reduce some potential biases, the employers' awareness of the limitations of each assessment is critical to heighten their ability to translate the test results to supplement their hiring decision accurately and effectively. For example, employers should carefully assess and consider the effectiveness of the personality assessments they utilize – and there are thousands on the market to choose from – in predicting positive future work performance varies significantly. Without careful consideration of the instrument being used, the results of those tests can limit the development of well-tailored and neurodiverse talent pools (Baez, 2013; Hurtz & Donovan, 2000; Le et al., 2011). The issue of social desirability in self-reports during personality tests is another relevant issue (Baez, 2013), and social desirability responses might especially disadvantage individuals with ASD who may not tailor their answers to company expectations in quite the same way that neurotypical candidates would. Using the results as a conversation point is a helpful strategy when interviewing candidates with disabilities, including Autistic candidates.

Research has shown that individuals with ASD reportedly have lower self-efficacy compared to their neurotypical peers (Lorenz & Heinitz, 2014), which may impact how they perform during an interview. *Self-efficacy* refers to the degree to which an individual believes in their abilities to perform and meet the demands of the given situation (Bandura, 1986), and interview or job self-efficacy reflects the extent to which people believe that they can perform well during job interviews (Tay et al., 2006). Low interview self-efficacy may result in underperformance that is not directly related to an ability to perform job functions (Latham & Budworth, 2006). Individuals with higher job search efficacy are more efficient in presenting and promoting themselves during job interviews, which results in more job offers (Moynihan et al., 2003).

Studies have shown that interventions to improve self-efficacy during job interviews led to higher ratings of interview performance (Kanfer et al., 2001; Latham & Budworth, 2006). Self-efficacy interventions often include multiple training components that consist of opportunities to iteratively demonstrate skills mastery, gain vicarious experience, engage in verbal self-guidance, and receive positive performance feedback (Liu et al., 2014; Peterson & Arnn, 2005). Mastery experience means having a successful experience after the performance. Having opportunities to experience what a successful performance looks like is one of the most powerful strategies that increase one's self-efficacy and confidence (Bandura, 1986). Vicarious experience refers to learning from other people and empathizing with others, and it is a useful strategy for people with limited interview experience to develop a sense of self-efficacy (Eden & Aviram, 1993). The practice of verbal self-guidance refers to increase positive internal dialogue as a strategy to promote a positive self-concept (Liu et al., 2014). Finally, receiving positive and constructive feedback also helps one develop self-efficacy (Liu et al., 2014).

Some research suggests that using only the employment interview as a selection method can lead to reliance on decision-makers' sometimes narrow or biased definitions of talent and an accompanying tendency to filter out individuals with atypical behaviors and social interactions (Krzeminska et al., 2019). This has led to an emphasis on screening and selection processes that deemphasize interviews or incorporate different strategies in the interview process such as activities, exercises, or demonstrations rather than the traditional question–answer structure for Autistic candidates (Krzeminska et al., 2019). Yet, even these approaches also carry important caveats, as personality and employment tests necessitate promoting disclosure in the application process to ensure appropriate accommodations, such as extra time or alterations to the test-taking environment or content, are provided and a fair assessment is conducted (Nester, 1993).

Video and Panel Interviews

The employment interview remains one of the most widely used selection methods. However, in recent years, there has been a precipitous growth in the use of delayed and asynchronous interaction through online, recorded, and video-based interviews (Levashina et al., 2014; Brenner et al., 2016). These new approaches to existing personnel selection methods create novel opportunities and challenges pertaining to the validity of new, asynchronous evaluation methods in identifying job qualifications and fit for hiring neurodiverse candidates. Traditional panel interviews are also still common, along with a growing reliance on video-based interviews. As with other technological applications, the use of synchronous and asynchronous video interviews, including those that utilize AI-based decision agents, offers novel efficiencies in employment screening and some potential to reduce interviewer bias around impressions of physical appearance, vocal and facial attributes, and use of social cues (Suen et al., 2019). However, these methods might still pose risks of assigning applicants to favorable/unfavorable categories on the basis of disability-related factors like delayed response time associated with assistive device usage. One interesting trend that may help overcome some of these barriers is the use of online interviews in which participants are offered the opportunity to conduct the interview with the video showing the applicant switched off, removing some potentially biasing factors from the interviewers' view and consideration, such as physical attractiveness and mannerisms (Meena, 2016).

While the reliability and predictive validity of panel interviews in personnel selection has been widely studied and supported (McDaniel et al., 1994;

Dixon et al., 2002), the validity of existing selection procedures specifically with regard to people with disabilities remains an open question (Posthuma et al., 2002). Researchers have noted that employer and interviewer perceptions about demeanor, enthusiasm, listening skills, and other factors often hinge on unconscious biases and normative expectations about how an interviewee should convey desirable attributes (Booth, 2016). Additionally, face-to-face interviews sometimes employ strategies or conditions that disadvantage Autistic applicants. These can include sensory distractions or discomforts (e.g., bright lights, noises, or smells in the interview room), expectations of immediate answers, or deliberately stressful question–answer formats that aim to measure an employee's critical thinking skills (Booth, 2016). Many of these tactics can have the common effect of measuring autism characteristics rather than actual job performance (Booth, 2016). Recent research has focused on the use of video modeling, response prompting, virtual reality, and mock interview skill training for Autistic individuals to improve job interview performance (Hayes et al., 2015), but often, this reinforces normative (and biased) focus on self-stimulatory behaviors, hygiene, and personal presentation, which can be systematically exclusionary.

Concerns over employment interview processes can also involve the final employment decision-making processes and the potential disconnect between affirmative/inclusive hiring practices at the front end and the actual hiring decision at the back end of the recruitment process. Research from other areas suggests that barriers to inclusive hiring may occur at the point of developing recruitment/talent "pools" and in the final stages of selection. Rivera (2012) conducted a case study analysis of elite professional firms' recruitment practices and examined why the firms struggle to create a racially diverse workforce by asking what hiring professionals look for in job candidates. The authors noted two barriers that prevent inclusive hiring: (1) employers generally believed that the lack of diversity at work is due to a lack of qualified applicants of color, often focusing on the social capital of coming from an elite educational institution; (2) decision-makers did not usually focus on diversity when evaluating the candidates and making the hiring decision, despite affirmative recruitment efforts, so selection criteria tended to diverge from diversity initiatives at the final selection stage, resulting in a discrepancy between the organizational intentions and actual hiring results (Rivera, 2012).

Additional Relevant Factors in the Interview Process

It is worth further delineating employer expectations about the desirability of "hard" and "soft" skills as outlined in the literature because employer assessments of these skills can weigh heavily on the selection process (Buck & Barrick, 1987). Employer skill preferences vary by region, sector, and occupation, and it has been noted that "skills" assessments often blend assessments of a job seeker's personal/behavioral characteristics (e.g., soft skills as well as their hard skills and prior qualifications) (Huffcutt, 2011; Newton et al., 2005; Jones et al., 2017). Many research studies (Baxter & Young, 1982; Hazler & Lotto, 1987; Casner-Lotto & Barrington, 2006; Rasul et al., 2013; Chowdhury & Miah, 2016; Matsouka & Mihail, 2016) that investigated the ideal attributes of entry-level job candidates focused on a wide range of employment skills. Often, candidates are assessed on both technical and nontechnical skills that support job performance (Buck & Barrick, 1987). The types of skills examined during an application process can generally be categorized into hard and soft skills. The hard skill dimension generally incorporates both basic skill sets (e.g., knowledge and skills of listening and writing) and technical skill sets (i.e., job-related skills). Soft skills are necessary skills for one to successfully apply basic and job-related skills and excel at work (Casner-Lotto & Barrington, 2006), which may include the concepts of work ethic, dependability, or interpersonal, communication, and social skills. However, the results of these studies showed mixed findings regarding what employers consider the most important attributes within each skill dimension, and most of the studies that examined employability skills focused on either general populations or individuals with disabilities but not both.

Given the limited comparative research, Ju et al. (2012) examined the difference in employers' expectations of employability skills between entry-level employees with and without disabilities and found that skills that are related to attitudes (e.g., work ethics) and basic skills (e.g., following instructions) are valued as essential attributes of an employee regardless of disability status. The employers also rated basic skills (e.g., ability to read and write or convey ideas) as the most important skills, compared to other employability skill categories (e.g., social skills or personal traits), for entry-level positions. However, there were two differences found in employers' ratings. First, employers rated the ability to stay safe as more important for employees with disabilities compared to employees without a disability. Employers also showed higher expectations in employees without a disability than employees with disabilities when rating employability skills. Both findings underscore a persistent misconception that people with disabilities are "less able" compared to people without disabilities. Employment interventions that are designed to support people with ASD often include an emphasis on training in social skills, which is based on the understanding of limited communication and socialization skills, which are the critical obstacles that prevent successful employment of people with ASD, and that social skills are highly valued by employers (Lawer et al., 2009; Lynas, 2014). Having social and communication skills (i.e., ability to self-promote) is a more prominent influencer than hard skills for Autistic people on employment success (Scott et al., 2015).

Making a good impression is essential in that it increases a candidate's chance to succeed in an interview (Cortez, Marshall et al., 2017; Rasmussen, 1984; Ruben et al., 2015). To better understand the ideal job interview attributes, other research focused on the impact of verbal and nonverbal (e.g., smile, gaze, pitch, or speech rate) cues. However, limited research has examined verbal and nonverbal behaviors of job seekers with ASD that regulate the social engagement during an interview process, as well as employers'/managers' and coworkers' perception of those behaviors, which in turn influences job success. For example, Bublitz et al. (2017) found that ASD individuals who are open to disclosing disability status are less likely to elaborate on their strengths as a person with ASD. For employers with limited knowledge of autism, disclosing disability without advocating strengths or educating the employers might not be beneficial for both the employers and interviewee in the interview process (Bublitz et al., 2017). As we begin to understand the role that social skills and behavior cues play for job seekers with ASD, more studies are needed to examine employers' perspectives on, and values of, these indicators with regard to individuals with ASD during the interview process and how that may influence their hiring decisions.

Research has identified key job interview evaluation constructs as including (a) demonstration of job-related skills/knowledge (e.g., job knowledge, procedural skills, declarative knowledge, and motivation); (b) interviewee performance (e.g., impression-management tactics, social influence behaviors, interpersonal presentation), and (c) personal/demographic characteristics' (e.g., candidate attractiveness, cultural background, attitudinal/behavioral similarity, race, gender, disability, etc.) effects on interview ratings and outcomes (Huffcutt, 2011). Interestingly, an empirical review found that assessments of interviewee performance correlate more strongly with interview assessments than assessments of job skills/knowledge (Huffcutt, 2011). Outside of organizational practices, some successful interventions identified in the literature for improving job interview and/or job performance for people with ASD include such approaches as covert audio coaching (Bennett et al., 2013) and virtual reality job interview training (Smith et al., 2014).

Research grounded in social identity theory and demographic theories has suggested that individuals tend to attract or receive more favorable feedback from others who share similar personal characteristics (Diaz et al., 2019). Not only was it evident that job seekers' characteristics and identities (e.g., race, gender, disability, or appearance) impact employment outcomes (e.g., Ameri et al., 2018), research that explored the possibilities of the influence of recruiters' or employers' identity on hiring decision outcomes also suggests evaluation bias when the recruiters or employers and applicants share similar identities (Diaz et al., 2019; Graves & Powell, 1996; O'Leary et al., 2009). For example, female recruiters are more likely to report a positive experience with female applicants than male applicants (Graves & Powell, 1996), and Black females are more likely to give more favorable ratings to résumés that indicate similar backgrounds (O'Leary et al., 2009). However, most research experiments that consider the evaluator's identity impact only focused on how evaluators rate résumés, which involved little interaction between recruiters and job candidates. Interestingly, Bagues and Esteve-Volart (2010) explored the impact of the evaluation committee's gender composition on the chance of female versus male candidates' success. They found that when both male and female candidates perform the same, male candidates receive higher ratings and are more likely to be hired from a female-majority committee. Male committee members rated the male candidate higher when they are sitting in a female-majority committee group. Their findings highlight that the influence of evaluators' identity is complex. It appears that personal identity does impact interviewers' perceptions of candidates' performance; in this case, female evaluators are likely to overstate the competency of male candidates. The results of such studies suggest that organizations need to provide more support to evaluators to promote fair assessment during the interview process in addition to balancing the representation of different identities in the committee group.

Adapting the Interview Process

Booth (2016) recommends that if the traditional interview must be used, employers provide Autistic applicants with: (a) more opportunities to prepare for the interview; (b) adequate notice and specified start/end times; (c) information about the venue (directions, sensory environment, accessibility); (d) details about the interview's format (number of interviewers, questions, practice or test scenarios); (e) details about dress code and what to bring; and (f) information about how to request adjustments/accommodations. Such opportunities to improve interview outcomes for individual applicants on the autism spectrum could benefit many different types of candidates. Since employers might not know that applicants are Autistic and they may be unwittingly eliminate them, designing protocols that will give all candidates these opportunities would serve the ultimate purpose of a more inclusive interview process. This would be a step toward ensuring more equitable outcomes from the interview and selection process. Additionally, it would be helpful if interviewees could have the option of bringing support workers/companions (e.g., mentors or job coaches), are given time to acclimate to the room before the interview starts and time to process questions and formulate answers, and are offered space to present on prior experience rather than solely adhering to a question–answer format (Booth, 2016). The goal should be to adapt the interview so that candidates are judged on their ability to perform essential job functions rather than on the basis of social factors such as eye contact, sitting still in a chair, or other social behaviors. An interviewer's perception of body language and nonverbal behavior in job interviews may be partially contingent on the demographic characteristics of the interviewee (Levine & Feldman, 2002). This is also an area that needs further research as to how intersectional identities for job seekers with ASD impact the perception of nonverbal cues in interviews. Although such accommodations (coaches and mentors present) are likely to help candidate performance during interviews, there may be unintended consequences of doing so that may inhibit employment, and this merits further research regarding the effects of adaptations on employment outcomes.

Many of these recommendations were mirrored in preliminary findings from a qualitative study performed by the authors (Bruyère et al., 2020), based on semistructured interviews and focus groups with employers with autism-focused hiring initiatives, service providers, and employed individuals with ASD. Employer respondents highlighted two strategies for improving neurodiverse hiring practices: (1) providing autism awareness and sensitivity training for HR and hiring professionals *prior to interviews*, and (2) modifying interview protocols or establishing alternative interview protocols (Bruyère et al., 2020). The training efforts described would be proximal to conducting the interview, and they focus on improving the professional(s)' understanding of neurodiversity, strategies for supporting candidates throughout the process, and overcoming a latent bias towards social cues (e.g., eye contact, body language and movement).

The second strategy – modifying or replacing interview protocols – was described as a means to allow candidates to showcase their qualifications in unconventional ways. Examples of these modifications/replacements included: (a) allowing opportunities to demonstrate technical skills by solving a problem; (b) selectively or completely removing interview panels, which can be intimidating and create communication complexities, in favor of shorter, one-to-one or two-to-one interview settings; (c) avoiding rapid-fire questioning strategies; (d) eliminating open-ended interview questions; (e) providing interview questions to interviewees in advance; and (f) introducing applicants to the work environment prior to starting the interview as an ice breaker. One potential tradeoff of modifying the number of interviewers may be lowering reliability and validity, which has been demonstrated to be higher for panels (McDaniel et al., 1994). With regard to modifying interview questions – including by prompting interviewers for more specific information and self-reflection, providing additional guidance on how to respond, and adapting question structure to facilitate understanding – there is early evidence that small modifications to question structure may mitigate differential job interview performance for neurodiverse job seekers (and, by extension, potentially increase the validity of the interview as a predictor of future job performance for these individuals; Maras et al., 2020). Research evidence indicates that the associations drawn by interviewers between candidate self-presentation and actual job performance may be particularly spurious in unstructured interviews (Barrick et al., 2009). Respondents also indicated the importance of organizational openness to allowing modifications and interview strategies to evolve over time, allowing for flexibility and exceptions within the screening and selection process, and looking to other companies in their sector or industry for examples of practices that work (e.g., use of Autism hiring networks to promote awareness and exchange best practices) (Bruyère et al., 2020).

Preliminary findings from respondents with ASD pointed to similar issues. In qualitative findings from interviews/focus groups with currently employed individuals with ASD, participants focused on two primary challenges that they experienced during traditional interviews: (1) the types of questions asked and (2) the interview structure and environment (Bruyère et al., 2020). Participants described their experiences with traditional interview questions that often center on idiomatic work-based social interactions or vague "personality profiles." These could include both generic open-ended questions (e.g., "Tell me about yourself") and/or hypothetical questions (e.g., "How would you handle conflict between you and a coworker?"). This need not entail eliminating such questions, as questions about behavior have been demonstrated as valid predictors of job performance. Recent research suggests that modifications and guidance within even behavioral questions may facilitate more equitable job interview success for candidates with autism (Maras et al., 2020). Participants indicated that these question structures sometimes do not play to their strengths, because these types of social experiences may not have been as salient to them in their life or prior work as they are to their peers without ASD, or because they do not understand the actual skill sets or personality characteristics that the questions are trying to elicit (Bruyère et al., 2020). Participants indicated that they felt occasional anxiety about "faking" socially appropriate responses to questions of this nature and indicated that they would have been able to provide stronger, more definitive answers had the questions centered on their specific skill sets. Despite these challenges, participants noted that with experience or exposure, they could adapt to the traditional interview questions and that they would have benefited from having the questions in advance or having an opportunity to better understand what the questions were trying to elicit more explicitly (Bruyère et al., 2020).

Regarding interview structure and environment, the respondents further noted that large-group interviews (either "cohort" interviews or interviews with a large panel of interviewers), hearing multiple people talking, or looking multiple people in the eyes can be some of the common challenges for an individual with ASD. Environmental unpredictability and overstimulation were other factors described as adversely impacting the interview experience and performance. Respondents indicated the importance of having clear instructions on job application websites and application materials, concise and explicit interview questions, incorporating a strength-based interview approach, and offering opportunities to adapt to environmental stimuli, such as within-interview breaks and opportunities to familiarize themselves with the workspace and interview room prior to the interview. Participants also noted the upside of disclosing their disability to the employer and noted that employer sensitivity and understanding of ASD increased their likelihood of disclosing earlier in the process (Bruyère et al., 2020).

Finally, service provider participants expanded on some of the training and interview structure themes, noting that candidates with ASD respond better when they are in a quiet environment and when they do not feel rushed. Provider participants mentioned alternative interview methods (e.g., a "portfolio" allowing opportunities for prerecorded skills demonstrations), use of specific and closed-ended interview questions that allow interviewees with ASD to more-accurately describe their qualifications without navigating confusing social context, and utilizing supportive environments and hiring professional sensitivity to enhance *mutuality* of understanding during the interview process (e.g., treating interviews as nonrigid settings in which interviewers allow candidates to self-advocate and are open to improvising questions and requirements through a "calibration/incremental approximation" model rather than a pure observation/assessment model) (Bruyère et al., 2020).

Learnings from an annual internship/experiential learning program at Cornell University's Industrial and Labor Relations (ILR) School may also inform this discussion. Each year, undergraduates from the ILR School's human resources academic degree program are placed with companies that are considering, planning, or have already initiated neurodiversity hiring programs, and the cohort performs interviews with their host company. Results from the 2018 cohort employer interviews (including five tech, finance, and professional services companies) provide instructive case examples for some of the strategies discussed thus far and highlight alternative approaches that companies with existing or burgeoning neurodiversity initiatives are currently undertaking. Importantly, these steps include efforts across the application process, from affirmative steps to ensuring that neurodiverse applicants are included in "talent pools" to inclusive alterations to the interview and selection process. Examples of specific neurodiversity features within these five companies included: (1) prescreening of candidates with external community employment service provider partners, who identify and refer candidates based on position fit/job match, skills, and education level; (2) making efforts to audit and modify interview processes so that they are less preoccupied with subjective social skills judgments and more focused on job features, skills demonstrations, and grounding in organizational skills/talent needs rather than impressions of soft skills; and (3) incorporating alternative skills demonstration opportunities to supplement or replace the traditional interview, including observational assessments and opportunities for creative problem solving that involve not only hiring personnel but also anticipated supervisors, and providing preinterview sensitivity and awareness training to these interviewers/recruiters (Bruyère, 2018).

Conclusion

In this chapter, we have summarized some of the admittedly sparse but growing research on employer-side practices in candidate screening, interviewing, and selection as they apply to individuals with ASD. While broad employer research and corresponding evidence-based interventions are currently lacking on the ways that selection and interview processes can be modified to move beyond the biases in traditional screening and selection processes to ensure that neurodiverse populations are not weeded out, there are, nevertheless, a number of opportunities for employers to critique their own processes and consider methods for removing processual barriers that are not directly correlated with predicting future job performance. If developing neurodiverse talent pools is an organizational priority, then simple alterations or flexibilities (e.g., carefully vetting screening software and vendors for inclusive practices, providing interview questions in advance, making efforts to limit sensory overstimulation during interviews, ensuring synergies between affirmative recruitment efforts and final decision-making practices) in the cultivation of candidate pools, design and methods used in the interview, and ultimate selection criteria, can help improve organizational hiring practices, while also facilitating a more inclusive application process that is welcoming to a broader array of applicants.

I/O psychologists can play a critical role in enhancing employment opportunities for Autistic individuals through research and consulting that enables auditing existing selection and interview practices for fairness and designing steps for implementing more neurodiversity-inclusive interview processes. Much of the existing research in the rehabilitation field focuses on barriers in the selection and interview process, and supplemental efforts by vocational rehabilitation service providers (including innovative technological applications) might offer alternative approaches that will assist in overcoming these barriers. However, many validated approaches may not incorporate biases that disparately impact neurodiverse applicants. Additional work is needed that specifies the ways that employers can develop and implement assessment criteria and approaches that are inclusive of individuals with ASD. The existing literature highlights potential minor alterations to processes that might decrease barriers and increase inclusivity without fundamentally changing the validity of the processes as predictors of job performance. This is where I/O psychologists can assist in moving the needle by conducting research on direct alterations/interventions in employer practices that will demonstrate improved hiring outcomes rather than just focusing on barriers and the contributions that providers external to the employer can make in preparing the candidates better for the interview process. Only when both the candidate and the work environment are enhanced in their ability to make the job match, will we mitigate and transcend the historical barriers that have prevented Autistic individuals from successfully navigating the interview process and kept them out of the workplace and workforce.

References

Ameri, M., Schur, L., Adya, M., Bentley, F. S., McKay, P., & Kruse, D. (2018). The disability employment puzzle: A field experiment on employer hiring behavior. *ILR Review, 71*(2), 329–364.

Angwin, J., Larson, J., Mattu, S., & Kirchner, L. (2016). *Machine bias: There's software used across the country to predict future criminals. And it's biased against blacks*. Retrieved from www.propublica.org/article/machine-bias-risk-assessments-in-criminal-sentencing

Austin, R. D., & Pisano, G. P. (2017). Neurodiversity as a competitive advantage. *Harvard Business Review, 95*(3), 96–103.

Autism Speaks. (n.d.). *Autism statistics and facts*. Retrieved from www.autismspeaks.org/autism-statistics

Baez, H. (2013, January 26). Personality tests in employment selection: Use with caution. *Cornell HR Review*. Retrieved from http://digitalcommons.ilr.cornell.edu/chrr/59

Bagues, M. F., & Esteve-Volart, B. (2010). Can gender parity break the glass ceiling? Evidence from a repeated randomized experiment. *The Review of Economic Studies*, 77(4), 1301–1328.

Baldwin, S., Costley, D., & Warren, A. (2014). Employment activities and experiences of adults with high-functioning Autism and Asperger's Disorder. *Journal of Autism and Developmental Disorders, 44*, 2440–2449. https://doi.org/10.1007/s10803-0142112-z

Bandura, A. (1986). *Social foundations of thought and action: A social cognitive theory*. Englewood Cliffs, NJ: Prentice-Hall.

Barrick, M. R., Shaffer, J. A., & DeGrassi, S. W. (2009). What you see may not be what you get: Relationships among self-presentation tactics and ratings of interview and job performance. *Journal of Applied Psychology, 94*, 1394–1411. https://doi.org/10.1037/a0016532

Baxter, M. B., & Young, J. L. (1982). Survey report what do employers expect from high school graduates? *NASSP Bulletin, 66*(458), 93–98.

Bennett, K. D., Ramasamy, R., & Honsberger, T. (2013). The effects of covert audio coaching on teaching clerical skills to adolescents with Autism Spectrum Disorder. *Journal of Autism and Developmental Disorders, 43*, 585–593. https://doi.org/10.1007/s10803-012-1597-6

Berkelaar, B. L., & Buzzanell, P. M. (2015). Online employment screening and digital career capital: Exploring employers' use of online information for personnel selection. *Management Communication Quarterly, 29*(1), 84–113. https://doi.org/10.1177/0893318914554657

Bobko, P., & Roth, P. L. (2013). Reviewing, categorizing, and analyzing the literature on black-white mean differences for predictors of job performance: Verifying some perceptions and updating/correcting others. *Personnel Psychology, 66*(1), 91–126.

Booth, J. (2016). *Autism Equality in the workplace: Removing barriers and challenging discrimination*. London: Jessica Kingsley Publishers.

Born, M. P., & Taris, T. W. (2010). The impact of the wording of employment advertisements on students' inclination to apply for a job. *The Journal of Social Psychology, 150*(5), 485–502.

Brenner, F. S., Tuulia, M., Ortner, T. M., & Fay, D. (2016). Asynchronous video interviewing as a new technology in personnel selection: The applicant's point of view. *Frontiers in Psychology*, 7(836), 1–11. https://doi.org/10.3389/fpsyg.2016.00863

Brooke, V., Brooke, A. M., Schall, C., Wehman, P., McDonough, J., Thompson, K., & Smith, J. (2018). Employees with autism spectrum disorder achieving long-term employment success: A retrospective review of employment retention and intervention. *Research and Practice for Persons with Severe Disabilities, 43*(3), 181–193. https://doi.org/10.1177/1540796918783202

Bruyère, S. M. (2018). *Summary of findings from ILR School HR credit internship: Undergraduate student interviews of companies with autism at work programs, Spring, 2018*. Ithaca, NY: Cornell University, ILR School, Yang-Tan Institute on Employment and Disability.

Bruyère, S. M., Chang, H.-Y., & Saleh, M. C. (2020). *Preliminary Report Summarizing the Results of Interviews and Focus Groups with Employers, Autistic Individuals, Service Providers, and Higher Education Career Counselors on Perceptions of Barriers and Facilitators for Neurodiverse Individuals in the Job Interview and Customer Interface Processes.* A report from the work of the Track B-1 (AI and Future Jobs) Empowering Neurodiverse Populations for Employment through National Science Foundation (NSF) Inclusion AI and Innovation Science (B-6970), RAISE C-Accel Phase I Grant funded to Vanderbilt University, Frist Center for Autism and Innovation, Nashville, TN; PTE Federal Award No.: 1936970, Subaward No.; UNIV61108. Ithaca, NY: Cornell University, ILR School, K. Lisa Yang and Hock E. Tan Institute on Employment and Disability. https://digitalcommons.ilr.cornell.edu/edicollect/1381/

Bublitz, D. J., Fitzgerald, K., Alarcon, M., D'Onofrio, J., & Gillespie-Lynch, K. (2017). Verbal behaviors during employment interviews of college students with and without ASD. *Journal of Vocational Rehabilitation, 47*(1), 79–92. https://doi-org.proxy.library.cornell.edu/10.3233/JVR-170884

Buck, L. L., & Barrick, R. K. (1987). They're trained, but are they employable? *Vocational Education Journal, 62*(5), 29–31.

Buolamwini, J., & Gebru, T. (2018). Gender shades: Intersectional accuracy disparities in commercial gender classification. MIT Media Lab. *Proceedings of Machine Learning Research, 81*(1), 1–15. Retrieved from www.media.mit.edu/publications/gender-shades-intersectional-accuracy-disparities-in-commercial-gender-classification/

Burke, R. V., Allen, K. D., Howard, M. R., Downey, D., Matz, M. G., & Bowen, S. L. (2013). Tablet-based video modeling and prompting in the workplace for individuals with autism. *Journal of Vocational Rehabilitation, 38*, 1–14.

Bury, S. M., Hedley, D., Uljarević, M., Dissanayake, C., & Gal, E. (2019). If you've employed one person with autism: An individual difference approach to the autism advantage at work. *Autism, 23*(6), 1607–1608.

Casner-Lotto, J., & Barrington, L. (2006). *Are they really ready to work? Employers' perspectives on the basic knowledge and applied skills of new entrants to the 21st century US workforce.* Washington, DC: Partnership for 21st Century Skills. 1 Massachusetts Avenue NW Suite 700, Washington, DC 20001.

Chapman, D. S., & Webster, J. (2003). The use of technologies in the recruiting, screening, and selection processes for job candidates. *International Journal of Selection and Assessment, 11*(2/3), 113–120. https://doi.org/10.1111/1468-2389.00234

Chappel, S. L., & Somers, B. C. (2010). Employing persons with autism spectrum disorders: A collaborative effort. *Journal of Vocational Rehabilitation, 32*, 117–124.

Chen, C.-C., Lin, M.-M., & Chen, C.-M. (2012). Exploring the mechanisms of the relationship between website characteristics and organizational attraction. *The International Journal of Human Resource Management, 23*(4), 867–885.

Chien, C.-F., & Chen, L.-F. (2008). Data mining to improve personnel selection and enhance human capital: A case study in high-technology industry. *Expert Systems with Applications, 34*(1), 280–290. https://doi.org/10.1016/j.eswa.2006.09.003

Chowdhury, T. A., & Miah, M. K. (2016). Employability skills for entry-level human resources management positions: Perceptions of students and employers. *Australian Journal of Career Development, 25*(2), 55–68.

Ciston, S. (2019). Intersectional AI is essential: Polyvocal, multimodal, experimental methods to save artificial intelligence. *Journal of Science and Technology of the Arts, 11*(2), 3–8. https://doi.org/10.7559/citarj.v11i2.665

Collins, C. J., & Han, J. (2004). Exploring applicant pool quantity and quality: The effects of early recruitment practice strategies, corporate advertising, and firm reputation. *Personnel Psychology, 57*(3), 685–717. https://doi.org/10.1111/j.1744-6570.2004.00004.x

Cortez, R., Marshall, D., Yang, C., & Luong, L. (2017). First impressions, cultural assimilation, and hireability in job interviews: Examining body language and facial expressions' impact on employer's perceptions of applicants. *Concordia Journal of Communication Research, 4*(1), 4.

Crespi, B. J. (2016). Autism as a disorder of high intelligence. *Frontiers in Neuroscience, 10*(300). https://doi.org/10.3389/fnins.2016.00300

Diaz, A. B., Marín, J., & Díaz, F. J. M. (2019). The irony of choice in recruitment: When similarity turns recruiters to other candidates. *M@n@gement, 22*(3), 466–486.

Ditchman, N. M., Miller, J. L., & Easton, A. B. (2018). Vocational rehabilitation service patterns: An application of social network analysis to examine employment outcomes of transition-age individuals with autism. *Rehabilitation Counseling Bulletin, 61*, 143–153. https://doi.org/10.1177/0034355217709455

Dixon, M., Wang, S., Calvin, J., Dineen, B., & Tomlinson, E. (2002). The panel interview: A review of empirical research and guidelines for practice. *Public Personnel Management, 31*(3), 397–428. https://doi.org/10.1177/009102600203100310

Dow, M. J., Lund, B. D., & Douthit, W. K. (2020). Investigating the link between unemployment and disability. *The International Journal of Information, Diversity, & Inclusion (IJIDI), 4*(1).

Dwork, C., Hardt, M., Pitassi, T., Reingold, O., & Zemel, R. (2012). Fairness through awareness. In Proceedings of the 3rd Innovations in Theoretical Computer Science Conference on-ITCS'12 (pp. 214–226). New York: ACM Press. https://doi.org/10.1145/2090236.2090255

EARN/PEAT (2020). *Checklist for employers: Facilitating the hiring of people with disabilities through the use of eRecruiting screening systems, including AI.* Washington, DC: U.S. Department of Labor, Office of Disability Employment Policy, Employer Assistance Resource Network/Partnership on Employment & Accessible Technology.

Eden, D., & Aviram, A. (1993). Self-efficacy training to speed reemployment: Helping people to help themselves. *Journal of Applied Psychology, 78*(3), 352.

Erickson, W., Malzer, V., & Saleh, M. (2020). *Disability outreach and inclusion messaging: Career page assessment of forty fortune 500 companies.* Washington, DC: U.S. Department of Labor, Office of Disability Employment Policy, Employer Assistance Resource Network.

Flower, R. L., Hedley, D., Spoor, J. R., & Dissanayake, C. (2019). An alternative pathway to employment for autistic job-seekers: A case study of a training and assessment program targeted to autistic job candidates. *Journal of Vocational Education & Training, 71*(3), 407–428.

Gallois, C., Callan, V., & Palmer, J. (1992). The influence of applicant communication style and interviewer characteristics on hiring decisions. *Journal of Applied Social Psychology, 22*, 1041–1060.

Gallup. (2020). *State of the American workplace report.* New York: Gallup. Retrieved from www.gallup.com/workplace/285818/state-american-workplace-report.aspx

Gaucher, D., Friesen, J., & Kay, A. C. (2011). Evidence that gendered wording in job advertisements exists and sustains gender inequality. *Journal of Personality and Social Psychology, 101*(1), 109.

Gilson, C., & Carter, E. (2016). Promoting social interactions and job independence for college students with autism or intellectual disability: A pilot study. *Journal of Autism & Developmental Disorders, 46*, 3583–3596. https://doi.org/10.1007/s10803-016-2894-2

Graves, L. M., & Powell, G. N. (1996). Sex similarity, quality of the employment interview and recruiters' evaluation of actual applicants. *Journal of Occupational and Organizational Psychology, 69*(3), 243–261.

Griffith, R. L., & McDaniel, M. (2006). The nature of deception and applicant faking behavior. In R. L. Griffith (Ed.), *A closer examination of applicant faking behavior*. Charlotte, NC: (IAP) Information Age Publishing.

Harwell, D. (2019, November 6). A face-scanning algorithm increasingly decides whether you deserve the job. *The Washington Post*. Retrieved from www.washingtonpost.com/technology/2019/10/22/ai-hiring-face-scanning-algorithm-increasingly-decides-whether-you-deserve-job/

Hayes, G. R., Custodio, V. E., Haimson, O. L., Nguyen, K., Ringland, K. E., Ulgado, R. R., & Weiner, R. (2015). Mobile video modeling for employment interviews for individuals with autism. *Journal of Vocational Rehabilitation, 43*, 275–287. https://doi.org/10.3233/JVR-150775

Hendricks, D. (2010). Employment and adults with autism spectrum disorders: Challenges and strategies for success. *Journal of Vocational Rehabilitation, 32*(2), 125–134.

Hmoud, B., & Laszlo, V. (2019). Will artificial intelligence take over human resources recruitment and selection? *Network Intelligence Studies*, 7(13), 21–30.

Huffcutt, A. I. (2011). An empirical review of the employment interview construct literature. *International Journal of Selection and Assessment, 19*(1), 62–81. https://doi.org/10.1111/j.1468-2389.2010.00535.x

Hurlbutt, K., & Chalmers, L. (2004). Employment and adults with Asperger syndrome. *Focus on Autism and Other Developmental Disabilities, 19*(4), 215–222.

Hurtz, G. M., & Donovan, J. J. (2000). Personality and job performance: The Big Five revisited. *Journal of Applied Psychology, 85*(6), 869.

Jaeger, P. (2011). *Disability and the internet: Confronting a digital divide*. Boulder, CO: Lynne Rienner Publishers.

Jones, M., Baldi, C., Phillips, C., & Waikar, A. (2017). The hard truth about soft skills: What recruiters look for in business graduates. *College Student Journal, 50*(3), 422–428.

Ju, S., Zhang, D., & Pacha, J. (2012). Employability skills valued by employers as important for entry-level employees with and without disabilities. *Career Development and Transition for Exceptional Individuals, 35*(1), 29–38.

Kanfer, R., Wanberg, C. R., & Kantrowitz, T. M. (2001). Job search and employment: A personality – Motivational analysis and meta-analytic review. *Journal of Applied psychology, 86*(5), 837.

Kochhar, R. (2020). Unemployment rose higher in three months of COVID-19 than it did in two years of the Great Recession. *Pew Research Foundation*. Retrieved from www.pewresearch.org/fact-tank/2020/06/11/unemployment-rose-higher-in-three-months-of-covid-19-than-it-did-in-two-years-of-the-great-recession/

Konradt, U., Garbers, Y., Böge, M., Erdogan, B., & Bauer, T. N. (2017). Antecedents and consequences of fairness perceptions in personnel selection: A 3-year longitudinal study. *Group & Organization Management, 42*(1), 113–146. https://doi.org/10.1177/1059601115617665

Krome, L. R. (2016). *Attracting women to STEM programs: The influence of goal-orientations and the use of gendered wording in recruitment materials* (Doctoral dissertation). Kansas State University.

Krzeminska, A., Austin, R. D., Bruyère, S. M., & Hedley, D. (2019). The advantages and challenges of neurodiversity employment in organizations. *Journal of Management & Organization, 25*(4), 453–463.

Latham, G. P., & Budworth, M.-H. (2006). The effect of training in verbal self-guidance on the self-efficacy and performance of Native North Americans in the selection interview. *Journal of Vocational Behavior, 68*(3), 516–523. https://doi.org/10.1016/j.jvb.2005.11.005

Lawer, L., Brusilovskiy, E., Salzer, M. S., & Mandell, D. S. (2009). Use of vocational rehabilitative services among adults with autism. *Journal of Autism and Developmental Disorders, 39*(3), 487–494.

Le, H., Oh, I. S., Robbins, S. B., Ilies, R., Holland, E., & Westrick, P. (2011). Too much of a good thing: Curvilinear relationships between personality traits and job performance. *Journal of Applied Psychology, 96*(1), 113.

Levashina, J., Hartwell, C. J., Morgeson, F. P., & Campion, M. A. (2014). The structured employment interview: Narrative and quantitative review of the research literature. *Personnel Psychology, 67*, 241–293. https://doi.org/10.1111/peps.1205

Levine, S. P., & Feldman, R. S. (2002). Women and men's nonverbal behavior and self-monitoring in a job interview setting. *Applied HRM Research*, 7(1), 1–14.

Liu, S., Huang, J. L., & Wang, M. (2014). Effectiveness of job search interventions: A meta-analytic review. *Psychological Bulletin, 140*(4), 1009.

Lorenz, T., & Heinitz, K. (2014). Aspergers – Different, not less: Occupational strengths and job interests of individuals with Asperger's syndrome. *PloS One, 9*(6), e100358.

Lynas, L. (2014). Project ABLE (Autism: Building Links to Employment): A specialist employment service for young people and adults with an autism spectrum condition. *Journal of Vocational Rehabilitation, 41*(1), 13–21. https://doi-org.proxy.library.cornell.edu/10.3233/JVR-140694

Macan, T. H., & Hayes, T. L. (1995). Both sides of the employment interview interaction: Perceptions of interviewers and applicants with disabilities. *Rehabilitation Psychology, 40*(4), 261–278. https://doi.org/10.1037/0090-5550.40.4.261

Maras, K., Norris, J. E., Nicholson, J., Heasman, B., Remington, A., & Crane, L. (2020). *Ameliorating the disadvantage for Autistic job seekers: An initial evaluation of adapted employment interview questions*. Bath: Centre for Applied Autism Research.

Markel, K. S., & Elia, B. (2016). How human resource management can best support employees with Autism: Future directions for research and practice. *Journal of Business and Management, 22*(1), 71–86.

Matsouka, K., & Mihail, D. M. (2016). Graduates' employability: What do graduates and employers think? *Industry and Higher Education, 30*(5), 321–326.

Mazurek, M. O., Shattuck, P. T., Wagner, M., & Cooper, B. P. (2011). Prevalence and correlates of screen-based media use among youths with Autism Spectrum Disorders. *Journal of Autism and Developmental Disorders, 42*, 1757–1767. https://doi.org/10.1007/s10803-011-1413-8

McCarthy, J. M., Bauer, T. N., Truxillo, D. M., Anderson, N. R., Costa, A. C., & Ahmed, S. M. (2017). Applicant perspectives during selection: A review addressing "so what?," "what's new?," and "where to next?" *Journal of Management, 43*(6), 1693–1725. https://doi.org/10.1177/0149206316681846

McDaniel, M. A., Whetzel, D. L., Schmidt, F. L., & Maurer, S. D. (1994). The validity of employment interviews: A comprehensive review and meta-analysis. *The Journal of Applied Psychology, 79*, 599–616.

Meena, K. (2016). Blind recruitment: The new hiring buzz for diversity inclusion. *International Journal of Business and General Management, 5*(5), 25–28.

Morgan, H. (2016). How social recruiting impacts job search. *Career Planning and Adult Development Journal, 32*(2), 33.

Moynihan, L. M., Roehling, M.V., LePine, M. A., & Boswell, W. R. (2003). A longitudinal study of the relationships among job search self-efficacy, job interviews, and employment outcomes. *Journal of Business and Psychology, 18*(2), 207–233.

Nester, M.A. (1993). Psychometric testing and reasonable accommodation for persons with disabilities. *Rehabilitation Psychology, 38*(2), 75–85. https://doi.org/10.1037/h0080292

Newton, B., Hurstfield, J., Miller, L., Page, R., & Akroyd, K. (2005). *What employers look for when recruiting the unemployed and inactive: skills, characteristics and qualifications* (Research Report No. 295). London: Department for Work and Pensions.

O'Leary, B. J., Durham, C. R., Weathington, B. L., Cothran, D. L., & Cunningham, C. J. (2009). Racial identity as a moderator of the relationship between perceived applicant similarity and hiring decisions. *Journal of Black Psychology, 35*(1), 63–77.

O'Neil, C. (2016). *Weapons of math destruction: How big data increases inequality and threatens democracy*. New York: Crown Publishing.

Partnership on Employment & Accessible Technology (PEAT). (2015). *eRecruiting & accessibility: Is HR technology hurting your bottom line?* Retrieved from www.peatworks.org/content/erecruiting-accessibility-report

Peterson, T. O., & Arnn, R. B. (2005). Self-efficacy: The foundation of human performance. *Performance Improvement Quarterly, 18*(2), 5–18.

Posthuma, R. A., Morgeson, F. P., & Campion, M. A. (2002). Beyond employment interview validity: A comprehensive narrative review of recent research and trends over time. *Personnel Psychology, 55*(1), 1–81. https://doi.org/10.1111/j.1744-6570.2002.tb00103.x

Rasmussen, K. G. (1984). Nonverbal behavior, verbal behavior, resumé credentials, and selection interview outcomes. *Journal of Applied Psychology, 69*(4), 551.

Rasul, M. S., Abd Rauf, R. A., & Mansor, A. N. (2013). Employability skills indicator as perceived by manufacturing employers. *Asian Social Science, 9*(8), 42.

Rivera, L. A. (2012). Diversity within reach: Recruitment versus hiring in elite firms. *The ANNALS of the American Academy of Political and Social Science, 639*(1), 71–90. https://doi.org/10.1177/0002716211421112

Robertson, S. M. (2010). Neurodiversity, quality of life, and autistic adults: Shifting research and professional focuses onto real-life challenges. *Disability Studies Quarterly, 30*(1).

Ruben, M. A., Hall, J. A., & Schmid Mast, M. (2015). Smiling in a job interview: When less is more. *Journal of Social Psychology, 155*(2), 107–126. https://doi-org.proxy.library.cornell.edu/10.1080/00224545.2014.972312

Saleh, M. C. (2020). *Career pages and online outreach to people with disabilities: Literature review.* Washington, DC: U.S. Department of Labor, Office of Disability Employment Policy, Employer Assistance Resource Network.

Saleh, M. C., & Bruyère, S. M. (2018). Leveraging employer practices in global regulatory frameworks to improve employment outcomes for people with disabilities. *Social Inclusion, 6*(1), 18–28. https://doi.org/10.17645/si.v6i1.1201

Schmidt, F. L., & Hunter, J. E. (1998). The validity and utility of selection methods in personnel psychology: Practical and theoretical implications of 85 years of research findings. *Psychological Bulletin, 124*(2), 262–274.

Scott, M., Falkmer, M., Girdler, S., & Falkmer, T. (2015). Viewpoints on factors for successful employment for adults with Autism Spectrum Disorder. *PLoS One, 10*(10), 1–15. https://doi-org.proxy.library.cornell.edu/10.1371/journal.pone.0139281

Sharma, N. (2014). Recruitment strategies: A power of E-Recruiting and social media. *International Journal of Core Engineering & Management (IJCEM), 1*(5).

Smith, M. J., Ginger, E. J., Wright, K., Wright, M. A., Taylor, J. L., Humm, L. B., Olsen, D. E., Bell, M. D., & Fleming, M. F. (2014). Virtual reality job interview training in adults with Autism Spectrum Disorder. *Journal of Autism and Developmental Disorders, 44*(10), 2450–2463. https://doi.org/10.1007/s10803-014-2113-y

Suen, H.Y., Chen, M.Y. C., & Lu, S. H. (2019). Does the use of synchrony and artificial intelligence in video interviews affect interview ratings and applicant attitudes? *Computers in Human Behavior, 98*, 93–101. https://doi.org/10.1016/j.chb.2019.04.012

Tay, C., Ang, S., & Van Dyne, L. (2006). Personality, biographical characteristics, and job interview success: A longitudinal study of the mediating effects of interviewing self-efficacy and the moderating effects of internal locus of causality. *Journal of Applied Psychology, 91*(2), 446.

Taylor, J. L., & Seltzer, M. M. (2011). Employment and post-secondary educational activities for young adults with autism spectrum disorders during the transition to adulthood. *Journal of Autism and Developmental Disorders, 41*(5), 566–574. https://doi.org/10.1007/s10803-010-1070-3

Trewin, S. (2018). *AI fairness for people with disabilities: Point of view*. Retrieved from https://arxiv.org/abs/1811.10670v1

Van Laarhoven, T., Carreon, A., Bonneau, W., & Lagerhausen, A. (2018). Comparing mobile technologies for teaching vocational skills to individuals with autism spectrum disorders and/or intellectual disabilities using universally-designed prompting systems. *Journal of Autism and Developmental Disorders, 48*, 2516–2529.

von Schrader, S., Malzer, V., & Bruyère, S. M. (2014). Perspectives on disability disclosure: The importance of employer practices and workplace climate. *Employer Rights and Responsibilities Journal, 26*, 237–255. https://doi.org/10.1007/s10672-013-9227-9

Wehman, P., Brooke V., Brooke, A. M., Ham, W., Schall, C., McDonough, J., Lau, S., Seward, H., & Avellone, L. (2016). Employment for adults with autism spectrum disorders: A retrospective review of a customized employment approach. *Research in Developmental Disabilities, 53–54*, 61–72. https://doi.org/10.1016/j.ridd.2016.01.015

Wehman, P., Schall, C. M., McDonough, J., Graham, C., Brooke, V., Riehle, J. E., & Avellone, L. (2017). Effects of an employer-based intervention on employment outcomes for youth with significant support needs due to autism. *Autism: The International Journal of Research & Practice, 21*, 276–290. https://doi.org/10.1177/1362361316635826

Whelpley, C. E., Banks, G. B., Bochantin, J., & Sandoval, R. (2020). Tensions on the spectrum: An inductive investigation of employee and manager experiences of autism. *Journal of Business and Psychology*. Advance online publication. https://doi.org/10.1007/s10869-019-09676-1

5

NEURODIVERSITY AND THE DISCLOSURE DILEMMA

Alecia M. Santuzzi and Robert T. Keating

Neurodiversity Versus Disability: The Impact of Perspective on Disclosure

Neurological differences including autism spectrum disorder (ASD), learning disabilities, attention deficit/hyperactivity disorder (ADHD), and other developmental and intellectual differences create diversity in cognitive abilities and behavior patterns among working adults (Singer, 1999). If an employing organization takes a neurodiversity perspective to cognitive differences, cognitive differences among workers are to be accepted as part of normal human variation (Kapp et al., 2013; Krzeminska et al., 2019). However, in order for this redefinition of human variation to be realized, the workplace environment and procedures must adjust to reflect neurodiverse features as normal variation (Bruyère & Barrington, 2012). These adjustments may include creating a positive workplace climate for human cognition differences and creative job design to capitalize on worker talent. Although recent trends (including perspectives in this edited volume) support the definition of neurodiversity as normal human variation, the workplace context reinforces the labelling of neurodivergent individuals as deviant and often socially stigmatized identities.

With some exceptions, current workplace practices have not yet embraced a neurodiversity perspective and manage neurodivergence as disability. Similar to current approaches to disability in the workplace, some limitations may be severe and directly conflict with job requirements; this creates a situation in which a worker is not qualified for the job because they cannot complete the essential functions with or without accommodations. However, for many neurodivergent workers, the divergence from the norm or typical patterns of cognitive functioning may be viewed as disabling but not in direct conflict with job duties. These

DOI: 10.4324/9781003023616-5

neurodivergent workers may require accommodations to the work environment or job design in order to be successful in a neurotypical environment. Also, workers with neurodivergent features are susceptible to experiences of unemployment, underemployment, and wage discrimination, similar to workers with other disabilities, and thus may require legal protections against unfair practices and barriers to successful employment.

In order for workers to benefit from legal protections and accommodation procedures in the workplace, employers need to know that workers have neurodivergent features, and those features must be evaluated as qualifying under the definition for a disability. Although the designation of disability is not automatic with a medical diagnosis, several neurodivergent conditions, including autism and intellectual disability, are explicitly identified by the U.S. Department of Labor's Office of Federal Contract Compliance Programs (OFCCP, 2020) as potentially qualifying as disabilities. A key characteristic to consider is that neurodivergence is largely *concealable*; thus, workers may have to willingly disclose their cognitive differences in order for the employer to know about them and react accordingly. Formal disclosures to an employing organization are a required step toward legally mandated protections and accommodations described in the Americans with Disabilities Act (1990). Beyond formal disclosure, workers who accept neurodivergence as a large part of their identities as individuals might risk feeling low authenticity unless they informally share these important features of themselves with coworkers and others. Even with the noted benefits of formal and informal disclosure, disclosure decisions are not easy and may require a careful consideration of the social and work-related costs compared to the expected benefits of disclosure. Moreover, workers with neurodivergent conditions may have some unique internal functioning and social experiences that change the disclosure decision for them, as compared to other types of disabilities and stigmatized social identities.

In this chapter, we will describe the research on disclosure and identity management decisions among adults with neurodivergent features. Although neurodiversity is a relatively new framework for discussing disclosure and other workplace social challenges, we can borrow lessons from existing literature on how workers manage concealable stigmatized identities (CSIs) – devalued attributes or social identities that can be hidden from others (Crocker et al., 1998; Quinn, 2006) – at work, with literature on concealable or invisible disabilities providing the most relevant insights (Santuzzi et al., 2014). We then analyze experiences that may be specific to neurodiversity that might modify existing conclusions about concealable identity management in the workplace. Finally, we outline future directions for both research and practices in industrial-organizational psychology, human resource management, and related disciplines to improve identity management experiences for neurodivergent workers. As much of the disclosure experience is contingent on workplace environments, we also provide some guidance for research and development endeavors as workplaces progress toward embracing a neurodiversity perspective.

The Disclosure Experience for Neurodivergent Workers

In general, revealing personal aspects about the self in social interaction facilitates relationship development in the workplace and other social settings (Collins & Miller, 1994). However, this general rule may be qualified if the feature being shared with others is socially stigmatized. Stigmatized features are devalued by others, contributing to a negative impression of the individual (Crocker et al., 1998; Goffman, 1963). Moreover, the negative evaluation of features such as disabilities can lead to generalized negative impressions through negative stereotypes and inaccurate beliefs about how the feature affects overall ability and function (Santuzzi & Cook, 2020). Individuals with CSIs, as well as stigmas more broadly, are generally aware of the social stigma attached to these features and expect to be classified as "stigmatized" should their identity be revealed to others (Bosson et al., 2005).

To navigate the stigma associated with neurodivergence or other concealable stigmatized identities (CSIs), workers might engage in a variety of identity management strategies to manage what and how much others know about their identity (Clair et al., 2005; King et al., 2017). In the broadest sense, identity management strategies take the form of revealing (actively disclosing the identity to others) or concealing (efforts to hide the identity from others). Either strategy can be applied by the same individual at different times and to varying degrees (Jones & King, 2014). For example, some workers with neurodivergent features may publicly discuss those features in formal and informal social interactions at work. Some workers might disclose formally in confidential settings but keep the information concealed in informal social interactions. Others may keep the information strictly hidden from all others in the workplace, even if it requires effort. Still others might calculate whether and how to incorporate neurodiversity into conversations on a case-by-case basis. At the interpersonal level, workers might engage in behaviors known as signaling (Jones & King, 2014; King et al., 2017) to determine if the current interaction partner and situation are safe for revealing. Importantly, when features are concealable – as most neurodivergent features are – workers have a variety of identity management strategies to consider, ranging from fully open and public to fully concealed.

Although there are a variety of ways in which workers might manage their concealable identities, the most common strategy when the identity is stigmatizing involves concealing. Workers with concealable disabilities and other CSIs might generally expect negative reactions from others if they disclose. Expectations of stigma may threaten one's sense of belonging in the workplace (Bosson et al., 2012), motivating workers who can conceal their stigmatized identities to do so in order to protect or improve their social standing at work. For example, one study found that workers with CSIs (i.e., mental illness, invisible physical disabilities, poverty) reported that they would be more likely to choose to conceal than reveal their identity and that they believed that disclosing their identity would have negative impacts on their relationships at work (Newheiser & Barreto, 2014). Furthermore, workers with CSIs may use a variety of concealing strategies that can vary in the degree of effort required. In a qualitative study of workers with invisible disabilities, including some neurodivergent features (e.g., Asperger's, ADHD, memory deficiency), participants reported several strategies for effortfully concealing their identities at work, such as avoiding situations where their identity would be relevant, controlling symptoms that would signal one's identity to others, monitoring potential disclosure targets for cues to how they might react, and adapting their work environment (e.g., using objects to keep hands busy while fidgeting; Santuzzi et al., 2019). Thus, workers with CSIs may go to great lengths to avoid perceived social threats from others' knowledge of their identity, even if it requires considerable effort as demanded by the type of concealing strategy or features of the impairment (e.g., symptomatology).

The trends in disclosure rates for adults with neurodivergent features appear to be consistent with patterns in the general CSI identity management literature. For example, one report suggested that one-third of college students with ASD did not disclose in college (Shattuck et al., 2012), which may predict behavior later in their career paths. Madaus and colleagues have published several papers reporting low rates of workplace disclosure among workers with learning disabilities. In one study, 73% of workers with learning disabilities reported experiencing some challenges at work due to the disability, but only 55% disclosed the learning disability at work, and only 12% requested accommodations. Of those who did disclose, only 11% disclosed during the job application process (Madaus, 2008). A similarly low rate of disclosure of learning disability was reported by Madaus et al. (2002), with only 30% of workers with learning disabilities disclosing to an employer despite 90% of workers experiencing disability-related challenges at work. In this study, only 15.7% of those who disclosed did so during the application process. Across both studies, there is a large gap between the number of workers with learning disabilities who experience interference due to disability at work and the number of those workers who disclose the learning disability to employers, suggesting a tendency to conceal at work. The very low percentage of workers who disclose early in the employment process (e.g., application) is also meaningful. The timing of disclosure has been shown to affect employer judgments, such that delaying disclosure may yield worse evaluations after an interview than if disclosure occurred earlier in the interview process (Roberts & Macan, 2006). As noted later in this chapter, however, the relative benefits from early disclosure (compared to delayed disclosure) may not generalize across neurodivergent conditions.

Consequences of Not Disclosing

At first, concealability seems like a net benefit as workers with concealable identities are not immediately treated as targets of stigma and prejudice (Quinn, 2006). However, the general tendency to not disclose neurodivergence or other concealable identities may come with some notable costs to the worker's performance and well-being (Follmer et al., 2019; Santuzzi et al., 2014), which can contribute to downstream challenges at the organizational level.

Worker Performance

Most directly, concealing may mean forfeiting needed accommodations for work performance or protections against discrimination in workplaces, especially in workplaces that are not yet using inclusive work design and practices. Without these protections in place, workers with neurodivergent features might risk poor work performance and corresponding costs to their reputation at work. Madaus et al. (2002) found that the most commonly reported reasons for disclosing learning disabilities to employers were instrumental to work performance, including to gain access to specialized technology, receive additional time or more detailed instructions, or to be better understood by the supervisor and coworkers to avoid misinterpretation of the worker's atypical behaviors in the workplace. More generally, research suggests that concealing an identity can yield lower levels of task-related self-confidence (Barreto et al., 2006), which may interfere with worker performance by extension. If the neurodivergent features directly interfere with work performance or work evaluations, disclosure might be necessary to gain access to accommodations or to prevent negative work evaluations due to misunderstandings about their behavior. Also, disclosure may be needed in order to give the employing organization an opportunity to "train the system" to better accommodate workers with neurodivergent features. Disclosure events may prompt employers to learn best practices for effective accommodations, inclusion, and integration to better support the performance of workers with neurodivergent features.

Several researchers have also argued that the cognitive effort involved with concealing a CSI may affect performance indirectly via displaced mental resources (DeJordy, 2008; Jones & King, 2014; Pachankis, 2007; Van Laar et al., 2019). Employees who conceal a CSI might be at an increased risk of high cognitive demands due to thought suppression while trying not to think about their stigmatizing feature, vigilance to cues of others' knowledge of the identity, and suspicion that others know about the identity and are negatively evaluating them (Pachankis, 2007). These additional cognitive demands may put workers with CSIs at a disadvantage relative to their counterparts with visible or no stigmatized features. Empirical research is limited in this area, but a few studies have offered some support. Smart and Wegner (1999) found that female undergraduates assigned to conceal an eating disorder while being asked questions relevant to the eating disorder reported more stigma-relevant thought intrusion and attempts at thought suppression during the interview than those who did not conceal. More recently, a qualitative study examined relationships between mental health coping strategies and performance among workers with psychological impairments.

Interview responses from 80% of participants revealed negative impacts of concealing behaviors on self-perceived job performance (Hennekam et al., 2020). In sum, evidence suggests that concealing a CSI in general can present unique cognitive demands not shared by other workers who are not concealing a stigmatized identity, and these demands might have deleterious effects on work performance. As with other parallels between neurodiverse features and CSIs mentioned thus far, it is reasonable to expect similar impacts of concealing for workers with neurodiverse features, especially those who perceive those features to be targets of stigma. As discussed in a subsequent section, workers with neurodivergent features that tax cognitive processes might be especially susceptible to the extra cognitive costs of identity management.

Worker Well-Being

Expending effort to conceal neurodivergence also might have negative consequences for worker well-being, even if doing so avoids immediate negative social consequences (Pachankis, 2007; Quinn, 2006). Effort comes with costs to psychological and physical health. Research suggests that concealing a concealable stigmatized identity is associated with psychological distress and more physical illness (Quinn & Chaudoir, 2009). Recent research has connected concealing traumatic brain injury (TBI) to social anxiety, low self-esteem, and loneliness (Hagger & Riley, 2017). Although not yet examined in empirical research, one concern is that the cost of effort spent in impression or identity management might be especially impactful for neurodivergent individuals who already experience taxed cognitive and/or social functioning.

Costs to individual well-being are also expected when neurodivergent workers feel inauthentic in the workplace (and other social environments) as a consequence of not revealing an important aspect of themselves to others. Experimental research in social psychology has shown that concealing a stigmatized identity threatens one's intrapersonal need for self-coherence (conversely, revealing a stigmatized identity threatened one's sense of belonging; Bosson et al., 2012). This finding converges with other research showing that individuals who concealed (versus those who revealed) a CSI (e.g., mental illness, LGB, poverty) in a social interaction reported decreased feelings of belonging and decreased sense of authenticity (Newheiser & Barreto, 2014). Recent research by Sarrett (2017) revealed that adults with autism felt that failing to disclose to others would risk low authenticity and incongruence with how they viewed themselves, consequences that provided motivation to be open about autism in the workplace. The deleterious effects of concealing on authenticity could result in self-directed negative affect (i.e., guilt and shame), which can have negative impacts on work-related self-confidence (Barreto et al., 2006). Together, these findings illustrate that when an individual is compelled to hide an important aspect of their identity, even if it is socially stigmatized, it can result in psychological strain.

Concealing neurodivergent features also can decrease psychological well-being, as it limits positive and rewarding roles that might emerge through the experience of being known as neurodivergent. Recent research suggested that some workers disclose concealable disabilities to be able to advocate for other workers with disabilities in the workplace or more generally (Santuzzi et al., 2019). Similar reports emerged from adults with traumatic brain injury who generally disclosed to others (Riley & Hagger, 2015) and workers with autism when asked why they disclosed in the workplace (Sarrett, 2017). With neurodivergent workers, disclosure also might allow others to observe firsthand the unique talents and other positive features of neurodiverse individuals (Sarrett, 2017). Disclosure allows others in the workplace to have firsthand experience with neurodivergence and its positive features in their work environment. Without disclosure, neurodivergent workers would forgo the benefits to psychological well-being associated with advocacy and increasing awareness of the unique talents among neurodivergent individuals.

Poor psychological well-being can also provide an indirect route by which concealing neurodivergent features can interfere with worker performance and job attitudes. Research among sexual minority workers found that not disclosing due to fear of stigma was associated with negative impacts on job attitudes, job-related stress and anxiety, and career outcomes (Ragins et al., 2007). Similar research by Newheiser et al. (2017) showed that concealing predicted lower job satisfaction and organizational commitment. Research also suggests that the damage to well-being and job attitudes may translate into lower productivity, negative experiences in appraisal processes, and more turnover (DeJordy, 2008; Jones & King, 2014; Newheiser et al., 2017). Therefore, the internal experiences of poor psychological well-being as a consequence of concealing neurodivergence might also interfere with individual work performance and organizational outcomes through lower productivity, commitment, and retention of workers.

Conditional Benefits of Disclosure

Given the negative consequences of concealing, disclosure may appear to be the optimal identity management strategy for neurodivergent workers; however, findings on the benefits of disclosure are mixed. A recent review of the CSI disclosure literature reported that disclosure was generally related to several beneficial work outcomes and psychological well-being outcomes, but these effects varied greatly across studies. In some cases, there was zero association or negative associations between disclosure and psychological well-being and job attitudes (Follmer et al., 2019). For example, Jones et al. (2016) showed decreased physical well-being after women disclosed pregnancy in the workplace. Research also suggests that disclosing mental illness in the workplace may lead to more personal discrimination (Elliot & Doane, 2015) and may be associated with increased employee withdrawal behaviors (Follmer & Jones, 2018). Research also suggests potential negative impacts of disclosure on work-related attitudes, including increased turnover intentions (Law et al., 2011).

Negative effects of disclosure are at least partly due to the cognitive and emotional burden of the decision itself (Quinn & Chaudoir, 2009), as well as the negative psychological consequences of stigma-based reactions to individuals with CSIs (Schmitt et al., 2014). Thus, weighing the cognitive and emotional costs of concealing against the threat of stigma and its associated negative health consequences from disclosure complicates the disclosure decision-making process, especially when workers have strong but conflicting motivations to reveal (e.g., for work accommodations) and conceal (e.g., high-stigma work environment). This disclosure dilemma may become even more complicated for workers with neurodivergent features, as individuals and organizations may be shifting from a disability focus to a neurodiversity perspective in different ways and at different rates.

The benefits of disclosure may not be realized unless conditions in the organization and individual workers are constructed in a way to ensure disclosure will yield net positive outcomes. To intervene at either the organizational or individual level, we must consider what barriers exist at the organizational and individual levels that might preclude disclosure and/or create a risk of negative consequences for disclosure of neurodivergent features in the workplace.

Barriers to the Benefits of Disclosure

To the extent that neurodiversity is interpreted as a stigmatized identity similar to disability, we can borrow lessons from the literature on disclosing concealable stigmatized identities in the workplace to understand the barriers to disclosing and experiencing a net benefit to disclosing neurodivergent features in the workplace. However, there may be some unique experiences for neurodivergent workers that contribute to their disclosure decisions and experiences. In the next section, we identify key environmental and individual barriers to the benefits of disclosing a concealable identity, highlighting lessons that may be consistent with the general experience of disclosing CSIs and conclusions that might need to be revisited in light of unique experiences of neurodivergent workers.

Experienced and Expected Stigma in the Work Environment

As a potentially stigmatized identity in the workplace, workers with neurodivergent features risk being targets of stigma, or negative social reactions, if others in the workplace are aware of those features. Based on extensive research on the experiences of CSIs in the workplace, a main reason that workers conceal their identities is due to expectations or experiences of stigma in their immediate work environments (Clair et al., 2005; Jones & King, 2014; Ragins, 2008). Stigma may be expected in workplaces with unsupportive supervisors and/or coworkers, creating a negative organizational climate. Importantly, the negative climate discourages workers from disclosing a potentially stigmatized identity at work (Ragins et al., 2007). von Schrader et al. (2014) surveyed 780 workers with disabilities and found that, among those who reported not disclosing their disability at their most recent job (n = 115), 78% reported fear of being fired or not hired, and more than 60% reported that unsupportive supervisors and coworkers and expectations of differential treatment were main reasons for not disclosing their disability at work.

The negative reactions of stigma might be driven by stereotypical beliefs held by supervisors and coworkers about the nature of neurodivergent conditions. Given the alignment with disability, neurodivergence likely cues disability stereotypes that target a worker's competence, independence, and general abilities (Santuzzi & Cook, 2020; Colella & Stone, 2005). Also, emotional reactions to disability tend to be ambivalent, as they incorporate perceptions of low competence but cue social responsibility and desires to promote justice (Fiske et al., 2002), although the positive regard may translate into pity and yield negative consequences in performance domains such as the workplace (Santuzzi & Cook, 2020).

Beyond general disability stereotypes, neurodivergent workers might be especially susceptible to damaging beliefs about their ability to complete job tasks and general mental capacity to function in a work environment. This is discouraging given the literature acknowledging the high level of talent, intellect, or specialized ability of some neurodivergent workers in the workplace (Austin & Pisano, 2017). The psychological and cognitive characteristics associated with neurodivergence might elicit concerns about predictability. Furthermore, many neurodivergent features might be interpreted as mental illness, which can yield higher degrees of social stigma compared to other features referred to as disabilities (e.g., mobility impairments). As research has shown, mental challenges yield some of the most severe reactions of stigma (Corrigan & Watson, 2002; Follmer & Jones, 2018). The stigma may be especially pronounced in performance domains such as the workplace, where cognitive and social functions are deemed critical to good employee performance and organizational outcomes. Research shows that employment discrimination may be higher for those who are perceived to have psychiatric as compared to physical impairments (Spirito et al., 2008) and that the stigma and stereotypes associated with psychiatric impairments have negatively affected experiences among working adults with ADHD (Patton, 2009).

Workers' concerns about stigma in the workplace (e.g., Black et al., 2020) are validated by the evidence of discrimination against neurodivergent workers in education and employment. Neurodivergent workers are more likely unemployed or underemployed and receive lower wages than other working age adults. Butterworth et al. (2015) reported an employment rate of 23.4% among individuals with cognitive disabilities. A similar overall estimate was reported in a recent study of individuals with ASD; however, only 14% reported being employed in a general community setting that also employed people without disabilities. An additional 15% of individuals with ASD were employed by facilities that mainly supported workers with disabilities (Roux et al., 2017). Even among those whose ASD was unaccompanied by an intellectual disorder, only 23% reported having community-based paid employment (Roux et al., 2017). These reports are especially concerning when one considers that general employment rates among adults in the U.S. and other economically developed nations typically exceed 70% (Black et al., 2020; Organisation for Economic Co-operation and Development [OECD], 2021).

Descriptive data from Roux and colleagues (2017) also showed that workers with ASD earned a median biweekly income of $194, which is far less than the median biweekly income of approximately $1,600 for the general population the same year data were collected (Bureau of Labor Statistics, 2015). Furthermore, workers with ASD were represented more in some occupations – groundskeeping and maintenance (28%), food preparation and services (18%), and retail (17%) – than other occupations – manufacturing (7%), office and administrative support (6%), and material handling and mail distribution (4%; Roux et al., 2017). Other research has shown that employment disparities also exist within the white-collar employment sector, with workers with ADHD and learning disabilities being far more represented in entrepreneurial as compared to management positions (Halmoy et al., 2009; Logan, 2009). Together, these statistics confirm structural barriers to employment reflected in employment rates and representation in some areas or sectors in employment.

Expectations of stigma may also come from experiences of discrimination at an interpersonal level following prior disclosures at work, resulting in a general fear of disclosure (Chaudoir & Quinn, 2010; Ragins et al., 2007). The rate at which instances of CSI disclosure in the workplace result in discriminatory reactions is unclear in the current literature; however, some studies have documented the nature of these experiences when they happen. For example, in one study of disclosure experiences among workers with HIV, several workers reported negative and discriminatory reactions by their employers, including their employer wanting to inform human resources and employees due to perceived risks to other workers, placing restrictions on their work duties, and being the subject of gossip at work (Stutterheim et al., 2017). In a mixed-methods study on the experiences of workers with CSIs, Santuzzi et al. (2019) found that workers who disclosed or cued (via symptomology) a disability at work experienced a variety of negative or stigmatizing reactions, including scrutiny from others about the legitimacy or severity of the condition, misattribution of symptoms or behaviors related to the condition to rudeness or lack of social skill, and strained interpersonal relationships with supervisors and coworkers. Discriminatory reactions to CSI disclosure can have negative effects on psychological well-being. Meta-analytic research shows a moderate relationship between perceived discrimination and psychological strain that is especially pronounced among individuals with CSIs compared to those with visible stigmatized features (Schmitt et al., 2014). Furthermore, bearing a CSI in general is associated with decreased physical and psychological well-being (Chaudoir & Quinn, 2010), and in some cases, these outcomes have been linked directly to CSI disclosure (e.g., Jones, 2017). This suggests that some of the negative health and occupational consequences of bearing a CSI might be uniquely explained by disclosure experiences.

Importantly, workers with neurodivergent features are aware of the stigma and risk of discrimination that they face in the workplace. Workers with ASD, ADHD, learning disabilities, and other neurodivergent conditions may worry about confirming negative stereotypes and other generalizations that affect social and work-related opportunities. The concerns about stigma discourage disclosure of neurodivergence in the workplace. For example, Madaus et al. (2002) reported that workers with learning disabilities who did not disclose to the employer worried that disclosing would negatively affect relationships with supervisors and coworkers and possibly threaten job security. Fear of stigma discourages disclosure generally among adults with concealable cognitive and mental health disabilities (Beatty & Kirby, 2006; Jans et al., 2012) and specifically among autistic workers (Johnson & Joshi, 2016; Sarrett, 2017) and adults with traumatic brain injury (Riley & Hagger, 2015). Related to stigma is the concern about being misunderstood, such that behaviors related to the neurodivergent condition are misinterpreted as indicators of poor performance, low commitment, or low motivation to succeed (Madaus et al., 2002; Santuzzi et al., 2019; Sarrett, 2017).

Together, these findings suggest that workers with CSIs may have good reasons to actively choose to hide their identity due to a perceived or experienced threat of social stigma and other negative interpersonal consequences. Fear of stigma can result from perceptions that their feature is generally stigmatized, personal experiences with stigma, or assessments of their work climate. Moreover, the negative reactions from others as a consequence of disclosure can have far-reaching implications for personal health and well-being as well as work attitudes and performance.

Internal Challenges of Neurodivergence

Although the vast majority of the literature on concealable stigmatized identities broadly and concealable disabilities more specifically point to the work environment as the primary factor predicting disclosure decisions and their outcomes, some recent research and discussions in the literature suggest that internal experiences among workers with neurodivergence and other concealable disabilities are also important to disclosure experiences.

Concealable disabilities, by definition, can be hidden and thus not detected by others unless the conditions are disclosed. However, many concealable disabilities, including those that fit into neurodivergence, come with features and symptoms that are also not easily detected *by the individual who has them* (Santuzzi et al., 2014). This may be especially problematic for workers who have conditions that are low in severity and create mild or temporary interference with work tasks

(Markel & Elia, 2016; Seltzer et al., 2003). For example, adults with learning disabilities may not have a clear interpretation of their learning challenges as indicative of a disability as compared to variation that fits within typical levels (Licht, 1983). Adults with ADHD might receive conflicting diagnoses and feedback from professionals, which adds ambiguity to their own personal experiences (Higgins et al., 2002). Also, some features of neurodivergent conditions are not salient to a worker until they are in a specific context that conflicts with the neurodivergent features (e.g., learning disabilities; Wadlington et al., 2006) or challenges are compounded by other stressors in the environment (e.g., ADHD). Ambiguity could also arise as the severity of features might change across time and developmental period (Seltzer et al., 2003). In a state of ambiguity, a worker experiencing neurodivergent symptoms is left to wonder if what they are experiencing is different from what others normally experience or if it is different enough to be classified as "divergent." If a worker does not detect their cognitive differences as divergent, then the worker likely sees disclosure as irrelevant. Neurodivergent workers also might see disclosure as irrelevant if their features are not salient in the specific situation (e.g., workplace) or do not feel the features are interfering with their work (Madaus et al., 2002: Santuzzi et al., 2019).

One of the internal challenges that might be unique to neurodivergent workers that is not experienced by all who have concealable disabilities is that the features of neurodivergence can directly interfere with identity management in the workplace (Johnson & Joshi, 2014). Seltzer et al. (2003) identified several features of autistic adolescents and adults that extend beyond cognitive task performance. These include social, behavioral, and communication challenges and developing friendships. Primary features of several neurodivergent conditions include differences in attending to and processing social cues and other information in the work environment (Markel & Elia, 2016; Hendricks, 2010). In some cases, the lack of weight placed on the importance of some cues (e.g., facial expressions) might be offset by increased acuity in other perceptions. However, conveying social information through subtle social cues might be taken for granted among those who are neurotypical or expect to interact with neurotypical others. Importantly, neurodivergent workers might not attend to or weight subtle social cues in their decisions about identity management in the workplace. If neurodivergent workers do not weight social reactions as much as neurotypical others, they might not feel the same pressure to effortfully manage their neurodiverse identities. Experienced or anticipated social stigma might not be experienced the same way for neurodivergent workers who perceive social cues differently. This does not suggest that there is no negative impact of social stigma on neurodivergent workers; the statistics on employment discrimination among neurodivergent workers clearly suggest otherwise. However, the cues for such threat might not be detected or interpreted as threatening as a neurotypical worker might view them.

This challenges the generalizability of findings related to disclosure experiences and identity management among individuals with disabilities and other concealable identities (Johnson & Joshi, 2014). The existing literature on identity management in the workplace seems to rest on an assumption that a worker detects a social threat in the environment, which cues effort toward identity management strategies with the goal of reducing the threat or negative consequences of it. Even if explicitly informed of a pending social threat, workers with neurodivergent features that interfere with social communication might experience challenges in effective identity management. To the extent that the neurodiverse feature compounds the social complexity of monitoring others' reactions and adjusting behavior to shape impressions, identity management strategies might be less common or less effective if used.

Another internal factor that likely affects disclosure experiences is the extent to which the neurodivergent features are accepted as part of a worker's identity. The concealable nature of many neurodivergent conditions gives workers flexibility not only in their selected identity management strategies when presenting themselves to others but also control over if and how they define themselves in light of their cognitive differences. The extent to which workers develop a disability identity for the neurodivergent features may depend on a number of internal and social experiences in the workplace and other social environments (Santuzzi & Waltz, 2016).

Workers with neurodivergent features also might accept a neurodiversity identity rather than a disability identity. For example, autistic workers might take a neurodiversity perspective and self-identify as autistic as the preferred identity, embracing value in their cognitive differences as an important part of their self-definition. This also might be accompanied by a preference for identity-first rather than person-first language. This indicates more value and centrality to their identity and likely a desire to be verified for such features that are important to them (Swann, 2012). The neurodiversity perspective is relatively young, with the term emerging only twenty years ago in the literature (Singer, 1999) and only recently becoming part of the diversity and inclusion discussions in employing organizations (Doyle, 2017). Thus, the term may be new to a large proportion of the workforce who may not have considered it an option when integrating their neurodivergent features into an identity. More likely, the current generation of workers defaults to a medical model and views their neurodiverse identities as features to make up for and overcome to succeed in the workplace. For those workers, disclosure decisions may be quite consistent with the experiences of other concealable disabilities that are assumed to be devalued by others and the worker that has them. Future research will determine how these disclosure experiences might evolve when the worker, employing organization, or both fully embrace a neurodiversity perspective to cognitive differences.

What Can Industrial-Organizational Psychology Do to Encourage Disclosure?

For both organizational response and worker well-being, disclosure of neurodivergent features in the workplace has value. However, organizations must work to create an environment that minimizes the social and work-related costs to disclosure in order for workers to appreciate the value of disclosing this personal information. If disclosure is expected to yield negative consequences such as social exclusion, fewer opportunities to network or advance in the organization, and felt pressure to compensate for stereotypes, the cost of disclosure might be viewed as higher than the benefits to psychological well-being and authenticity. Moreover, the psychological costs could even contradict the intended benefits if disclosure cues the need for effortful identity management to compensate for stigma and stereotypes. To ensure the best outcomes, organizations should encourage disclosure and prepare the organization to ensure positive and supportive response to the disclosure.

Recent research in inclusion and diversity management practices provides some starting points for continued research and development of best practices, but continued work is needed to refine the precise mechanisms for success. As noted previously, the diversity climate within organizations predicts worker identity management decisions and strategies. Providing signals of inclusion through practices such as diversity statements and policies and related training opportunities for employees may lead job candidates and current workers to anticipate inclusion in the organization. Gilbride et al. (2003) offer procedures among organizations employing workers with disabilities; these practices include increased flexibility with policies, openness to accommodations, focus on matching employee abilities to jobs, and demonstrating an ability to supervise a diverse workforce.

Beyond recruitment, inclusive organizations may build trust with the employees, and this trust can translate into more job satisfaction, commitment to the organization, and organizational citizenship behaviors (Shore et al., 2011). Of particular relevance, recent work also suggests that inclusion is associated with positive reactions to formal disclosure requests in the employing organization (Santuzzi et al., 2021). More inclusion was associated with more positive affect, less negative affect, and higher levels of perceived appropriateness in reaction to receiving the Voluntary Self-Identification of Disability form (VSID). Less anticipated stigma in the workplace also predicted less concern about privacy and less concern about others' reactions to their disclosure responses on the VSID. Taken together, the findings suggest that inclusiveness in the work environment can facilitate both formal and informal disclosure of disabilities and divergent abilities.

For many organizations, providing an opportunity to disclose formally on forms such as the VSID is considered an inclusive practice (Gasper et al., 2019). However, recent research focusing on the terminology used in those forms can significantly affect whether a worker will disclose a divergent ability or health condition. Across two large samples of adult workers from an online platform, findings indicated that changing the response options on the VSID from asking about "disability" to instead asking about a "qualifying condition" significantly increased the disclosure frequency among workers. The impact was especially pronounced among workers with psychological disabilities (Santuzzi et al., 2020). This suggests that organizations can improve the disclosure experience and disclosure rates by adjusting terminology on formal disclosure requests. This modification is consistent with qualitative research suggesting that workers with concealable disabilities rarely described their limitations as "disabilities," instead preferring to describe them as a general "condition" or by citing a medical diagnosis (Santuzzi et al., 2019).

Fostering positive interpersonal relationships in the workplace may also be a key ingredient to facilitating positive disclosure experiences among neurodivergent workers. Although focused on mental illness rather than neurodiversity, Pahwa et al. (2017) found that mental illness disclosure was selective; individuals chose specific individual partners to disclose to and not others. This is consistent with the patterns that emerged in Santuzzi et al. (2019) for concealable disability disclosure, with the evaluated relationship of an interaction partner being the most common strategy used when deciding whether to disclose a disability (see also Sarrett, 2017, for experiences specific to adults with autism). The preferred identity management strategies among workers who can conceal disabilities and divergent abilities is to evaluate their interaction partners on a case-by-case basis to determine whether and how to reveal the information to them. Organizations can take this lesson as a cue to develop interpersonal allies in the workplace through ally training and mentoring programs to foster positive relationships within the workplace (Nittrouer, 2019).

In addition to developing allies within the employing organization to directly improve the climate for neurodiversity, organizations could also demonstrate support for neurodivergent workers by creating partnerships with community organizations that support adults with neurodivergent conditions (Markel & Elia, 2016). Such partnerships not only symbolize the employing organization's efforts toward an inclusive work environment but also may create recruitment opportunities for the employing organization to attract more neurodiversity into their employee case.

Future Research Directions

The recommendations listed here are largely motivated by research on disability and illness. Neurodiversity and divergence shares a number of key features with the disability literature, including impact on mental processes, negative stereotypes, and perceived misfit with work tasks. Thus, we can apply many of the lessons learned from the literature on disabilities and illness to inform development of inclusive practices and work environments.

However, there also might be some unique features of neurodiversity that should be considered in future research and lend some caution to immediate application of past research to the neurodiversity challenges in the workplace. For example, some revisions and additional strategies may be required if a worker does not see the neurodivergent condition as a "disability" and instead embraces the individual difference as variation in neurodiversity. Two main areas in need of continued research to inform disclosure experiences of workers with neurodivergent features are in the neurodiversity identity and positive features of neurodivergent conditions.

The Neurodiverse Identity

Similar to other areas of disability research (Bogart, 2014; Hahn & Belt, 2004; Santuzzi & Waltz, 2016), recent work suggests that workers may vary in the extent to which they develop an identity that highlights their neurodivergent features. Identity has been most evident in research on autism but could extend into other neurodiverse features. Developing a positive disability identity has been linked to social support and psychological well-being (Bogart, 2014). It may also buffer negative experiences such as discrimination and microaggressions (Bogart et al., 2018; Branscombe et al., 1999).

The role of disability identity in disclosure of neurodivergent features remains understudied in the empirical literature. Dalgin and Gilbride (2003) emphasized the importance of disability identity in disclosure of psychiatric disabilities at work. Not identifying the impairment as a disability made disclosure seem irrelevant. Also, like many other studies, the researchers noted the importance of stigma risk and work environment in guiding those disclosure decisions.

We might expect a similar pattern to occur for workers with neurodivergent features. If they identify the features as "disabilities," they might see them as relevant to legal protections and accommodation opportunities. Developing a disability identity for the neurodivergent features may facilitate disclosure (Santuzzi & Waltz, 2016), but they also would likely face the same dilemmas about identity management and disclosure that have been reported in research on workers with concealable disabilities (Santuzzi et al., 2019).

The research is not yet well established on the neurodiverse identity to determine if it functions similarly to a disability identity in disclosure decisions and experiences. On the one hand, developing a positive neurodiverse identity should bring an experience of value for the neurodivergent features as individual differences and not limitations (Singer, 1999). This might parallel the emergence of the Deaf identity and associated community of individuals who do not see their differences in hearing ability as limitations but rather valued individual variation. Some evidence of this also appears among individuals with autism who celebrate their cognitive differences (Gobbo & Shmulsky, 2016).

The difference between developing a neurodiverse identity and a disability identity might be more than just labeling. Disability implies a limitation, which is acknowledged in legal definitions of disability such as by the Americans with Disabilities Act (ADA) of 1990. By identifying as a person with a disability (PWD), a worker might be accepting a social identity and see value in connecting with the larger community of others with disabilities. However, the identity also may be instrumental, as it acknowledges structural disadvantages and opens the door for workers to be eligible for protections and accommodations if needed.

Adopting and disclosing a neurodiverse identity might not serve the same instrumental purpose. The neurodiverse identity could serve the same positive benefits as any valued group identity, which should be evident in positive psychological well-being and social buffers against transgressions. However, the neurodiverse identity celebrates individual differences as normal variation, variation that should not be in conflict with workplace processes and environments. The decision to disclose, then, would likely serve a social purpose to build intimacy and relationships with others in the workplace. Similar to work cited previously, disclosure for instrumental purposes such as accommodations becomes irrelevant if the features are not defined as disabilities (Dalgin & Gilbride, 2003).

Continued research also should consider the extent to which individual self-definitions of neurodiversity are congruent with organizational definitions and policies for neurodiversity. One possible trend is that organizations may continue to adopt the term "neurodiversity" to indicate their goal of inclusion for cognitive differences. However, the organization's practices and social environment might not fully reflect a neurodiversity perspective. A worker who adopts a neurodiversity identity might be especially discouraged to find out that their employing organization sent signals that they value their identity, but that value did not come through in the organization's day-to-day practices and social interactions with others in the organization. Continued research is needed to determine the impact of employing organizations displaying definitions of neurodiversity that differ from a worker's definition of a neurodiverse identity. Moreover, research should identify how organizations can be better prepared to fully display their value for neurodiversity in ways that are genuine to workers.

The perceived risks of sharing information about neurodiverse features also might be driven by the type of identity adopted by workers with such features. Communication privacy management theory (Petronio, 1991, 2013) points to conditions guiding decisions to reveal or conceal disability (or other private information with consequences). The theory suggests that workers might evaluate the risk of allowing others to share their private information. These risks include forfeiting control over who may learn the information and negative reactions to the information. If the information is believed to be stigmatized, workers might conceal the information to be sure it remains private. Only trusted others will learn the information. The identity adopted for the features as disability or neurodiversity might move the threshold for risk among workers who are deciding whether to disclose, with those who adopt neurodiversity as having a higher risk tolerance and disclosing more often than those with a disability identity. Future research is needed to explore this phenomenon.

The Talent Advantages of Neurodiverse Workers

Another area that is an emerging area of study and invites continued research is in understanding of the talents and performance advantages among neurodiverse workers. The term "disability" is often discussed as creating disadvantages for workers in the workplace with few exceptions (cf. Samosh, 2020). Unlike the tradition of the disability literature, the emerging neurodiversity literature seems to be highlighting work-related advantages among workers with neurodiverse or divergent features, referring to neurodivergent workers as specialists (Doyle, 2017) rather than generalists.

Specializations among neurodivergent workers might include task-related features such as high intellectual functioning, whereas others are associated with general traits such as honesty. Recent research notes the high levels of talent, intellectual functioning, and specialized abilities that autistic workers might demonstrate in the workplace. In accordance, several major companies, such as Microsoft, JPMorgan Chase, Ford, and Dell, have implemented human resource policies aimed at recruiting neurodiverse talent to perform such jobs as data analytics, software testing, and customer support (Austin & Pisano, 2017). To the extent that these task-related advantages and traits are valued by employing organizations, workers might capitalize on those benefits by disclosing their neurodivergent features. In this way, disclosure of neurodivergent features may be instrumental, as it punctuates fit with job tasks in which the workers' features show an advantage. This creates an interesting shift from the existing literature relying on a disability perspective, in which disclosure is perceived as risking misfit to job tasks. The favorability of specific talents might shift as job designs change or in consideration for opportunities to advance into leadership positions which might be tailored to those with more general talent profiles. Future research should examine how neurodiverse workers manage the favorable features of their neurodivergence. Do employers have similar evaluations of workers with specific favorable talents as compared to those with general talents? Are employers willing to redesign higher-level positions in organizations to fit the talents of neurodivergent employees who might be eligible for advancing into leadership positions? If not, disclosure might be discouraged so that the employees are not seen as having a narrow talent profile that could preclude advancement opportunities.

Conclusion

The shift in perspective from disability to neurodiversity when discussing neurodivergent features associated with conditions such as autism, ADHD, and learning disabilities creates additional complexity in the disclosure process in the workplace. From a disability perspective, disclosure presents a dilemma of whether the costs of making a stigmatized identity known are outweighed by the benefits of protections against discrimination and eligibility for accommodations at work. It is possible that workers with disabilities also see their disabilities as stigmatizing, adding motivation to keep a disability concealed to deny the disability identity within themselves. Workers who embrace neurodiversity in their self-definitions accept their features as part of a continuum of normal variation in abilities. Disclosure may risk social stigma, but not necessarily, because the individual endorses a stigmatizing label for themselves. Rather, they might be concerned about stigma because others have not embraced a neurodiversity perspective. Disclosure may also be beneficial to workers with neurodivergent features as organizations gain more awareness of the specialist talents among neurodivergent workers. Those workers might rely on disclosure to highlight those specialist talents as a fit to the organization's goals. This allows workers to disclose for instrumental reasons. However, the instrumental goal might be different from those who adopt a disability perspective. Whereas disclosing disability may be instrumental to preventing negative consequences of discrimination or poor work performance evaluations due to limitations, disclosure of neurodiverse features might be instrumental to affirm specialized talents and present authentically at work. A neurodiversity perspective also may allow workers to view their features as individual differences that should be disclosed for the purposes of developing intimate relationships rather than as instrumental steps toward accommodations and protections. Until workplaces embrace neurodiversity in their interpretations of worker ability differences, workers who adopt a neurodiversity perspective for themselves may still face organizational policies and practices grounded in a disability perspective (e.g., case-by-case accommodations). Thus, disclosure dilemmas still emerge for these workers, as their features are viewed as disabilities that require accommodations in the workplace. As research continues on the individual and organizational definitions of neurodiversity and, importantly, practices adjust accordingly, the disclosure dilemma may evolve from being a decision about revealing a stigmatized identity to protect oneself to decisions about providing relevant personal information to foster positive relationships in the workplace. Such positive disclosure experiences have the potential to facilitate social networking among coworkers, which can promote team cohesion and performance. Furthermore, positive disclosures can serve as cues of organizational inclusion to other workers that can influence future disclosures of neurodiverse features as well as other attributes and identities that have been historically stigmatized in the workplace. In this way, adoption of a neurodiversity perspective may support inclusion of individual attributes traditionally perceived as "disabilities" as components of organizational diversity that can contribute to the social and performance-related success of organizations.

References

Americans with Disabilities Act of 1990, Pub. L. No. 101–336, 104 Stat. 328 (1990). Retrieved from www.ada.gov/pubs/ada.htm

Austin, R. D., & Pisano, G. P. (2017). Neurodiversity as a competitive advantage. *Harvard Business Review, 95*(3), 96–103. Retrieved from https://hbr.org/2017/05/neurodiversity-as-a-competitive-advantage

Barreto, M., Ellemers, N., & Banal, S. (2006). Working under cover: Performance-related self-confidence among members of contextually devalued groups who try to pass. *European Journal of Social Psychology, 36*, 337–352. https://doi.org/10.1002/ejsp.314

Beatty, J. E., & Kirby, S. L. (2006). Beyond the legal environment: How stigma influences invisible identity groups in the workplace. *Employee Responsibilities and Rights Journal, 18*, 29–44. https://doi.org/10.1007/s10672-005-9003-6

Black, M. H., Mahdi, S., Milbourn, B., Scott, M., Gerber, A., Esposito, C., . . . Girdler., S. (2020). Multi-informant international perspectives on the facilitators and barriers to employment for autistic adults. *Autism Research*, 1–20. https://doi.org/10.1002/aur.2288

Bogart, K. R. (2014). The role of disability self-concept in adaptation to congenital or acquired disability. *Rehabilitation Psychology*, *59*(1), 107–115. https://doi.org/10.1037/a0035800

Bogart, K. R., Lund, E. M., & Rottenstein, A. (2018). Disability pride protects self-esteem through the rejection-identification model. *Rehabilitation Psychology*, *63*(1), 155–159. https://doi.org/10.1037/rep0000166

Bosson, J. K., Prewitt-Freilino, J. L., & Taylor, J. N. (2005). Role rigidity: A problem of identity misclassification? *Journal of Personality and Social Psychology*, *89*(4), 552–565. https://doi.org/10.1037/0022-3514.89.4.552

Bosson, J. K., Weaver, J. R., & Prewitt-Freilino, J. L. (2012). Concealing to belong, revealing to be known: Classification expectations and self-threats among persons with concealable stigmas. *Self and Identity*, *11*, 114–135. https://doi.org/10.1080/15298868.2010.513508

Branscombe, N. R., Schmitt, M. T., & Harvey, R. D. (1999). Perceiving pervasive discrimination among African Americans: Implications for group identification and well-being. *Journal of Personality and Social Psychology*, *77*, 135–149. https://doi.org/10.1037/0022-3514.77.1.135

Bruyère, S. M., & Barrington, L. (2012). *Employment and work.* Thousand Oaks, CA: SAGE.

Bureau of Labor Statistics. (2015). *The Economics Daily, Median usual weekly earnings of full-time wage and salary workers by occupation and sex.* U.S. Department of Labor, Bureau of Labor Statistics. Retrieved from www.bls.gov/opub/ted/2015/median-usual-weekly-earnings-of-full-time-wage-and-salary-workers-by-occupation-and-sex.htm

Butterworth, J., Hiersteiner, D., Engler, J., Bershadsky, J., & Bradley, V. (2015). National Core Indicators ©: Data on the current state of employment of adults with IDD and suggestions for policy development. *Journal of Vocational Rehabilitation*, *42*(3), 209–220. https://doi.org/10.3233/jvr-150741

Chaudoir, S. R., & Quinn, D. M. (2010). Revealing concealable stigmatized identities: The impact of disclosure motivations and positive first disclosure experiences on fear of disclosure and well being. *Journal of Social Issues*, *66*, 570–584. https://doi.org/10.1111/j.1540-4560.2010.01663.x

Clair, J. A., Beatty, J. E., & MacLean, T. L. (2005). Out of sight but not out of mind: Managing invisible social identities in the workplace. *Academy of Management Review*, *30*, 78–95. https://doi.org/10.5465/amr.2005.15281431

Colella, A., & Stone, D. L. (2005). Workplace discrimination toward persons with disabilities: A call for some new research directions. In R. Dipboye & A. Colella (Eds.), *Discrimination at work: The psychological and organizational bases* (pp. 227–253). Mahwah, NJ: Lawrence Erlbaum.

Collins, N. L., & Miller, L. C. (1994). Self-disclosure and liking: A meta-analytic review. *Psychological Bulletin*, *116*, 457–475. https://doi.org/10.1037/0033-2909.116.3.457

Corrigan, P. W., & Watson, A. C. (2002). Understanding the impact of stigma on people with mental illness. *World Psychiatry: Official Journal of the World Psychiatric Association*, *1*(1), 16–20. Retrieved from www.ncbi.nlm.nih.gov/pmc/articles/PMC1489832/

Crocker, J., Major, B., & Steele, C. (1998). Social stigma. In D. T. Gilbert, S. T. Fiske, & G. Lindzey (Eds.), *The handbook of social psychology* (4th ed., Vol. 2., pp. 504–553). New York: McGraw-Hill.

Dalgin, R. S., & Gilbride, D. (2003). Perspectives of people with psychiatric disabilities on employment disclosure. *Psychiatric Rehabilitation Journal, 26*(3), 306. https://doi.org/10.2975/26.2003.306.310

DeJordy, R. (2008). Just passing through: Stigma, passing, and identity decoupling in the work place. *Group & Organization Management, 33*, 504–531. https://doi.org/10.1177/1059601108324879

Doyle, N. (2017). Neurodiversity at work. In British Psychological Society (Ed.), *Psychology at work: Improving wellbeing and productivity in the workplace* (pp. 44–62). Leicester: British Psychological Society.

Elliott, M., & Doane, M. J. (2015). Stigma management of mental illness: Effects of concealment, discrimination, and identification on well-being. *Self and Identity, 14*(6), 654–674. https://doi.org/10.1080/15298868.2015.1053518

Fiske, S. T., Cuddy, A. J. C., Glick, P., & Xu, J. (2002). A model of (often mixed) stereotype content: Competence and warmth respectively follow from perceived status and competition. *Journal of Personality and Social Psychology, 42*(6), 878–902. https://doi.org/10.1037//0022–3514.82.6.878

Follmer, K. B., & Jones, K. S. (2018). Mental illness in the workplace: An interdisciplinary review and organizational research agenda. *Journal of Management, 44*(1), 325–351. https://doi.org/10.1177/0149206317741194

Follmer, K. B., Sabat, I. E., & Siuta, R. L. (2019). Disclosure of stigmatized identities at work: An interdisciplinary review and agenda for future research. *Journal of Organizational Behavior, 41*(2), 169–184. https://doi.org/10.1002/job.2402

Gasper, J., Palan, M., & Muz, B. (2019). *Survey of employer policies on the employment of people with disabilities: Final report (for U.S. Department of Labor)*. Rockville, MD: Westat.

Gilbride, D., Stensrud, R., Vandergoot, D., & Golden, K. (2003). Identification of the characteristics of work environments and employers open to hiring and accommodating people with disabilities. *Rehabilitation Counseling Bulletin, 46*(3), 130–137. https://doi.org/10.1177/00343552030460030101

Gobbo, K., & Shmulsky, S. (2016). Autistic identity development and postsecondary education. *Disability Studies Quarterly, 36*(3). https://doi.org/10.18061/dsq.v36i3.5053

Goffman, E. (1963). *Stigma: Notes on the management of spoiled identity*. Englewood Cliffs, NJ: Prentice-Hall.

Hagger, B. F., & Riley, G. A. (2017). The social consequences of stigma-related self-concealment after acquired brain injury. *Neuropsychological Rehabilitation, 29*(7), 1129–1148. https://doi.org/10.1080/09602011.2017.1375416

Hahn, H. D., & Belt, T. L. (2004). Disability identity and attitudes toward cure in a sample of disabled activists. *Journal of Health and Social Behavior, 45*(4), 453–464. https://doi.org/10.1177/002214650404500407

Halmøy, A., Fasmer, O. B., Gillberg, C., & Haavik, J. (2009). Occupational outcome in adult ADHD: impact of symptom profile, comorbid psychiatric problems, and treatment: A cross-sectional study of 414 clinically diagnosed adult ADHD patients. *Journal of Attention Disorders, 13*(2), 175–187. https://doi.org/10.1177/1087054708329777

Hendricks, D. (2010). Employment and adults with autism spectrum disorders: Challenges and strategies for success. *Journal of Vocational Rehabilitation, 32*(2), 125–134. https://doi.org/10.3233/jvr-2010-0502

Hennekam, S., Richard, S., & Grima, F. (2020). Coping with mental health conditions at work and its impact on self-perceived job performance. *Employee Relations: The International Journal, 42*(3), 626–645. https://doi.org/10.1108/er-05-2019-0211

Higgins, E. L., Raskind, M. H., Goldberg, R. J., & Herman, K. L. (2002). Stages of acceptance of a learning disability: The impact of labeling. *Learning Disability Quarterly, 25*, 3–18.

Jans, L. H., Kaye, H. S., & Jones, E. C. (2012). Getting hired: Successfully employed people with disabilities offer advice on disclosure, interviewing, and job search. *Journal of Occupational Rehabilitation, 22*(2), 155–165. https://doi.org/10.1007/s10926-011-9336-y

Johnson, T. D., & Joshi, A. (2014). Disclosure on the spectrum: Understanding disclosure among employees on the autism spectrum. *Industrial and Organizational Psychology*, 7(2), 278–281. https://doi.org/10.1111/iops.12149

Johnson, T. D., & Joshi, A. (2016). Dark clouds or silver linings? A stigma threat perspective on the implications of an autism diagnosis for workplace well-being. *Journal of Applied Psychology, 101*(3), 430–449. https://doi.org/10.1037/apl0000058

Jones, K. P. (2017). To tell or not to tell? Examining the role of discrimination in the pregnancy disclosure process at work. *Journal of Occupational Health Psychology, 22*(2), 239–250. https://doi.org/10.1037/ocp0000030

Jones, K. P., & King, E. B. (2014). Managing concealable stigmas at work: A review and multilevel model. *Journal of Management, 40*, 1466–1494. https://doi.org/10.1177/0149206313515518

Jones, K. P., King, E. B., Gilrane, V. L., McCausland, T. C., Cortina, J. M., & Grimm, K. J. (2016). The baby bump: Managing a dynamic stigma over time. *Journal of Management, 42*(6), 1530–1556. https://doi.org/10.1177/0149206313503012

Kapp, S. K., Gillespie-Lynch, K., Sherman, L. E., & Hutman, T. (2013). Deficit, difference, or both? Autism and neurodiversity. *Developmental Psychology, 49*(1), 59–71. https://doi.org/10.1037/a0028353

King, E. B., Mohr, J. J., Peddie, C. I., Jones, K. P., & Kendra, M. (2017). Predictors of identity management: An exploratory experience-sampling study of lesbian, gay, and bisexual workers. *Journal of Management, 43*(2), 476–502. https://doi.org/10.1177/0149206314539350

Krzeminska, A., Austin, R. D., Bruyère, S. M., & Hedley, D. (2019). The advantages and challenges of neurodiversity employment in organizations. *Journal of Management & Organization, 25*(4), 453–463. https://doi.org/10.1017/jmo.2019.58

Law, C. L., Martinez, L. R., Ruggs, E. N., Hebl, M. R., & Akers, E. (2011). Transparency in the workplace: How the experiences of transsexual employees can be improved. *Journal of Vocational Behavior, 79*(3), 710–723. https://doi.org/10.1016/j.jvb.2011.03.018

Licht, B. G. (1983). Cognitive-motivational factors that contribute to the achievement of learning-disabled children. *Journal of Learning Disabilities, 16*, 483–490. https://doi.org/10.1177/002221948301600812

Logan, J. (2009). Dyslexic entrepreneurs: The incidence; their coping strategies and their business skills. *Dyslexia, 15*(4), 328–346. https://doi.org/10.1002/dys.388

Madaus, J. W. (2008). Employment self-disclosure rates and rationales of university graduates with learning disabilities. *Journal of Learning Disabilities, 41*(4), 291–299. https://doi.org/10.1177/0022219407313805

Madaus, J. W., Foley, T. E., McGuire, J. M., & Ruban, L. M. (2002). Employment self-disclosure of postsecondary graduates with learning disabilities: Rates and rationales. *Journal of Learning Disabilities, 35*(4), 364–369. https://doi.org/10.1177/00222194020350040701

Markel, K. S., & Elia, B. (2016). How human resource management can best support employees with autism: Future directions for research and practice. *Journal of Business Management, 22*(1), 71–85. Retrieved from https://jbm.johogo.com/issue/2201.php

Newheiser, A.-K., & Barreto, M. (2014). Hidden costs of hiding stigma: Ironic interpersonal consequences of concealing a stigmatized identity in social interactions. *Journal of Experimental Social Psychology, 52*, 58–70. https://doi.org/10.1016/j.jesp.2014.01.002

Newheiser, A.-K., Barreto, M., & Tiemersma, J. (2017). People like me don't belong here: Identity concealment is associated with negative workplace experiences. *Journal of Social Issues, 73*, 341–358. https://doi.org/10.1111/josi.12220

Nittrouer, C. L. (2019). *Allies as intermediaries: Strategies that promote hiring people with intellectual disabilities* (Unpublished doctoral dissertation). Houston, TX: Rice University. Retrieved from https://hdl.handle.net/1911/105432

Office of Federal Contract Compliance Programs. (2020). *Voluntary self-identification of disability* (Form CC-305, OMB Control Number 1250–0005). Retrieved from www.dol.gov/agencies/ofccp/self-id-forms

Organisation for Economic Co-operation and Development (OECD). (2021). *Employment rate (indicator)*. Retrieved from https://doi.org/10.1787/1de68a9b-en

Pachankis, J. E. (2007). The psychological implications of concealing a stigma: A cognitive-affective-behavioral model. *Psychological Bulletin, 133*, 328–345. https://doi.org/10.1037/0033-2909.133.2.328

Pahwa, R., Fulginiti, A., Brekke, J. S., & Rice, E. (2017). Mental illness disclosure decision making. *American Journal of Orthopsychiatry, 87*(5), 575–584. https://doi.org/10.1037/ort0000250

Patton, E. (2009). When diagnosis does not always mean disability: The challenge of employees with attention deficit hyperactivity disorder (ADHD). *Journal of Workplace Behavioral Health, 24*(3), 326–343. https://doi.org/10.1080/15555240903176161

Petronio, S. (1991). Communication boundary management: A theoretical model of managing disclosure of private information between marital couples. *Communication Theory, 1*(4), 311–335. https://doi.org/10.1111/j.1468-2885.1991.tb00023.x

Petronio, S. (2013). Brief status report on communication privacy management theory. *Journal of Family Communication, 13*(1), 6–14.

Quinn, D. M. (2006). Concealable versus conspicuous stigmatized identities. In S. Levin & C. van Laar (Eds.), *Stigma and group inequality: Social psychological perspectives* (pp. 83–104). Mahwah, NJ: Lawrence Erlbaum Associates.

Quinn, D. M., & Chaudoir, S. R. (2009). Living with a concealable stigmatized identity: The impact of anticipated stigma, centrality, salience, and cultural stigma on psychological distress and health. *Journal of Personality and Social Psychology, 97*, 634–651. https://doi.org/10.1037/a0015815

Ragins, B. R. (2008). Disclosure disconnects: Antecedents and consequences of disclosing invisible stigmas across life domains. *Academy of Management Review, 33*(1), 194–215. https://doi.org/10.5465/amr.2008.27752724

Ragins, B. R., Singh, R., & Cornwell, J. M. (2007). Making the invisible visible: Fear and disclosure of sexual orientation at work. *Journal of Applied Psychology, 92*(4), 1103–1118. https://doi.org/10.1037/0021-9010.92.4.1103

Riley, G. A., & Hagger, B. F. (2015). Disclosure of a stigmatized identity: A qualitative study of the reasons why people choose to tell or not tell others about their traumatic brain injury. *Brain Injury, 29*(12), 1480–1489. https://doi.org/10.3109/02699052.2015.1071427

Roberts, L. L., & Macan, T. H. (2006). Disability disclosure effects on employment interview ratings of applicants with nonvisible disabilities. *Rehabilitation Psychology, 51*(3), 239–246. https://doi.org/10.1037/0090-5550.51.3.239

Roux, A. M., Shattuck, P. T., Rast, J. E., Anderson, K. A. (2017). *National autism indicators report: Developmental disability services and outcomes in adulthood*. Philadelphia, PA: Life Course Outcomes Research Program, A.J. Drexel Autism Institute, Drexel University. Retrieved from https://drexel.edu/autismoutcomes/publications-and-reports/publications/National-Autism-Indicators-Report-Developmental-Disability-Services-and-Outcomes-in-Adulthood/

Samosh, D. (2020). The three-legged stool: Synthesizing and extending our understanding of the career advancement facilitators of persons with disabilities in leadership positions. *Business & Society*. https://doi.org/10.1177/0007650320907134

Santuzzi, A. M., & Cook, L. (2020). Disability stereotypes. Chapter to appear. In J. Nadler & E. Voyles (Eds.), *Stereotypes: The thinking person's guide to today's reality in the U.S.* (pp. 243–263). Santa Barbara, CA: Praeger Publishing.

Santuzzi, A. M., & Waltz, P. R. (2016). Disability in the workplace: A unique and variable identity. *Journal of Management, 42*(5), 1111–1135. https://doi.org/10.1177/0149206315626269

Santuzzi, A. M., Keating, R. T., & Martinez, J. M. (2020, June). Response options affect psychological reactions and disability disclosure rates. In D. Samosh, B. J. Lyons, & D. C. Baldridge (Chairs), *Contemporary barriers to the recruitment and inclusion of persons with disabilities*. Alternative session conducted at the 35th Annual Conference of the Society for Industrial Organizational Psychology, Virtual.

Santuzzi, A. M., Keating, R., Martinez, J., Finkelstein, L., Rupp, D., & Strah, N. (2019). Uncovering antecedents and consequences of identity management strategies for workers with concealable disabilities. *Journal of Social Issues, 75*(3), 847–880. https://doi.org/10.1111/josi.12320

Santuzzi, A. M., Martinez, J. M., & Keating, R. T. (2021). *The benefits of inclusion for disability measurement in the workplace*. Advance online publication. https://doi.org/10.1108/EDI-06-2020-0167

Santuzzi, A. M., Waltz, P. R., Finkelstein, L. M., & Rupp, D. E. (2014). Invisible disabilities: Unique challenges for employees and organizations. *Industrial and Organizational Psychology*, 7(2), 204–219. https://doi.org/10.1111/iops.12134

Sarrett, J. (2017). Interviews, disclosures, and misperceptions: Autistic adults' perspectives on employment related challenges. *Disability Studies Quarterly, 37*(2). https://doi.org/10.18061/dsq.v37i2.5524

Schmitt, M. T., Branscombe, N. R., Postmes, T., & Garcia, A. (2014). The consequences of perceived discrimination for psychological well-being: A meta-analytic review. *Psychological Bulletin, 140*(4), 921–948. https://doi.org/10.1037/a0035754

Seltzer, M. M., Krauss, M. W., Shattuck, P. T., Orsmond, G., Swe, A., & Lord, C. (2003). The symptoms of autism spectrum disorders in adolescence and adulthood. *Journal of Autism and Developmental Disorders, 33*(6), 565–581. https://doi.org/10.1023/b:jadd.0000005995.02453.0b

Shattuck, P. T., Narendorf, S. C., Cooper, B., Sterzing, P. R., Wagner, M., & Taylor, J. L. (2012). Postsecondary education and employment among youth with an autism spectrum disorder. *Pediatrics, 129*(6), 1042–1049. https://doi.org/10.1542/peds.2011-2864

Shore, L. M., Randel, A. E., Chung, B. G., Dean, M. A., Holcombe Ehrhart, K., & Singh, G. (2011). Inclusion and diversity in work groups: A review and model for future research. *Journal of Management, 37*(4), 1262–1289. https://doi.org/10.1177/0149206310385943

Singer, J. (1999). "Why can't you be normal for once in your life?" From a problem with no name to the emergence of a new category of difference. In M. Corker & S. French (Eds.), *Disability discourse* (pp. 59–67). Buckingham: Open University Press.

Smart, L., & Wegner, D. M. (1999). Covering up what can't be seen: Concealable stigma and mental control. *Journal of Personality and Social Psychology*, *77*, 474–486. https://doi.org/10.1037/0022-3514.77.3.474

Spirito Dalgin, R., & Bellini, J. (2008). Invisible disability disclosure in an employment interview: Impact on employers' hiring decisions and views of employability. *Rehabilitation Counseling Bulletin*, *52*(1), 6–15. https://doi.org/10.1177/0034355207311311

Stutterheim, S. E., Brands, R., Baas, I., Lechner, L., Kok, G., & Bos, A. E. R. (2017). HIV status disclosure in the workplace: Positive and stigmatizing experiences of health care workers living with HIV. *Journal of the Association of Nurses in AIDS Care*, *28*(6), 923–937. https://doi.org/10.1016/j.jana.2017.06.014

Swann, W. B., Jr. (2012). Self-verification theory. In P. A. M. Van Lange, A. W. Kruglanski, & E. T. Higgins (Eds.), *Handbook of theories of social psychology* (p. 23–42). Thousand Oaks, CA: SAGE.

Van Laar, C., Meeussen, L., Veldman, J., Van Grootel, S., Sterk, N., & Jacobs, C. (2019). Coping with stigma in the workplace: Understanding the role of threat regulation, supportive factors, and potential hidden costs. *Frontiers in Psychology*, *10*. https://doi.org/10.3389/fpsyg.2019.01879

von Schrader, S., Malzer, V., & Bruyère, S. (2014). Perspectives on disability disclosure: The importance of employer practices and workplace climate. *Employee Responsibilities and Rights Journal*, *26*, 237–255. https://doi.org/10.1007/s10672-013-9227-9

Wadlington, E. M., Wadlington, P. L., & Rupp, D. E. (2006). Teachers with dyslexia and dyscalculia: Effects on life. *Academic Exchange Quarterly*, *10*, 110–123. Retrieved from https://www3.psych.purdue.edu/reprints/index.php?page=request_article&site_id=27&article_id=1720

6

DO TRADITIONAL LEADERSHIP THEORIES WORK IN A NEURODIVERSE CONTEXT?

Stephanie R. Seitz

Leadership is an interpersonal process "whereby intentional influence is exerted by one person over other people to guide, structure, and facilitate activities and relationships in a group or organization" (Yukl, 2006, p. 8). It is a topic that has been studied robustly in the organizational sciences, with research encompassing a focus not only on the leader but on the entire leadership relationship, including followers, peers, context/environment, and culture (for a review, see Avolio et al., 2009). However, although leaders are leading increasingly diverse sets of employees, research on appropriately managing diversity is in relative infancy (see, for example, Chrobot-Mason & Ruderman, 2004; Kirton & Greene, 2015). Additionally, scholars have noted that the term "diversity" often excludes disability, even though it is considered a core dimension of diversity in organizations (McLaughlin et al., 2004; Shore et al., 2009).

Early leadership research rested on the assumption that followers were sufficiently homogenous to be considered as one and that leaders treated them, on average, in about the same manner (Dansereau et al., 1975). Leadership research has certainly grown from this primitive view, recognizing followers as individuals with varying relationships with leaders (e.g., Dansereau et al., 1995). However, even this more modern perspective assumes that followers generally have a neurotypical baseline. As the demographics of the modern workforce change, including increased neurodiversity, and organizations strive to comply with accommodations required of the Americans with Disabilities Act, such an assumption is increasingly flawed. Various conditions falling under the umbrella of neurological atypicality are defined as disability, and those with such conditions often seek and obtain employment, just like their neurotypical counterparts.

The assumption that traditional theories work for all is inaccurate, and it stems from a foundation of "abled" organizations (Morgan, 1986), an idea that runs

DOI: 10.4324/9781003023616-6

parallel to a more familiar term of "gendered" organizations (e.g., Acker, 1990; Martin & Collinson, 2002; Williams et al., 2012) as well as the racial foundations (or "whiteness") of organizations (Ashcraft & Allen, 2003). The crux of these ideas is that traditional theories and notions of organizations often have at their core the default worker, who is male, white, and abled. Theory and research drawn from this default are necessarily flawed. Additionally, this "ideology is predicated on the assumption that organizations are neutral work environments in which the same rules applied to everyone will yield equitable rewards of pay, prestige, and upward mobility" (Harlan & Robert, 1998, p. 398). In challenging the idea of the neutral organizations, scholars have argued that elements of diversity must not simply be treated as individual characteristics but as integral elements of organizational culture (Harlan & Robert, 1998). In order to do this, organizational paradigms must shift drastically. It can be radical to question whether long-standing and well-respected theories apply in changing contexts, but it can open the door to new understanding (see, for example, Hofstede, 1980).

Scholars and practitioners alike are discovering that diversity alone does not bring automatic benefits, but rather it is the proper management of diversity, including focus on retention and promotion of individuals from underrepresented groups, that reaps organizational rewards (Cook & Glass, 2014; Giscombe & Mattis, 2002; Hom et al., 2008). In terms of neurodiversity, research has already uncovered common organizational practices and theories that tend to apply differently and/or detrimentally to those who are not neurotypical. For example, traditional selection practices may be ineffective at selecting appropriate candidates. Neurodivergent candidates who may perform well on the job often don't do well in traditional interviews specifically because of differences in social interactions from neurotypical peers (Sarrett, 2017). Additionally, personality tests and other selection tools may have adverse impact when applied to neurodivergent candidates (Risavy & Hausdorf, 2011; see also Saleh, Chang, Bruyère, & Vogus, in this volume). Assessment tools may also be flawed when applied to neurodivergent employees (see, for example, Hunter & Hunter, in this volume). For example, employees with learning disabilities may have difficulty with documenting and describing their own accomplishments and work experiences, regardless of actual achievement, and would thus be at a disadvantage compared to their neurotypical counterparts (Sumner & Brown, 2015). Many organizations use some form of self-evaluation within their performance management systems, and if an employee's ability in written expression is impaired, they may be denied promotion or advancement opportunities even if they have high performance. In addition, promotability is often highly related to perceived similarity and likability, and thus subordinates who are perceived as socially different may experience discrimination (Wayne & Liden, 1995). In light of these discoveries, it is prudent to explore whether and how the leadership theories and research put forth to date are applicable to this growing sector of the workforce. This chapter will explore traditional and modern theories of leadership in the context of current knowledge about neurodiverse workers.

Importance of Leadership to Neurodiversity Initiatives

In exploring leadership application to a neurodiverse workforce, it is first important to elucidate *why* leadership is an essential element to any neurodiversity initiative. Of course, scholars and practitioners alike understand the benefits of effective leadership generally. Leadership is particularly important for diversity initiatives because of the need for accountability structures (Matton & Hernandez, 2004). Additionally, neurodivergent employees may benefit from purposeful support and guidance (Seitz & Smith, 2016).

Although research in this arena is still developing, we can look to examples of what seems to be working (or not) for organizations in practice. In their investigation of the neurodiversity initiatives of two high-tech firms, Loiacono and Ren (2018) found some commonalities in the success of these programs. First, executives at both firms stressed the cruciality of managerial support, citing managerial education and training as contributors to an environment of accommodation and appropriate support. This is in line with previous research showing that when there was a commitment from top management, hiring of employees with disabilities increased (Erickson et al., 2014). Additionally, advocacy and policy are crucial to the cultural shift needed for neurodiversity initiatives to succeed. "For high-tech companies, or any company for that matter, to truly engage with and accept those who are neurodiverse, top executives must show leadership and support for the effort" (Loiacono & Ren, 2018, p. 269).

Deutsche Bank instituted an internship program for autistic graduates, which was the focus of a qualitative study on expectations and outcomes (Remington & Pellicano, 2019). Similar to what was reported at the high tech firms described above, the interns who reported positive outcomes felt they had the support of their managers without being "mollycoddled" (p. 16). Appropriate accommodations and understanding from leadership were also key to positive experiences for interns and managers alike. In contrast, some interns who were less positive about their experiences reported that managers were unfamiliar with their condition and didn't know how to support them.

Van den Bosch and colleagues (2019) described an exploratory qualitative study of a Dutch organization run by and for individuals on the autism spectrum. They concluded that one of the most important elements of the success of that organization was ensuring that those on the spectrum were put at the center of the decision-making process so that solutions were geared toward improving their own outcomes. The research also uncovered the importance of visibility and "being seen as a full adult" (p. 13); recognition of the diversity within the autism spectrum; and acknowledgement that those on the autism spectrum are just as capable of responsibility and leadership positions as those who are not.

The lesson that may be gleaned from this initial research is that effective leadership in neurodiverse organizations is essential and must be purposeful. Employees who are neurodivergent can thrive and greatly contribute when given the appropriate opportunities to do so. Although it may sound simple, evidence shows that managers may struggle in the face of a neurodiverse environment, especially with the insufficient HRM specialist support and/or resources typically found in managerial positions (Gibb, 2003; Mcguire et al., 2008). For example, Richards et al. (2019) found that line managers engaged in a great deal of emotional labor when managing neurodiverse employees. Many managers reported a dearth of information on the conditions falling under the neurodiversity umbrella, having received most of their information from neurodivergent employees themselves. They also reported having to engage in greater-than-average levels of interaction with neurodivergent employees as compared with neurotypical employees, and many characterized their experiences managing neurodivergent employees as "a time consuming and highly distracting commitment" (Richards et al., 2019, p. 24). It is worth noting that not all managers described their experiences as negative – in fact, some managers reported high degrees of satisfaction, and the authors noted that this occurred often "because the line manager drew on skill-sets unrelated to the wider management role" (p. 26). Although this research is just emerging, it is possible that issues with managing and leading a neurodiverse workforce arise due to old tools being used for new situations.

Application of Leadership Theories to Neurodiversity

In order to address the issue of leadership in neurodiverse contexts, we must examine leadership theory to understand whether what works *generally* will work *specifically* for neurodivergent employees. Dansereau and colleagues (2013) theorized that although the multitudes of leadership theories and styles have often been developed separately from one another, resulting in a rather siloed field, there may be a common thread to their effectiveness. They used self-expansion theory (Aron et al., 1991) to propose that leadership generally works when a relationship is formed between leader and follower that allows the follower to expand the "self" to include the leader and the leader's resources. Self-expansion is characterized as a fundamental human process, the foundation of which is the basic human motivation to self-expand and seek close relationships in order to increase the "physical and social resources, perspectives, and identities that facilitate achievement of any goal that might arise" (Aron et al., 2001, p. 478). Close relationships involve an expansion of the self because, in such a relationship, the other's experiences, perspectives, and identities are, to a certain extent, experienced as one's own (Aron et al., 2013). It is a process wherein "our cognitive construction of the other overlaps with (or shares activation potentials with) our cognitive construction of the self" (Aron et al., 2013, p. 102).

The process begins with a comparison of the current self to a potential future self that includes the leader (and the resources that accompany the leader). If the follower recognizes that the potential future self is an improvement on the current self, there will be motivation to self-expand with the leader (Aron et al., 2001; Dansereau et al., 2013). The expanded self results in an overlapping of resources – the follower has access to their own resources plus those of the leader. Both leader and follower are motivated to protect their own resources as well as the other's, and they will thus resist deexpansion (Aron & Aron, 2000).

The first question, then, to address is as follows: Is self-expansion universal, even for neurodivergent employees? If neurodivergent employees have goals and recognize the resources needed to accomplish those goals, the answer would be yes. We must take this in the context of the neurodiversity movement, which stipulates that neurodivergent individuals are an example of normal human variation (Jaarsma & Welin, 2012) and that neurodivergent individuals may approach problems differently and have different strengths and weaknesses compared to what is considered "typical." Thus, fundamental human processes such as self-expansion still apply in neurodiverse contexts, but the way self-expansion functions for neurodivergent employees or manifests within their relationships may be something that differentiates them from their neurotypical counterparts. I do not attempt here to delve into the specific ways that these manifestations may differ, with the acknowledgment that "neurodiversity" itself is a term that may include a wide range of conditions, including, for example, autism, nonverbal learning disorders, ADD/ADHD, and learning and mood disorders (Johnston-Tyler & Analla, 2015). What the next sections will explore, however, involves how different goals and resource needs may influence the self-expansion process for neurodivergent employees, and may thus shift how the leadership process evolves, as well as how leadership may be expanded to include the needs of a neurodiverse workforce.

Leadership theories can be organized into several different categories, based on the type of approach used. Dansereau et al. (2013) adapted a category structure for leadership theories based on groupings developed by Dansereau and Yammarino (1998a, 1998b) and Dansereau et al. (1995), and these categories are used here for ease of presentation. The categories and example theories within them will not provide an exhaustive list of all possible leadership theories, but they may be considered representative of the majority of leadership theories present in the extant literature.

Group-Oriented Leadership

Group-oriented leadership includes approaches that are either targeted at a group (rather than individuals) or arise within a group. These leadership approaches allow for self-expansion because engaging in these types of leadership activities helps to enhance group identity, and thus followers within the group may self-expand with the group and/or the leader (Dansereau et al., 2013). Examples of group-oriented leadership include initiating structure and shared leadership.

The concept of initiating structure arose from the Ohio State Leadership Studies, which strove to discover which leadership behaviors made for effective leadership (Stogdill, 1950). Its basic premise is that effective leadership depends on a leader shaping and organizing work goals, offering clear communication channels, and being goal oriented (Fleishman, 1973). Dansereau et al. (2013) theorized that followers self-expand in response to initiating structure primarily because of the heightened opportunity to achieve team goals, therefore developing a stronger identity with the group. Group identity indicates a baseline awareness of group membership, and the stronger the group identity, the more likely individuals in the group include other group members (including the group leader) into the self.

One of the issues neurodivergent employees may face with a leader engaging in initiating structure behaviors is if they are not treated as individuals and recognized for their unique potential contributions and needs. Previous research has shown that employees with autism, for example, benefit from clear instructions and individual support (Seitz & Smith, 2016), which may or may not be provided by a leader engaging in initiating structure behaviors. This is where another set of behaviors identified by the Ohio State Leadership Studies would be considered essential. Consideration describes the extent to which a "leader shows concern and respect for followers, looks out for their welfare, and expresses appreciation and support" (Judge et al., 2004, p. 36). If initiating structure and consideration are both present in the ensemble of a leader's behaviors, the benefits of team goal orientation and the individual attention that a neurodivergent employee may need would likely combine to allow for self-expansion. For neurotypical employees, initiating structure alone could be enough, if not ideal, for achieving goals. However, for neurodiverse groups, it is likely that a leader must provide both initiating structure and consideration.

Shared leadership also falls under the umbrella of group-oriented leadership and describes the extent to which leadership is shared among group members rather than being centered on one leader (Carson et al., 2007). The process by which shared leadership occurs often relies on the different tasks and goals a group must complete, with leadership aligned by the specific expertise and knowledge of the group members (Carson et al., 2007). Group members self-expand because as they share knowledge and experience in their particular leadership roles, they are providing resources to the rest of the group. Thus, self-expansion occurs with other individual group members as well as the group itself (Dansereau et al., 2013).

One of the major issues that neurodivergent workers report is that they often have misunderstandings with their colleagues, especially regarding displayed emotions, and especially in team meeting contexts (Morris et al., 2015). Additionally, in the case of autistic workers, due to stereotyping of the condition, employees' competency and skills may be doubted by coworkers and leaders (Whelpley et al., 2020). This presents a problem in a shared leadership context, where neurodivergent group members may have to rely on others to accept them as potential leaders and value their contributions. One of the boundary conditions of self-expansion in shared leadership theorized by Dansereau et al. (2013) is the distribution of task competence. In extending this idea, the perception of competence may also act as a boundary condition. In order for shared leadership to be effective in a neurodiverse workgroup, all members of the group must be educated on neurodiversity and understand the value of the neurodivergent group member (in particular with appropriate accommodations; Seitz & Smith, 2016).

Development-Based Leadership

Development-based leadership approaches are characterized by helping and encouraging followers to achieve goals and engage in self-development. "This category of traditional leadership approaches generally provides followers with a guided autonomy, where they are nudged along a path but are given the resources and responsibilities to achieve goals on their own" (Dansereau et al., 2013, p. 806). This generally promotes self-expansion because followers are offered appropriate resources to achieve mutually beneficial goals, so there is motivation to include the leader's resources in the self.

One of the most well-known leadership theories falling under the development-based leadership umbrella is path-goal theory, which describes motivating followers through incentives for goal achievement as well as aiding followers along the path to goal achievement by removing barriers and obstacles along the way (House, 1971). Characteristic of this approach is the shaping of leader behavior based on three factors: the follower, the task, and the situation. Leaders who are effective with the path-goal approach thus ideally tailor the resources they provide (House, 1971). Self-expansion occurs as a result of this leadership approach when followers recognize a shared purpose between themselves and their leader and that the leader is providing very specific resources related to the follower's needs.

Research on employees with autism shows that when leaders have appropriate knowledge and education and offer suitable accommodation, it can lead to more positive and successful employment experiences (Seitz & Smith, 2016). Additionally, employees with learning disabilities are better equipped to succeed with appropriate accommodations from their organizations and managers (Gerber & Price, 2003). These findings suggest that at least for some neurodivergent employees, a leader who understands their particular needs in relation to the task at hand and the context in which they're working (as with the path-goal approach) will promote the self-expansion process.

Individual-Based Leadership

Some leadership theories rely on the assumption that leaders use the same or similar leadership behaviors across all followers; however, individual-based leadership approaches assume that leaders do not lead uniformly (Dansereau et al., 2013). Leaders who use individual-based leadership approaches view and treat their followers as individuals (or are at least perceived to do so), and this allows for self-expansion because followers feel that they are valued and that they have a shared purpose with their leader.

One of the first leadership theories to resist the "average" leadership assumption was vertical-dyad linkage (VDL), and it focuses on the individual exchange relationships between leaders and followers (Dansereau, 1995). VDL theory "describes the process by which a leader and a member develop various behavioral interdependencies between their respective roles" (Graen & Schiemann, 1978, p. 206). VDL theory was the foundation for other leadership theories such as leader–member exchange (LMX) and individualized leadership, both of which focus on the relationship between leader and follower. LMX measures the quality of the relationship between leader and follower, in particular, mutual trust, respect and commitment (Liden & Maslyn, 1998). Similarly, individualized leadership describes an approach in which the leader shapes his or her leadership style based on the skills and needs of each individual follower, and relationships are formed between leader and follower independent of the leader's relationships with other followers (Dansereau et al., 1995).

Given that neurodiversity is defined by the variation from neurotypical, individual-based leadership approaches likely provide the space for leaders to provide neurodivergent employees unique resources as well as development opportunities based on their skills and abilities. However, Dansereau and colleagues theorized that the boundary conditions of these individual-based leadership approaches may involve (among other factors) interpersonal potential. For example, compatibility between leader and follower (Duchon et al., 1986; Tsui & O'Reilly, 1989) and the social effectiveness of the follower (political skill; Brouer et al., 2009; Harris et al., 2009) may limit the development of self-expansion. This is relevant for leadership of neurodivergent employees because some of the conditions under the neurodiversity umbrella, such as autism, ADHD, and mood disorders, may impede interpersonal relationships. It is careful understanding of these conditions and the unique ways they manifest for each individual employee that is crucial to developing productive leadership relationships (see, for example, Seitz & Smith, 2016). Without resources and training for the leaders themselves, this can lead to emotional labor and negative outcomes (Richards et al., 2019). Maintaining high-quality relationships with neurodivergent employees likely requires even more than the basic formulas for individual-based leadership, such as trust, respect, and commitment. These relational elements in neurodiverse contexts may act as a minimal baseline, with additional requirements of care, understanding, and flexibility, especially for employees who deviate from social norms due to their neurodivergence.

Vision-Based Leadership

Vision-based leadership approaches rely on the ability of the leader to tap into followers' sense of a big picture and overarching shared goal. The ability to present a clear picture of a vision allows followers to develop and adjust to work toward shared goals, which promotes self-expansion (Dansereau et al., 2013). The two theories most closely associated with this category are charismatic leadership and transformational leadership.

Transformational leadership is characterized by a leader effectively communicating a vision to followers and then empowering followers to reach shared goals associated with that vision (Bass, 1985). Four behavioral elements comprise transformational leadership: individualized consideration, idealized influence, inspirational motivation, and intellectual stimulation (Bass, 1985). "Inspirational leadership would include persuading followers to adopt shared goals; intellectual stimulation provides followers with the path to solve problems in new ways; individualized consideration takes into account the individual needs of the follower in achieving these shared goals" (Dansereau et al., 2013, p. 812). Each of these behavioral elements likely promotes self-expansion because the leader provides the motivation and tools for followers to succeed.

The effectiveness of transformational leadership to trigger self-expansion in neurodivergent followers likely depends a great deal on the individual-consideration behavioral element. Support and guidance that neurodivergent employees receive is most effective when it is specifically tailored to the needs of particular individuals – it is important to recognize that neurodivergent employees are not a singular block of similarities, and their conditions vary in type, manifestations, and level (Bewley & George, 2016). Thus, the other behavioral elements of transformational leadership would be bolstered by careful individual consideration and could be ineffective without it (see, for example, Seitz & Owens, 2020). For example, autistic employees in particular may struggle with leaders who enact transformational leadership behaviors by using abstract communication such as metaphors (Parr et al., 2013). Leaders who engage in individualized consideration may be better equipped to develop and manage relationships with employees who have difficulty going along with the traditional employee "script," such as some employees with ASD, because it would involve acknowledgment and familiarity with individual employee characteristics, skills, strengths, and needs.

Charismatic leadership is similar to transformational leadership in that both are associated with the effective communication of an overarching vision; charismatic leaders are characteristically able to "sell" a vision through the force of their ability to be charismatic (House & Baetz, 1979). This allows for self-expansion in followers because they buy into not only the vision but the leader as well (Dansereau et al., 2013). Charisma on its own is not something that has emerged in the neurodiversity literature as an especially effective technique for neurodivergent employees. This may be because the themes that the neurodiversity literature has produced are follower focused. The "magic" of a leader may be less important for neurodivergent workers than the leader's ability to support the needs of the follower. Although overarching goals and a clear vision may be helpful for workers, research is clear that this may be important but not sufficient for a neurodiverse workforce.

Outcome-Based Leadership

Outcome-based leadership approaches focus on task and goal completion (i.e., outcomes), with leaders providing followers the tools and resources needed for desired outcomes. Followers self-expand because leaders allow them to have small-scale, daily success with minimal effort, and they can then use their "saved" effort to grow and develop in other areas (Dansereau et al., 2013). Two prime examples of outcome-based leadership are transactional and pragmatic approaches.

Transactional and pragmatic leadership are actually quite similar in that both rely on the exchange relationship between leaders and followers. Transactional leadership, in particular, describes a relationship in which "both the leader and follower reach an agreement concerning what the follower will receive for achieving the negotiated level of performance. Rewards are then provided consistent with satisfactory completion of the agreement" (Howell & Avolio, 1993, p. 892). Pragmatic leadership theory goes just a bit further, describing leadership that is transactional and also takes into account the opportunities, threats, and realities of the situation in which the leader and follower are operating (Mumford et al., 2008).

For neurodivergent followers, outcome-based leadership approaches are what might be considered the bare minimum for their ensured success (this may, in fact, be the case for neurotypical employees as well). Seitz and Smith (2016), for example, found that autistic employees benefited from clear instructions and expectations while being allowed the space and time to complete tasks. Similarly, Mellifont (2019) found that personalized support improved long-term employment outcomes for neurodiverse employees. As with any other population of employees, personalized support is not the *only* criterion for leadership of neurodivergent employees; it is simply a starting point.

Other Contemporary Leadership Theories

Dansereau et al. (2013) include two other categories that they situate in a more contemporary leadership context: organizational leadership and nonleadership. Both of these categories represent a divergence from the more traditional theories of leadership in that they describe situations in which there is either no primary leadership figure (i.e., the organization or agent(s) of the organization act as leader) or where the follower is expected to self-lead in the absence of a leader or leadership behaviors. Followers may self-expand if they believe a leader and an organization are one in the same because the leader is perceived to have all the resources of the organization – this theoretical basis is formed from the romance of leadership theory, which, in contrast to the leadership theories previously discussed, is not about leadership behaviors, but rather the attributional process within followers (Meindl & Ehrlich, 1987). In the case of non-leadership, such as a laissez-faire style, followers may self-expand because of the autonomy they are given to be creative and self-develop in their work.

Both of these more contemporary categories of leadership may hinder or help the self-expansion process in neurodivergent workers, likely depending on many factors. First, organizational leadership generally, and the romance of leadership specifically, is about whether followers attribute the representation of the organization to a leader. While this *can* be cause for self-expansion, followers will likely only self-expand if the leader/organization represents a true resource for them. For neurodivergent followers, this would mean that the leader/organization is providing appropriate support and accommodations. Nonleadership, such as laissez-faire, may not give all neurodivergent employees what they need to succeed – this is also highly dependent on other contextual factors and the individual followers themselves. Employees with certain conditions that fall under the umbrella of neurodiversity, such as mood or learning disorders, may appreciate the freedom of nonleadership as a resource, as they could be free to work creatively in ways that best suit their needs, only using the leader as a "safety net" of sorts (Dansereau et al., 2013). Employees with other conditions such as autism may prefer or even need direct instruction and direction (Seitz & Smith, 2016).

Putting Leadership into Practice for Neurodiversity

In light of these considerations for how traditional leadership theories may operate for a neurodiverse workforce, I now turn to the more practical question of how, then, can the concept of leadership be expanded (or focused) so it works for all employees. The aspects of leadership that consistently stand out as essential to neurodivergent employees include individualization, accommodation, and support. The good news is that these are also leadership qualities that work for neurotypical employees. In order to put these qualities into practice in an effective way, we can look to other streams of research, such as disability and inclusion, and incorporate those findings as well.

In order to engage in the kind of leadership that is tailored and individualized for neurodivergent employees, it is important to understand how generalizations about disability can hinder the leadership process. Colella and Bruyère (2011) provided a synthesis of disability literature, explaining a number of reasons, based on psychological theories, for the biased treatment of people with disabilities. One such reason is stereotyping, and leaders who engage in stereotyping are, by definition, excluding the individual from the equation. Stereotypes are "shared beliefs about person attributes, usually personality traits, but often also behaviors, of a group of people" (Leyens et al., 1994, p. 11). When leaders are inexperienced with employees who have disabilities, they may rely on their own stereotypes to assess them, based on their group membership (disabled) rather than their individual qualities or behaviors (Kaye et al., 2011). This can lead to ratings of poor performance, poor attendance, and the perception of unease amongst coworkers (Nelissen et al., 2016).

Stereotypes about neurodiverse workers vary as widely as the conditions included in the definition of neurodiversity, from the belief that a person with autism is a "talented nerd lacking social graces" (Bury et al., 2019, p. 1607) to the stereotype that those with mood disorders are unable to make competent decisions or are dangerous to themselves or others (Lazowski et al., 2012). Although the definition of a stereotype is neither positive nor negative, the use of stereotypes can be damaging to those seeking individualized resources for their growth and development. Bury and colleagues (2019) described the problem with focusing on stereotypical traits of an autistic employee while ignoring that employee's preferences and desires:

> Let us return to composite John. With only two RRBI criteria required for diagnosis, John might not prefer repetitive work tasks, instead preferring to be challenged, to have variety in his work and to use his imagination. Invoking a stereotype that he is predisposed to enjoy repetitive work that others find monotonous could effectively sabotage his job satisfaction while undermining his strengths and potential contribution.
>
> (p. 1608)

Intergroup contact theory provides a framework for how leaders may reduce their bias and stereotyping of neurodivergent employees in order to provide individual resources and support. The theory asserts that, in general, personal contact with negatively stereotyped individuals reduces prejudice and improves attitudes (Allport, 1954). Of course, not all contact is positive, so there are certain conditions that provide for the ideal context in which to improve attitudes (Novak et al., 2011). First, there should be sufficient opportunities for personal interaction that go beyond surface level. Second, the interactions should allow for disconfirmation of stereotypes held about group membership. Third, the situation should be one in which those interacting should be perceived as equal status to one another. Fourth, the relationships between those interacting should be interdependent. Finally, there should be support from the organization or those in positions of authority for intergroup acceptance (Novak et al., 2011). What is most relevant to leading for neurodiversity is allowing for employees to be individuals rather than being defined by their disability. Thus, in line with intergroup contact theory, personal contact between leader and follower that is meaningful, respectful, and cooperative within an environment of inclusion sets the foundation for effective leadership.

As is evident from much of leadership thought as described earlier, leadership certainly does not happen in a vacuum. Theories such as pragmatic and situational leadership explicitly include the idea that leaders must focus on more than just their followers but also lead within an organizational (or industry or societal, etc.) context. This is where we can draw from disability literature again and highlight the importance of organizational culture and climate, which leaders often have a hand in shaping, for neurodivergent workers. Indeed, the highest level of leadership in an organization sets the tone for the organizational culture, and middle-/lower-level managers and leaders are the front lines of enacting that cultural tone; support from top management teams for diversity initiatives positively contributes to hiring people with disabilities (Erickson et al., 2014). Research has found that when supervisors and subordinates differ on disability status, there is a negative impact on LMX; this negative relationship, however, can be ameliorated by an organizational climate of inclusion (Dwertmann & Boehm, 2016). Additionally, a metasynthesis of qualitative research on the experiences of people with disabilities in the workplace revealed that, by and large, physical accommodations represent the absolute bare minimum for accessibility, and organizational culture in terms of acceptance and flexibility are crucial for success (Gewurtz & Kirsh, 2009). These findings are likely especially important for neurodiversity, as it can often be considered an invisible disability. If leaders are unable to individualize leadership via personal contact with followers and foster inclusive climates, they may never even learn of a disability at all, as neurodivergent employees often perceive barriers to disclosure in large part due to fear of noninclusive culture and practices (Santuzzi et al., 2014; Von Schrader et al., 2014). The role that leadership plays in this process is thus essential.

The disability literature points to a couple of practical strategies for ensuring a culture or climate of inclusion, which leaders may put into practice for a neurodiverse workforce. Each of the following strategies echoes the importance discussed of individualized forms of leadership appropriate to the strengths and preferences of neurodivergent employees. First, it is important to understand the extent to which disabled employees feel integrated into their workplace, which may be done through an assessment of integration (Wehman, 2003). Second, diversity training may be implemented by leaders (and, in particular, for leaders) that focuses on disability and, as is relevant to this chapter, neurodiversity (Phillips et al., 2016).

Future Research Directions

Although disability literature builds a foundation for understanding how to lead for neurodiversity, it really only scratches the surface. As Nota and colleagues (2014) found, employer attitudes can vary greatly depending on the type of disability that is presented. The most negative attitudes tended to be toward mental disabilities when compared with intellectual and sensory disabilities. There are other factors that may make neurodiversity a unique set of conditions that distinguish it from other types of disabilities. Often, disability is considered a surface-level difference (e.g., Ivancevich & Gilbert, 2000). In some cases, neurodiversity may be somewhat observable, but this depends on the type of condition and its severity. Many neurodivergent employees have what may be considered invisible disabilities, which includes "a wide range of physical and psychological conditions that often have no visible manifestation or have visible features that are not clearly connected to a disability" (Santuzzi et al., 2014, p. 204). Additionally, the definition of disability is extraordinarily broad, and it includes both medical diagnoses and social construction. That is, according to the Americans with Disabilities Act, employees may be considered disabled if they have an actual medical disability that substantially limits a major life activity *or* if they are simply regarded as having a disability (ADA, 1990). Future research must thus use general disability research as a beginning point for more specific research on neurodiversity and leadership.

Future research may also go beyond inclusion and integration for neurodivergent employees. These are, of course, essential but not sufficient. The greatest benefit of effective leadership for neurodiversity will likely come from recognizing and celebrating difference rather than assimilation. After all, proponents of neurodiversity assert that the neurological differences characteristic of neurodiversity should be considered as natural human variation; neurodiversity does not represent diseases that need to be cured but rather different ways of perceiving and reacting to the world (Austin & Pisano, 2017). A deeper understanding of how neurodivergent employees can contribute to organizations because of (rather than in spite of) their neurological differences will be crucial for leaders and organizations to harness their value.

A last consideration for scholars to consider is that, to date, virtually all literature centered on leadership and neurodiversity assumes that neurodivergent employees are subordinates. While neurotypical practitioners have the benefit of scholarship on the experience of leaders, that is not the case for those who are neurodivergent. The bias that research has found within organizations relating to the assumption that disabled employees are suited only for certain jobs (Nota et al., 2014) seems to have seeped into the research itself, and we have not yet considered that neurodivergent leaders exist and may have different processes, outcomes, and experiences. A case study conducted by Van den Bosch et al. (2019) is one exception, providing details on a Dutch organization run by and for people on the autism spectrum. Future research should build on this, exploring these experiences in greater depth as well as providing the kind of generalizability larger-scale projects may provide.

Conclusion

Leadership is one of the most robustly studied topics in the field of management, and yet much of this literature rests on the assumption that followers are neurotypical. This chapter questioned such an assumption and provided ways that we may look at leadership differently in order to ensure that neurodiversity is taken into account. Leadership that is built on individual relationships, offers individualized support, resources, and accommodations, and values neurodivergent employees will provide benefits to those employees as well as to leaders and organizations. Neurodivergent followers can benefit greatly from a nuanced approach to leadership, and they should also be considered and cultivated themselves for leadership positions. Part of breaking down the systems of "abled" organizations involves subverting the assumptions of not only who followers are but who successful and effective leaders may be.

References

Acker, J. (1990). Hierarchies, jobs, bodies: A theory of gendered organizations. *Gender & Society*, *4*(2), 139–158.

Allport, G. W. (1954). *The nature of prejudice*. Cambridge, MA: Addison-Wesley.

Americans with Disabilities Act of 1990. (1990). Public Law No. 101–336, 104 Stat. 328.

Aron, A., & Aron, E. N. (2000). Self-expansion motivation and including other in the self. In W. Ickes, & S. Duck (Eds.), *The social psychology of personal relationships* (pp. 109–129). New York: John Wiley & Sons.

Aron, A., Aron, E. N., & Norman, C. (2001). Self expansion model of motivation and cognition in close relationships and beyond. In G. Fletcher & M. Clark (Eds.), *Blackwell handbook of social psychology: Interpersonal processes* (pp. 478–501). Malden MA: Blackwell.

Aron, A., Aron, E. N., Tudor, M., & Nelson, G. (1991). Close relationships as including other in the self. *Journal of Personality and Social Psychology*, *60*(2), 241.

Aron, A., Lewandowski, G. W., Jr., Mashek, D., & Aron, E. N. (2013). The self-expansion model of motivation and cognition in close relationships. In J. A. Simpson & L. Campbell (Eds.), *Oxford library of psychology. The Oxford handbook of close relationships* (p. 90–115). Oxford: Oxford University Press.

Ashcraft, K. L., & Allen, B. J. (2003). The racial foundation of organizational communication. *Communication Theory*, *13*(1), 5–38.

Austin, R. D., & Pisano, G. P. (2017). Neurodiversity as a competitive advantage. *Harvard Business Review*, *95*(3), 96–103.

Avolio, B. J., Walumbwa, F. O., & Weber, T. J. (2009). Leadership: Current theories, research, and future directions. *Annual Review of Psychology*, *60*, 421–449.

Bass, B. M. (1985). *Leadership and performance beyond expectations*. New York: Free Press.

Bewley, H., & George, A. (2016). *Neurodiversity at work*. London: National Institute of Social and Economic Research.

Brouer, R. L., Duke, A., Treadway, D. C., & Ferris, G. R. (2009). Moderating effect of political skill on the demographic dissimilarity – leader – member exchange quality relationship. *The Leadership Quarterly*, *20*, 61–69.

Bury, S. M., Hedley, D., Uljarević, M., Dissanayake, C., & Gal, E. (2019). If you've employed one person with autism. . .: An individual difference approach to the autism advantage at work. *Autism*, *23*(6), 1607–1608.

Carson, J. B., Tesluk, P. E., & Marrone, J. A. (2007). Shared leadership in teams: An investigation of antecedent conditions and performance. *Academy of Management Journal*, *50*, 1217–1234.

Chrobot-Mason, D., & Ruderman, M. N. (2004). Leadership in a diverse workplace. In M. S. Stockdale & F. J. Crosby (Eds.), *The psychology and management of workplace diversity* (pp. 100–121). Hoboken, NJ: Blackwell Publishing.

Colella, A., & Bruyère, S. (2011). Disability and employment: New directions for industrial and organizational psychology. In S. Zedeck (Ed.), *APA handbook of industrial and organizational psychology* (Vol. 1, pp. 473–504). Washington, DC: American Psychological Association.

Cook, A., & Glass, C. (2014). Above the glass ceiling: When are women and racial/ethnic minorities promoted to CEO? *Strategic Management Journal, 35*(7), 1080–1089.

Dansereau, F. (1995). A dyadic approach to leadership: Creating and nurturing this approach under fire. *The Leadership Quarterly, 6*, 479–490.

Dansereau, F., Graen, G., & Haga, W. J. (1975). A vertical dyad linkage approach to leadership within formal organizations: A longitudinal investigation of the role making process. *Organizational Behavior and Human Performance, 13*(1), 46–78.

Dansereau, F., Seitz, S. R., Chiu, C. Y., Shaughnessy, B., & Yammarino, F. J. (2013). What makes leadership, leadership? Using self-expansion theory to integrate traditional and contemporary approaches. *The Leadership Quarterly, 24*(6), 798–821.

Dansereau, F., & Yammarino, F. J. (1998a). *Leadership: The multiple-level approaches contemporary and alternative*. Stamford, CT: Jai Press.

Dansereau, F., & Yammarino, F. J. (1998b). A multiple-level leadership mosaic. In F. Dansereau, & F. J. Yammarino (Eds.), *Leadership: The multiple-level approaches contemporary and alternative*, (Vol. 24, pp. 327–349). Stamford, CT: Jai Press.

Dansereau, F., Yammarino, F. J., Markham, S. E., Alutto, J. A., Newman, J., Dumas, M., . . . Lee, S. (1995). Individualized leadership: A new multiple-level approach. *The Leadership Quarterly, 6*(3), 413–450.

Duchon, D., Green, S. G., & Taber, T. D. (1986). Vertical dyad linkage: A longitudinal assessment of antecedents, measures, and consequences. *Journal of Applied Psychology, 71*, 56–60.

Dwertmann, D. J., & Boehm, S. A. (2016). Status matters: The asymmetric effects of supervisor – Subordinate disability incongruence and climate for inclusion. *Academy of Management Journal, 59*(1), 44–64.

Erickson, W., von Schrader, S., Bruyère, S., VanLooy, S., & Matteson, D. (2014). Disability-inclusive employer practices and hiring of individuals with disabilities. *Journal of Rehabilitation Research, Policy and Education, 28*(4), 309–328.

Fleishman, E. A. (1973). Twenty years of consideration and structure. In E. A. Fleishman & J. G. Hunt (Eds.), *Current developments in the study of leadership* (pp. 1–40). Carbondale, IL: Southern Illinois University Press.

Gerber, P. J., & Price, L. A. (2003). Persons with learning disabilities in the workplace: What we know so far in the Americans with Disabilities Act era. *Learning Disabilities Research & Practice, 18*(2), 132–136.

Gewurtz, R., & Kirsh, B. (2009). Disruption, disbelief and resistance: A meta-synthesis of disability in the workplace. *Work, 34*(1), 33–44.

Gibb, S. (2003). Line manager involvement in learning and development: Small beer or big deal? *Employee Relations, 25*(3), 281–293.

Giscombe, K., & Mattis, M. C. (2002). Leveling the playing field for women of color in corporate management: Is the business case enough? *Journal of Business Ethics, 37*(1), 103–119.

Graen, G., & Schiemann, W. (1978). Leader – member agreement: A vertical dyad linkage approach. *Journal of Applied Psychology, 63*, 206–212.

Harlan, S. L., & Robert, P. M. (1998). The social construction of disability in organizations: Why employers resist reasonable accommodation. *Work and Occupations, 25*(4), 397–435.

Harris, K. J., Harris, R. B., & Brouer, R. L. (2009). LMX and subordinate political skill: Direct and interactive effects on turnover intentions and job satisfaction. *Journal of Applied Social Psychology, 39*, 2373–2395.

Hofstede, G. (1980). Motivation, leadership, and organization: Do American theories apply abroad? *Organizational Dynamics*, *9*(1), 42–63.

Hom, P. W., Roberson, L., & Ellis, A. D. (2008). Challenging conventional wisdom about who quits: Revelations from corporate America. *Journal of Applied Psychology*, *93*(1), 1–34.

House, R. J. (1971). A path goal theory of leader effectiveness. *Administrative Science Quarterly*, *24*, 321–339.

House, R. J., & Baetz, M. (1979). Leadership: Some generalizations and new directions. In B. Staw (Ed.), *Research in organizational behavior* (pp. 341–423). Greenwich, CT: JAI Press.

Howell, J. M., & Avolio, B. J. (1993). Transformational leadership, transactional leadership, locus of control, and support for innovation: Key predictors of consolidated-business-unit performance. *Journal of Applied Psychology*, *78*, 891–902.

Ivancevich, J. M., & Gilbert, J. A. (2000). Diversity management: Time for a new approach. *Public Personnel Management*, *29*(1), 75–92.

Jaarsma, P., & Welin, S. (2012). Autism as a natural human variation: Reflections on the claims of the neurodiversity movement. *Health Care Analysis*, *20*(1), 20–30.

Johnston-Tyler, J., & Analla, Y. (2015). Addressing neurodiverse employment needs: Working with Autism Spectrum Disorder I, NVLD, ADHD, learning and mood disordered clients. *Career Planning & Adult Development Journal*, *31*(4), 172–178.

Judge, T. A., Piccolo, R. F., & Ilies, R. (2004). The forgotten ones? The validity of consideration and initiating structure in leadership research. *Journal of Applied Psychology*, *89*, 36–51.

Kaye, H. S., Jans, L. H., & Jones, E. C. (2011). Why don't employers hire and retain workers with disabilities? *Journal of Occupational Rehabilitation*, *21*(4), 526–536.

Kirton, G., & Greene, A. M. (2015). *The dynamics of managing diversity: A critical approach*. Routledge.

Lazowski, L., Koller, M., Stuart, H., & Milev, R. (2012). Stigma and discrimination in people suffering with a mood disorder: A cross-sectional study. *Depression Research and Treatment*, *2012*, 1–9.

Leyens, J. P., Yzerbyt, V., & Schadron, G. (1994). *Stereotypes and social cognition*. Thousand Oaks, CA: SAGE.

Liden, R. C., & Maslyn, J. M. (1998). Multidimensionality of leader – member exchange: An empirical assessment through scale development. *Journal of Management*, *24*, 43–72.

Loiacono, E. T., & Ren, H. (2018). Building a neurodiverse high-tech workforce. *MIS Quarterly Executive*, *17*(4), 263–279.

Martin, P. Y., & Collinson, D. (2002). Over the pond and across the water: Developing the field of gendered organizations. *Gender, Work & Organization*, *9*(3), 244–265.

Matton, J. N., & Hernandez, C. M. (2004). A new study identifies the "makes and breaks" of diversity initiatives. *Journal of Organizational Excellence*, *23*(4), 47–58.

Mcguire, D., Stoner, L., & Mylona, S. (2008). The role of line managers as human resource agents in fostering organizational change in public services. *Journal of Change Management*, *8*(1), 73–84.

McLaughlin, M. E., Bell, M. P., & Stringer, D. Y. (2004). Stigma and acceptance of persons with disabilities: Understudied aspects of workforce diversity. *Group & Organization Management*, *29*(3), 302–333.

Meindl, J. R., & Ehrlich, S. B. (1987). The romance of leadership and the evaluation of organizational performance. *Academy of Management Journal*, *30*, 91–109.

Mellifont, D. (2019). DESerting clients? A study investigating evidence-based measures supporting the long-term employment of neurodiverse Australians. *Management and Labour Studies, 44*(4), 455–466.

Morgan, G. (1986). *Images of organization.* Newbury Park, CA: SAGE.

Morris, M. R., Begel, A., & Wiedermann, B. (2015, October). Understanding the challenges faced by neurodiverse software engineering employees: Towards a more inclusive and productive technical workforce. In *Proceedings of the 17th International ACM SIGACCESS Conference on Computers & Accessibility* (pp. 173–184). New York: ACM.

Mumford, M. D., Antes, A. L., Caughron, J. J., & Friedrich, T. L. (2008). Charismatic, ideological, and pragmatic leadership: Multi-level influences on emergence and performance. *The Leadership Quarterly, 19*, 144–160.

Nelissen, P. T., Hülsheger, U. R., van Ruitenbeek, G. M., & Zijlstra, F. R. (2016). How and when stereotypes relate to inclusive behavior toward people with disabilities. *International Journal of Human Resource Management, 27*(14), 1610–1625.

Nota, L., Santilli, S., Ginevra, M. C., & Soresi, S. (2014). Employer attitudes towards the work inclusion of people with disability. *Journal of Applied Research in Intellectual Disabilities, 27*(6), 511–520.

Novak, J., Feyes, K. J., & Christensen, K. A. (2011). Application of intergroup contact theory to the integrated workplace: Setting the stage for inclusion. *Journal of Vocational Rehabilitation, 35*(3), 211–226.

Parr, A. D., Hunter, S. T., & Ligon, G. S. (2013). Questioning universal applicability of transformational leadership: Examining employees with autism spectrum disorder. *The Leadership Quarterly, 24*(4), 608–622.

Phillips, B. N., Deiches, J., Morrison, B., Chan, F., & Bezyak, J. L. (2016). Disability diversity training in the workplace: Systematic review and future directions. *Journal of Occupational Rehabilitation, 26*(3), 264–275.

Remington, A., & Pellicano, E. (2019). 'Sometimes you just need someone to take a chance on you': An internship programme for autistic graduates at Deutsche Bank, UK. *Journal of Management & Organization, 25*(4), 516–534.

Richards, J., Sang, K., Marks, A., & Gill, S. (2019). "I've found it extremely draining" Emotional labour and the lived experience of line managing neurodiversity. *Personnel Review, 48*(7), 1903–1923.

Risavy, S. D., & Hausdorf, P. A. (2011). Personality testing in personnel selection: Adverse impact and differential hiring rates. *International Journal of Selection and Assessment, 19*(1), 18–30.

Santuzzi, A. M., Waltz, P. R., Finkelstein, L. M., & Rupp, D. E. (2014). Invisible disabilities: Unique challenges for employees and organizations. *Industrial and Organizational Psychology*, 7(2), 204–219.

Sarrett, J. (2017). Interviews, disclosures, and misperceptions: Autistic adults' perspectives on employment related challenges. *Disability Studies Quarterly, 37*(2).

Seitz, S. R. & Owens, B. P. (2020). Transformable? A multi-dimensional exploration of transformational leadership and follower implicit person theories. *European Journal of Work and Organizational Psychology*. https://doi.org/10.1080/1359432X.2020.1830761

Seitz, S. R., & Smith, S. A. (2016). Working toward neurodiversity: How organizations and leaders can accommodate for autism spectrum disorder. *Journal of Business and Management, 22*(1), 135–152.

Shore, L. M., Chung-Herrera, B. G., Dean, M. A., Ehrhart, K. H., Jung, D. I., Randel, A. E., & Singh, G. (2009). Diversity in organizations: Where are we now and where are we going? *Human Resource Management Review, 19*(2), 117–133.

Stogdill, R. M. (1950). Leadership, membership and organization. *Psychological Bulletin*, *47*, 1–14.

Sumner, K. E., & Brown, T. J. (2015). Neurodiversity and human resource management: Employer challenges for applicants and employees with learning disabilities. *The Psychologist-Manager Journal*, *18*(2), 77–85.

Tsui, A. S., & O'Reilly, C. A. (1989). Beyond simple demographic effects: The importance of relational demography in superior – subordinate dyads. *Academy of Management Journal*, *32*, 402–423.

Van den Bosch, K. E., Krzeminska, A., Song, E.Y., Van Hal, L. B., Waltz, M. M., Ebben, H., & Schippers, A. P. (2019). Nothing about us, without us: A case study of a consumer-run organization by and for people on the autism spectrum in the Netherlands. *Journal of Management & Organization*, *25*(4), 464–480.

Von Schrader, S., Malzer, V., & Bruyère, S. (2014). Perspectives on disability disclosure: The importance of employer practices and workplace climate. *Employee Responsibilities and Rights Journal*, *26*(4), 237–255.

Wayne, S. J., & Liden, R. C. (1995). Effects of impression management on performance ratings: A longitudinal study. *Academy of Management Journal*, *38*(1), 232–260.

Wehman, P. (2003). Workplace inclusion: Persons with disabilities and coworkers working together. *Journal of Vocational Rehabilitation*, *18*(2), 131–141.

Whelpley, C. E., Banks, G. C., Bochantin, J. E., & Sandoval, R. (2020). Tensions on the spectrum: An inductive investigation of employee and manager experiences of autism. *Journal of Business and Psychology*. Advance online publication. https://doi.org/10.1007/s10869-019-09676-1

Williams, C. L., Muller, C., & Kilanski, K. (2012). Gendered organizations in the new economy. *Gender & Society*, *26*(4), 549–573.

Yukl, G. (2006). *Leadership in organizations*. Upper Saddle River, NJ: Pearson Custom Publishing, Pearson Education.

7

THE ROLE OF COLLEAGUES IN WORK EXPERIENCES OF EMPLOYEES WITH AUTISM

Natalie H. Longmire and Julie L. Taylor

Introduction

Neurodiversity[1] is increasingly emerging as a focal topic among organizations. For example, large technology and software companies such as Microsoft, Dell, and SAP have created hiring programs aimed at recruiting individuals on the autism spectrum. In addition, a variety of small businesses have adopted the mission of providing employment for adults with autism. These initiatives have arisen in part from the acknowledgement that neurodiversity, like other forms of diversity, has the potential to promote performance, creativity, and innovation through more unique knowledge and perspectives (Bell et al., 2011). However, a key challenge involves avoiding or overcoming interpersonal friction among coworkers in order to harness the full potential of neurodiversity (Harrison & Klein, 2007; Jehn et al., 1999). Neurodiversity, which is most often associated with autism unaccompanied by intellectual disability,[2] poses particular challenges due to the social and interpersonal difficulties that this population tends to experience. Thus, understanding colleague relationships is important in any diversity context, but it is particularly important for understanding the experiences and outcomes of neurodiverse employees.

Chapter Purpose

The aim of this chapter is to review research findings relevant to the role of coworkers in work experiences for employees with autism. We first summarize the literature on the impact of coworkers on employees' work experiences generally. Next, we delve into the literature on disability and coworkers, ending with a focus on autism specifically. Because there is little research directly examining

DOI: 10.4324/9781003023616-7

colleague relationships for employees with autism, we follow our summary of the literature by focusing on important avenues for future research. These focus largely on the ways in which aspects of autism might interact with what is known about how social processes unfold between colleagues. Finally, we suggest some points of practical guidance for stakeholders interested in supporting colleague relationships in neurodiversity initiatives. Coworkers are an important, though commonly overlooked, factor in the success (or failure) of Autistic employees' work experiences.

Autism and Employment

Although adults with autism[3] are often fully capable of gainful employment, they are disproportionately underemployed. Recent estimates of employment rates for adults on the autism spectrum without an intellectual disability range from 37% to 67% (Arnold et al., 2019; Helles et al., 2016; Mason et al., 2018; Ohl et al., 2017; Taylor et al., 2015, 2019). There is also emerging research to suggest that once employment positions are obtained, Autistic adults have a very difficult time maintaining those positions over time (Taylor et al., 2015; Taylor & DaWalt, 2017). A number of factors have been associated with whether adults on the autism spectrum are employed, such as daily living skills, availability of services, and social communication impairments associated with their autism (Holwerda et al., 2012; Lord et al., 2020; Taylor et al., 2015; Taylor & Mailick, 2014; Walsh et al., 2014).

Persistent, pervasive difficulty with social communication and interaction is one of the two core components of an autism diagnosis (American Psychiatric Association, 2013). Of relevance to interactions in organizational contexts, key challenges include difficulty understanding norms of reciprocity (Gouldner, 1960) in everyday conversation and in relationships more broadly. Employees with autism might find it challenging to infer coworkers' unique perspectives and emotional states (Baron-Cohen et al., 1985), which can have a negative impact on a number of employee outcomes (Côté, 2014; Longmire & Harrison, 2018). In addition, the workplace is a unique context in that some roles are highly formalized, creating a set of social expectations that can vary vastly across different contexts and interactions (Holmes, 2000). Difficulty intuiting these types of nuances is an explicit marker of autism (American Psychiatric Association, 2013). Finally, Autistic employees' common misunderstandings of both the verbal and nonverbal nuances of everyday small talk at work can be a major source of stress (Methot et al., 2020).

Recent trends in the workplace have, if anything, exacerbated the potential challenges stemming from social and communication difficulties. Work has become increasingly interdependent and team based, and economies have shifted from majority manufacturing jobs to majority service and knowledge-based jobs. Both of these trends bring relationships with colleagues to the forefront of definitions of work effectiveness (Grant & Parker, 2009). Thus, it is particularly important to understand how relationships with coworkers might impact the employment experiences of Autistic adults.

The Vital Role of Coworkers

The idea that coworkers play a formative role in shaping employees' work experiences – for better *or* worse – is not new to the organizational literature (Chiaburu & Harrison, 2008; Schneider, 1987). However, we suggest that relative to their "neurotypical" peers, relationships with coworkers are likely even more consequential for employees on the autism spectrum. Imagine one woman with autism who is hired for a job in retail. She tries to get to know her coworkers but has a hard time engaging in the give-and-take of everyday conversation. Oftentimes, she feels that they are speaking a language she cannot quite grasp, full of slang terms and idioms, and with ease that they seem to take for granted. She feels much more comfortable when she can talk about her extensive knowledge of meteorology, a topic she has intensely studied since childhood. Over time, her coworkers might grow to dislike her for what they see as interpersonal "blunders," avoiding her in the store and excluding her from get-togethers outside of work. One day, they decide to convince her that she should take the keys to the store home after closing, with the intent of causing trouble for her with their manager. Taking the suggestion at face value, she falls for their deception. Her manager has no choice but to let her go for violating company policy.

Another scenario – one that turns out quite differently – is that of a man who is recruited for a position as a software developer through a neurodiversity-focused program in the organization. When he is hired, the company assigns a coworker to guide him not only in his work role but also in the social aspects of the job. For example, the coworker suggests that he learn who will be in attendance at a meeting beforehand so that he can have a better sense of what to expect. The coworker also helps this employee by explaining that when arriving late to a meeting, it would be best to skip a greeting and instead take a seat without interrupting the speaker. As a result, this employee feels increasingly confident in navigating the unwritten rules of workplace interactions, and he knows he can always approach this coworker if he needs more advice. Without the added stress of wondering how to navigate the nuances of every coworker interaction, this employee is able to focus his attention and energy on the job for which he was hired. The opportunity to form positive relationships enables him to collaborate well with others and contribute important perspectives to team-based projects. Moreover, the work unit as a whole is able to harness the benefits of neurodiversity by sidestepping harmful interpersonal dynamics that could have arisen due to misunderstandings.

Both of these scenarios are informed by real experiences of people on the autism spectrum. In each, the employee experiences challenges when trying to navigate the interpersonal aspects of their work. This can be a challenge for any employee, but the social and communication difficulties that are inherent in an autism diagnosis greatly compound those difficulties. At the same time, the divergent outcomes between these two examples illustrate the vital role colleagues can play in shaping the work experience of Autistic employees. In the former example, coworkers sought to undermine the employee, and this behavior eventually contributed to her termination from the organization. In the latter example, coworkers enabled the employee not only to maintain his job but to thrive in it, benefitting both him and the work unit as a whole.

Overview of Relevant Literature

Effects of Colleague Relationships on Employee Outcomes

Relationships with coworkers can take a number of different forms and fulfill a variety of needs and functions. Evidence suggests that employees see coworker relationships as serving purposes far beyond providing work or career-related advice only. For example, a qualitative investigation uncovered a typology of six different functions of workplace relationships: task assistance, career advancement, emotional support, friendship, personal growth, and giving to others (Colbert et al., 2016). Along these lines, social network researchers tend to define coworker relationships as either instrumental or expressive, characterized by an exchange of task-related or socioemotional resources, respectively (Burt et al., 2013; Kilduff & Brass, 2010). Multiplex relationships are ones that involve a combination of these resource classes (Methot et al., 2016). Some have noted that workplace relationship functions can change across time. New relationships might be characterized largely by instrumentality, whereas ones that have been growing and developing over a longer period of time are more likely to be centered around loyalty and trust (Ferris et al., 2009). Finally, it is important to note that coworkers can have high-quality and deeply meaningful coworker relationships *with or without* experiencing that relationship as friendship (Dutton & Heaphy, 2003; Kahn, 2007). Thus, coworker relationships have the potential to be both rich and complex.

Employees need high-quality connections with coworkers for a number of reasons. First, most adults spend the majority of their waking hours at work, so coworkers can have a significant impact on general well-being. Connections with coworkers have the power to be "life-giving or life-depleting" (Dutton & Heaphy, 2003, p. 263). Simply feeling known by one's colleagues can bolster well-being by fulfilling a core need for identity confirmation, affirming the essential features of what makes a person who they are (Swann et al., 2004). When employees actively and respectfully engage with those around them, they are more likely to experience a sense of vitality and learning at work, which in turn supports psychological growth and health (Dutton & Heaphy, 2003; Spreitzer et al., 2005). Experiencing friendship with coworkers can lead to more positive emotions at work (Colbert et al., 2016). Employees also experience greater life satisfaction if they feel that their coworkers are sources of personal growth and closeness (Ehrhardt & Ragins, 2018). Finally, researchers have noted that because the quality of a person's work relationships can be career defining, they should be considered an important end in and of themselves (rather than simply a means to other goals) (Gersick et al., 2000).

In addition to supporting general well-being, high-quality coworker relationships can contribute to more positive job attitudes and overall effectiveness at work. During the socialization process, coworkers play an important role in newcomers' adjustment (Song et al., 2017). Cumulative evidence underscores the link between coworker support and job satisfaction, job involvement, and organizational commitment (Chiaburu & Harrison, 2008). Specifically, employees experience higher job satisfaction when they feel supported by coworkers either in their work role or in their broader career advancement (Colbert et al., 2016). Positive relationships with coworkers also support effectiveness in one's work role and in the organization more broadly (Chiaburu & Harrison, 2008). In addition, cumulative evidence suggests that workplace friendship centrality (an indicator of prominence or popularity) is linked to both job performance and long-term career success (Fang et al., 2015).

Alternatively, research underscores the destructive impacts of unsupportive or antagonistic coworkers. Experiencing aggressive behaviors from coworkers, such as bullying or incivility, leads to lower job satisfaction and well-being, as well as higher turnover intentions (Hershcovis, 2011). In addition, more subtle behaviors such as social undermining in early experiences with coworkers can create a foundation for negative work outcomes later on (Kammeyer-Mueller et al., 2013). When employees are socially excluded by coworkers, feelings of loneliness can create circumstances that contribute to lower job performance (Ozcelik & Barsade, 2018). Further consequences of ostracism at work include more negative emotions, self-perceptions, and job attitudes, along with lower overall well-being and increased likelihood of job turnover (Howard et al., 2020). Importantly, the negative impacts of unsupportive or antagonistic relationships likely outweigh the positive effects of supportive ones (Duffy et al., 2002; Labianca & Brass, 2006).

Positive interpersonal processes and relationships are also a vital component of teamwork. Friendship has been shown to bolster the performance of work teams overall (Balkundi & Harrison, 2006; Chung et al., 2017), likely due to both motivational and task coordination benefits (Ellemers et al., 2004, 2013; Gruenfeld et al., 1996; Harrison et al., 2003). Particularly when interpersonal differences are salient within a team, one friendship can act as a bridge across differences, whereas a contentious relationship can trigger performance-damaging effects (Ren et al., 2014). Similarly, interpersonal conflict in just one dyad can poison performance for the entire team, due at least in part to inhibited information exchange among all team members (Humphrey et al., 2017). In particular, conflicts that are personal in nature (rather than task oriented) detract attention and energy from productive team processes (Jehn, 1995). Thus, high-quality relationships with coworkers are important not only for individual outcomes but also for collective functioning and performance.

Autism and Colleague Relationships

Now that we have established the multiple facets of colleague relationships and the extent of their impact on employees' work experiences, we turn to a discussion of autism and colleague relationships. The research directly addressing this topic is sparse and often plagued by methodological limitations such as small sample sizes and cross-sectional designs. Thus, we begin by considering the relevance of what is known about coworker relationships for employees with intellectual disabilities or with mental illness. Then we review the small body of research that provides some insight into colleague relationships for Autistic employees specifically.

Colleague Relationships for Employees in Other Populations

Because there is little research to date on the impact of coworker relationships on employees with autism, we begin by considering findings from research focusing on the role of coworkers for employees with intellectual disabilities or with mental illness. Like employees with autism, those with a mental illness or intellectual disability might face social or communication challenges in their relationships with coworkers as well as potential stigmatization associated with their diagnosis. Some research has examined colleague relationships for employees with intellectual disabilities, and these findings might be relevant for understanding coworker relationships for employees on the autism spectrum. For example, a review of the literature on work relationships for employees with intellectual disabilities concluded that, unsurprisingly, social and communication skills are a key factor in workplace social integration (Chadsey, 2007). In a large multinational study of adults in supportive employment (the majority of whom had an intellectual disability), severity of disruptive behaviors was negatively associated with social adjustment at work (Jenaro et al., 2002). While adults with social and behavioral challenges might have difficulty initiating relationships with their coworkers, research also suggests that peer coworkers (without intellectual disabilities) tend to avoid self-disclosing to employees with intellectual disabilities (Ohtake & Chadsey, 1999). In other words, even when adults with intellectual disabilities attempt to build positive relationships with their coworkers, those attempts might not be returned in kind. Reciprocal self-disclosure is a crucial foundation for positive relationship development (Altman & Taylor, 1973), so this finding suggests ongoing challenges for connecting across developmental differences.

It is important to note a few key distinctions of the research summarized in this section that might limit its applicability to Autistic employees – particularly those who don't have an intellectual disability. First, these studies are virtually always conducted in the context of understanding formal supports for employees with disabilities. Employees with autism, particularly those without intellectual disability, often do not receive formal workplace supports (Ohl et al., 2017). This could be because they live in a state in which services are only funded for those who have significant support needs, or they may choose not to seek out or take advantage of such services (we address the topic of diagnosis disclosure more fully in what follows). Thus, relative to those with intellectual disabilities, we would expect that adults with autism (without intellectual disability) are less likely to be receiving formal help navigating social relationships at work. Relatedly, because formal workplace supports are often visible to coworkers, and because developmental disabilities are typically associated with cognitive limitations, coworkers clearly understand that the employee has a disability. For employees with autism, coworkers might not connect their social challenges to an underlying disability, particularly when that employee chooses not to disclose his or her autism diagnosis.

To this point, a study of adults with severe mental illness found that those who participated in a supported employment program experienced greater social support from coworkers than did a group with no on-site support (Rollins et al., 2002). Discriminatory treatment from coworkers toward employees with mental illness can include insensitive, patronizing, or condescending remarks, as well as exclusion from social interaction and activities (Russinova et al., 2011). Receiving support from both supervisors and coworkers is likely a key factor in maintaining employment for people with mental illness (Corbière et al., 2014).

Colleague Relationships for Employees with Autism

A few studies provide insights into the role of colleague relationships in the work experiences of employees with autism. Interestingly, a study of 130 Autistic employees (without an intellectual disability) found that coworker relationships were considered among both the most positive *and* the most negative aspects of the work experience (Baldwin et al., 2014). Specifically, 45% of respondents named positive relationships with colleagues as the best part of their job; and at the same time, 46% noted social challenges such as misunderstandings, criticism, and exclusion as some of the most negative aspects of their experience at their organization. In another small qualitative study of adults with autism spectrum disorder (N = 18), difficulty navigating social interactions in the workplace was the most frequently named obstacle to employment success (Müller et al., 2003). That employees with autism would make this connection is unsurprising, given the demonstrated link between building relationships with colleagues and successful social integration for any newcomer to an organization (Ellis et al., 2017). Thus, the existing data provide some (albeit limited) evidence that the impact of coworker relationships on work experiences for this population – for both better and worse – is not unlike that of the general population.

Despite the apparent importance of supportive coworker relationships for this group, a number of factors specific to autism spectrum disorders might impede or derail relationship development with coworkers. The extant literature largely focuses on beginning stages of coworker relationships, such as initial attitudes, first impressions, and potential stigmatization. First, the extent of coworkers' awareness and understanding of autism spectrum disorder can be a barrier to relationship development (Annabi & Locke, 2019). Some data suggest that the general population is more aware of the positive symptoms associated with autism than the negative or challenging ones and that people tend to overestimate the prevalence of positive symptoms, such as having specialized knowledge of specific topics (Jensen et al., 2016). On one hand, this could mean that most employees have an overall neutral to positive attitude toward having an Autistic coworker. On the other hand, unrealistic expectations could be problematic for coworker relationships between employees with and without an autism spectrum disorder. For example, coworkers might have unrealistic performance expectations of an employee with autism and be disappointed to discover that her skills are actually in line with those of everyone else. Underestimating the challenges associated with autism can lead coworkers to react with a lack of empathy when difficult behaviors arise.

Decisions and dynamics surrounding disclosure of an autism spectrum disorder to colleagues can also impact relationships with colleagues. Many employees on the autism spectrum do not disclose their disability (Ohl et al., 2017). As with other invisible disabilities or stigmatized identities, employees must weigh the potential psychological and accommodation benefits with the potential for further stigmatization and discrimination (Clair et al., 2005; Ragins, 2008; Santuzzi et al., 2014; Santuzzi & Keating, in this volume). Yet autism disclosure is likely to be particularly complicated and fraught for two reasons. First, the social and communication symptoms associated with autism, though not physically visible, are not easily concealed (Santuzzi et al., 2014). Second, due to challenges with navigating the nuances of individual supervisor or coworker interactions, employees with autism might have difficulty discerning the appropriate timing, target, and delivery of a disclosure conversation (Johnson & Joshi, 2014). As a result, Autistic adults might take a number of different approaches to disclosure at work, and they have reported a wide variety of both positive and negative outcomes, whether they choose to disclose or pass regarding their diagnosis (Sarrett, 2017).

Some Autistic adults report positive consequences of disclosing their disability (Sarrett, 2017). Research suggests that adults with autism who disclose their disability make more favorable first impressions than adults who choose not to disclose (Sasson & Morrison, 2019). Moreover, disclosure of an autism spectrum disorder has been linked to job stability (Ohl et al., 2017). Other evidence suggests negative outcomes of disclosure. If an employee chooses to disclose only to a supervisor, coworkers might question the fairness of any accommodations made for that employee (Colella, 2001; Colella et al., 2004). Further, disclosing an autism spectrum disorder to a supervisor or coworker was found to be associated with greater perceptions of stigma-related threat in the workplace, but only for those who had received their diagnosis later in life (Johnson & Joshi, 2016).

Even without disclosing an autism spectrum disorder, it is still possible for employees with autism to be stigmatized by colleagues (Hurley-Hanson et al., 2020). Specific behaviors associated with an autism spectrum disorder could lead coworkers to stigmatize an employee as having poor "fit" with the culture of the organization or being rude or disengaged (Patton, 2019). For example, an Autistic employee might find "small talk" with coworkers to be particularly challenging or confusing and prefer to avoid it. Although its label might imply triviality, the omission of small talk as an interaction ritual in the workplace can signal a lack of care or recognition of others (Coupland, 2003; Methot et al., 2020). Along these same lines, because social interaction with coworkers is not typically an explicit part of one's job description, employees with autism might not immediately understand its intrinsic function or value. As a result of those employees neglecting to engage, coworkers might conclude that they are simply rude or self-centered. In more structured settings, such as scheduled meetings, Autistic employees might face challenges understanding the fluid and unwritten rules of when and how to contribute. Speaking too frequently could be evaluated as attempts to dominate the meeting, while someone who speaks too little could be seen as disengaged. All of these patterns might contribute to the subjective assessment that an employee simply does not fit with the organization.

Directions for Future Research: Theorizing Beyond First Impressions

Taken together, the literature suggests that coworkers are a key but often overlooked component in neurodiversity initiatives. Based on the evidence available, we can tentatively conclude that supportive colleague relationships are important to Autistic employees and that negative attitudes and potential stigmatization from coworkers are two potential barriers to high-quality relationships. However, the literature provides few insights beyond these initial attitudinal outcomes. Given the importance of colleague relationships for all employees and the interpersonal challenges often experienced by those on the autism spectrum, it is vital to better understand the nature of coworker relationship dynamics for this population.

For example, one clear connection between theories of work relationships and characteristics of autism spectrum disorders is that of relational norms. Outside of work, relationships are characterized largely by socioemotional goals, informal roles, and communal exchange norms, whereas workplace relationships are focused on instrumental goals, formal roles, and norms of social exchange (Pillemer & Rothbard, 2018). This means that the majority of neurotypical employees approach coworker relationships differently from how they would treat family members or friends outside of work. It is generally understood that coworker relationships exist primarily to achieve the goals laid out by the organization, not the employees' own social and emotional needs. Further, relationships outside of an organizational context are often informal, whereas work relationships often take on formal roles, such as supervisor–subordinate, service provider–customer, supplier–buyer, etc. These different roles can be accompanied by unwritten rules of communication and interaction that must be flexibly adjusted across relationships and across contexts. Finally, norms of social exchange are perhaps the most important aspect of workplace relationships, as reciprocity forms the foundation for trust and cooperation at work (Cropanzano & Mitchell, 2005; Lyons & Scott, 2012).

Employees with autism might find it particularly difficult to navigate these aspects of work relationships with different rules and expectations than relationships outside of work. These potential challenges are unlikely to be ameliorated by the social interventions and supports that are typically accessed by Autistic children and adults. Autism interventions are concentrated largely in early childhood, and much of what is taught about navigating relationships is likely to apply only to the rules and norms of nonwork relationships. Similarly, social skills trainings targeted toward adolescents and adults with autism focus on friendships and relationships outside of the work context (Sasson & Morrison, 2019). Transition and work-related supports and interventions often focus on the technical aspects of the job or interviewing skills to get the job rather than how to navigate the interpersonal nuances of coworker relationships once a job is procured.

A few isolated violations of the norms of social exchange can set coworker relationships on a downward spiral. Especially when an employee is new to an organization, one negative event with a coworker can lead to a relationship characterized by competition rather than trust and cooperation (Ballinger & Rockmann, 2010). Attempts to repair trust must follow a nuanced set of expectations from coworkers; attempts to apologize are not always successful (Kim et al., 2004). Research on relationship networks in organizations has found that when employees neglect to offer help to their coworkers, they are less likely to receive support or help from those coworkers (Venkataramani & Dalal, 2007). This might be particularly problematic for Autistic employees, who may feel that their disability renders their assistance less valuable to their coworkers. Even if employees with autism do not mean harm, behaviors that are interpreted as incivility can break the process of trust development and lead coworkers to exclude that employee. Moreover, this might be especially true if the employee has demonstrated a lack of understanding of exchange norms in prior interactions (Scott et al., 2013). Finally, research has found that simply having negative feelings toward an employee can lead to less helping and more harming behavior toward that employee (Lyons & Scott, 2012). As we discussed previously, the interpersonal challenges associated with autism increase the likelihood of coworkers' negative attitudes toward them. By incorporating neurodiversity into theorizing about work relationships, new insights into these negative dynamics (and how to avoid them) might be uncovered.

Another direction for future research is to better understand how social challenges associated with autism can impact performance. When an employee violates a coworker's trust, their performance can suffer because important work-related resources and supports are cut off (Dirks & Skarlicki, 2009). Similarly, employees who report feelings of loneliness at work experience a subsequent decline in performance (Ozcelik & Barsade, 2018). Interpersonal discrimination behaviors in face-to-face interactions with colleagues can also inhibit motivation and performance for Autistic employees (Hebl et al., 2016). As we speculated before, performance declines for employees with autism might be viewed in a particularly negative light by coworkers. Coworkers who previously held unrealistic expectations about people with autism having highly specialized knowledge and skills might be especially disappointed when these expectations are violated. Conversely, coworkers who were previously skeptical that an Autistic person would be a valuable colleague might see performance declines as confirmation of such beliefs. Thus, performance declines due to social challenges faced by neurodiverse employees might be particularly difficult for them to overcome, given the preexisting performance expectations held by their coworkers.

A third avenue for future research could target difficulties surrounding relationship repair for Autistic employees. Research suggests that successfully repairing a coworker relationship requires a highly nuanced understanding of trust processes, social exchange norms, and culturally based rituals (Dirks et al., 2009; Ren & Gray, 2009). One problem could be that the employee with autism fails to discern that a coworker relationship is deteriorating. If one party is unaware of the need for relationship repair, the restoration process is more likely to be unsuccessful (Olekalns et al., 2019). Even if both parties sense the relationship is suffering, they must then come to some agreement regarding the nature and severity of the fracture (Bottom et al., 2002; Okimoto & Wenzel, 2014). Perspective taking, which plays a key role in constructing these mutual understandings (Wright et al., 2000), is a skill that some people with autism find particularly challenging (Mathersul et al., 2013).

Finally, and perhaps most importantly, it is prudent to gain insights into the potential myriad of positive relational consequences of neurodiversity initiatives. Research suggests that discrimination in the workplace can negatively impact the culture of the entire organization (Hebl et al., 2016). On the other hand, employees feel good when they help their coworkers (George & Brief, 1992; Koopman et al., 2016). Thus, involving coworkers in appropriate accommodations for Autistic employees could be an enriching experience for all parties. Moreover, tackling the stigmatization of autism through interpersonal discourse with colleagues might lead to positive social change and a more inclusive organizational environment (Lyons et al., 2017). Like employees with other disabilities, neurodiverse employees are likely to experience microaggressions at work in the form of insulting, patronizing, or otherwise degrading forms of interpersonal behavior (Hebl et al., 2016; Sue, Capodilupo, Torino et al., 2007). As perpetrators of these forms of discrimination, "neurotypical" coworkers might have benign or even benevolent intentions, but their effects are harmful nonetheless. Enlisting allies and empowering neurodiverse employees to speak up against ableist microaggressions in the workplace can educate both perpetrators and bystanders, as well as reinforce norms of respect and inclusion (Hebl et al., 2016; Sue, Alsaidi, Awad et al., 2019).

In addition, organizations' initiatives to support employees with autism might have positive spillover effects for their coworkers. For example, recognizing that Autistic employees might prefer to communicate with their coworkers virtually rather than face-to-face, managers might offer more flexibility in all employees' choice of communication channels when possible. It is likely that employees beyond those with autism would benefit from this increased autonomy in selecting a communication channel that best fits the situation (Barry & Fulmer, 2004; Brodsky, 2020). As another example, the kind of social support offered to the Autistic employee in our second opening vignette would certainly be valuable to any newcomer in an organization (Nelson & Quick, 1991).

Practical Implications

As organizations seek to promote neurodiversity, we suggest a few strategies that might promote supportive coworker relationships. First, Autistic adults themselves emphasize the importance of coworkers' autism education and awareness (Sarrett, 2017). If coworkers have realistic expectations about the potential strengths and challenges associated with autism spectrum disorder, employees with autism might be less anxious about disclosing their disability and less likely to experience stigma postdisclosure. Formalizing such training might also signal to both potential and current Autistic employees that their disclosure will be received positively.

The diversity training literature suggests that focusing on inclusiveness and similarities across groups is less likely to result in backlash against diversity initiatives (Bezrukova et al., 2012). Specifically, focusing on a common group identity (without diminishing smaller intergroup differences) and focusing on an alternate shared identity are two strategies that have proven effective in general diversity training initiatives (Paluck & Green, 2009). Thus, when incorporating autism awareness into training initiatives, it could be beneficial to focus on the "spectrum" part of autism spectrum disorder. Even if someone does not have a diagnosis of autism, all employees can be placed at some point on the spectrum of differences in patterns and preferences of relating to others. For example, employees who are low in characteristics such as extraversion (Wilmot et al., 2019), emotional intelligence (Côté, 2014), or self-monitoring (Kilduff & Day, 1994) would find ways to identify with some aspects of the autism diagnosis. Neurodiversity reflects variations across the entire population, not simply a diagnostic binary or categorical distinction. Making this salient could be effective for creating allies against interpersonal discrimination directed toward employees who have an autism diagnosis (Hebl et al., 2016).

Another potentially effective strategy for incorporating coworkers in neurodiversity initiatives targets perspective taking and empathy (Paluck & Green, 2009). Both perspective taking and empathy are simple yet potentially powerful tools for reducing prejudicial attitudes and behaviors in organizations (Longmire & Harrison, 2018). Perspective-taking interventions could consist of experiential exercises (e.g., "imagine yourself in the shoes of this person"), firsthand narratives, or media (e.g., books or films) presenting nuanced experiences of Autistic people. In addition, a more immersive intervention has been shown to promote perspective taking and empathy. *Auti-sim* is a publicly available virtual reality program that simulates sensory overload, a common experience for people on the autism spectrum. Researchers found that participants who engaged in this program reported greater perspective taking, empathy, and helping intentions relative to those who simply observed the simulation or read a similar text vignette (Sarge et al., 2020).

Another key theme of autism awareness training should focus on diversity of characteristics within the autism diagnosis. A beloved quote in the autism community comes from Autistic professor Dr. Stephen Shore: "If you've met one person with autism, you've met one person with autism." This sentiment resonates so strongly with Autistic adults because although autism symptoms typically fall into a few main categories, they can manifest in a myriad of ways and to widely varying degrees. Thus, it is important for coworkers to understand that simply knowing that an employee has autism does not substitute for getting to know that person's unique strengths and challenges.

Importantly, managers must continuously engage in creating an inclusive and supportive environment, as autism awareness alone will be unlikely to result in a change of behavior toward employees on the autism spectrum (Bezrukova et al., 2012). Such efforts should focus not solely on training Autistic employees to better adapt to their coworkers but on all parties working together toward the goal of inclusion. Involving all stakeholders could be particularly important in the context of conflict resolution (Okimoto & Wenzel, 2014).

In addition, designating a "bridging" role between the employee with autism and other members of the organization can be helpful (Johnson, 2016). For example, an Autistic employee might be assigned a specific coworker as a safe resource for help with the interpersonal challenges of the organization. Harkening back to our opening example, the coworker could act as a vital sensemaking partner for everything from meeting protocols to office politics. In addition, this coworker could aid broader social inclusion by serving as a third-party advocate if the employee with autism does violate relational norms with other colleagues (Hebl et al., 2016). In support of this idea, a recent investigation found that a racial diversity training program was only efficacious for those employees who had already developed cross-race friendships at work (Ragins & Ehrhardt, 2020). However, it is important to note that not all coworkers would be an appropriate fit for such a role. Managers should be careful to identify potential mentors as employees who understand both the nature of autism and the social landscape of the organization.

Conclusion

In this chapter, we address the role of colleagues in the work experiences of employees with autism. As in the general population, research suggests that Autistic employees view supportive relationships with coworkers as a key factor for effectiveness and thriving at work. However, due to the interpersonal challenges commonly experienced by adults on the autism spectrum, navigating relationships with coworkers can be particularly difficult. Limited evidence suggests that employees with autism might experience negative first impressions or stigmatization, which complicate dynamics around self-disclosure. We suggest important avenues for future research that extends theory beyond these initial stages to better understand the role of coworkers in the ongoing work experiences of neurodiverse employees.

Notes

1. We recognize that autism is not the only source of neurodiversity. More broadly, neurodiversity refers to natural variation in neurocognitive function across individuals, which would also include differences in, for example, attention deficit hyperactivity disorder (ADHD) or dyslexia. For the purposes of this chapter, we focus specifically on the autism population, because autism in particular is associated with social challenges that have unique implications for coworker relationships.
2. This would coincide with the former diagnosis of Asperger syndrome. In the most recent iteration of the *Diagnostic and Statistical Manual of Mental Disorders* (DSM-5), Asperger syndrome was folded into the definition of autism spectrum disorder and is no longer a separate diagnosis.
3. There is disagreement within the autism community about how to refer to individuals with this condition. Many self-advocates (though not all) prefer identity-first language (e.g., Autistic adult), whereas many clinicians and researchers (though not all) use person-first language (e.g., adult with autism or adult with autism spectrum disorder). In this chapter, we reflect this diversity of thought by using the terms "Autistic adults," "adults with autism spectrum disorder," and "adults with autism" interchangeably.

References

Altman, I., & Taylor, D. A. (1973). *Social penetration: The development of interpersonal relationships*. New York: Holt, Rinehart and Winston.

American Psychiatric Association. (2013). *Diagnostic and statistical manual of mental disorders, 5th edition: DSM-5* (5th ed.). Washington, DC: American Psychiatric Publishing.

Annabi, H., & Locke, J. (2019). A theoretical framework for investigating the context for creating employment success in information technology for individuals with autism. *Journal of Management & Organization, 25*(4), 499–515. https://doi.org/10.1017/jmo.2018.79

Arnold, S., Foley, K.-R., Hwang, Y. I. (Jane), Richdale, A. L., Uljarevic, M., Lawson, L. P., Cai, R. Y., Falkmer, T., Falkmer, M., Lennox, N. G., Urbanowicz, A., & Trollor, J. (2019). Cohort profile: The Australian Longitudinal Study of Adults with Autism (ALSAA). *BMJ Open*, *9*(12), e030798. https://doi.org/10.1136/bmjopen-2019-030798

Baldwin, S., Costley, D., & Warren, A. (2014). Employment activities and experiences of adults with high-functioning autism and Asperger's Disorder. *Journal of Autism and Developmental Disorders*, *44*(10), 2440–2449. https://doi.org/10.1007/s10803-014-2112-z

Balkundi, P., & Harrison, D. A. (2006). Ties, leaders, and time in teams: Strong inference about network structure's effects on team viability and performance. *The Academy of Management Journal*, *49*(1), 49–68. https://doi.org/10.2307/20159745

Ballinger, G. A., & Rockmann, K. W. (2010). Chutes versus ladders: Anchoring events and a punctuated-equilibrium perspective on social exchange relationships. *Academy of Management Review*, *35*(3), 373–391. https://doi.org/10.5465/AMR.2010.51141732

Baron-Cohen, S., Leslie, A. M., & Frith, U. (1985). Does the Autistic child have a "theory of mind"? *Cognition*, *21*(1), 37–46. https://doi.org/10.1016/0010-0277(85)90022-8

Barry, B., & Fulmer, I. S. (2004). The medium and the message: The adaptive use of communication media in dyadic influence. *Academy of Management Review*, *29*(2), 272–292. https://doi.org/10.5465/amr.2004.12736093

Bell, S. T., Villado, A. J., Lukasik, M. A., Belau, L., & Briggs, A. L. (2011). Getting specific about demographic diversity variable and team performance relationships: A meta-analysis. *Journal of Management*, *37*(3), 709–743. https://doi.org/10.1177/0149206310365001

Bezrukova, K., Jehn, K. A., & Spell, C. S. (2012). Reviewing diversity training: Where we have been and where we should go. *Academy of Management Learning & Education*, *11*(2), 207–227. https://doi.org/10.5465/amle.2008.0090

Bottom, W. P., Gibson, K., Daniels, S. E., & Murnighan, J. K. (2002). When talk is not cheap: Substantive penance and expressions of intent in rebuilding cooperation. *Organization Science*, *13*(5), 497–513. https://doi.org/10.1287/orsc.13.5.497.7816

Brodsky, A. (2020). Virtual surface acting in workplace interactions: Choosing the best technology to fit the task. *Journal of Applied Psychology*. Advance online publication. https://doi.org/10.1037/apl0000805

Burt, R. S., Kilduff, M., & Tasselli, S. (2013). Social network analysis: Foundations and frontiers on advantage. *Annual Review of Psychology*, *64*(1), 527–547. https://doi.org/10.1146/annurev-psych-113011-143828

Chadsey, J. (2007). Adult relationships. In S. L. Odom, R. H. Horner, M. E. Snell, & J. Blacher (Eds.), *Handbook of developmental disabilities* (pp. 449–466). New York: Guilford Press.

Chiaburu, D. S., & Harrison, D. A. (2008). Do peers make the place? Conceptual synthesis and meta-analysis of coworker effects on perceptions, attitudes, OCBs, and performance. *Journal of Applied Psychology*, *93*(5), 1082–1103. https://doi.org/10.1037/0021-9010.93.5.1082

Chung, S., Lount, R. B., Park, H. M., & Park, E. S. (2017). Friends with performance benefits: A Meta-analysis on the relationship between friendship and group performance. *Personality and Social Psychology Bulletin*, *44*(1), 63–79. https://doi.org/10.1177/0146167217733069

Clair, J. A., Beatty, J. E., & Maclean, T. L. (2005). Out of sight but not out of mind: Managing invisible social identities in the workplace. *Academy of Management Review*, *30*(1), 78–95. https://doi.org/10.5465/AMR.2005.15281431

Colbert, A. E., Bono, J. E., & Purvanova, R. K. (2016). Flourishing via workplace relationships: Moving beyond instrumental support. *Academy of Management Journal, 59*(4), 1199–1223. https://doi.org/10.5465/amj.2014.0506

Colella, A. (2001). Coworker distributive fairness judgments of the workplace accommodation of employees with disabilities. *Academy of Management Review, 26*(1), 100–116. https://doi.org/10.5465/AMR.2001.4011984

Colella, A., Paetzold, R. L., Belliveau, M. A., & Hollenbeck, J. (2004). Factors affecting coworkers' procedural justice inferences of the workplace accommodations of employees with disabilities. *Personnel Psychology, 57*(1), 1–23. https://doi.org/10.1111/j.1744-6570.2004.tb02482.x

Corbière, M., Villotti, P., Lecomte, T., Bond, G. R., Lesage, A., & Goldner, E. M. (2014). Work accommodations and natural supports for maintaining employment. *Psychiatric Rehabilitation Journal, 37*(2), 90–98. https://doi.org/10.1037/prj0000033

Côté, S. (2014). Emotional intelligence in organizations. *Annual Review of Organizational Psychology and Organizational Behavior, 1*(1), 459–488. https://doi.org/10.1146/annurev-orgpsych-031413-091233

Coupland, J. (2003). Small talk: Social functions. *Research on Language and Social Interaction, 36*(1), 1–6. https://doi.org/10.1207/S15327973RLSI3601_1

Cropanzano, R., & Mitchell, M. S. (2005). Social exchange theory: An interdisciplinary review. *Journal of Management, 31*(6), 874–900. https://doi.org/10.1177/0149206305279602

Dirks, K. T., Lewicki, R. J., & Zaheer, A. (2009). Introduction to special topic forum: Repairing relationships within and between organizations: Building a conceptual foundation. *The Academy of Management Review, 34*(1), 68–84. https://doi.org/10.5465/amr.2009.35713285

Dirks, K. T., & Skarlicki, D. P. (2009). The relationship between being perceived as trustworthy by coworkers and individual performance. *Journal of Management, 35*(1), 136–157. https://doi.org/10.1177/0149206308321545

Duffy, M. K., Ganster, D. C., & Pagon, M. (2002). Social undermining in the workplace. *Academy of Management Journal, 45*(2), 331–351. https://doi.org/10.2307/3069350

Dutton, J., & Heaphy, E. (2003). The power of high quality connections. In K. S. Cameron, J. E. Dutton, & R. E. Quinn (Eds.), *Positive organizational scholarship: Foundations of a new discipline* (pp. 263–278). San Francisco, CA: Berrett-Koehler.

Ehrhardt, K., & Ragins, B. R. (2018). Relational attachment at work: A complementary fit perspective on the role of relationships in organizational life. *Academy of Management Journal, 62*(1), 248–282. https://doi.org/10.5465/amj.2016.0245

Ellemers, N., De Gilder, D., & Haslam, S. A. (2004). Motivating individuals and groups at work: A social identity perspective on leadership and group performance. *The Academy of Management Review, 29*(3), 459–478. https://doi.org/10.2307/20159054

Ellemers, N., Sleebos, E., Stam, D., & de Gilder, D. (2013). Feeling included and valued: How perceived respect affects positive team identity and willingness to invest in the team. *British Journal of Management, 24*(1), 21–37. https://doi.org/10.1111/j.1467-8551.2011.00784.x

Ellis, A. M., Nifadkar, S. S., Bauer, T. N., & Erdogan, B. (2017). Newcomer adjustment: Examining the role of managers' perception of newcomer proactive behavior during organizational socialization. *Journal of Applied Psychology, 102*(6), 993–1001. https://doi.org/10.1037/apl0000201

Fang, R., Landis, B., Zhang, Z., Anderson, M. H., Shaw, J. D., & Kilduff, M. (2015). Integrating personality and social networks: A meta-analysis of personality, network position, and work outcomes in organizations. *Organization Science, 26*(4), 1243–1260. https://doi.org/10.1287/orsc.2015.0972

Ferris, G. R., Liden, R. C., Munyon, T. P., Summers, J. K., Basik, K. J., & Buckley, M. R. (2009). Relationships at work: Toward a multidimensional conceptualization of dyadic work relationships. *Journal of Management, 35*(6), 1379–1403. https://doi.org/10.1177/0149206309344741

George, J. M., & Brief, A. P. (1992). Feeling good-doing good: A conceptual analysis of the mood at work-organizational spontaneity relationship. *Psychological Bulletin, 112*(2), 310–329. https://doi.org/10.1037/0033-2909.112.2.310

Gersick, C. J. G., Dutton, J. E., & Bartunek, J. M. (2000). Learning from academia: The importance of relationships in professional life. *Academy of Management Journal, 43*(6), 1026–1044. https://doi.org/10.5465/1556333

Gouldner, A. W. (1960). The norm of reciprocity: A preliminary statement. *American Sociological Review, 25*(2), 161–178. https://doi.org/10.2307/2092623

Grant, A. M., & Parker, S. K. (2009). Redesigning work design theories: The rise of relational and proactive perspectives. *The Academy of Management Annals, 3*(1), 317–375. https://doi.org/10.1080/19416520903047327

Gruenfeld, D. H., Mannix, E. A., Williams, K. Y., & Neale, M. A. (1996). Group composition and decision making: How member familiarity and information distribution affect process and performance. *Organizational Behavior and Human Decision Processes, 67*(1), 1–15. https://doi.org/10.1006/obhd.1996.0061

Harrison, D. A., & Klein, K. J. (2007). What's the difference? Diversity constructs as separation, variety, or disparity in organizations. *Academy of Management Review, 32*(4), 1199–1228. https://doi.org/10.5465/AMR.2007.26586096

Harrison, D. A., Mohammed, S., McGrath, J. E., Florey, A. T., & Vanderstoep, S. W. (2003). Time matters in team performance: Effects of member familiarity, entrainment, and task discontinuity on speed and quality. *Personnel Psychology, 56*(3), 633–669. https://doi.org/10.1111/j.1744-6570.2003.tb00753.x

Hebl, M., Ruggs, E., Martinez, L., Trump-Steele, R., & Nittrouer, C. (2016). Understanding and reducing interpersonal discrimination in the workplace. In T. D. Nelson (Ed.), *Handbook of prejudice, stereotyping, and discrimination* (pp. 387–407). New York: Psychology Press.

Helles, A., Gillberg, I. C., Gillberg, C., & Billstedt, E. (2016). Asperger syndrome in males over two decades: Quality of life in relation to diagnostic stability and psychiatric comorbidity: *Autism, 21*(4), 458–469. https://doi.org/10.1177/1362361316650090

Hershcovis, M. S. (2011). "Incivility, social undermining, bullying . . . oh my!": A call to reconcile constructs within workplace aggression research. *Journal of Organizational Behavior, 32*(3), 499–519. https://doi.org/10.1002/job.689

Holmes, J. G. (2000). Social relationships: The nature and function of relational schemas. *European Journal of Social Psychology, 30*(4), 447–495. https://doi.org/10.1002/1099-0992(200007/08)30:4<447::AID-EJSP10>3.0.CO;2-Q

Holwerda, A., van der Klink, J. J. L., Groothoff, J. W., & Brouwer, S. (2012). Predictors for work participation in individuals with an Autism spectrum disorder: A systematic review. *Journal of Occupational Rehabilitation, 22*(3), 333–352. https://doi.org/10.1007/s10926-011-9347-8

Howard, M. C., Cogswell, J. E., & Smith, M. B. (2020). The antecedents and outcomes of workplace ostracism: A meta-analysis. *Journal of Applied Psychology, 105*(6), 577–596. https://doi.org/10.1037/apl0000453

Humphrey, S. E., Aime, F., Cushenbery, L., Hill, A. D., & Fairchild, J. (2017). Team conflict dynamics: Implications of a dyadic view of conflict for team performance. *Organizational Behavior and Human Decision Processes, 142*, 58–70. https://doi.org/10.1016/j.obhdp.2017.08.002

Hurley-Hanson, A. E., Giannantonio, C. M., & Griffiths, A. J. (2020). The stigma of autism. In A. E. Hurley-Hanson, C. M. Giannantonio, & A. J. Griffiths (Eds.), *Autism in the workplace: Creating positive employment and career outcomes for Generation A* (pp. 21–45). London: Springer International Publishing. https://doi.org/10.1007/978-3-030-29049-8_2

Jehn, K. A. (1995). A multimethod examination of the benefits and detriments of intragroup conflict. *Administrative Science Quarterly, 40*(2), 256–282. https://doi.org/10.2307/2393638

Jehn, K. A., Northcraft, G. B., & Neale, M. A. (1999). Why differences make a difference: A field study of diversity, conflict, and performance in workgroups. *Administrative Science Quarterly, 44*(4), 741–763. https://doi.org/10.2307/2667054

Jenaro, C., Mank, D., Bottomley, J., Doose, S., & Tuckerman, P. (2002). Supported employment in the international context: An analysis of processes and outcomes. *Journal of Vocational Rehabilitation, 17*(1), 5–21.

Jensen, C. M., Martens, C. S., Nikolajsen, N. D., Skytt Gregersen, T., Heckmann Marx, N., Goldberg Frederiksen, M., & Hansen, M. S. (2016). What do the general population know, believe and feel about individuals with autism and schizophrenia: Results from a comparative survey in Denmark. *Autism, 20*(4), 496–508. https://doi.org/10.1177/1362361315593068

Johnson, T. D. (2016). *Scaling cliffs and crossing chasms: Unpacking the micro-processes of inclusion through the lens of autism job coaches*. Retrieved from https://etda.libraries.psu.edu/catalog/q524jn76v

Johnson, T. D., & Joshi, A. (2014). Disclosure on the spectrum: Understanding disclosure among employees on the autism spectrum. *Industrial and Organizational Psychology, 7*(2), 278–281. https://doi.org/10.1111/iops.12149

Johnson, T. D., & Joshi, A. (2016). Dark clouds or silver linings? A stigma threat perspective on the implications of an autism diagnosis for workplace well-being. *Journal of Applied Psychology, 101*(3), 430–449. https://doi.org/10.1037/apl0000058

Kahn, W. (2007). Meaningful connections: Positive relationships and attachments at work. In J. E. Dutton & B. R. Ragins (Eds.), *Exploring positive relationships at work: Building a theoretical and research foundation* (pp. 189–206). New York: Routledge.

Kammeyer-Mueller, J., Wanberg, C., Rubenstein, A., & Zhaoli, S. (2013). Support, undermining, and newcomer socialization: Fitting in during the first 90 days. *Academy of Management Journal, 56*(4), 1104–1124. https://doi.org/10.5465/amj.2010.0791

Kilduff, M., & Brass, D. J. (2010). Organizational social network research: Core ideas and key debates. *The Academy of Management Annals, 4*(1), 317–357. https://doi.org/10.1080/19416520.2010.494827

Kilduff, M., & Day, D.V. (1994). Do chameleons get ahead? The effects of self-monitoring on managerial careers. *The Academy of Management Journal, 37*(4), 1047–1060. https://doi.org/10.2307/256612

Kim, P. H., Ferrin, D. L., Cooper, C. D., & Dirks, K.T. (2004). Removing the shadow of suspicion: The effects of apology versus denial for repairing competence-versus integrity-based trust violations. *Journal of Applied Psychology, 89*(1), 104–118.

Koopman, J., Lanaj, K., & Scott, B.A. (2016). Integrating the bright and dark sides of OCB: A daily investigation of the benefits and costs of helping others. *Academy of Management Journal, 59*(2), 414–435. https://doi.org/10.5465/amj.2014.0262

Labianca, G. J., & Brass, D. J. (2006). Exploring the social ledger: Negative relationships and negative asymmetry in social networks in organizations. *The Academy of Management Review, 31*(3), 596–614. https://doi.org/10.2307/20159231

Longmire, N. H., & Harrison, D. A. (2018). Seeing their side versus feeling their pain: Differential consequences of perspective-taking and empathy at work. *Journal of Applied Psychology, 103*(8), 894–915.

Lord, C., McCauley, J. B., Pepa, L. A., Huerta, M., & Pickles, A. (2020). Work, living, and the pursuit of happiness: Vocational and psychosocial outcomes for young adults with autism: *Autism*. https://doi.org/10.1177/1362361320919246

Lyons, B. J., Pek, S., & Wessel, J. L. (2017). Toward a "sunlit path": Stigma identity management as a source of localized social change through interaction. *Academy of Management Review, 42*(4), 618–636. https://doi.org/10.5465/amr.2015.0189

Lyons, B. J., & Scott, B. A. (2012). Integrating social exchange and affective explanations for the receipt of help and harm: A social network approach. *Organizational Behavior and Human Decision Processes, 117*(1), 66–79. https://doi.org/10.1016/j.obhdp.2011.10.002

Mason, D., McConachie, H., Garland, D., Petrou, A., Rodgers, J., & Parr, J. R. (2018). Predictors of quality of life for Autistic adults. *Autism Research, 11*(8), 1138–1147. https://doi.org/10.1002/aur.1965

Mathersul, D., McDonald, S., & Rushby, J. A. (2013). Understanding advanced theory of mind and empathy in high-functioning adults with autism spectrum disorder. *Journal of Clinical and Experimental Neuropsychology, 35*(6), 655–668. https://doi.org/10.1080/13803395.2013.809700

Methot, J. R., Lepine, J. A., Podsakoff, N. P., & Christian, J. S. (2016). Are workplace friendships a mixed blessing? Exploring tradeoffs of multiplex relationships and their associations with job performance. *Personnel Psychology, 69*(2), 311–355. https://doi.org/10.1111/peps.12109

Methot, J. R., Rosado-Solomon, E. H., Downes, P., & Gabriel, A. S. (2020). office chit-chat as a social ritual: The uplifting yet distracting effects of daily small talk at work. *Academy of Management Journal*. https://doi.org/10.5465/amj.2018.1474

Müller, E., Schuler, A., Burton, B., & Yates, G. (2003). Meeting the vocational support needs of individuals with Asperger syndrome and other autism spectrum disabilities. *Journal of Vocational Rehabilitation, 18*(3), 163–175.

Nelson, D. L., & Quick, J. C. (1991). Social support and newcomer adjustment in organizations: Attachment theory at work? *Journal of Organizational Behavior, 12*(6), 543–554. https://doi.org/10.1002/job.4030120607

Ohl, A., Grice Sheff, M., Small, S., Nguyen, J., Paskor, K., & Zanjirian, A. (2017). Predictors of employment status among adults with Autism Spectrum Disorder. *Work, 56*(2), 345–355. https://doi.org/10.3233/WOR-172492

Ohtake, Y., & Chadsey, J. G. (1999). Social disclosure among coworkers without disabilities in supported employment settings. *Mental Retardations, 37*(1), 25–35.

Okimoto, T. G., & Wenzel, M. (2014). Bridging diverging perspectives and repairing damaged relationships in the aftermath of workplace transgressions. *Business Ethics Quarterly, 24*(3), 443–473. https://doi.org/10.5840/beq201471515

Olekalns, M., Caza, B. B., & Vogus, T. (2019). Gradual drifts, abrupt shocks: From relationship fractures to relational resilience. *Academy of Management Annals, 14*(1), 1–28. https://doi.org/10.5465/annals.2017.0111

Ozcclik, H., & Barsade, S. G. (2018). No employee an island: Workplace loneliness and job performance. *Academy of Management Journal, 61*(6), 2343–2366. https://doi.org/10.5465/amj.2015.1066

Paluck, E. L., & Green, D. P. (2009). Prejudice reduction: What works? A review and assessment of research and practice. *Annual Review of Psychology, 60*(1), 339–367. https://doi.org/10.1146/annurev.psych.60.110707.163607

Patton, E. (2019). Autism, attributions and accommodations: Overcoming barriers and integrating a neurodiverse workforce. *Personnel Review, 48*(4), 915–934. https://doi.org/10.1108/PR-04-2018-0116

Pillemer, J., & Rothbard, N. P. (2018). Friends without benefits: Understanding the dark sides of workplace friendship. *Academy of Management Review, 43*(4), 635–660. https://doi.org/10.5465/amr.2016.0309

Ragins, B. R. (2008). Disclosure disconnects: Antecedents and consequences of disclosing invisible stigmas across life domains. *Academy of Management Review, 33*(1), 194–215. https://doi.org/10.5465/AMR.2008.27752724

Ragins, B. R., & Ehrhardt, K. (2020). Gaining perspective: The impact of close cross-race friendships on diversity training and education. *Journal of Applied Psychology*. Advance online publication. https://doi.org/10.1037/apl0000807

Ren, H., & Gray, B. (2009). Repairing relationship conflict: How violation types and culture influence the effectiveness of restoration rituals. *Academy of Management Review, 34*(1), 105–126. https://doi.org/10.5465/amr.2009.35713307

Ren, H., Gray, B., & Harrison, D. A. (2014). Triggering faultline effects in teams: The importance of bridging friendship ties and breaching animosity ties. *Organization Science, 26*(2), 390–404. https://doi.org/10.1287/orsc.2014.0944

Rollins, A. L., Mueser, K. T., Bond, G. R., & Becker, D. R. (2002). Social relationships at work: Does the employment model make a difference? *Psychiatric Rehabilitation Journal, 26*(1), 51–61. https://doi.org/10.2975/26.2002.51.61

Russinova, Z., Griffin, S., Bloch, P., Wewiorski, N. J., & Rosoklija, I. (2011). Workplace prejudice and discrimination toward individuals with mental illnesses. *Journal of Vocational Rehabilitation, 35*(3), 227–241.

Santuzzi, A. M., Waltz, P. R., Finkelstein, L. M., & Rupp, D. E. (2014). Invisible disabilities: Unique challenges for employees and organizations. *Industrial and Organizational Psychology*, 7(2), 204–219. https://doi.org/10.1111/iops.12134

Sarge, M. A., Kim, H.-S., & Velez, J. A. (2020). An autism intervention: The role of perspective taking in combating public stigma with virtual simulations. *Cyberpsychology, Behavior, and Social Networking, 23*(1), 41–51. https://doi.org/10.1089/cyber.2019.0678

Sarrett, J. (2017). Interviews, disclosures, and misperceptions: Autistic adults' perspectives on employment related challenges. *Disability Studies Quarterly, 37*(2). https://doi.org/10.18061/dsq.v37i2.5524

Sasson, N. J., & Morrison, K. E. (2019). First impressions of adults with autism improve with diagnostic disclosure and increased autism knowledge of peers. *Autism: The International Journal of Research and Practice, 23*(1), 50–59. https://doi.org/10.1177/1362361317729526

Schneider, B. (1987). The people make the place. *Personnel Psychology, 40*(3), 437–453. https://doi.org/10.1111/j.1744-6570.1987.tb00609.x

Scott, K. L., Restubog, S. L. D., & Zagenczyk, T. J. (2013). A social exchange-based model of the antecedents of workplace exclusion. *Journal of Applied Psychology, 98*(1), 37–48. https://doi.org/10.1037/a0030135

Song, Y., Liu, Y., Shi, J., & Wang, M. (2017). Use of proactive socialization tactics and socialization outcomes: A latent growth modeling approach to understanding newcomer socialization process. *Academy of Management Discoveries, 3*(1), 42–63.

Spreitzer, G., Sutcliffe, K., Dutton, J., Sonenshein, S., & Grant, A. M. (2005). A socially embedded model of thriving at work. *Organization Science, 16*(5), 537–549. https://doi.org/10.1287/orsc.1050.0153

Sue, D. W., Alsaidi, S., Awad, M. N., Glaeser, E., Calle, C. Z., & Mendez, N. (2019). Disarming racial microaggressions: Microintervention strategies for targets, white allies, and bystanders. *American Psychologist, 74*(1), 128–142. https://doi.org/10.1037/amp0000296

Sue, D. W., Capodilupo, C. M., Torino, G. C., Bucceri, J. M., Holder, A. M. B., Nadal, K. L., & Esquilin, M. (2007). Racial microaggressions in everyday life: Implications for clinical practice. *American Psychologist, 62*, 271–286. http://dx.doi.org/10.1037/0003-066X.62.4.271

Swann, W. B., Polzer, J. T., Seyle, D. C., & Ko, S. J. (2004). Finding value in diversity: Verification of personal and social self-views in diverse groups. *The Academy of Management Review, 29*(1), 9–27. https://doi.org/10.2307/20159006

Taylor, J. L., & DaWalt, L. S. (2017). Brief report: Postsecondary work and educational disruptions for youth on the autism spectrum. *Journal of Autism and Developmental Disorders, 47*(12), 4025–4031. https://doi.org/10.1007/s10803-017-3305-z

Taylor, J. L., DaWalt, L. S., Marvin, A. R., Law, J. K., & Lipkin, P. (2019). Sex differences in employment and supports for adults with autism spectrum disorder. *Autism, 23*(7), 1711–1719. https://doi.org/10.1177/1362361319827417

Taylor, J. L., Henninger, N. A., & Mailick, M. R. (2015). Longitudinal patterns of employment and postsecondary education for adults with autism and average-range IQ. *Autism, 19*(7), 785–793. https://doi.org/10.1177/1362361315585643

Taylor, J. L., & Mailick, M. R. (2014). A longitudinal examination of 10-year change in vocational and educational activities for adults with autism spectrum disorders. *Developmental Psychology, 50*(3), 699–708. https://doi.org/10.1037/a0034297

Venkataramani, V., & Dalal, R. S. (2007). Who helps and harms whom? Relational antecedents of interpersonal helping and harming in organizations. *Journal of Applied Psychology, 92*(4), 952–966. https://doi.org/10.1037/0021-9010.92.4.952

Walsh, L., Lydon, S., & Healy, O. (2014). Employment and vocational skills among individuals with Autism Spectrum Disorder: Predictors, impact, and interventions. *Review Journal of Autism and Developmental Disorders, 1*(4), 266–275. https://doi.org/10.1007/s40489-014-0024-7

Wilmot, M. P., Wanberg, C. R., Kammeyer-Mueller, J. D., & Ones, D. S. (2019). Extraversion advantages at work: A quantitative review and synthesis of the meta-analytic evidence. *Journal of Applied Psychology, 104*(12), 1447–1470. https://doi.org/10.1037/apl0000415

Wright, C. R., Manning, M. R., Farmer, B., & Gilbreath, B. (2000). Resourceful sensemaking in product development teams. *Organization Studies, 21*(4), 807–825. https://doi.org/10.1177/0170840600214006

8

WORKPLACE ACCOMMODATION CONSIDERATIONS FOR A NEURODIVERSE WORKFORCE

Eric Patton

Introduction

Over the last five years, a remarkable development has occurred, both in the workplace and in management research: an emphasis on the employment of individuals on the autism spectrum and, more broadly, neurodiversity in the workplace. Neurodiversity, similar to other forms of diversity, represents natural variations in human beings that include less common neurodivergent conditions such as autism (Ortega, 2009; Waisman-Nitzan et al., 2019). In line with established research findings on the business benefits of workplace diversity (Hubbard, 2007; Page, 2007), many companies such as SAP, Ford, Microsoft, and Ernst & Young have hired individuals on the autism spectrum for the skills they bring to the workplace (Austin & Pisano, 2017; Wright, 2016), and many service organizations such as Specialisterne and the Arc are working to connect individuals on the spectrum with possible employers to provide meaningful work to this often neglected segment of the workforce.

Over the last several years, there has been a lively and important debate in the neurodiversity/autism community over the appropriateness of medical models of autism (i.e., autism as a disorder to be treated/cured) and social/identity models (i.e., autism as another form of diversity similar to race, gender, sexual orientation), with an emphasis on terminology, dignity, and resources (Baron-Cohen, 2017; Bottema-Beutal et al., 2020; Kapp et al., 2013; Lollini, 2018). Much of this work rejects the disorder language but embraces a difference-and-disability viewpoint, which underlines diversity while acknowledging that individuals can experience disability in certain contexts and require supports/accommodations. Overall, several facts are clear: First, from a legal standpoint, organizations may be required to accommodate workers with autism under the Americans with Disabilities Act

DOI: 10.4324/9781003023616-8

(ADA) and other disability legislation across the globe. Second, individuals with autism have been severely disadvantaged in the workplace due to a host of barriers (Patton, 2019). Third, the number of young adults with autism who will be joining the ranks of employable adults is going to grow by leaps and bounds in the coming decade (Chu, 2015; Johnson & Joshi, 2016). Finally, the underemployment of individuals on the autism spectrum represents both an untapped source of competitive advantage for organizations (Austin & Pisano, 2017) and unnecessarily high costs and lost productivity to society (Knapp et al., 2009).

The purpose of this chapter is to explore what workplace accommodations can be implemented to create truly inclusive workplaces for individuals on the autism spectrum. On the one hand, companies are often legally required to offer reasonable workplace accommodations to individuals with physical or neurocognitive conditions. On the other hand, many of the success stories and examples of companies that employ individuals on the spectrum are cases of fitting the individual to the job rather than fitting the job to the individual. While individuals on the high end of the spectrum have found success in information technology, and individuals on the lower end of the spectrum have found low-level jobs such as bagging groceries, such connections are ones that require less effort and less change on the part of employers, as these positions are well suited to specific minorities within the neurodiversity community (Doyle, 2020). Although these successes are laudable and positive, disability researchers have long recognized that employee–organization "fit" generally constitutes a barrier to employment for differently abled individuals (Erickson et al., 2014; Ren et al., 2008). To be truly inclusive, employers need to consider *all* reasonable accommodations regardless of natural fit with the position. As reported by Skibell (2017), experts are beginning to worry that people with autism are in danger of being pigeonholed in certain technical fields (e.g., computer programming, database management, electrical wiring) to the exclusion of wider workforce participation. Furthermore, the law makes no reference to employee–job fit when it comes to legally required workplace accommodations. The chapter will consider three areas: First, an overview of autism will be presented along with a consideration of the legal aspects of workplace accommodations including the barriers that exist for individuals with autism in requesting such accommodations. Second, a number of possible accommodations will be described, both during the selection process and on the job. Third, the role of supervisors and coworkers in successful implementation of accommodations will be discussed.

Overview of Autism Spectrum and Legally Required Accommodation Policies

According to the *Diagnostic and Statistical Manual of Mental Disorders*, 5th edition (American Psychiatric Association, 2013), autism is a neurodevelopmental disorder that is characterized by persistent deficits in social communication and social interaction across multiple contexts, including deficits in social reciprocity, nonverbal communicative behaviors used for social interactions, and skills in developing, maintaining, and understanding relationships. While the previous version of the DSM defined several conditions separately (e.g., autism, Asperger's, childhood disintegrative disorder), the DSM-V groups these conditions under the umbrella of autism spectrum disorder (ASD), thus underlining the spectrum characteristic of the condition. Consistent with the concept of autism as spectrum, one of the most well-known adages concerning autism, which was coined by Dr. Stephen Shore, himself an individual on the spectrum, is: "When you've met one person with autism, you've met one person with autism" (Chu, 2015; Skibell, 2017). Indeed, in some cases, autistic individuals may be unable to speak, have physical or intellectual impairments, and require life-long support and constant care, while in other cases, autism can be completely invisible to observers, coworkers, and managers (Van Wieren et al., 2008). As noted, the spectrum reality also negates the stereotype that all individuals with autism are interested or adept in information technology.

Still, to some degree, most individuals with autism tend to have some level of difficulty with verbal and nonverbal communication, which can be manifested through challenges expressing wants and needs, difficulties understanding the subtleties of idioms, humor, and sarcasm, idiosyncrasies in volume, pitch, and rhythm of speech, difficulties in maintaining eye contact, and an inability to properly interpret body language and facial expressions. Another common set of challenges for people across the spectrum involves social interactions, characterized by difficulty in starting conversations, difficulty in comforting or showing interest in the feelings or preferences of others, aversion to physical contact, and not responding when spoken to or even when praised. Finally, individuals on the spectrum often have a pattern of ritualized or repetitive behaviors, which lead to tight adherence to routine and rules, strong resistance to and discomfort over change or unplanned events, repeated verification and questions, and excessive focus/conversation on a very limited set of topics (American Psychiatric Association, 2013; World Health Organization, 2013).

At the same time, there is a growing emphasis on the strength-based model of neurodiversity, which underlines the strengths that neurominorities possess that make them valuable contributors to the workforce (Wong et al., 2018). The same characteristics that are framed as deficits in the DSM-V have been highlighted as positives by many researchers (Austin & Pisano, 2017; Lorenz & Heinitz, 2014). The different ways of thinking and processing information, the laser focus on specific areas, the attention to detail, and visual-spatial abilities in nonverbal tasks are all characteristics that can add value to organizations. Furthermore, employed individuals with autism are described as typically very hardworking, loyal, honest, reliable, nonjudgmental, punctual, not partaking in office politics, and take fewer sick days (Hurlbutt & Chalmers, 2004; Hillier et al., 2007; Khalifa et al., 2020; Parr et al., 2013). Not surprisingly, individuals with autism generally receive satisfactory or strong performance evaluations at work (Parr et al., 2013).

Unfortunately, despite these strengths and the efforts of a limited number of forward-looking companies, most work environment still seem to be unwelcoming places for the vast majority of individuals with autism. While the employment rate of working-age individuals with any disability is less than half the rate of individuals without disabilities in the United States (38% vs. 80%, according to Erickson et al., 2020) the participation of individuals on the spectrum is far lower. According to the National Autistic Society (NAS), in the United Kingdom, only 15% of adults of working age with autism are employed in full-time jobs (Mavranezouli et al., 2014; Rosenblatt, 2008). Furthermore, 80% of individuals with the highest functioning level of autism (previously known as Aspergers) are unemployed (Austin & Pisano, 2017; Barnard et al., 2001; Parr et al., 2013). Of those who are employed, underemployment in low-level, unskilled jobs not corresponding to their intelligence, education, and abilities is another common phenomenon (Bjelland et al., 2010).

While this lack of workforce participation can represent a barrier to personal success and cut off an important source of meaning and accomplishment for individuals on the spectrum, the societal costs are also high when talented individuals who are willing and able to work are not provided sufficient opportunities. Over the course of an individual with autism's life, the societal costs of caring and supporting an unemployed person on the spectrum has been estimated to be between 1.4 to 2.4 million U.S. dollars in the United Kingdom and the United States (Harmuth et al., 2018). Families are also affected, as many individuals on the spectrum live with their parents. Katz et al. (2015) reported that 73% of adults with autism aged 22 and older live with their parents, and that 32% have no social involvement outside their families. Related to this, Hillier and Galizzi (2014) found that nearly half the parents they interviewed reported lost income and career difficulties due to providing care and support to their adult children on the spectrum.

Overall, a picture emerges in which a segment of the population that is motivated, hardworking, and often highly skilled and intelligent is being denied employment opportunities that would benefit the individuals themselves, their families, employers, and society as a whole. However, beyond these individual fairness, social benefits, and pragmatic business reasons for making work more accessible to the autism community, there are also legal reasons to provide accommodations in the workplace. While the legislative reasons for providing workplace accommodations have not been sufficient to bring about inclusion for neurodivergent individuals, the language of accommodations is closely tied to the law, and in many ways, laws set the context around which accommodations will occur. As such, an important place to start when introducing the concept of accommodations is the legal aspect.

Autism, Accommodations, and the Law

The latter part of the 20th century saw a host of countries pass legislation aimed at protecting the rights of individuals with disabilities. Most of these laws included protections for mental health conditions and aimed to remove barriers in the workplace. On the global level, Article 23 of the 1948 United Nations Universal Declaration of Human Rights states that everyone, including any member of a vulnerable population, has a right to work, to just and fair working conditions, to protection against unemployment, and to equal pay for equal work (UN General Assembly, 1948). In 2008, the United Nations ratified the Convention on the Rights of Persons with Disabilities to promote, protect, and ensure the full enjoyment of human rights by people with disabilities and ensure that they enjoy full equality under the law. Specific to work and employment, Article 27 of the convention prohibits discrimination in obtaining work or career advancement on the basis of disability, protects individuals with disabilities from harassment at work and unsafe/unfair working conditions and pay, promotes entrepreneurship and access to education/vocational training for individuals with disabilities, and aims to ensure that reasonable accommodations are provided to persons with disabilities in the workplace (United Nations, 2006). The Convention on the Rights of Persons with Disabilities has been signed or ratified by more than 180 countries and the European Union. As noted by Waisman-Nitzan et al. (2019) and Jaarsma and Welin (2012), the vulnerability of those with neurodivergence, including autism, makes such conventions very important to individuals on the spectrum. Furthermore, the 17 United Nations Sustainable Development Goals (SDG), set by the General Assembly in 2015, include *reducing inequalities*, *decent work & economic growth*, and *good health & well-being*, which are relevant to employment opportunities for neurominorities.

Of course, enforceable legislation resides at the country level. In the United States, the 2008 amendments to the 1990 Americans with Disabilities Act (ADA) defined disability as a physical or mental impairment that substantially limits a major life activity, including the ability to work, and protected qualified individuals with a disability from workplace discrimination whether or not they required an accommodation to perform the essential functions of a job. The 2008 amendments relaxed the standards for the "substantial limitations" and made clear that the determination of a disability should be construed in favor of broad coverage (Martin et al., 2011). In light of the 2008 amendments, the civil rights enforcement agency in the United States, the Equal Employment Opportunity Commission (EEOC), released new regulations for the ADA and listed autism in their examples of impairments that would be covered under the ADA as a disability (Martin et al., 2011; Hensel, 2017). In this vein, the EEOC has filed several successful lawsuits on behalf of workers with autism against employers for workplace discrimination. Comfort Suite Hotels ($132,500 in 2011), Randstad ($60,000 in 2012), Golden Corral ($85,000 in 2018), and Party City ($155,000 in 2019) all made settlement payments and implemented policy changes in response to lawsuits by the EEOC alleging discrimination against individuals on the autism spectrum (EEOC, 2011, 2012, 2018, 2019). (Further information about autism-at-work programs and the interface with the regulatory environment can be found in the chapter by Saleh and Bernick in this volume.) As will be discussed in what follows, however, issues around disclosure, questions around essential functions of a job, and lack of self-advocacy/failure to file complaints limit the effectiveness of the ADA in protecting individuals with autism. In the United Kingdom, the Equality Act of 2010 protects workers with physical and mental/psychological health conditions, while both Australia's Disability Discrimination Act and Canada's Human Rights Act do the same. All of these laws stipulate that individuals with disabilities, including autism, cannot be discriminated against in the hiring process and require employers to provide reasonable accommodations that do not place undue hardship on the employer but assist workers in meeting the essential functions of a job.

Using the Americans with Disabilities Act as a model, Title I of the ADA requires employers with 15 or more employees to make good-faith efforts to provide workplace accommodations of three potential types. First, accommodations may consist of modifications to the application, recruitment, and selection process in order to provide qualified applicants with a fair opportunity for a position. Second, accommodations may involve modifying certain job tasks or physical features of the work environment. Third, accommodations may require employers to modify certain rules or elements of workplace culture to ensure that employees with disabilities are not deprived of workplace rights and privileges (Gold et al., 2012).

Two issues surrounding legislation and the ability to receive accommodations that are particularly challenging for neurodivergent minorities are: (1) determining what is an *essential* job function that will allow for a *reasonable* accommodation and (2) the requirement that individuals needing accommodations must initiate the process by both disclosing and requesting accommodations from employers. Given the emphasis on soft skills in management over the last 40 years that place a premium on interpersonal skills, communication skills, networking abilities, and so on, many of today's job descriptions/requirements for high-paying jobs may appear to be out of reach for individuals with autism if such skills are viewed as essential (Patton, 2019). While the essential nature of these characteristics is certainly questionable (Doyle, 2020; Patton, 2019), they can represent a barrier to members of neurominorities, especially given the fact that individuals with autism often have difficulty advocating for themselves (Hillier & Galizzi, 2014). While the EEOC states that autism is a protected disability, and despite some EEOC victories for individuals with autism previously highlighted, Van Wieren et al. (2012) found only 170 complaints from individuals with autism in the EEOC Integrated Mission System from 1992 to 2008 compared to 45,560 complaints about back ailments, 14,151 complaints relating to diabetes, 2,028 complains about speech impairments, 5,045 for HIV, and 6,717 for learning disabilities. The number of complaints is much lower than the prevalence of the condition suggests should exist, which indicates that, similar to research on the lack of EEOC complaints by individuals with intellectual disabilities (Unger et al., 2005), there is a lack of motivation to file allegations with the EEOC (Van Wieren et al., 2012). This difficulty in self-advocacy also exacerbates the other issue that leads to individuals with autism not receiving accommodations they are legally entitled to: the requirement to self-disclose. Unless a disability is clear and evident, the ADA requires accommodation seekers to self-disclose. Given that many job seekers with autism do not have an obvious and clear disability, the onus falls on them to self-disclose. Beyond lack of self-advocacy, there are other reasons an individual on the spectrum might choose nondisclosure. Researchers have found that individuals with disabilities often choose nondisclosure due to concerns over being fired, lack of support, being passed over for promotion, being treated/viewed differently by supervisors, and fears of being bullied by coworkers, especially when the disability is invisible (von Schrader, Malzer, et al., 2014; von Schrader, Xu, et al., 2014). Specific to autism, Johnson and Joshi (2016) found that individuals on the spectrum overwhelmingly chose to avoid disclosing their condition out of fear of stereotypes and stigmatization. Similarly, given the continuing disability bias present in American society, particularly around neurological and psychological disabilities, Hensel (2017) suggests that it is often advantageous for a worker with autism to refrain from voluntarily disclosing their condition. Still, the "advantages" of nondisclosure seem quite weak since, as previously noted, even individuals on the very high-functioning end of the spectrum have an unemployment rate of 80% (Richards, 2012). An upcoming section on coworkers and supervisors will highlight that although individual's on the less severe end of the spectrum do not demonstrate a disability, their behaviors can still lead to negative outcomes in the workplace. (Further discussion on neurodiversity and the disclosure dilemma can be found in the chapter by Santuzzi and Keating in this volume.)

From a legal standpoint, every individual who discloses their autism is, at minimum, entitled to have their situation considered from an accommodation standpoint. At the same time, the laws in effect are clearly not enough to secure individuals on the spectrum the supports they require. The extremely high unemployment rates are evidence of this fact. Some common characteristics of the laws enacted to help people with protected conditions actually make it less likely that eligible individuals will receive the accommodations to which they are entitled. A prime example are the restrictions on employers about asking questions regarding potential disabilities (Clark, 1997), which act as a disincentive for employers to even broach the subject out of (a) fear they may violate the ADA and face legal action by asking a question that could help an employee or (b) perhaps more cynically, prefer nondisclosure as it will save the costs/hassles of accommodations. While costs associated with accommodations have been widely shown to be very inexpensive (Gewurtz et al., 2016; Schur et al., 2014) employers are often concerned about perceptions of coworkers in terms of fairness and resource allocation (Schur et al., 2014). While the supervisor and coworker dynamics of requesting accommodations will be covered in an upcoming section, it is important to discuss the nature of accommodations that can help neurodivergent individuals with autism gain employment and thrive in the workplace.

Accommodations for the Worker with Autism: Before the Job and Once on the Job

Apart from the legal imperatives of providing reasonable accommodations, researchers have underlined how such supports benefit organizations and individuals alike. On the organization side, Gold et al. (2012) underline that providing workplace accommodations leads to increased job performance, less turnover, and higher job satisfaction on the part of the focal individual and also has organization-wide benefits. General personal well-being is also enhanced by disclosure, as Sarrett (2017) and Newheiser et al. (2017) note that concealing a disability leads to social isolation, stress, depression, and other negative health outcomes. Given that the visible nature of a medical condition is a strong predictor of obtaining an accommodation (von Schrader, Xu, et al., 2014), individuals on the high-functioning end of the autism spectrum, who may be able to conceal their condition and choose nondisclosure, are at risk of these negative personal consequences. In this vein, Konrad et al. (2013) found strong evidence that accommodations increase life satisfaction for workers with disabilities and reduce perceived disability-related discrimination. Still, many individuals with invisible disabilities choose nondisclosure due to fears of disparate treatment in hiring, negative workplace interactions, and barriers in career advancement (von Schrader, Malzer, et al., 2014).

At the same time, requesting accommodations is not always a matter of helping with a disability. In fact, von Schrader, Xu, et al. (2014) found that individuals both with and without a disability are apt to request accommodations. Using 2012 census-level data from the U.S. Department of Labor, they found that the vast majority of workers with disabilities do not request accommodations, with only 15.8% of workers with cognitive disabilities requesting accommodations. In fact, perhaps due to a lack of concern of stigma and/or discrimination, their study reported that close to 9% of workers without disabilities request accommodations, signifying that 95% of individuals requesting accommodations around policies or physical changes in the workplace were people without disabilities (i.e., close to 12 million accommodation requests from workers without disabilities compared to roughly 600,000 requests from workers with disabilities). Furthermore, despite fears to the contrary, there is a great deal of evidence indicating that most accommodations involve little or no cost to employers (Gewurtz et al., 2016; Schur et al., 2014). Overall, fears and misconceptions around accommodations seem to weigh as heavily as legal entitlements for both employers and individuals. Developing an inclusive organizational culture around disability and/or a culture in which all employees are comfortable requesting reasonable accommodation regardless of the root cause of the request may be the best avenue for ensuring that employees get the support they need (Gewurtz et al., 2016; Gold et al., 2012; von Schrader, Malzer, et al., 2014).

In the case of individuals with autism, the timing of these accommodations will typically be required at two different phases of the individual-organizational relationship: during the recruitment phase and once the individual is in the job.

Accommodations During the Interview Phase

In the United States, the Americans with Disabilities Act applies to all aspects of employment, including job advertisements, job applications, job interviews, and postoffer medical examinations. As such, employers have an obligation to make reasonable accommodations to enable applicants with disabilities to participate in the interview process (Whetzel, 2014; EEOC, 2002; also see Saleh, Chang, Bruyère, & Vogus in this volume). Accommodations during this phase are particularly important for individuals on the spectrum, as the common social interaction deficiencies can make the interview process especially challenging. As previously noted, many employers now look for proficiency in soft people skills, and the ability to display such skills during interviews is advantageous and can influence employers' perceptions of candidates (Lindsay et al., 2015). Many employers hope for job candidates to be personable and a good fit with coworkers (Richards, 2017), which, as previously noted, can represent a barrier (Erickson et al., 2014) for individuals with disabilities. This superficial lack of "fit" can manifest itself upon initial contact. Furthermore, all interviews, regardless of the nature of the position, require candidates to adopt a certain dress code and behavior, make eye contact, and have a good understanding of employer expectations, verbal cues, body language, and so on, all of which can represent challenges to even individuals on the high-functioning end of the spectrum (Katz et al., 2015). In addition to perhaps not making the desired first impression, the social anxiety brought on by the interview process can cause individuals with autism to freeze up, make thinking difficult, and prevent the interviewee from demonstrating their knowledge and qualifications (Whetzel, 2014; also see Saleh et al., in this volume).

As previously noted, the onus is on the job applicant to disclose a disability under the Americans with Disabilities Act, and this includes during the application process. In fact, it is against the law for a potential employer to ask any disability-related questions during the preoffer stage of employment, nor can an employer ask any question that would potentially elicit information about a disability (Clark, 1997). As explained by Clark (1997), if a medical condition is obvious, then an employer has greater latitude on asking about job-related questions that could involve the disability. In fact, according to the ADA, an obvious impairment (e.g., an applicant using a wheelchair) would require a potential employer to provide reasonable accommodations during the interview process. Still, as highlighted by Richards (2017), high-functioning autistic individuals will not be obviously eligible for ADA protection in the interview process, and since many individuals will choose not to disclose their diagnosis due to stigmas, some manifestations of autism can make an interviewer view social difficulties as a negative character flaw.

When an individual with autism discloses their diagnosis to a potential employer or if their condition is obvious, there are several accommodations that potential employers should and could be required to provide. At the outset, however, it is important that individuals with autism conduct a proper job search and, once an application is submitted and an invitation for an interview is offered, prepare for the encounter. In terms of applying, Whetzel (2014) notes that individuals with autism must understand how they learn and work, ensure that their education and experience relate to the position they are applying for, and understand the environments they are comfortable working in. While these recommendations clearly also make good sense for anyone considering any potential position, they are essential for an individual with autism. While a neurotypical person may believe that any job or work experience may be valuable to some extent, the risk of failure for a member of a neurominority is higher, and careful consideration of a potential job can also inform the types of accommodations that should be requested. In terms of preparation before an interview, Whetzel (2014) suggests that practice and role-playing are important and should be conducted with the aid of trusted helpers who will provide honest feedback such as a job specialist, a coach, or a parent. Whetzel, who has served as the lead consultant for the cognitive/neurological team for the Job Accommodation Network, also notes that the preparation work does not only involve helping with the social interaction difficulties associated with autism but also the repetitive/ritualistic aspects of the condition, which can involve excessive talk or focus on certain topics. In interviews with parents of young adults with autism seeking employment, Hillier and Galizzi (2014) found that these families spent an average of four hours a week in job interview preparation. On the corporate side, as part of their program to hire and incorporate individuals with autism into their workplace, Microsoft invites qualified applicants to a week-long preparatory program focused on success in the hiring process featuring practice interviews and mock projects (Westover et al., 2018).

In terms of specific accommodations, both the Job Accommodation Network (JAN) in the United States and the Job Accommodation Services of the Canadian Council on Rehabilitation and Work offer several examples related to job interviews. Whetzel (2104) suggests requesting fewer interviewers to mitigate social anxiety, requesting that the initial interview be held over the phone, requesting interview questions in advance, and asking that the interview take place at a specific time during the day can all be effective accommodations at mitigating issues around social anxiety and routines. Of course, given the diversity within the autism community, any accommodations should be tailored to the specific individual. For example, for some individuals on the spectrum, a phone interview would be worse than an in-person experience. In some cases, a helpful accommodation could be to have an employment support worker or even a parent present during the job interview (Gewurtz et al., 2016). Rather than relying on verbal communication, online or written alternatives can be considered so that employers can focus on skills and not performance in the interview (Lindsay et al., 2015).

This nod to skills and qualifications is also a reminder that some practices that can be helpful for the recruitment of individuals with autism simply represent best practices in general. Gewurtz et al. (2016) recommends that interviews for individuals with autism should follow standard procedures, be based on job analysis, and use rating scales which are in line with evidence-based research that structured interviews are more valid than unstructured interviews across contexts (Rynes et al., 2002; Schmidt & Hunter, 1998).

Overall, laws such as the Americans with Disabilities Act require employers to provide an accommodation, if needed, to enable an applicant to have equal opportunity in the interview process (EEOC, 2002). For both the organization and the individual, it is essential that hiring managers, human resources personnel, and employers look beyond the disability to identify job candidates who can contribute to the organization (Gewurtz et al., 2016).

On-the-Job Accommodations

Given the spectrum reality of autism, developing a definitive list of accommodations is not feasible in the same way one could generate guidelines to accommodate individuals with vision, hearing, or mobility impairments. Depending on where an individual falls on the spectrum and the specific manifestations/deficits they need support with, and job requirements and context, accommodations can take many forms. The Job Accommodations Network (2019), however, suggests seven questions that employers should ask when exploring accommodations for employees with autism: (1) What limitations is the employee experiencing? (2) How do these limitations affect the employee and the employee's job performance? (3) What specific job tasks are problematic as a result of these limitations? (4) What accommodations are available to reduce or eliminate these problems, and are all possible resources being used to determine possible accommodations? (5) Has the employee been consulted regarding possible accommodations? (6) Once accommodations are in place, would it be useful to meet with the employee to evaluate the effectiveness of the accommodations and to determine whether additional accommodations are needed? (7) Do supervisory personnel and employees need training? This last question will be considered more fully in the next section on supervisors and coworkers.

In terms of products, services, and strategies that can be used to accommodate workers with autism in fulfilling their duties, the Job Accommodations Network suggests that job coaches can help overcome deficits relating to attentiveness/concentration, time management, and organizing/planning/prioritizing. Khalifa et al.'s (2020) review of autism modifications indicated that job coaches can be helpful for performing environmental assessments and recommending workplace modifications and could also provide individual training both on-site and off-site. A review of autism accommodations by Harmuth et al. (2018) also highlighted that the use of professionals to work alongside adults is common during the initial weeks of employment and also as an on-going maintenance support throughout job tenure. In this vein, The Home Depot uses job coaches extensively in its autism employment initiative, with every new employee with autism having an assigned coach who works with the trainee for at least three months, after which the interactions decrease in frequency (Owens, 2010; Westover et al., 2018). Whetzel (2014) notes that a support person/coach can be a form of reasonable accommodation under the ADA and underlines that a support person may be particularly important in helping with stress and emotions by providing comfort, encouragement, and support, especially during performance evaluations or a disciplinary meeting.

Beyond the services of a coach/support person, tools and environmental modifications can be relevant accommodations. Sound-related accommodations such as noise-cancelling headphones/headsets, noise-abatement and control mechanisms such as environmental sound machines, sound absorption and soundproof paneling can help with issues relating to attentiveness/concentration, executive functioning, noise sensitivity, and stress intolerance (Job Accommodations Network, 2019; Khalifa et al., 2020; Lindsay et al., 2019). Other environmental modifications that can represent reasonable accommodations include alternative lighting, cubicle doors/shades, ergonomic equipment, and modified workspaces. In terms of organization and clarity of instructions/communication, wall calendars and planners, written instructions, color-coded systems, checklists, task flow charts, and a variety of software applications for organization/timing/reminders can be options (Job Accommodations Network, 2019; Khalifa et al., 2020; Lindsay et al., 2019; Richardson et al., 2019). For individuals with severe deficits, using pictures, speech-enhancing software, and special "signal words" that can be used to calm workers with autism or indicate that they are perhaps speaking too loud can also be useful (Job Accommodations Network, 2019; Richardson et al., 2019).

Finally, to accommodate routines/rituals and manage stress, flexible schedules, modified break schedules, fidget devices, remote work, and stress-reduction apps can all be employed (Job Accommodations Network, 2019). Modifying work assignments or other elements such as avoiding business travel or providing private rooms when traveling for business have also been reported as effective (Lindsay et al., 2019).

Although there is variation among these accommodations, most of these are very inexpensive or no cost, which is common for most disabilities (Gewutz et al., 2016; Schur et al., 2014; von Schrader, Xu, et al., 2014). As previously noted, however, the societal and family costs associated with unemployed adults with autism can be enormous (Harmuth et al., 2018; Hillier & Galizzi, 2014).

While potential costs are certainly a concern of employers, the reviews by Khalifa et al. (2020) and Lindsay et al. (2019) highlight that employers report that most accommodations are not burdensome, but what employers often lack is information and confidence around employing individuals with disabilities. Individuals with disabilities and support organizations identify misconceptions, fears, and excessive focus on costs as barriers to hiring individuals with disabilities and to providing accommodations (Gold et al., 2012). Overall, legal incentives are often not sufficient to insure equal opportunity and fair treatment for neurominorities in the workplace. Much depends on a supportive workplace and the attitudes of coworkers and supervisors.

Creating an Inclusive Neurodiversity Culture: The Role of Coworkers and Supervisors

While legal requirements, individual success, and organizational benefits would seem to be strong enough reasons for organizations to implement workplace accommodations for neurominorities, the reality is that barriers around workplace dynamics often make disclosure less likely and sometimes make supervisors hesitant to implement supports. Furthermore, factors that should really not be considered when it comes to accommodations often enter into the equation for managers. For example, von Schrader, Xu, et al. (2014) found that employee characteristics and personality traits, such as neuroticism and agreeableness, were significantly related to accommodation receipt, while Florey and Harrison (2000) demonstrated that managers were more likely to approve accommodation requests from disabled workers with good past performance as opposed to poor.

For individuals with invisible disabilities, fear of discrimination from coworkers and managers can loom large. As Russinova et al. (2011) note, perceptions still exist in our society that neurodivergent people or anyone with any mental illness are dangerous, unpredictable, unreliable, lacking in self-control and will thus be poor or problem employees. From a legal standpoint, it is important to note that fears around "danger" and "problem employees" do not mean that employers lack recourse against employees who break disciplinary rules if they are recipients of a workplace accommodation. The Equal Employment Opportunity Commission (EEOC) in the United States allows companies to discipline employees who break rules surrounding insubordination, inappropriate and disrespectful behavior, and other conduct standards such as yelling, cursing, or making obscene gestures even if a disability is at the root of these behaviors (Hensel, 2017). As long as such disciplinary action does not target neurodivergent employees exclusively and is related to business necessity, employers are unencumbered in taking action. While there is no evidence that individuals with autism are any more violent than neurotypical people (Im, 2016), certain manifestations of autism can be perceived as rude or inappropriate (Hensel, 2017; Richards, 2012). Given that most people will have negative reactions to workplace colleagues who tend to lose their temper easily, are perceived as arrogant, have difficulty asking for help, and have odd idiosyncrasies (Bliss & Edmonds, 2008; Meyer, 2001; Richards, 2012), individuals with autism with certain behavioral manifestations caused by their condition may be perceived as difficult people who are undesirable team members. Unlike many other conditions covered under the ADA and similar laws, the milder forms of autism may be even more stigmatizing, as others in the workplace will not perceive that a disability exists or may trivialize/discount the condition

(Hurley-Hanson & Giannantonio, 2017; Johnson & Joshi, 2016). Johnson and Joshi (2016) identify high-functioning autism as a disability that others may view with suspicion (e.g., "everyone has issues") and/or view as controllable (e.g., "he's just throwing a fit to get what he wants").

Overall, fears and misconceptions can represent a serious barrier for needed accommodations for people with invisible disabilities. In fact, von Schrader, Xu, et al. (2014) found that most individuals with disabilities do not request or receive workplace accommodation. Factors that influence the decision to conceal a disability, as reported by individuals with conditions entitling them to accommodations, include the risk of being fired/not hired, concerns that the supervisor may focus on disability, resulting in limited promotion opportunities and general lack of support, fears of being treated differently by supervisors/coworkers, and of being bullied by coworkers (von Schrader, Malzer, et al., 2014). Having one's professional competence discredited, patronizing behavior, condescending remarks, and social exclusion are also concerns for neurodivergent individuals in the workplace (Russinova et al., 2011).

While few accommodations involve expenses that would cause undue hardship to an employer and thus would be irrelevant to the granting of an accommodation, Gold et al. (2012) found that an excessive focus on costs was also perceived to be a barrier preventing workplace accommodations. Another barrier that can cause an employer to deny or attempt to avoid providing accommodations is the fear that neurotypical workers will view accommodations as unfair (Colella, 2001). Legally, employers are prohibited from disclosing health information about employees to their coworkers, which opens the door to perceived injustice on the part of neurotypical employees when they have no explanation for an autistic employee's special accommodations. Furthermore, the nature of autism can also exacerbate feelings of unfairness by coworkers. On the one hand, as previously noted, some of the manifestations of autism can be perceived as rudeness or unpleasantness. Consistent with Stone and Colella's (1996) theoretical model suggesting that disabled workers who have a pleasant interpersonal style will face fewer barriers in the workplace, perceived special or preferential treatment for an unpleasant coworker would understandably be poorly received by colleagues who are in the dark as to the reasons for the accommodations. On the other hand, as highlighted at the beginning of the chapter, neurodivergent employees with autism are often excellent workers, have strong attendance records, are valued by organizations, and receive favorable performance evaluations. While strong performers have been shown to receive accommodations more easily from supervisors, Florey and Harrison (2000), Paetzold et al. (2008) found that coworkers were more accepting of accommodations for disabled colleagues who were poor performers, and viewed accommodations for strong performers as unfair.

In sum, the message is that legislation is not enough. For individuals to be comfortable requesting accommodations and for accommodations to be successful, less emphasis must be placed on the law and more emphasis must be placed on developing a supportive organizational culture.

A particularly important element of creating an inclusive workplace environment culture in which employees will be willing to disclose and where accommodations will be respected is leadership and support from the highest levels of the organization. Erickson et al. (2014) found that strong senior management commitment was found to be the most important factor in recruiting and selecting people with disabilities, and Bruyère et al. (2004) reported that "top management commitment" was rated as the most important means of reducing employment/advancement barriers for disabled workers by human resource professionals. Wright (2016) found that for many managers and senior leaders who have championed autism-at-work initiatives, the interest in helping workers with autism stems from an autism diagnosis of a family member.

Beyond senior leadership, von Schrader, Malzer, et al. (2014) found that individuals with hidden health conditions ranked "having a supportive supervisor relationship" as very important in the decision to disclose. Gold et al. (2012) emphasize the need to build trust between supervisors and individuals with invisible disabilities in order to promote disclosure and receipt of accommodations. Results of their study demonstrated that employers acknowledge that employees must take a leap of faith and trust that employers have employees' best interests in mind, even if that trust takes time to develop. Furthermore, both employers and employees pointed out that employees must be honest in their disclosures of disabilities, as lying or concealing destroys any chance for mutual trust and respect (Gold et al., 2012). In terms of supervisors and/or senior leaders gaining the trust of employees with autism, traditional emotion-based leadership styles such as transformational leadership (Bass, 1985) have proven ineffective, especially the elements relating to inspirational motivation, emotional appeals to a great cause, and challenging followers (Parr et al., 2013). Instead, the individualized consideration component of transformational leadership and authentic leadership (Boekhorst, 2015; Dwertmann & Boehm, 2016; Walumbwa et al., 2008) have been identified as pathways towards reaching neurodivergent employees (Hurley-Hanson & Giannantonio, 2017; Parr & Hunter, 2014).

While coworkers can represent a barrier to accommodations, they can also be a help. As noted by Schur et al. (2014), coworker cooperation and support are needed for the successful implementation of some accommodations, the support of coworkers can set the tone for subsequent accommodation requests and requests by other employees who may not have felt confident making a request in the past, and, as previously highlighted, supervisors will often afford great consideration to coworkers when deciding to implement accommodations. A way that is emerging from examples and research to create inclusion for workers with autism is to actively engage coworkers as mentors or coaches. Companies such as SAP, Freddie Mac, and Hewlett Packard have created support circles made up of coworkers, created mentoring programs, and developed buddy systems to help colleagues on the spectrum (Austin & Pisano, 2017; Wright, 2016), while the job coaches at Home Depot described by Westover et al. (2018) were coworkers. Although such programs require workers with autism to disclose their diagnosis to all, the benefits are high for all parties. Coworkers have been shown to generally be very supportive of special accommodations for differently abled colleagues when they are aware of the issue (Schur et al., 2014), and inclusion efforts that focus on the participation of all employees can create a strong and positive culture. In fact, von Schrader, Malzer, et al. (2014) report that workers, both typical employees and especially employees with disabilities, who perceive that their workplace has an inclusive climate feel higher levels of psychological empowerment on the job and higher levels of organizational support. Also, similar to senior leaders, Wright (2016) notes that many neurotypical employees are happy to engage in these inclusion efforts because they have family members/children on the spectrum.

In terms of how to facilitate a culture of neurodiversity inclusion in the workplace, Olsheski et al. (2002) recommend a multipronged approach designed to remove or minimize the effect of various organizational- or systems-level barriers that hinder job accommodations and continued employment of employees with disabilities. Beyond reviewing policies and procedures regarding disability issues, they advocate the development of a disability management program led by an employee–management steering committee, which would serve as the organizational vehicle for program development, implementation, and operation. Olsheski et al. (2002) underline the need for all stakeholders (e.g., management, union officials, employees) to be committed to the mission, goals, and objectives of the disability management program, and training for all. In terms of training, the Job Accommodation Network (JAN) stresses that training for all managers around accommodation requests is essential, regardless of who is actually responsible for processing such requests (Job Accommodations Network, 2017). They note that ADA complaints often stem from managers not realizing that an accommodation request is being made under the ADA and that managers sometimes are unaware of how to deal with these requests even when recognized. Specific to autism, JAN recommends autism awareness training for all members of organizations given the misunderstandings and misattributions that some manifestations of autism can lead to (Job Accommodations Network, 2015). Although specific employee–coworker training interventions would require the permission of the worker with autism, when coworkers are aware of the unique communication differences that individuals with autism exhibit, they may be more understanding, be able to find better ways to interact with their colleagues with autism, and ensure they are being understood as well. This better two-way communication can be beneficial for the employee with autism as well, as they will be able to rely on the feedback of coworkers to make needed adjustments if possible. Overall, as previously underlined, coworkers have been shown to be very supportive of their colleagues with autism when they are aware and informed of the circumstances (Schur et al., 2014).

Conclusion and the Road Ahead

A clear message that emerges from this review is that legislation and needing supports are insufficient to create a neurodiversity-friendly workplace. Many of the barriers to a more inclusive workplace for neurominorities involve fears, stigmas, perceptions, and misattributions on the part of managers, coworkers, and individuals with autism as well. These more perceptual and psychological factors are the domain of I-O psychologists, and as researchers, we must strive to help develop evidence-based solutions to neurodiversity issues. Specifically, we will need to move beyond our neurotypical ideas about leadership, communication, job performance, teamwork, and ability in order to question the underlying assumptions of our theories and practices and reframe our conception of work and "good" employees. A takeaway from the work to date is that some organizations are making great efforts toward integrating individuals on the spectrum, while other employers seem lost due to uncertainties and a lack of information. I-O psychologists can help bridge this gap and also expand the current success stories beyond jobs that easily fit the individual's strengths to include jobs that are possible with reasonable accommodations and fit the individual's interests and capabilities. On the nature of accommodations, more research is needed on job analysis, alternative work arrangements, physical layout, and communication. Relating to barriers to accommodations, researchers need to take inspiration from other areas in diversity research to uncover implicit bias and adverse impact of seemingly fair policies and procedures, and examine the dynamics of social identities. Most accommodations are inexpensive. There exists a disconnect between fears and misapprehension on the one hand and success stories and inclusive cultures on the other. This gap can be bridged by better information about the nature of autism and neurodiversity, evidence-based research on accommodations, and highlighting positive outcomes. The challenge is to develop the knowledge to help neurotypical workers to consider the neurodivergent view of work and to help demonstrate the benefits of accommodations to and for all.

References

American Psychiatric Association. (2013). *Diagnostic and statistical manual of mental disorders* (5th ed.). Washington, DC: Author.

Austin, R. D., & Pisano, G. P. (2017). Neurodiversity as a competitive advantage. *Harvard Business Review, 95*, 96–103.

Barnard, J., Harvey, V., Potter, D., & Prior, A. (2001). *The reality for adults with autism spectrum disorders*. London: National Autistic Society.

Baron-Cohen, S. (2017). Editorial perspective: Neurodiversity-a revolutionary concept for autism and psychiatry. *Journal or Child Psychology and Psychiatry, 58*(6), 744–747.

Bass, B. M. (1985). *Leadership and performance beyond expectations*. New York: Free Press.

Bjelland, M. J., Bruyère, S. M., von Schrader, S., Houtenville, A. J., Ruiz-Quintanilla, A., & Webber, D. A. (2010). Age and disability employment discrimination: Occupational rehabilitation implications. *Journal of Occupational Rehabilitation, 20*, 456–471.

Bliss, E., & Edmonds, G. (2008). *A self-determined future with Asperger syndrome*. London: JKP.

Boekhorst, J. A. (2015). The role of authentic leadership in fostering workplace inclusion: A social information processing perspective. *Human Resource Management, 54*, 241–264.

Bottema-Beutel, K., Kapp, S. K., Lester, J. N., Sasson, N. J., & Hand, B. N. (2020). Avoiding ableist language: Suggestions for autism researchers. *Autism in Adulthood, 3*, 18–29. https://doi.org/10.1089/aut.2020.0014

Bruyère, S. M., Erickson, W. A., & VanLooy, S. (2004). Comparative study of workplace policy and practices contributing to disability nondiscrimination. *Rehabilitation Psychology, 49*, 28–38.

Chu, F. (2015, June). Making it work. *Inc. Magazine*, p. 34.

Clark, T. L. (1997). A map for the labyrinth: How to conduct job interviews and obtain medical information without violating the Americans with Disabilities Act. *The Labor Lawyer, 13*(1), 121.

Colella, A. (2001). Co-worker distributive fairness judgments of the workplace accommodation of employees with disabilities. *Academy of Management Review, 26*, 100–116.

Doyle, N. (2020). Diamond in the rough? Neurodiversity inclusion in practice. In *Symposium presentation at the Society for Industrial and Organizational Psychology (SIOP) 2020 Virtual Conference.*

Dwertmann, D. J. G., & Boehm, S. A. (2016). Status matters: The asymmetric effects of supervisor – subordinate disability incongruence and climate for inclusion. *Academy of Management Journal, 59*, 44–64.

Equal Employment Opportunity Commission (EEOC). (2002). *Enforcement guidance: Reasonable accommodation and undue hardship under the Americans with Disabilities Act.* Retrieved from www.eeoc.gov/policy/docs/accommodation.html#general

Equal Employment Opportunity Commission (EEOC). (2011, November 7). *Comfort suites to pay $132,500 for disability discrimination against clerk with autism* [Press release]. Retrieved from www.eeoc.gov/newsroom/comfort-suites-pay-132500-disability-discrimination-against-clerk-autism

Equal Employment Opportunity Commission (EEOC). (2012, May 10). *Randstad US, LP to pay $60,000 to settle EEOC disability bias suit* [Press release]. Retrieved from www.eeoc.gov/newsroom/randstad-us-lp-pay-60000-settle-eeoc-disability-bias-suit

Equal Employment Opportunity Commission (EEOC). (2018, July 13). *Golden corral franchisee to pay $85,000 to settle EEOC disability and sex harassment lawsuit* [Press release]. Retrieved from www.eeoc.gov/newsroom/golden-corral-franchisee-pay-85000-settle-eeoc-disability-and-sex-harassment-lawsuit

Equal Employment Opportunity Commission (EEOC). (2019, April 22). *Party city to pay $155,000 to settle EEOC disability discrimination lawsuit* [Press release]. Retrieved from www.eeoc.gov/newsroom/party-city-pay-155000-settle-eeoc-disability-discrimination-lawsuit

Erickson, W., Lee, C., & von Schrader, S. (2020). *Disability statistics from the 2018 American Community Survey (ACS).* Ithaca, NY: Cornell University Yang-Tan Institute (YTI). Retrieved from www.disabilitystatistics.org

Erickson, W. A., von Schrader, S., Bruyère, S. M., VanLooy, S. A., & Matteson, S. (2014). Disability-inclusive employer practices and hiring of individuals with disabilities. *Rehabilitation Research, Policy, and Education, 28*(4), 309–328.

Florey, A. T., & Harrison, D. A. (2000). Responses to informal accommodation requests from employees with disabilities: Multistudy evidence on willingness to comply. *Academy of Management Journal, 43*, 224–233.

Gewurtz, R. E., Langan, S., & Shand, D. (2016). Hiring people with disabilities: A scoping review. *Work: Journal of Prevention, Assessment & Rehabilitation, 54*(1), 135–148. https://doi.org/10.3233/WOR-162265

Gold, P. B., Oire, S. N., Fabian, E. S., & Wewiorski, N. J. (2012). Negotiating reasonable workplace accommodations: Perspectives of employers, employees with disabilities, and rehabilitation service providers. *Journal of Vocational Rehabilitation, 37*(1), 25–37.

Harmuth, E., Silletta, E., Bailey, A., Adams, T., Beck, C., & Barbic, S. P. (2018). Barriers and facilitators to employment for adults with autism: A scoping review. *Annals of International Occupational Therapy, 1*(1), 31–40. https://doi.org/10.3928/24761222-20180212-01

Hensel, W. F. (2017). People with autism spectrum disorder in the workplace: An expanding legal frontier. *Harvard Civil Rights-Civil Liberties Law Review, 52*(1), 73–102.

Hillier, A., Campbell, H., Mastriani, K., Izzo, M.V., Kool-Tucker, A., Cherry, L., & Beversdorf, D. Q. (2007). Two-year evaluation of a vocational support program for adults on the autism spectrum. *Career Development for Exceptional Individuals, 30*, 35–47.

Hillier, A., & Galizzi, M. (2014). Employment outcomes for young adults with autism spectrum disorders. *Review of Disability Studies: An International Journal, 10*(1/2), 69.

Hubbard, E. E. (2007). *The diversity scorecard: Evaluating the impact of diversity on organizational performance*. New York: Routledge.

Hurlbutt, K., & Chalmers, L. (2004). Employment and adults with Asperger syndrome. *Focus on Autism and Other Developmental Disabilities, 19*, 215–222.

Hurley-Hanson, A. E., & Giannantonio, C. M. (2017). LMX and autism: Effective working relationships. In T. A. Scandura & E. Mouriño-Ruiz (Eds.), *Leading diversity in the 21st century* (pp. 281–302). Charlotte, NC: IAP Information Age Publishing.

Im, D. S. (2016). Template to perpetrate: An update on violence in autism spectrum disorder. *Harvard Review of Psychiatry, 24*(1), 14–35.

Jaarsma, P., & Welin, S. (2012). Autism as a natural human variation: Reflections on the claims of the neurodiversity movement. *Health Care Analysis, 20*(1), 20–30.

Job Accommodations Network. (2015). *Autism Spectrum Disorders (ASD) and disability awareness training*. https://askjan.org/blogs/jan/2015/04/autism-spectrum-disorders-asd-and-disability-awareness-training.cfm

Job Accommodations Network. (2017). *Effective Accommodation Practices Series (EAP) Series: Five practical tips for providing and maintaining effective job accommodations*. Retrieved from https://askjan.org/articles/EAPS/upload/FivePracticalTips.doc

Job Accommodations Network. (2019). *Accommodation and compliance series: Employees with autism spectrum*. Retrieved from https://askjan.org/disabilities/Autism-Spectrum.cfm

Johnson, T. D., & Joshi, A. (2016). Disclosure on the spectrum: Understanding disclosure among employees on the autism spectrum. *Industrial and Organizational Psychology: Perspectives on Science and Practice*, 7(2), 278–281. https://doi.org/10.1111/iops.12149

Kapp, S. K., Gillespie-Lynch, K., Sherman, L. E., & Hutman, T. (2013). Deficit, difference, or both? Autism and neurodiversity. *Developmental Psychology, 49*(1), 59–71.

Katz, N., Dejak, I., & Gal, E. (2015). Work performance evaluation and QoL of adults with High Functioning Autism Spectrum Disorders (HFASD). *Work, 51*(4), 887–892. https://doi.org/10.3233/WOR-152001

Khalifa, G., Sharif, Z., Sultan, M., & Di Rezze, B. (2020). Workplace accommodations for adults with autism spectrum disorder: A scoping review. *Disability and Rehabilitation, 42*(9), 1316–1331. https://doi.org/10.1080/09638288.2018.1527952

Knapp, M., Romeo, R., & Beecham, J. (2009). Economic cost of autism in the UK. *Autism, 13*(3), 317–336.

Konrad, A. M., Moore, M. E., Ng, E. S.W., Doherty, A. J., & Breward, K. (2013). Temporary work, underemployment and workplace accommodations: Relationship to well-being for workers with disabilities. *British Journal of Management, 24*(3), 367–382. https://doi.org/10.1111/j.1467-8551.2011.00809.x

Lindsay, S., McDougall, C., Sanford, R., Menna-Dack, D., Kingsnorth, S., & Adams, T. (2015). Exploring employment readiness through mock job interview and workplace role-play exercises: Comparing youth with physical disabilities to their typically developing peers. *Disability and Rehabilitation: An International, Multidisciplinary Journal, 37*(18), 1651–1663. https://doi.org/10.3109/09638288.2014.973968

Lindsay, S., Osten, V., Rezai, M., & Bui, S. (2019). Disclosure and workplace accommodations for people with autism: A systematic review. *Disability and Rehabilitation, 42*, 1–14 https://doi.org/10.1080/09638288.2019.1635658

Lollini, A. (2018). Brain equality: Legal implications of neurodiversity in a comparative perspective. *New York University Journal of International Law and Politics, 51*(1), 69–134.

Lorenz, T., & Heinitz, K., (2014). Aspergers – different, not less: Occupational strengths and job interests of individuals with Asperger's syndrome. *PLoS One, 9*(6), e100358. https://doi.org/10.1371/journal.pone.0100358

Martin, E., Cleary, L., & Caner, K. D. (2011, April 7). EEOC releases new regulations for the Americans with Disabilities Act. *Mondaq*. Retrieved from https://advance.lexis.com/api/document?collection=news&id=urn:contentItem:52JW-G9N1-F03R-N2B6-00000-00&context=1516831

Mavranezouli, I., Megnin-Viggars, O., Cheema, N., Howlin, P., Baron-Cohen, S., & Pilling, S. (2014). The cost-effectiveness of supported employment for adults with autism in the United Kingdom. *Autism: The International Journal of Research and Practice, 18*(8), 975–984.

Meyer, R. (2001). *Asperger syndrome employment workbook: An employment workbook for adults with Asperger syndrome*. London: JKP.

Newheiser, A., Barreto, M., & Tiemersma, J. (2017). People like me don't belong here: Identity concealment is associated with negative workplace experiences. *Journal of Social Issues, 73*(2), 341–358. https://doi.org/10.1111/josi.12220

Olsheski, J. A., Rosenthal, D. A., & Hamilton, M. (2002). Disability management and psychosocial rehabilitation: Considerations for integration. *Work: Journal of Prevention, Assessment & Rehabilitation, 19*(1), 63–70.

Ortega, F. (2009). The cerebral subject and the challenge of neurodiversity. *BioSocieties, 4*(4), 425–445.

Owens, D. M. (2010, June 1). Hiring employees with autism: As more people with autism enter the workforce, employers are tapping a new source of talent. *HR Magazine, 55*(6), 84.

Paetzold, R. L., Garcia, M. F., Colella, A., Ren, L. R., Triana, M. C., & Ziebro, M. (2008). Perceptions of people with disabilities: When is accommodation fair? *Basic & Applied Social Psychology, 30*, 27–35.

Page, S. E. (2007). Making the difference: Applying a logic of diversity. *Academy of Management Perspectives, 21*(4), 6–20. https://doi-org.ezproxy.sju.edu/10.5465/AMP.2007.27895335

Parr, A. D., & Hunter, S. T. (2014). Enhancing work outcomes of employees with autism spectrum disorder through leadership. *Autism, 18*, 545–554.

Parr, A. D., Hunter, S. T., & Ligon, G. S. (2013). Questioning universal applicability of transformational leadership: Examining employees with autism spectrum disorder. *The Leadership Quarterly, 24*, 608–622.

Patton, E. (2019). Autism, attributions and accommodations: Overcoming barriers and integrating a neurodiverse workforce. *Personnel Review, 48*(4), 915–934. https://doi-org.ezproxy.sju.edu/10.1108/PR-04-2018-0116

Ren, L. R., Paetzold, R. L., & Colella, A. (2008). A meta-analysis of experimental studies on the effects of disability on human resource judgments. *Human Resource Management Review, 18*(3), 191–203. https://doi.org/10.1016/j.hrmr.2008.07.001

Richards, J. (2012). Examining the exclusion of employees with Asperger syndrome from the workplace. *Personnel Review, 41*(5), 630–646. https://doi.org/10.1108/00483481211249148

Richards, K. (2017). Social skills training: An intervention for adults with high-functioning autism. *BU Journal of Graduate Studies in Education, 9*(2), 42–46.

Richardson, L., McCoy, A., & McNaughton, D. (2019). "He's worth the extra work": The employment experiences of adults with ASD who use augmentative and alternative communication (AAC) as reported by adults with ASD, family members, and employers. *Work, 62*(2), 205–219. https://doi.org/10.3233/WOR-192856

Rosenblatt, M. (2008). *I exist: The message from adults with autism in England.* London: National Autistic Society.

Russinova, Z., Griffin, S., Bloch, P., Wewiorski, N. J., & Rosoklija, I. (2011). Workplace prejudice and discrimination toward individuals with mental illnesses. *Journal of Vocational Rehabilitation, 35*(3), 227–241.

Rynes, S. L., Colbert, A. E., & Brown, K. C. (2002). HR professionals' beliefs about effective human resource practices: Correspondence between research and practice. *Human Resource Management, 41*, 149–174.

Sarrett, J. (2017). Interviews, disclosures, and misperceptions: Autistic adults' perspectives on employment-related challenges. *Disability Studies Quarterly, 37*, 1–22.

Schmidt, F. L., & Hunter, J. E. (1998). The validity and utility of selection methods in personnel psychology: Practical and theoretical implications of 85 years of research findings. *Psychological Bulletin, 124*, 262–274.

Schur, L., Nishii, L., Adya, M., Kruse, D., Bruyère, S., & Blanck, P. (2014). Accommodating employees with and without disabilities. *Human Resource Management, 53*, 593–621.

Skibell, A. (2017). More people with autism are getting training for technology jobs: Some worry the push forecloses other job prospects. *Tech Directions*, 77(4), 22–24.

Stone, D. L., & Colella, A. (1996). A model of factors affecting the treatment of disabled individuals in organizations. *Academy of Management Review, 21*, 352–401.

Unger, D., Campbell, L., & McMahon, B. T. (2005). Workplace discrimination and mental retardation: The national EEOC ADA research project. *Journal of Vocational Rehabilitation, 23*, 145–154.

United Nations. (2006). *Convention on the Rights of Persons with Disabilities.* Treaty Series, 2515, 3. Retrieved from www.un.org/development/desa/disabilities/convention-on-the-rights-of-persons-with-disabilities/convention-on-the-rights-of-persons-with-disabilities-2.html

United Nations General Assembly. (1948). *Universal declaration of human rights.* Retrieved from www.un.org/en/universal-declaration-human-rights/index.html

Van Wieren, T. A., Armstrong, A. J., & McMahon, B. T. (2012). Autism spectrum disorders and intellectual disabilities: A comparison of ADA Title I workplace discrimination allegations. *Journal of Vocational Rehabilitation, 36*, 159–169.

Van Wieren, T. A., Reid, C. A., & McMahon, B. T. (2008). Workplace discrimination and autism spectrum disorders: The National EEOC Americans with Disabilities Act Research project. *Work, 31*, 299–308.

von Schrader, S., Malzer, V., & Bruyère, S. (2014). Perspectives on disability disclosure: The importance of employer practices and workplace climate. *Employee Responsibilities & Rights Journal, 26*(4), 237.

von Schrader, S., Xu, X., & Bruyère, S. M. (2014). Accommodation requests: Who is asking for what? *Rehabilitation Research, Policy, and Education, 28*, 329–344.

Waisman-Nitzan, M., Gal, E., & Schreuer, N. (2019). Employers' perspectives regarding reasonable accommodations for employees with autism spectrum disorder. *Journal of Management and Organization, 25*(4), 481–498.

Walumbwa, F. O., Avolio, B. J., Gardner, W. L., Wernsing, T. S., & Peterson, S. J. (2008). Authentic leadership: Development and validation of a theory-based measure. *Journal of Management, 34*, 89–126.

Westover, J. H., Hughes, K., & Cardon, T. (2018). Autism in the workplace today: A literature review and examination of five autism programs. *International Journal of Interdisciplinary Organizational Studies, 13*(3/4), 1–13. https://doi.org/10.18848/2324-7649/CGP/v13i02/1-13

Whetzel, M. (2014). Interviewing tips for applicants with autism spectrum disorder (ASD). *Journal of Vocational Rehabilitation, 40*(2), 155–159. https://doi.org/10.3233/JVR-140668

Wong, P. S., Donelly, M., Neck, P. A., & Boyd, B. (2018). Positive autism: Investigation of workplace characteristics leading to a strengths-based approach to employment of people with autism. *Review of International Comparative Management/Revista de Management Comparat International, 19*(1), 15–30. https://doi.org/10.24818/rmci.2018.1.15

World Health Organization. (2013). *Autism spectrum disorders and other developmental disorders: From raising awareness to building capacity*. Geneva: WHO Document Production Services.

Wright, A. D. (2016, October). Autism speaks, and employers listen. *HR Magazine, 61*(8), 60–64.

9

PERFORMANCE MANAGEMENT AND CAREER DEVELOPMENT FOR EMPLOYEES WITH AUTISM

Uncovering Hidden Requirements

Samuel T. Hunter and Melissa D. Hunter

Neurodiverse employees often possess skills and abilities that make them valuable assets to organizations (Jiang et al., 2015; Krzeminska et al., 2019; Remington et al., 2009; Scott et al., 2017). Although it is important to recognize that autism is a *spectrum* disorder, meaning there is variability in skills, interests, and abilities across individuals, evidence does suggest that employees with autism spectrum disorder (ASD) often demonstrate strong levels of reliability and lower levels of absenteeism (e.g., Baldwin et al., 2014; de Schipper et al., 2016; Scott et al., 2019; Woo, 2019). Neil Barnett, the director of inclusive hiring at Microsoft described employees with ASD as "being good at problem solving, coding. [These employees] have a strong attention to detail" (Sardon, 2019) and companies such as Ernst and Young seek out employees on the autism spectrum as sources of innovation and novel insight (Twaronite, 2019). Such observations have led companies such as Microsoft, SAP, and Ford Motor Company to create autism hiring programs with notable success.

Despite these examples of recent successes, the general employment outlook for individuals on the autism spectrum is, all too often, bleak. Individuals with ASD are often unemployed or underemployed and report greater dissatisfaction with employment. More conservative estimates of unemployment suggest that approximately 50% of individuals with ASD are unemployed (Ohl et al., 2017). Factoring in underemployment (i.e., working at a lower capacity for which one is qualified) estimates in addition to unemployment, however, reveal upper bound estimates to be as high as 85% to 90% (Krzeminska et al., 2019; Roux et al., 2015). Moreover, although individuals with disabilities face employment challenges at a greater rate than those without disabilities, individuals with autism face a particularly austere employment outlook (Roux et al., 2015; Scott et al., 2019). Those that do find employment are typically paid less than their peers (Ohl et al.,

DOI: 10.4324/9781003023616-9

2017; Roux et al., 2015). There is also indication that turnover rates are higher for those on the spectrum and for younger individuals in particular (Wei et al., 2018). Finally, and most relevant to our chapter, is the fact that individuals with ASD who do find employment report lower levels of satisfaction on the job, often noting the social challenges of work as key factors in that dissatisfaction (Hurlbutt & Chalmers, 2004; Ohl et al., 2017; Pfeiffer et al., 2018).

Such employment difficulties have implications for a range of issues in industrial and organizational psychology, many of which are covered in this book, including interviewing and selection/hiring (Saleh et al., in the current volume), leadership (Parr & Hunter, 2014; Seitz, in this volume), socialization (Volpone et al., in this volume), recruitment (Giannantonio & Hurley, in this volume), and onboarding and teamwork training (Longmire & Taylor, in this volume). In our chapter, we discuss the importance of performance management and career development as key factors not only to improving the general employment outlook for individuals with ASD but in improving the quality of employment for the long-term success of organizations as well as the well-being of those employed.

Performance Management and Hidden Performance Requirements

According to DeNisi and Murphy (2017), performance management is defined as the "variety of activities, policies, procedures, and interventions designed to help employees improve their performance" (p. 421) and is linked to firm performance (DeNisi & Smith, 2014). Given the potentially confusing overlap, it is worth noting that performance management subsumes the concept of performance appraisal that involves the formal assessment and measurement of work completed by employees. More precisely, successful performance management flows from and is typically built upon the information gathered during performance appraisal. Although other models of performance management exist (see DeNisi & Smith, 2014, as an example), we utilize as a foundation the framework presented by Kinicki and colleagues (2013) due to the model's focus on common human resource practices and stages of performance.

The performance management model proposed by Kinicki and colleagues (2013) involves four primary stages, offered in sequence and ultimately feeding back into each other in cyclical fashion. The first stage outlined by the authors is to define performance goals with the aim of making clear to both the assessor (e.g., manager or supervisor) and employee what the expectations for performance are. Research is clear on the criticality of goal setting as the cornerstone of effective performance (Buchner, 2007; Locke & Latham, 1990) and is one of the foundational behaviors of effective leadership (Judge et al., 2004; Stogdill, 1950). The second stage of performance management involves evaluating performance, including the quantification and measurement of associated behaviors (DeNisi & Murphy, 2017). The third stage involves reviewing performance with the aim of delivering useful feedback on performance to employees as well as developmental activities such as coaching (Liu & Batt, 2010). The fourth and final stage is to establish the consequences of performance (e.g., Podsakoff et al., 1982). Such consequences in the best-case scenarios involve rewards for good performance but also may include punitive measures should an employee find themselves underperforming on a consistent basis with little justification or reasonable rationale for performing below expectations.

Performance Management for Employees with ASD

A key assumption of models such as those presented by Kinicki and colleagues (2013) and others (DeNisi & Smith, 2014) is that performance and associated expectations are quantifiable and can, within reasonable parameters, be clearly conveyed to an employee. That is, there is an implicit view that performance management represents the management of in-role behaviors or those behaviors explicitly outlined as part of a job (Srivastava & Shree, 2019; Van Dyne & LePine, 1998). The reality of organizational life, however, is that not all requisite behavior is made explicit in performance management systems. Some components of a job are *extra-role*. Extra-role work behavior has significant conceptual overlap with constructs such as contextual performance (e.g., Motowidlo & Van Scotter, 2000) and organizational citizenship behavior (e.g., Organ, 1988). Contextual performance is generally viewed as a set of behaviors that contribute to the social fabric of the organization rather than core task functions of the organization (Krzeminska et al., 2019). Given our focus on performance management rather than, say, organizational climate, we utilize extra-role behavior as the focus, although it is arguable that the terms are synonymous. Most critical here is that extra-role behavior is not formally part of a performance management system and, instead, is picked up through informal interaction and unwritten norms (Srivastava & Shree, 2019). It is important to acknowledge, however, that extra-role behaviors may be implicitly linked to evaluations of formal task performance (Johnson, 2001; Van Scotter & Motowidlo, 2000), proving particularly challenging for employees with ASD, who may struggle with the unknown or "hidden" behaviors tied to perceptions of employee success.

Lessons From the Education Literature and the Hidden Curriculum

Notably, there are parallel constructs in the education literature relating to extra-role behavior that can serve as key sources of guidance on managing workplace issues. Namely, a common focus of intervention research related to adolescents with ASD in education settings is referred to as the "hidden curriculum." Alsubaie (2015) defines the hidden curriculum as "the unspoken or implicit values, behaviors, procedures, and norms that exist in the educational setting" (p. 125). Although the term "hidden curriculum" is now used widely to describe a set of skills that are important for the social success of students with autism, it was originally introduced by Anyon (1980) to describe differential teaching of students in schools based on their social class. Anyon argued that students from the working class, for example, were taught to follow procedural steps, while students perceived to be in the professional class were engaged more in creative or independent activities. This differential teaching, in turn, reinforced expectations for future employment and social class (Anyon, 1980; Sulaimani & Gut, 2019). While this term has since been adopted by ASD researchers, the connection between understanding the hidden curriculum and future employment success as originally noted by Anyon (1980) supports the assertion that the hidden curriculum is an important component of supporting neurodiverse individuals in the workplace.

Similar to extra-role behavior in the workplace, the hidden curriculum develops in school settings as a result of unspoken and unwritten rules and expectations regarding social behaviors, attitudes and values, and procedures and norms within the setting (Alsubaie, 2015; Jerald, 2006) and is communicated indirectly and without specific intent (Jerald, 2006). To understand the hidden curriculum, individuals in the environment must interpret and respond to visual, auditory, and social cues from others. The hidden curriculum is a complex set of skills, encompassing teacher expectations, peer expectations and motives, and understanding of behaviors that elicit positive and negative reactions from others (Myles & Simpson, 2001). For example, in educational settings, social norms might dictate that students use slang when speaking to each other at lockers but avoid doing so when speaking to their teachers or use quiet voice volume in the classroom but louder voice volume in the cafeteria. These social expectations are never taught or directly addressed; rather, students are simply expected to learn them from cues and experiences in the environment. However, several authors have noted specific and consistent deficits in the ability of students with ASD to identify the hidden curriculum within the educational environment, resulting in negative long-term impacts (Lee, 2011; Myles & Simpson, 2001; Myles & Smith, 2005; Thomas & Boellstorff, 2017).

Specific characteristics of those diagnosed with ASD contribute to difficulty understanding the hidden curriculum; in particular, deficits in theory of mind. Theory of mind is defined as "an individual's ability to understand that everyone has their own thoughts, beliefs, emotions, and attitudes, which may differ from one's own" (Sulaimani & Gut, 2019, p. 32). Sometimes called "mindreading" (Baron-Cohen, 2001), theory of mind requires individuals to infer the thoughts and beliefs of others by relying on cues such as tone of voice, gestures and posture, facial expressions, and contextual factors (Baron-Cohen, 2000). Significant evidence (Baron-Cohen, 2000; Begeer et al., 2003; Kaland et al., 2008; Peterson et al., 2007; Zelazo et al., 2002; Ziatas et al., 1998) indicates that theory of mind is a core deficit for individuals with ASD, underlying many of the diagnostic features of ASD. For example, deficits in theory of mind lead people with ASD to assume that others are experiencing thoughts and feelings similar to their own, which can impair empathy and perspective-taking and may explain inappropriate emotional reactions sometimes demonstrated by individuals with ASD. Deficits in theory of mind also increase the likelihood that individuals with ASD will fail to ask for clarification or help if they are unsure of what to do in a situation, because they may not understand that another person possesses information that they do not have.

Identifying and understanding the hidden curriculum can also be challenging for individuals with ASD because of its dynamic nature. The hidden curriculum may vary depending on the age of the individual (e.g., behaviors that are socially acceptable for a 16-year-old may not be so for a 25-year-old), gender, sexuality, ethnicity and culture, and setting (Lee, 2011). Thus, while an employee with ASD may have successfully navigated the hidden curriculum of a high school or college environment, demonstrating those same behaviors may not be successful in the work environment.

Although there have been limited research studies examining the role of extra-role behavior in performance management for employees with autism, the education and applied behavior analysis literature provide a rich base of intervention research for addressing the hidden curriculum for individuals with autism. The hidden curriculum of educational environments shares similar features with the concept of extra-role behavior in the work environment. Sulaimani and Gut (2019) state, "The hidden curriculum outlines the general standards a community holds everyone responsible for, despite the fact that most persons may not be aware of them or take them for granted" (p. 32). Similarly, Van Dyne and LePine (1998) define extra-role behavior as voluntary and discretionary behavior of employees that is targeted toward benefiting the organization. While high school students with ASD are not formally evaluated on their ability to successfully navigate the hidden curriculum, mastery of the skills that comprise the hidden curriculum is vital for social success in high school and future success in other settings (Sulaimani & Gut, 2019). In the workplace, employees who demonstrate extra-role behavior are often viewed positively despite a lack of formal reward system for these behaviors (Johnson, 2001; Organ, 1988; Van Scotter & Motowidlo, 2000; Vigoda-Gadot, 2007; Whiting et al., 2008).

Consider the following hypothetical scenario of extra-role performance. Imagine a sales organization with 25 employees housed in a typical brick-and-mortar office. In our hypothetical office, there is a communal breakroom, and kept in that breakroom is a coffee maker that is shared by employees. Although never explicitly stated to new hires, employees learn that if they do use the coffee maker, they are expected bring in coffee and filters from time to time to share with others using the machine. Employees who do not do engage in this unwritten norm are viewed negatively by their peers. When such negative perceptions occur, offending employees may not be given sales leads or offered help when dealing with multiple customers during a particularly busy period. They may be left out of social invitations after work at which strategies are formed or even more social norms are established. Key here is that buying coffee for the communal coffee maker would not be discussed in a formal performance management system, nor would a supervisor formally view such behavior as poor performance. Instead, an employee must be socially aware and adept enough to learn such unspoken rules, just as with the concept of the hidden curriculum in our earlier examples. As may be surmised, for employees with ASD, learning these unspoken rules is challenging if not insurmountable without explicit intervention.

One of the critical aspects of the example is that although components of job expectations are not expressly outlined in a performance management system (i.e., extra-role behaviors), such behaviors can impact bottom-line components that are part of a performance management system (Wright et al., 1993; Van Dick et al., 2008). In other words, failing to participate in unwritten rules and norms in an organization cannot only be ostracizing and negatively harm an employee's well-being, such inactivity can also negatively albeit indirectly impact in-role performance (Alkahtani, 2015; Srivastava & Shree, 2019). Thus, as we consider ways to improve the work-lives of employees with ASD, not only must we consider ways to improve typical forms of performance management, we must also consider those extra-role behaviors that fall outside of typical performance management systems to ensure employees with ASD are not indirectly being impacted due to the social nature of their disability.

Recommendations for Managing Hidden Performance Requirements

For individuals with autism, we recommend the Myles et al. (2013) manual titled "The Hidden Curriculum of Getting and Keeping a Job: Navigating the Social Landscape of Employment" as an excellent resource for understanding the hidden curriculum in the workplace. From the perspective of the supervisor, we pull from the applied behavior analysis (ABA),[1] and education literature to provide the following recommendations for performance management of neurodiverse individuals, noting that performance management models have a number of implications for supporting employees on the autism spectrum. We walk through each of the four stages of performance management outlined by Kinicki and colleagues (2013), with a focus on providing recommendations for managing performance issues that may be hidden from employees with ASD.

Defining Performance Goals

When performance goals are clearly defined and are a good fit, the unique characteristics of individuals with autism, including their tendency to adhere to rules and routine and attention to detail, will allow for strong performance in the workplace. Clearly defined goals are important for any performance management system (Locke & Latham, 1990). However, for individuals with autism, the challenge is in understanding that deficits in theory of mind and difficulty identifying important extra-role behaviors may require greater clarification or specific identification of the expected behaviors. We turn to the applied behavior analysis and education literature to provide the following recommendations:

It is important for managers of neurodiverse employees to recognize that social interactions may be highly demanding for individuals with autism, as attending to social cues such as body language or tone of voice is difficult. We recommend that goals are written in clear language and that employees with autism have a chance to review the goals prior to discussion with the supervisor. In some cases, it may be appropriate for the employee to generate their own ideas for performance goals and then refine those goals in conjunction with the supervisor. Supervisors should be specific in defining multiple aspects of the goal. What are the parameters for completion of the goal: time, product, or other dimensions? If the goal is to "improve" in some area, how is improvement defined? Supervisors should also examine their own personal biases or expectations for extra-role behaviors, and how such behaviors are weighing into performance evaluation, they should be clearly specified.

A large body of research supports the use of visual supports for developing skills for individuals with autism across a variety of settings (Dettmer et al., 2000; Hart-Barnett et al., 2018). Visual supports are a diverse set of tools that present abstract verbal or social information in visual format (Dettmer et al., 2000). Perhaps the most commonly utilized visual support in education and treatment settings is the visual schedule, which uses written text, pictures, or icons to identify steps that should be completed within a specified time period. Given the strong research base for visual supports as useful tools for individuals with ASD, we recommend the supervisor develop a written schedule of activities with their neurodiverse employees. The format and content of the schedule will vary based on the preferences and needs of the employee as well as the nature of the task and should be developed in conjunction with the employee. Visual schedules can reduce anxiety for individuals with ASD by clarifying expectations and reducing the need for reliance on reading social cues (Dettmer et al., 2000).

Another useful visual support for the work environment is called "work jigs." First introduced by the creators of the TEACCH model of intervention for individuals with autism, work jigs are a series of pictures that detail the sequence of steps involved in a task (Schople et al., 1995). For example, consider a new employee with ASD working as a landscaper for the physical plant of a university. For the task of planting seasonal plants in the lawn of a central building, a work jig could be created simply by taking photos of the steps involved in planting, placing the photos in order on a document with a brief description of each step, indicating what the employee should do when the task is finished, and providing the employee with a copy of the document when she is asked to complete the task. The work jig allows for autonomy in the workplace while reducing the need for relying on verbal instructions. In some situations, a simple list of task steps or expected activities could clarify expectation effectively. In addition, identifying task priority using color-coding or other strategies could support individuals with ASD in understanding how they should prioritize their time at work (Van Bourgondien & Schopler, 1996).

Finally, when setting performance goals for individuals with ASD, it is important to note the difference between predictability and repetition. While predictability reduces anxiety for individuals with ASD, just as is true for neurotypical employees, engaging in the same repetitive task on the job every day may negatively impact motivation and work performance (Van Bourgondien & Woods, 1992). Neurodiverse individuals may do well with repetitive tasks for a specified period of time, but we caution against the notion that these employees will prefer to do the same task throughout their career. Visual supports such as schedules or work jigs provide an opportunity to introduce variety into work tasks while still creating a sense of predictability. For instance, new tasks can be introduced on the visual schedule, with work jigs created to illustrate the steps in the task (Hendricks, 2010). In this way, the role of the neurodiverse employee can continue to grow or change while addressing the need for predictability.

Evaluating and Reviewing Performance

Again, we stress here that the key to effective performance evaluation for neurodiverse employees is clarity and specificity. Supervisors should avoid vague feedback like "keep up the good work" or "I'd like to see you be more of a team player." This type of feedback does not provide clear direction and will be confusing for employees with autism, and likely for most other employees as well. Another important consideration is clear identification of when a task is considered completed or if a task should be ongoing, as well as what the employee should do when a task is complete. Consider this example: an individual with autism is working on a coding package for an IT firm. When the task is complete, the employee spends many hours playing a role-play game at his desk. When a fellow employee complains to the supervisor, the individual with autism is written up for poor use of company time. However, in this example, there was no clear direction for the employee about what should be done when the task was complete. From the employee's perspective, he has done his job, and due to deficits in theory of mind, he cannot predict that the supervisor likely has another task for him to complete or how his coworkers may react to his game playing at work, so he does not ask what should be done next or respond to social pressure from coworkers to begin a new task. Thus, performance evaluation should include guidance about all aspects of performance.

Again pulling from the education and applied behavior analysis literature bases, we suggest two possible strategies for effective performance feedback for employees with ASD: video feedback and self-management. In a video feedback system, the employee is filmed completing a specific performance objective or task, then the supervisor and employee view the video together. The supervisor provides praise or corrective feedback, or likely both, during the review of the footage (Barnes, 2014). Tasks, moreover, may be drawn from standardized and validated approaches developed in work samples (Schneider & Schmitt, 1986). Although such samples are often used in assessment, they would have applicability as a training tool given their standardization and representativeness of the job. Video feedback has been shown to be effective in teaching a variety of social and communication skills to children with ASD, and more recently, it has been utilized to teach vocational skills to young adults with autism. For example, English and colleagues (2017) utilized a video feedback system to teach gardening skills to three adults with autism, while Allen and colleagues (2010) utilized a video-based procedure to teach adolescents and young adults with autism to work as a mascot in a retail-based setting. Although not relevant for all job tasks (e.g., coding), video feedback does allow for a clear and specific discussion of many work behaviors that are relevant to performance evaluation.

Alternatively, self-management strategies ask the employee to monitor and review their own performance on a regular basis. In a 2015 review of self-management interventions for individuals with ASD, Aljadeff-Abergel and colleagues (2015) suggest that self-management involves recording the occurrence or nonoccurrence of a target behavior, administering a consequence for performance, evaluating performance against a predetermined goal, and creating antecedents to increase the probability of correct performance. Self-management strategies have been effective in both reducing nondesired behaviors (stereotypic behavior, disruptive behavior, and off-task behavior) and increasing desired behaviors (complimenting others, conversation skills, academic accuracy, compliance, schedule following, and task completion) for children and adolescents with autism in school, home, and community settings (Wilczynski et al., 2009).

Self-management systems are easily integrated into visual schedules or work jigs as described by simply including a checkmark or other way to note when a task is complete. In the workplace, these systems could also include a rating of performance that the neurodiverse employee assigns to their own work, with specific examples included to clearly define each component of the rating. Self-evaluations are a common component of performance review, although typically only at scheduled evaluations. Self-management strategies for neurodiverse individuals are similar but are best used more frequently, such as on a daily or weekly basis, and should include clearly defined goals that describe specific behaviors to be performed. Self-management strategies can also be useful in teaching social skills that may be part of extra-role behaviors or the hidden curriculum in the workplace (Lee et al., 2007). Consider our example about social behaviors in the break room. A weekly self-management checklist could serve as a reminder to the employee to bring in coffee filters or to practice greeting at least three coworkers each week.

The strategies recommended here, including visual supports, video feedback, and self-management tools, can all be easily created with the use of cell phones, tablets, or laptops. Creating performance management tools using technology allows neurodiverse employees to use strategies to increase their workplace success while minimizing stigma. We suggest that supporting individuals with autism in the development of these strategies in a way that integrates well with the workplace is a role for human resources personnel, diversity coordinators, and/or technology specialists.

Determining Consequences of Performance

In keeping with our theme, we again stress the importance of clarity and specificity of consequences in the performance management process for neurodiverse employees. Consequences for performance should be documented in a written format that avoids vague language and instead indicates how specific behaviors lead to specific outcomes. Furthermore, managers may need to meet more frequently with employees with ASD to provide frequent feedback on progress. Again, such meetings should be characterized by clarity and specificity. Finally, managers and supervisors may need to make explicit whether more optional work tasks are expected of employees. This may include, for example, working overtime hours or continuing making coding progress on a software package once goals have been met for a given performance period.

Another important factor to consider in motivating employees with autism is the concept of choice-making. Choice-making has been widely utilized in the applied behavior analysis literature as a strategy for increasing desired behaviors and reducing avoidance of tasks or activities (e.g., Dunlap et al., 1994; Moes, 1998; Northgrave et al., 2019; Watanabe & Sturmey, 2003). Cannella and colleagues (2005) argue that choice-making skills have a positive impact on personal functioning, while Shogren and colleagues (2015) include choice-making as an important component of their definition of self-determination. In the workplace, choice-making could include opportunities to decide what project to work on in the long term or what task to accomplish on a day-to-day basis as well as input on the branch or team that the neurodiverse employee will work with. When providing choices to employees with autism, the manager should clearly specify which tasks or roles should take priority and which might be less important.

Research on motivation to complete tasks for individuals with ASD also indicates that this population is more likely to have difficulty delaying reinforcement than their peers (Whiting & Dixon, 2015). Two possible strategies to address this concern are providing more frequent access to reinforcement or providing a representation of later reinforcement. Consider a common scenario in which employees receive quarterly bonuses based on performance. As we discuss in what follows, individuals with ASD often have difficulty maintaining goal-directed, future-oriented behavior, so long-term incentives may not be the most appropriate motivating tool. However, employers can create a system whereby the neurodiverse employee receives smaller portions of the bonus at shorter increments of time. Alternatively, a visual tool could be utilized daily or weekly by the employee and her supervisor to note progress toward the goal.

Perhaps what is most important to understand is that due to deficits in social communication and theory of mind (ToM), individuals with ASD will not often spontaneously request or discuss their preferences or even understand that options are available. Motivation in the workplace often involves a component of peer acknowledgment or even competition, which neurodiverse individuals may not attend to consistently. Further, neurodiverse employees may have difficulty expressing their wants or needs in a social interaction with the supervisor. Visual supports provide another useful option here. For example, supervisors can provide neurodiverse employees with a menu of possible motivators or rewards, with clearly written descriptions of the motivator and the criteria for earning the motivator. Strategies like this one are similar to preference assessments, which have long been utilized in ABA to effectively identify preference and increase desired behavior for individuals with ASD (Leaf et al., 2015).

TABLE 9.1 Recommendations for Managing Performance for Employees with ASD

Stages of performance management (adapted from Kinicki et al., 2013)	*Unique challenges for employees with ASD*	*Recommendations for organizations*
Defining performance goals	• Difficulty perceiving extra-role behaviors/hidden curriculum • Social communication deficits (e.g., difficulty understanding figurative language, reading body language) • Theory-of-mind deficits	• Clearly define performance goals, in writing, using visual supports as needed, specifying important dimensions of performance and giving a clear definition of completion of the goal • Allow the employee to review performance goals prior to meeting with supervisor • Explicitly clarify the importance of extra-role behaviors, or describe specific extra-role behaviors that should be performed • Use visual supports or work jigs as strategies for guiding performance of tasks

(*Continued*)

TABLE 9.1 (Continued)

Stages of performance management (adapted from Kinicki et al., 2013)	*Unique challenges for employees with ASD*	*Recommendations for organizations*
Evaluating performance & reviewing performance	• Difficulty accepting or understanding feedback due to ToM deficits • Difficulty understanding vague or indirect feedback • Uncertainty about what to do when a task or work activity is completed	• Use video feedback systems to review performance • Create self-management tools to allow the employee with ASD to consistently evaluate their own performance • Provide feedback in alternate formats, such as written format to complement in-person • Utilize technology (e.g., cell phones, tablets, etc.) to ensure the performance evaluation systems are portable and work with the structure of the organization and technology access and ability of the individual
Determining consequences of performance	• Less ability to delay access to reward relative to neurotypical peers • Social communication deficits and ToM, which may result in the employee with autism failing to discuss their preferences	• Provide opportunities for choice-making as much as possible • Consider smaller goals that allow rewards to be earned more frequently • Provide a visual support that allows for frequent documentation (e.g., daily or weekly) of progress toward performance goals • Provide a written or visual menu of possible rewards or other consequences for performance

Career Development and Unique Considerations for Employees with ASD

Whereas performance management represents the processes of facilitating proximal or short-term performance in an organization, career development is "the process by which both individuals and their employers manage the various tasks, behaviors, and experiences within and across jobs and organizations over time, with implications for employees' work-related identity" (Zacher et al., 2019, p. 357). As such, performance management is one of the mechanisms available to support the longer-term goal of successful career development. Inherent in this view of career development, moreover, is that employees are learning and growing, gaining new skills, and facing new challenges. Also underpinning such views on career development is that by facilitating learning and growth, organizations both retain those employees and benefit from their improved skill sets (Wang & Wanberg, 2017).

There have been a number of theoretical frameworks and paradigms used to study career management as well as career development. Although the focus of such approaches is varied, each paradigm offers guidance on how to best support employees over a length of their career and, as such, are noted here. Person–environment fit models (Parsons, 1909), for example, propose that facilitating a fit between an employee's interests and work requirements (i.e., environment) results in job satisfaction on the part of the employee and ultimately higher performance for the organization. In contrast to person–environment fit models, life span models are often based on developmental psychology and suggest that as an employee's life changes, so too will changes be observed in work and work expectations (Wang & Wanberg, 2017). Moreover, such models stress that when there are changes, periods of transition will be required to make such adjustments (e.g., having a child, graduating with a new degree, changes in health). Finally, cognitive and social cognitive theories (e.g., Dreher & Bretz, 1991) propose that choices about careers are based on a rational weighing of one's abilities and whether such abilities will allow oneself to pursue career outcomes of value (e.g., pay, promotion).

As is the case with performance management, the career development programs based on these paradigms have typically been based on the needs and functions of neurotypical employees. As such, these programs may disproportionally advantage neurotypical employees while potentially disadvantaging employees with ASD. Moreover, as is the case with performance management and extra-role behavior, such disadvantage may not be readily apparent, requiring explicit consideration to limit the disparate impact universal application may cause. Consider a personal example of an adult family member of the authors who was diagnosed with autism in college. Now in his 40s, the individual has worked for more than 15 years in a technical role for an international company and has been asked to apply for promotion or management positions but has declined to do so. When asked why, he responded, "Why would I want to give up doing the job I like doing to tell other people how to do the job I like doing?" If traditional career development approaches are the only options offered, this individual will likely miss opportunities for growth in his career. Considering barriers to career development and other pathways to development is imperative for employees with ASD.

Career Development for Employees with ASD

Given the limitations of career development models in that they are built on the needs of neurotypical employees, it is important to consider specific, unique factors that may impact the career development of individuals with ASD relative to their coworkers. Notably, Mynatt and colleagues (2014) outline issues individuals with ASD may face with regard to career development. The first is that given challenges with social skills, employees with ASD may find it challenging to seek out new opportunities. Moreover, employees with ASD may have concerns about forming new friendships and social connections associated with a new position. As such, it is incumbent on managers and supervisors to make new opportunities available, demonstrating how such opportunities will lead to tangible growth in the future as well as building efficacy around their ability to develop new social connections in those positions. Second, Mynatt and colleagues (2014) discuss the narrowed set of interests that accompany disabilities such as ASD (Hurlbutt & Handler, 2010). Finding areas of growth, then, can be a challenge, as employees with ASD may be more fixated on one area of work or the job. Third, employees with ASD may demonstrate sensory issues that also limit their growth opportunities. Moving from a quiet office where the job task was organizing files to a noisier, brighter warehouse job where the task is organizing boxes may be particularly challenging for employees with ASD, for example. Finally, as noted previously, some employees with ASD may lack a strong theory of mind, having less insight into their own feelings or mental states (Dritschel et al., 2010). They may simply be less aware of their own wants and needs, again, making it incumbent on managers to have careful and thoughtful discussions about what tasks and opportunities may be best suited for them. Moreover, managers must be cognizant that new positions may require an increase in social interaction or responsibility and set appropriate expectations (Wanous, 1989) about those new positions as keys to long-term success.

In addition to considering the limitations of career development programs as outlined by Mynatt and colleagues (2014), it is useful to consider the educational literature that emphasizes key areas of functioning and their relationship to educational performance. Drawing on what we know about educational performance, we can make recommendations about how such functions translate to job performance, addressing two key areas of functioning: executive functioning skills and social communication skills.

Executive functions are a set of cognitive functions that include a broad range of higher-order skills such as abstract reasoning, social decision-making, self-regulation, flexibility, working memory, and planning and organizing. These are skills that are considered crucial for future-oriented and goal-directed behavior (Hofmann et al., 2012). Impairments in executive functions have been widely cited for individuals with ASD (e.g., Russell, 1997; Ozonoff et al., 1991) and are supported by findings from brain imaging studies that find structural and functional differences in the prefrontal cortex of the brain, which is thought to be the center of executive functions (e.g., Gilbert et al., 2009; Luna et al., 2002; Castelli et al., 2002). Wolf and colleagues (2009) found that executive function deficits were common for individuals with ASD in college settings, especially planning, organizing, and timely completion of assignments. Furthermore, Lopez et al. (2005) hypothesized that executive dysfunction explains the rigidity, perseverative behaviors, and difficulty with change that is often demonstrated by individuals with ASD.

Many employment activities are influenced by executive functions, such as time management, keeping materials organized, following schedules and coping with schedule changes, and planning for and completing long-term tasks (Wolf et al., 2009). For adults with ASD, executive functioning deficits often take the form of difficulty initiating new tasks, difficulty planning ahead to reach goals, or inability to inhibit inappropriate responses (e.g., focusing on a perseveration rather than an appropriate topic) (Hill, 2004). Wolf and colleagues (2009) reported that while most adults can project outcomes and subsequently demonstrate goal-directed behavior for a timeline six months in the future, college students with Level One ASD may experience projection as short as 48 hours due to executive function deficits (Wolf et al., 2009). This has important implications for goal-setting and future orientation for neurodiverse employees. That is, if career development can be considered a future-oriented process that requires planning for long-term goals and developing new roles within an organization, deficits in executive functions can be hypothesized to directly and negatively impact career development for individuals with ASD.

In addition to executive function deficits, individuals with autism experience impairment in social communication skills that are a core diagnostic feature of ASD (American Psychiatric Association, 2013) and are well documented across age (Billstedt et al., 2007), gender (Rivet & Matson, 2011), culture (Matson et al., 2017), and cognitive ability (Simonoff et al., 2019). Adults with ASD describe social interaction as a stressful experience that comes at considerable psychological cost (Schupp et al., 2013). Communication and social difficulties with other employees and supervisors are reported by adult employees with ASD to be a primary barrier to success at work (Hendricks, 2010) and may even increase the likelihood of termination (Bolman, 2008).

These costs associated with social interaction can be viewed through the lens of resource and ego depletion theories such as the conservation-of-resource theory (Hobfoll, 2001). Such theories stress that resources are finite, including cognitive resources. To the extent such resources are "spent" on demands such as social interaction, fewer resources are available for other functions. Such losses can increase stress, further exacerbating effects and resulting in a "loss spiral" (Hayward, 2019). Key here is that employees with ASD are particularly susceptible to stress and strain from social interaction and may find themselves with less capacity to perform other job functions as a result (Bishop-Fitzpatrick et al., 2016; Hayward et al., 2019).

Along such lines, the importance of job-related social communication skills for individuals with ASD is receiving increased attention in the literature in recent years. For example, Grob et al. (2019) indicate that social communication skills are critical to job success, helping to create a positive relationship between employees with ASD and their coworkers and supervisors. Job-related social communication skills vary by setting and task but may include asking for help when needed, knowing how to respond to feedback, acknowledging when an instruction has been given, or notifying a supervisor when a task is completed (Partington & Mueller, 2015). Given that these skills are associated with positive job outcomes but are known challenges for individuals with ASD, we suggest that intentional steps to support social communication and the development of social relationships in the workplace is crucial for career development. We turn again to the education and applied behavior analysis literature for recommendations for supporting career development for individuals with ASD by addressing needs in the areas of social communication and executive functioning.

Provide Exposure to Growth Roles

Given that career development may inherently include the concept of change, this is likely a challenging process for individuals with ASD, who may have limited ability to visualize themselves in alternative roles (Quirici, 2015) within an organization or difficulty considering how change in the workplace may impact their day-to-day lives as well as long-term outcomes. As always, supervisors should be clear in describing any proposed changes in roles or tasks, using written or visual strategies (Hagner & Cooney, 2005). In addition, we recommend allowing neurodiverse employees to "try on" different roles in the organization. For example, providing a one-week trial period may give the individual with autism an opportunity to understand the new role in a variety of ways. If a trial period is not possible, shadowing someone who is already in the role or viewing videos of others working in the role could also offer an opportunity to understand the role in a way that goes beyond just a verbal description (Lattimore et al., 2008). Accepting and adjusting to change is difficult for many neurodiverse employees, but as noted, avoiding a career that involves the same repetitive task for long periods of time is also important. Allowing a trial period or preview of new or alternative roles may allow the employee with autism to better understand the possible benefits of change within their work role.

Provide Alternative Strategies for Communication

As noted, social stress is a major barrier to successful employment of individuals with ASD. Providing alternative strategies for communication can help to relieve some of the stress that neurodiverse employees experience in the workplace. Fortunately, technology provides many opportunities for alternative forms of communication, such as email, text, videoconferencing, or working in shared documents. For example, consider an employee with ASD who has an innovative idea in the workplace. In order to advance the idea, it must be shared with a team, which can be a difficult scenario for the individual, and it is possible that this barrier would prevent the employee from sharing the idea and thereby limit career growth. Rather than presenting to a large group in person, the employee could create a presentation to be shared in a remote conference. Alternatively, with support from a peer mentor or other resource, the employee could develop a social script for the presentation. Social scripts are simply a written script of a verbal social interaction that the neurodiverse employee can rehearse and even refer to as needed during the social interaction. Social scripts have been recommended for social interaction of college students (Dipeolu et al., 2014). In a 2014 review, Sng and colleagues found that social scripts in auditory, visual, or written format were effective in teaching individuals with ASD social communication skills in a variety of settings. In general, we recommend that the supervisor and employee work together to identify alternative means of social communication that may reduce stress for the employee with autism.

Assign Peer Mentors and Create Opportunities for Relationship Development

While informal and formal social interactions may be stressful for individuals with autism in the workplace, we caution against the notion that individuals with autism are uninterested in social interaction. Bauminger and Kasari (2000) found that high-functioning children and adolescents with autism have a desire for relationships with others and often experience feelings of loneliness more intently than comparison children without autism. Furthermore, having available supportive social networks has been associated with higher quality of life for adults with autism (Renty & Roeyers, 2006). Peer mentoring programs have shown progress in college settings as effective strategies for supporting relationship building and social development for young adults with ASD and have been shown to increase the likelihood of continued attendance in college settings, reduce stress, and increase reports of happiness and well-being (Siew et al., 2017). Peer mentor programs typically pair an individual with autism with a neurotypical peer who has some training in supporting individuals with ASD to address specific goals, such as increased community integration or reduced stress related to social interaction. While there is limited research about peer mentoring in the workplace, given the success of these programs, we recommend that employers explore the development of peer mentor programs for neurodiverse employees.

Assess Supports and Determine Which Supports Can Be Faded

Finally, we pull again from the ABA research base to suggest that while implementing support strategies for neurodiverse employees is important, it is also

TABLE 9.2 Recommendations for Managing Career Development for Employees with ASD

Career development goal	*Unique challenges for employees with ASD*	*Recommendations for managers/ supervisors*
Expansion of employee roles or skills	• Difficulty with change may limit seeking of new opportunities • Narrowed set of interests	• Provide exposure to growth opportunities on a trial basis or allow shadowing of others in possible new roles • Use visual supports or videos to illustrate other roles or opportunities
Retention of the employee	• Deficits in executive functioning • Deficits in social communication skills	• Provide alternative strategies for communication (email, text) to reduce social stress • Create a peer mentor program to support social connection of neurodiverse employees
Develop autonomy and a sense of accomplishment	• Deficits in executive functioning	• Fade supports as needed, based on good assessment of what is working and what is no longer needed

critical to have a plan for fading these supports as the individual gains new skills and experiences success in the work environment. The need for specialized supports and accommodations, while necessary, may also lead to stigma in the workplace or contribute to a sense of unfairness among other employees. The process of identifying and implementing support strategies should be reviewed frequently, and those supports that are no longer needed should be gradually faded. Fading is the process of slowly removing interventions or supports and is important for ensuring independence and autonomy (MacDuff et al., 2001). Supervisors and their neurodiverse employees should frequently assess what tools or strategies are in place and whether those tools or strategies continue to serve a need or provide support for the individual with autism. The process of supporting career development for neurodiverse employees should be an ongoing one, with frequent review of the employees' strengths and needs within the organization.

Lessons from the Applied World: What Is Industry Doing to Support ASD Employment?

The earlier discussion highlights the importance of tailored approaches to performance management and career development to the well-being and retention of employees with ASD. Unfortunately, with a few notable exceptions (e.g., Coleman & Adams, 2018; Scott et al., 2019), there has been limited systematic research on best practices for supporting these activities for employees on the autism spectrum specifically, and as such, it may be beneficial to consider what the applied community is doing to address these issues. Although less systematic than rigorous academic investigation, inspection of the applied community may serve to inspire future research as well as provide some preliminary but tangible guidance for organizations seeking to support these performance management and career development activities.

As part of a small pilot program that began in 2016, for example, Ford Motor Company brought in four employees with ASD to work on product development (Diament, 2016). The program was viewed as a success, resulting in expanded hiring and a new program called FordInclusiveWorks. The company partnered with the Autism Alliance of Michigan to facilitate reasonable accommodations through the hiring process. Most relevant to this chapter, however, has been the focus not only on hiring but also on performance management of employees. The chief program officer noted that "some employees need checklists to stay on task" as an illustration. Program coordinators also acknowledge the unique demands from a career development perspective, with the chief program officer noting, "For a lot of these guys, it's not the actual job performance, it's all of the other things like getting to work on time, dressing and being ready to focus that can derail an opportunity." So far, the program has been a success, generating growing interest within the organization to hire and support more employees on the spectrum.

Perhaps the most visible and vocal organization promoting employment practices for those with ASD has been Microsoft (Sardon, 2019). For reasons similar to those that pushed the Ford Motor Company to approach hiring differently, Microsoft also makes accommodations in the hiring process such as limiting interviews for positions that require limited social interaction for in-role performance. With regard to performance management, Microsoft makes reasonable accommodations that support performance, including allowing employees to write code on their own laptops rather than more public forums such as a whiteboard or shared digital space where others can view progress in real time. Such accommodations can limit the anxiety associated with social interaction, allowing for these employees to engage in work activities in their own way and, ultimately, to shine (Sardon, 2019).

A growing number of companies have followed the lead set by Microsoft and others, including SAP, which has hired more than 175 employees on the autism spectrum to date. Not only has the company hired employees on the spectrum, however, they also report a retention rate of 90% (Woo, 2019), showing both care in the hiring process and a commitment to performance management and career development. As another example, Ernst & Young approaches neurodiversity from the perspective that diversity in perspectives helps reveal avenues for innovation (Twaronite, 2019). The company reports that in the first month, members of the pilot program "identified process improvements that cut the time of technical training in half." The company utilizes a four-step process that includes recruitment and accommodating hiring but also a focus on unique training and developing interpersonal skills in a customized manner as well as continued onboarding and long-term support. Other employers that are autism friendly include Walgreens, Home Depot, AMC, and CVS. Some organizations are autism focused, primarily employing those with ASD, and have demonstrated success as well.

Summary of Industry Trends and Remaining Unknowns

We must be cautious about interpreting such cases as a systematic investigation of best practices in supporting employees. Yet given the dearth of literature on career development and performance management of employees on the spectrum, we can draw some preliminary conclusions from these patterns. The first is that organizations with successful employment programs make accommodations in the hiring process and recognize the need to address the unique challenges faced by those on the autism spectrum. The second is that for organizations that successfully employ individuals with ASD, support does not stop at the hiring phase and, instead, continues beyond hiring to longer-term sustained employment. The nature of this support, however, is somewhat unclear given the nascent stages of such programs. Third, and most relevant to the chapter, there is limited systematic investigation within organizations of the best ways to support employees on the autism spectrum. Thus, although early signs from industry are that programs can be developed successfully, the precise nature of how to do so remains unclear. As such, we see value in considering perspectives outside of industry and the field of I-O psychology for cues on how progress may be made.

How Can I-O Psychologists Support Careers and Performance of Employees With ASD?

As we turn the corner on this decade, the field of I-O psychology has turned inward to ask questions of our future roles in both academic and applied areas (e.g., Aguinis et al., 2017; Bal et al., 2019; Zickar & Highhouse, 2017). Such reflections provide, among other things, a depiction of the "levers" we have for influence in our discipline. When reflecting on what I-O psychologists can do to support the processes of performance management and career development, four roles emerge in association with these levers. We outline these four roles and the way in which they can support the careers and enhance performance of employees with ASD in what follows.

Integrators

I-O psychology is a relatively young field, born from a blend of management, measurement, and related but older fields such as personality, experimental, and social psychology (see Katzell & Austin, 1992, for full discussion). Although we can debate the precise roots of the field, it is less debatable that we are natural integrators (Hunter et al., 2017). Even today, many I-O psychologists have found their homes in business schools rather than psychology departments, showcasing the inherent flexibility of the discipline (Aguinis et al., 2017). One of our biggest strengths is to draw from and connect disciplines in the service of solving complex problems and, in particular, work-oriented problems. The challenges employees with autism face represent one of those complex problems that benefits from our ability to reach out to and learn from other disciplines to support the resolution of such problems.

In this chapter, specifically, we drew directly from the education and school psychology literature as areas not traditionally utilized to solve workplace issues but as some that have also found that solutions from disciplines such as autism clinical science, developmental disability, special education, and vocational education were similarly informative. As we begin to consider what can be done to support employees on the autism spectrum, the educational areas are ripe with lessons to learn and must not be ignored as new frameworks are developed for the workplace. The reality is that school psychologists, applied behavior analysts, and related professionals have been asking themselves how they can support performance for students with autism for much longer than I-O psychologists have concerned themselves with employment issues around similar topics.

As integrators, it is critical that we do not stop reaching out to education and school literatures for these critical lessons. Of similar importance, however, is to also consider emerging areas such as technology (e.g., Morelli et al., 2017) to provide meaningful and rapid feedback in the service of performance management, as an example. Sensory issues associated with ASD also suggest that areas such as cognitive psychology and kinesthesiology are also critical avenues to consider that are not often associated with I-O psychology as a field or the subareas of performance management and career development.

Researchers

Along lines related to the discussion so far is that, as academics, we have tremendous power to study issues surrounding autism. Noted earlier, much of this work has traditionally been housed in the education literature. Although there are similarities and linkages between the education and workplace literatures, workplace issues often present a unique set of demands and, as such, opportunities for research. Moreover, as more individuals with autism begin to enter the workforce, it is incumbent upon us as a field to begin to ask critical research questions surrounding the world of employment using other disciplines as jumping-off points as we expand to the unique issues facing the world of work. Core research questions surrounding performance management and career development include but are hardly limited to: What does a new challenge look like for an employee with autism? How do we support employees with ASD who both seek out and find themselves in a position to supervise others? Is career progression unique for employees with ASD? Do individuals with autism detect extra-role behaviors in the workplace, and if so, do they respond appropriately? How frequently should employees with ASD receive performance feedback? Finally, how should researchers approach evaluation research in work settings?

Trainers/Training Developers

Using existing frameworks as well as new insights gathered from emerging research, I-O psychologists are poised to play a critical role in developing training programs for both supervisors and employees with ASD (Brown, 2017). This chapter lays out several recommendations for how managers can more effectively manage the performance and careers of employees with autism. Formal training programs that put to work these recommendations and those we have missed will be critical to fully instantiate improvements in the workplace. In particular, formal training programs allow participants to utilize exercises, consider in-depth cases, and engage in opportunities for application as critical tools not only to improve knowledge but also to build the behavioral habits required for substantive change to occur. Finally, although the focus of the chapter has been on providing recommendations to managers and supervisors of employees with autism, we have touched on tools and techniques employees with ASD can utilize themselves. Thus, training programs aimed at teaching employees with autism how to seek feedback effectively, navigate hidden performance expectations, and identify areas for growth and learning will supplement training programs aimed at managers and peers.

Policy Advocates

One final role we can engage in as a field is by serving as advocates for policy change. I-O psychologists and, in particular, the Society for Industrial and Organizational Psychology have begun to make effortful movement in the area of advocacy (Lewis-Burke, 2020). Recent changes in legislation such as the Americans with Disabilities Act of 1990 as amended by the Americans with Disabilities Act of 2008 have resulted in greater legal protection and incentivization for accommodating employees with autism (Hensel, 2017). In particular, employees with autism have the right to reasonable accommodation on the job. The precise nature of what represents a reasonable accommodation, however, is often in flux as subjected to cases that emerge. Given that I-O psychologists are in the unique position of having expertise in both psychology and the workplace, it is critical for us to leverage such expertise to serve as advocates and guides for those on the spectrum. Specifically, our expertise allows for meaningful and data-driven recommendations for what is a reasonable expectation for organizations and employees on the autism spectrum is well within the obligation of our discipline.

Closing Comments

In our chapter, we examined approaches to performance management and career development that were developed for neurotypical employees. In doing so, we observed ways in which organizations can adjust these approaches to support employees with ASD. In addition, we uncovered a number of hidden work requirements that may put employees at a disadvantage. Using literature from outside of I-O psychology and related fields such as human resource management, education, school psychology, and ABA, we were able to provide organizations with recommendations on how to manage these hidden requirements. We believe this intersection of disciplines provides for unique insight into supporting employees with ASD and recommend, going forward, that I-O psychology look to these literature bases not only for managing the performance and careers of employees with autism but also for a range of workplace issues. Lessons should flow both ways, with education learning from the world of work. Employees with ASD are certainly deserving of the effort to cross disciplinary boundaries as we have much to learn from each other.

Note

1. Applied behavior analysis, according to Fisher et al. (2013), "focuses on solving problems of social importance using the principles and procedures of behavior analysis" (p. 3). Applied behavior analysis focuses on external, observable behavior and assumes correlation with these behaviors and internal events or feelings. ABA explores environmental variables that impact behavior and utilizes the manipulation of those variables as a primary strategy for prediction and change of behavior (Fisher et al., 2013).

References

Aguinis, H., Ramani, R. S., Campbell, P. K., Bernal-Turnes, P., Drewry, J. M., & Edgerton, B. T. (2017). Most frequently cited sources, articles, and authors in industrial-organizational psychology textbooks: Implications for the science–practice divide, scholarly impact, and the future of the field. *Industrial and Organizational Psychology, 10*(4), 507–557.

Aljadeff-Abergel, E., Schenk, Y., Walmsley, C., Peterson, S. M., Frieder, J. E., & Acker, N. (2015). The effectiveness of self-management interventions for children with autism – A literature review. *Research in Autism Spectrum Disorders, 18*(5), 34–50.

Alkahtani, A. (2015). Organizational citizenship behavior (OCB) and rewards. *International Business Research, 8*(4), 210.

Allen, K. D., Wallace, D. P., Greene, D. J., Bowen, S. L., & Burke, R. V. (2010). Community-based vocational instruction using videotaped modeling for young adults with autism spectrum disorders performing in air-inflated mascots. *Focus on Autism and Other Developmental Disabilities, 25*(3), 186–192.

Alsubaie, M. A. (2015). Hidden curriculum as one of current issue of curriculum. *Journal of Education and Practice, 6*(33), 125–128.

American Psychiatric Association. (2013). *Diagnostic and statistical manual of mental disorders* (5th ed.). Washington, DC: Author.

Anyon, J. (1980). Social class and the hidden curriculum of work. *Journal of Education, 162*, 67–92.

Bal, P. M., Dóci, E., Lub, X., Van Rossenberg, Y. G., Nijs, S., Achnak, S., . . . Van Zelst, M. (2019). Manifesto for the future of work and organizational psychology. *European Journal of Work and Organizational Psychology, 28*(3), 289–299.

Baldwin, S., Costley, D., & Warren, A. (2014). Employment activities and experiences of adults with high-functioning autism and Asperger's disorder. *Journal of Autism and Developmental Disorders, 44*(10), 2440–2449.

Barnes A. (2014). *Using video feedback to increase eye-contact during mock job interviews for transition age adults with Autism Spectrum Disorders* (Graduate Thesis and Dissertations). Gainesville, FL: University of Florida.

Baron-Cohen, S. (2000). Theory of mind and autism: A fifteen-year review. *Understanding Other Minds: Perspectives from Developmental Cognitive Neuroscience, 2*, 3–20.

Baron-Cohen, S. (2001). Theory of mind in normal development and autism. *Prisme, 34*(1), 74–183.

Bauminger, N., & Kasari, C. (2000). Loneliness and friendship in high-functioning children with autism. *Child Development, 71*(2), 447–456.

Begeer, S., Rieffe, C., Terwogt, M. M., & Stockmann, L. (2003). Theory of mind – based action in children from the autism spectrum. *Journal of Autism and Developmental Disorders, 33*(5), 479–487.

Billstedt, E., Carina Gillberg, I., & Gillberg, C. (2007). Autism in adults: Symptom patterns and early childhood predictors. Use of the DISCO in a community sample followed from childhood. *Journal of Child Psychology and Psychiatry, 48*(11), 1102–1110.

Bishop-Fitzpatrick, L., Hong, J., Smith, L. E., Makuch, R. A., Greenberg, J. S., & Mailick, M. R. (2016). Characterizing objective quality of life and normative outcomes in adults with autism spectrum disorder: An exploratory latent class analysis. *Journal of Autism and Developmental Disorders, 46*(8), 2707–2719.

Bolman, W. M. (2008). Brief report: 25-year follow-up of a high-functioning autistic child. *Journal of Autism and Developmental Disorders, 38*(1), 181–183.

Brown, K. G. (Ed.). (2017). *The Cambridge handbook of workplace training and employee development*. Cambridge, UK: Cambridge University Press.

Buchner, T. W. (2007). Performance management theory: A look from the performer's perspective with implications for HRD. *Human Resource Development International, 10*(1), 59–73.

Cannella, H. I., O'Reilly, M. F., & Lancioni, G. E. (2005). Choice and preference assessment research with people with severe to profound developmental disabilities: A review of the literature. *Research in Developmental Disabilities, 26*(1), 1–15.

Castelli, F., Frith, C., Happé, F., & Frith, U. (2002). Autism, Asperger syndrome and brain mechanisms for the attribution of mental states to animated shapes. *Brain, 125*(8), 1839–1849.

Coleman, D. M., & Adams, J. B. (2018). Survey of vocational experiences of adults with autism spectrum disorders, and recommendations on improving their employment. *Journal of Vocational Rehabilitation, 49*(1), 67–78.

DeNisi, A. S., & Murphy, K. R. (2017). Performance appraisal and performance management: 100 years of progress? *Journal of Applied Psychology, 102*(3), 421.

DeNisi, A., & Smith, C. E. (2014). Performance appraisal, performance management, and firm-level performance: A review, a proposed model, and new directions for future research. *Academy of Management Annals, 8*(1), 127–179.

de Schipper, E., Mahdi, S., de Vries, P., Granlund, M., Holtmann, M., Karande, S., . . . Bölte, S. (2016). Functioning and disability in autism spectrum disorder: A worldwide survey of experts. *Autism Research, 9*(9), 959–969.

Dettmer, S., Simpson, R. L., Myles, B. S., & Ganz, J. B. (2000). The use of visual supports to facilitate transitions of students with autism. *Focus on Autism and Other Developmental Disabilities, 15*(3), 163–169.

Diament, M. (2016). *Ford expands autism hiring initiative*. Retrieved from www.disabilityscoop.com/2016/11/29/ford-expands-autism-hiring/23064/

Dipeolu, A. O., Storlie, C., & Johnson, C. (2014). Transition to college and students with high functioning Autism Spectrum Disorder: Strategy considerations for school counselors. *Journal of School Counseling, 12*(11), n11.

Dreher, G. F., & Bretz, R. D. (1991). Cognitive ability and career attainment: Moderating effects of early career success. *Journal of Applied Psychology, 76*(3), 392.

Dritschel, B., Wisely, M., Goddard, L., Robinson, S., & Howlin, P. (2010). Judgements of self-understanding in Vo adolescents with Asperger syndrome. *Autism, 14*(5), 509–518.

Dunlap, G., dePerczel, M., Clarke, S., Wilson, D., Wright, S., White, R., & Gomez, A. (1994). Choice making to promote adaptive behavior for students with emotional and behavioral challenges. *Journal of Applied Behavior Analysis, 27*(3), 505–518.

English, D. L., Gounden, S., Dagher, R. E., Chan, S. F., Furlonger, B. E., Anderson, A., & Moore, D. W. (2017). Effects of video modeling with video feedback on vocational skills of adults with autism spectrum disorder. *Developmental Neurorehabilitation, 20*(8), 511–524.

Fisher, W. W., Piazza, C. C., & Roane, H. S. (Eds.). (2013). *Handbook of applied behavior analysis*. New York: Guilford Press.

Flower, R. L., Hedley, D., Spoor, J. R., & Dissanayake, C. (2019). An alternative pathway to employment for autistic job-seekers: A case study of a training and assessment program targeted to autistic job candidates. *Journal of Vocational Education & Training, 71*(3), 407–428.

Gilbert, S. J., Meuwese, J. D., Towgood, K. J., Frith, C. D., & Burgess, P. W. (2009). Abnormal functional specialization within medial prefrontal cortex in high-functioning autism: A multi-voxel similarity analysis. *Brain, 132*(4), 869–878.

Grob, C. M., Lerman, D. C., Langlinais, C. A., & Villante, N. K. (2019). Assessing and teaching job-related social skills to adults with autism spectrum disorder. *Journal of Applied Behavior Analysis, 52*(1), 150–172.

Hagner, D., & Cooney, B. F. (2005). "I do that for everybody": Supervising employees with autism. *Focus on Autism and Other Developmental Disabilities, 20*(2), 91–97.

Hart-Barnett, J., Trillo, R., & More, C. M. (2018). Visual supports to promote science discourse for middle and high school students with autism spectrum disorders. *Intervention in School and Clinic, 53*(5), 292–299.

Hayward, S. M., McVilly, K. R., & Stokes, M. A. (2019). Autism and employment: What works. *Research in Autism Spectrum Disorders, 60*(5), 48–58.

Hendricks, D. (2010). Employment and adults with autism spectrum disorders: Challenges and strategies for success. *Journal of Vocational Rehabilitation, 32*(2), 125–134.

Hensel, W. F. (2017). People with autism spectrum disorder in the workplace: An expanding legal frontier. *Harvard Civil Rights-Civil Liberties Law Review, 52*, 73.

Hill, E. L. (2004). Executive dysfunction in autism. *Trends in Cognitive Sciences, 8*(1), 26–32.

Hobfoll, S. E. (2001). The influence of culture, community, and the nested-self in the stress process: Advancing conservation of resources theory. *Applied Psychology, 50*(3), 337–421.

Hofmann, W., Schmeichel, B. J., & Baddeley, A. D. (2012). Executive functions and self-regulation. *Trends in Cognitive Sciences, 16*(3), 174–180.

Hurlbutt, K., & Chalmers, L. (2004). Employment and adults with Asperger syndrome. *Focus on Autism and Other Developmental Disabilities, 19*(4), 215–222.

Hurlbutt, K. S., & Handler, B. R. (2010). High school students with Asperger syndrome: A career path binder project. *Intervention in School and Clinic, 46*(1), 46–50.

Hunter, S.T., Shortland, N. D., Crayne, M. P., & Ligon, G. S. (2017). Recruitment and selection in violent extremist organizations: Exploring what industrial and organizational psychology might contribute. *American Psychologist, 72*(3), 242.

Jerald, C. D. (2006). *The hidden costs of curriculum narrowing* (Issue brief). Center for Comprehensive School Reform and Improvement.

Jiang, Y. V., Palm, B. E., DeBolt, M. C., & Goh, Y. S. (2015). High-precision visual long-term memory in children with high-functioning autism. *Journal of Abnormal Psychology, 124*(2), 447–456.

Johnson, J. W. (2001). The relative importance of task and contextual performance dimensions to supervisor judgments of overall performance. *Journal of Applied Psychology, 86*(5), 984–996.

Judge, T. A., Piccolo, R. F., & Ilies, R. (2004). The forgotten ones? The validity of consideration and initiating structure in leadership research. *Journal of Applied Psychology, 89*(1), 36.

Kaland, N., Callesen, K., Møller-Nielsen, A., Mortensen, E. L., & Smith, L. (2008). Performance of children and adolescents with Asperger syndrome or high-functioning autism on advanced theory of mind tasks. *Journal of Autism and Developmental Disorders, 38*(6), 1112–1123.

Katzell, R. A., & Austin, J. T. (1992). From then to now: The development of industrial-organizational psychology in the United States. *Journal of Applied Psychology, 77*(6), 803.

Kinicki, A. J., Jacobson, K. J., Peterson, S. J., & Prussia, G. E. (2013). Development and validation of the performance management behavior questionnaire. *Personnel Psychology, 66*(1), 1–45.

Krzeminska, A., Austin, R. D., Bruyère, S. M., & Hedley, D. (2019). The advantages and challenges of neurodiversity employment in organizations. *Journal of Management & Organization, 25*(4), 453–463.

Lattimore, L. P., Parsons, M. B., & Reid, D. H. (2008). Simulation training of community job skills for adults with autism: A further analysis. *Behavior Analysis in Practice, 1*(1), 24–29.

Leaf, J. B., Leaf, R., Alcalay, A., Leaf, J. A., Ravid, D., Dale, S. & Oppenheim-Leaf, M. (2015). Utility of formal preference assessments for individuals diagnosed with autism spectrum disorder. *Education and Training in Autism and Developmental Disabilities, 50*(2), 199–212.

Lee, H. J. (2011). Cultural factors related to the hidden curriculum for students with autism and related disabilities. *Intervention in School and Clinic, 46*(3), 141–149.

Lee, S. H., Simpson, R. L., & Shogren, K. A. (2007). Effects and implications of self-management for students with autism: A meta-analysis. *Focus on Autism and Other Developmental Disabilities, 22*(1), 2–13.

Lewis-Burke Associates LLC. (2020). *Guide to federal outreach & advocacy*. https://www.siop.org/LinkClick.aspx?fileticket=W4qmCGsnOUM=&portalid=84

Liu, X., & Batt, R. (2010). How supervisors influence performance: A multilevel study of coaching and group management in technology-mediated services. *Personnel Psychology, 63*(2), 265–298.

Locke, E. A., & Latham, G. P. (1990). *A theory of goal setting & task performance*. Englewood Cliffs, NJ: Prentice-Hall, Inc.

Lopez, B. R., Lincoln, A. J., Ozonoff, S., & Lai, Z. (2005). Examining the relationship between executive functions and restricted, repetitive symptoms of autistic disorder. *Journal of Autism and Developmental Disorders, 35*(4), 445–460.

Luna, B., Minshew, N. J., Garver, K. E., Lazar, N. A., Thulborn, K. R., Eddy, W. F., & Sweeney, J. A. (2002). Neocortical system abnormalities in autism: An fMRI study of spatial working memory. *Neurology, 59*(6), 834–840.

MacDuff, G. S., Krantz, P. J., & McClannahan, L. E. (2001). Prompts and prompt-fading strategies for people with autism. In *Making a difference: Behavioral intervention for Autism* (pp. 37–50). Austin, TX: Pro-Ed.

Matson, J. L., Matheis, M., Burns, C. O., Esposito, G., Venuti, P., Pisula, E., & Ishitobi, M. (2017). Examining cross-cultural differences in autism spectrum disorder: A multinational comparison from Greece, Italy, Japan, Poland, and the United States. *European Psychiatry, 42*, 70–76.

Moes, D. R. (1998). Integrating choice-making opportunities within teacher-assigned academic tasks to facilitate the performance of children with autism. *Journal of the Association for Persons with Severe Handicaps, 23*, 319–328.

Morelli, N., Potosky, D., Arthur, W., & Tippins, N. (2017). A call for conceptual models of technology in IO psychology: An example from technology-based talent assessment. *Industrial and Organizational Psychology, 10*(4), 634–653.

Myles, B. S., Endow, J., & Mayfield, M. (2013). *The hidden curriculum of getting and keeping a job: Navigating the social landscape of employment: A guide for individuals with autism spectrum and other social-cognitive challenges*. Shawnee Mission, KS: AAPC Publications.

Myles, B. S., & Simpson, R. L. (2001). Understanding the hidden curriculum: An essential social skill for children and youth with Asperger syndrome. *Intervention in School and Clinic, 36*(5), 279–286.

Myles, B. S., & Smith, S. (2005). A look inside the hidden curriculum: The importance of teaching vague and elusive information to individuals with autism spectrum disorders. *Autism Spectrum Quarterly*, 22–29.

Mynatt, B. S., Gibbons, M. M., & Hughes, A. (2014). Career development for college students with Asperger's syndrome. *Journal of Career Development, 41*(3), 185–198.

Northgrave, J., Vladescu, J. C., DeBar, R. M., Toussaint, K. A., & Schnell, L. K. (2019). Reinforcer choice on skill acquisition for children with autism spectrum disorder: A systematic replication. *Behavior Analysis in Practice, 12*(2), 401–406.

Ohl, A., Grice Sheff, M., Small, S., Nguyen, J., Paskor, K., & Zanjirian, A. (2017). Predictors of employment status among adults with Autism Spectrum Disorder. *Work, 56*(2), 345–355.

Organ, D. W. (1988). *Organizational citizenship behavior: The good soldier syndrome*. Lexington, MA: Lexington Books/DC Heath and Com.

Ozonoff, S., Rogers, S. J., & Pennington, B. F. (1991). Asperger's syndrome: Evidence of an empirical distinction from high-functioning autism. *Journal of Child Psychology and Psychiatry, 32*(7), 1107–1122.

Parr, A. D., & Hunter, S. T. (2014). Enhancing work outcomes of employees with autism spectrum disorder through leadership: Leadership for employees with autism spectrum disorder. *Autism, 18*(5), 545–554.

Parr, A. D., Hunter, S. T., & Ligon, G. S. (2013). Questioning universal applicability of transformational leadership: Examining employees with autism spectrum disorder. *The Leadership Quarterly, 24*(4), 608–622.

Parsons, F. (1909). *Choosing a vocation*. Boston, MA: Houghton-Mifflin.

Partington, J. W., & Mueller, M. M. (2015). *The Assessment of Functional Living Skills (The AFLS): Independent living skills assessment protocol, an assessment, skills tracking system, and curriculum guide for skills that are essential for independence*. Behavior Analysts, Incorporated.

Peterson, C. C., Slaughter, V. P., & Paynter, J. (2007). Social maturity and theory of mind in typically developing children and those on the autism spectrum. *Journal of Child Psychology and Psychiatry, 48*(12), 1243–1250.

Pfeiffer, B., Brusilovskiy, E., Davidson, A., & Persch, A. (2018). Impact of person-environment fit on job satisfaction for working adults with autism spectrum disorders. *Journal of Vocational Rehabilitation, 48*(1), 49–57.

Podsakoff, P. M., Todor, W. M., & Skov, R. (1982). Effects of leader contingent and non-contingent reward and punishment behaviors on subordinate performance and satisfaction. *Academy of Management Journal, 25*(4), 810–821.

Quirici, M. (2015). Geniuses without imagination: Discourses of autism, ability, and achievement. *Journal of Literary & Cultural Disability Studies, 9*(1), 71–88.

Remington, A., Swettenham, J., Campbell, R., & Coleman, M. (2009). Selective attention and perceptual load in autism spectrum disorder. *Psychological Science, 20*(11), 1388–1393.

Renty, J., & Roeyers, H. (2006). Quality of life in high-functioning adults with autism spectrum disorder. *Autism, 10*(5), 511–524.

Rivet, T. T., & Matson, J. L. (2011). Review of gender differences in core symptomatology in autism spectrum disorders. *Research in Autism Spectrum Disorders, 5*(3), 957–976.

Roux, A. M., Shattuck, P. T., Rast, J. E., Rava, J. A., Edwards, A. D., Wei, X., & Yu, J. W. (2015). Characteristics of two-year college students on the autism spectrum and their support services experiences. *Autism Research and Treatment, 2015,* 391693.

Russell, J. E. (1997). *Autism as an executive disorder.* Oxford: Oxford University Press.

Schneider, B., & Schmitt, N. (1986). *Staffing organizations.* Glenview, IL: Scott Foresman & Co.

Schopler, E., Mesibov, G. B., & Hearsey, K. (1995). Structured teaching in the TEACCH system. In *Learning and cognition in autism* (pp. 243–268). Boston, MA: Springer.

Schupp, C. W., Simon, D., & Corbett, B. A. (2013). Cortisol responsivity differences in children with autism spectrum disorders during free and cooperative play. *Journal of Autism and Developmental Disorders, 43*(10), 2405–2417.

Scott, M., Jacob, A., Hendrie, D., Parsons, R., Girdler, S., Falkmer, T., & Falkmer, M. (2017). Employers' perception of the costs and the benefits of hiring individuals with autism spectrum disorder in open employment in Australia. *PloS One*, 12(5), 1–16.

Scott, M., Milbourn, B., Falkmer, M., Black, M., Bölte, S., Halladay, A., & Girdler, S. (2019). Factors impacting employment for people with autism spectrum disorder: A scoping review. *Autism, 23*(4), 869–901.

Shogren, K. A., Wehmeyer, M. L., Palmer, S. B., Rifenbark, G. G., & Little, T. D. (2015). Relationships between self-determination and postschool outcomes for youth with disabilities. *The Journal of Special Education, 48*(4), 256–267.

Siew, C. T., Mazzucchelli, T. G., Rooney, R., & Girdler, S. (2017). A specialist peer mentoring program for university students on the autism spectrum: A pilot study. *PLoS ONE, 12*(7), e0180854.

Simonoff, E., Kent, R., Stringer, D., Lord, C., Briskman, J., Lukito, S., & Baird, G. (2019). Trajectories in symptoms of autism and cognitive ability in autism from childhood to adult life: Findings from a longitudinal epidemiological cohort. *Journal of the American Academy of Child & Adolescent Psychiatry, 59*(12), 1342–1352.

Srivastava, A. P., & Shree, S. (2019). A review of extra role behavior as an organizational asset. *SAMVAD, 18,* 39–46.

Stogdill, R. M. (1950). Leadership, membership and organization. *Psychological Bulletin, 47*(1), 1.

Sulaimani, M. F., & Gut, D. M. (2019). Hidden curriculum in a special education context: The case of individuals with autism. *Journal of Educational Research and Practice, 9*(1), 3.

Thomas, H., & Boellstorff, T. (2017). Beyond the spectrum: Rethinking autism. *Disability Studies Quarterly, 37*(1).

Twaronite, K. (2019, May 10). A neurodiverse world is a better working world. *EY Magazine*. Retrieved from www.ey.com/en_us/diversity-inclusiveness/how-neurodiversity-is-driving-innovation-from-unexpected-places

Van Bourgondien, M. E., & Schopler, E. (1996). Intervention for adults with autism. *Journal of Rehabilitation, 62*(1), 65.

Van Bourgondien, M. E., & Woods, A.V. (1992). Vocational possibilities for high-functioning adults with autism. In E. Schopler & G. Mesibov (Eds.), *High-functioning individuals with autism* (pp. 227–239). Boston, MA: Springer.

Van Dick, R., van Knippenberg, D., Kerschreiter, R., Hertel, G., & Wieseke, J. (2008). Interactive effects of work group and organizational identification on job satisfaction and extra-role behavior. *Journal of Vocational Behavior, 72*(3), 388–399.

Van Dyne, L., & LePine, J. A. (1998). Helping and voice extra-role behaviors: Evidence of construct and predictive validity. *Academy of Management Journal, 41*(1), 108–119.

Van Scotter, J., Motowidlo, S. J., & Cross, T. C. (2000). Effects of task performance and contextual performance on systemic rewards. *Journal of Applied Psychology, 85*(4), 526–535.

Vigoda-Gadot, E. (2007). Redrawing the boundaries of OCB? An empirical examination of compulsory extra-role behavior in the workplace. *Journal of Business and Psychology, 21*(3), 377–405.

Wang, M., & Wanberg, C. R. (2017). 100 years of applied psychology research on individual careers: From career management to retirement. *Journal of Applied Psychology, 102*(3), 546.

Wanous, J. P. (1989). Installing a realistic job preview: Ten tough choices. *Personnel Psychology, 42*(1), 117–134.

Watanabe, M., & Sturmey, P. (2003). The effect of choice-making opportunities during activity schedules on task engagement of adults with autism. *Journal of Autism and Developmental Disorders, 33*(5), 535–538.

Wei, X., Yu, J. W., Wagner, M., Hudson, L., Roux, A. M., Shattuck, P., & Blackorby, J. (2018). Job searching, job duration, and job loss among young adults with autism spectrum disorder. *Journal of Vocational Rehabilitation, 48*(1), 1–10.

Whiting, S. W., & Dixon, M. R. (2015). Delayed reinforcement and self-control: Increasing tolerance for delay with children and adults with autism. In *Autism service delivery* (pp. 407–435). New York: Springer.

Whiting, S. W., Podsakoff, P. M., & Pierce, J. R. (2008). Effects of task performance, helping, voice, and organizational loyalty on performance appraisal ratings. *Journal of Applied Psychology, 93*(1), 125–139.

Wilczynski, S., Green, G., Ricciardi, J., Boyd, B., Hume, A., Ladd, M., & Rue, H. (2009). *National standards report: The national standards project: Addressing the need for evidence-based practice guidelines for autism spectrum disorders*. Randolph, MA: National Autism Center.

Wolf, L. E., Brown, J. T., & Bork, G. R. K. (2009). *Students with Asperger syndrome: A guide for college personnel*. Shawnee, KS: Autism Asperger Publishing.

Woo, E. (2019). *Autism at work: Encouraging neurodiversity in the workplace*. Retrieved from https://news.sap.com/2019/10/workplace-neurodiversity-autism-at-work-program/

Wright, G. C., Hubick, K. T., Farquhar, G. D., & Rao, R. N. (1993). Genetic and environmental variation in transpiration efficiency and its correlation with carbon isotope discrimination and specific leaf area in peanut. In *Stable isotopes and plant carbon-water relations* (pp. 247–267). New York: Academic Press.

Zacher, H., Esser, L., Bohlmann, C., & Rudolph, C. W. (2019). Age, social identity and identification, and work outcomes: A conceptual model, literature review, and future research directions. *Work, Aging and Retirement, 5*(1), 24–43.

Zelazo, P. D., Jacques, S., Burack, J. A., & Frye, D. (2002). The relation between theory of mind and rule use: evidence from persons with autism-spectrum disorders. *Infant and Child Development: An International Journal of Research and Practice*, *11*(2), 171–195.

Ziatas, K., Durkin, K., & Pratt, C. (1998). Belief term development in children with autism, Asperger syndrome, specific language impairment, and normal development: Links to theory of mind development. *Journal of Child Psychology and Psychiatry, 39*(5), 755–763.

Zickar, M. J., & Highhouse, S. (2017). Where has all the psychology gone? (Twenty years later). *Industrial and Organizational Psychology*, *10*(4), 616–621.

10

SUPPORTING THE MENTAL HEALTH AND WELL-BEING OF AUTISTIC AND OTHER NEURODIVERGENT EMPLOYEES IN THE WORK ENVIRONMENT

Simon M. Bury, Jennifer R. Spoor, Susan M. Hayward, and Darren Hedley

Introduction

People diagnosed with autism spectrum disorder (hereafter 'autism') experience high rates of co-occurring mental health challenges (Hollocks et al., 2019; Uljarević et al., 2020). Employment is linked to improved health and well-being in the general population (Boardman et al., 1999; Claussen et al., 1993; McKee-Ryan et al., 2005; Modini et al., 2016; Paul & Moser, 2009); however, there is limited research that has examined employment-related mental health benefits or costs in the autistic population[1] (Hedley, Cai, et al., 2018; Hedley, Spoor, et al., 2018; Hedley et al., 2019). This is pertinent given exceedingly high rates of under- and unemployment in this group worldwide (Australian Bureau of Statistics, 2019; Roux et al., 2017; The National Autistic Society, 2016). In this chapter, we suggest that these poor employment outcomes may partly reflect the complexities of mental health conditions commonly co-occurring with autism. Indeed, core autistic traits often do not impede successful work task completion, although they may contribute to workplace misunderstandings (Bury et al., 2020; Hayward et al., 2020). Thus, while workplace education concerning the characteristics of autism may be beneficial, there is additionally a mostly unacknowledged need for workplace-based, targeted (i.e., autism-specific) mental health supports.

In this chapter we first summarise common co-occurring psychiatric conditions in autistic people, focusing on depression, anxiety, and sleep disorders, as these are particularly prevalent in autism. We then discuss psychosocial stressors through the lens of job demands-resource (JD-R) theory (Bakker & Demerouti, 2017). We include case studies and narratives from individuals with lived experience of mental health concerns, focusing on how these concerns have affected their employment. These case studies are drawn from employees of our industry

DOI: 10.4324/9781003023616-10

partner DXC Technology, and their autism employment program the DXC Dandelion Program, an overview of which is provided in a case study in what follows. We then summarise conventional mental health and well-being supports aimed for the work environment and identify some limits of these initiatives in supporting autistic employees. Last, we discuss recently developed autism-specific mental health and well-being supports, outlining recommendations for embedding these into targeted autism employment programs. Although we focus on autism, we expect that the information and principles provided here will be applicable to other neurodivergent people as well as other workplace-based neurodiversity programs.

Autism and Mental Health and Well-Being

Depression and anxiety are the most common workplace mental health conditions in the general population and are associated with greater absenteeism and poor work functioning through presenteeism (Lerner et al., 2010; Plaisier et al., 2010). Co-occurring mental health concerns are common in autism and potentially impact employment rates and sustainability; however, no research to date has investigated the unique impact of co-occurring mental health on autism employment. Lifetime prevalence of depressive disorders in the autistic population ranges from 28% to 49%; about four times higher than that observed in the general population, which ranges from 11% to 17% (Hollocks et al., 2019; Hudson et al., 2018; Lai et al., 2019; Merikangas et al., 2010; Uljarević et al., 2020). Furthermore, depressive symptoms are strongly associated with suicide in this population (Dell'Osso et al., 2019; Hedley & Uljarević, 2018). Atypical presentations of depression in autism may include displays of anger and frustration, changes in special interests (e.g., focus on morbid or death-related interests), changes in self-care (e.g., hygiene), and more frequent 'meltdowns' (Attwood & Garnett, 2016). While specific factors are associated with depression in autistic populations (e.g., family history, IQ; Greenlee et al., 2016; Rai, Heuvelman, et al., 2018), risk factors associated with the social interaction and communication diagnostic criteria of autism (e.g., loneliness, reduced social support, bullying) are predictive of higher rates of depression (Hedley et al., 2018; Mazurek, 2014; Rai, Culpin, et al., 2018).

Anxiety disorders are also very common amongst individuals on the autism spectrum, and while estimates vary widely based on the study and measures used, large-scale studies and meta-analytic reviews suggest that up to 60% of autistic individuals meet the criteria for anxiety in their lifetime (Buck et al., 2014; Hollocks et al., 2019; Lever & Geurts, 2016; Uljarević et al., 2019). A recent meta-analysis of 12-month prevalence of different types of anxiety disorder in autistic adults (Hollocks et al., 2019) showed higher prevalence compared to the general population across all subtypes (American Psychiatric Association, 2013), including general anxiety disorder (18% vs 2.9%–3.6%), social anxiety disorder (29%

vs 2%–7%), and obsessive compulsive disorder (19% vs 1.1%–1.8%).[2] In addition, anxiety can display atypically in autistic populations. For example, 'social avoidance and distress' associated with social anxiety disorder may be less likely to be associated with the fear of social evaluation or judgement in autistic individuals compared to the general population (Kerns et al., 2014). Additionally, autistic individuals often report atypical specific phobias or anxieties, which may be associated with the repetitive and restrictive behaviours and interests diagnostic criteria (American Psychiatric Association, 2013), such as unexpected sensory input, changes in activity or routine, or being prevented from performing calming repetitive behaviours (Halim et al., 2018; Mayes et al., 2013). Given atypical presentation of anxiety in autism and a lack of autism-specific anxiety measures, prevalence of anxiety in autistic individuals may be underestimated.

Sleep problems in the general population are associated with decreased cognitive abilities and concentration, which can affect work performance and safety (Ford et al., 2011; Hui & Grandner, 2015). These issues can also distort perceptions of the work environment (e.g., perceive greater pressure and demands), potentially leading to increased stress. Thus, the effect of sleep on employment is reciprocal, whereby stress can lead to sleep problems and sleep problems to greater stress, which can lead to increased mental health challenges (de Lange et al., 2005; Törnroos et al., 2017).

Sleep disorders are common in adults on the autism spectrum (Carmassi et al., 2019), with some research showing higher rates of sleep disorders in autistic individuals (17.6%) compared to non-autistic individuals (9.6%; Croen et al., 2015). Common sleep problems amongst autistic individuals include difficulties falling asleep, low sleep quality and efficiency (Limoges et al., 2005; Tani et al., 2003), insomnia (Baker & Richdale, 2015; Tani et al., 2003), and circadian sleep–wake rhythm disorders (Baker & Richdale, 2017; Limoges et al., 2005). However, these studies are often limited by small sample size or participant characteristics (e.g., inclusion of adolescents). Social factors such as unemployment and social interactions have also been associated with sleep disorders in people on the autism spectrum (Baker et al., 2019; Hedley, Uljarević, Cameron, et al., 2017).

It is important to note that mental well-being is more than the absence of mental health challenges. Mental well-being is a multifaceted construct, which, in addition to reduced negative symptomology of mental health, also includes positive aspects of cognitive, emotional, and psychological well-being (Keyes et al., 2002). The World Health Organisation (2020) defines mental well-being as "a state of well-being in which every individual realizes his or her own potential, can cope with the normal stresses of life, can work productively and fruitfully, and is able to make a contribution to her or his community". In line with this definition, suggestions and recommendations in this chapter are aimed to not only improve negative mental health but to create environments and situations in which autistic individuals can reach their potential. Indeed, positive mental well-being has been shown to buffer the effects of negative mental health in employees on the autism spectrum (Hedley, Uljarević et al., 2019), thus providing an important avenue to support mental health in this population.

Case Example: Written by Jackson 'Jacky' Shin (pseudonym)

This case study was provided by Jacky, who was asked to write about his experience of mental health and autism and working in the information communication technology (ICT) sector as part of a three-year autism employment program. Jacky's story highlights the unique ways mental health can impact autistic people, as well as difficulties and available workplace supports. Jacky was a part of the program for three years but has since graduated and has been employed in a similar field for the past two years. Jacky writes:

> *While living with autism has been challenging, the fact of living with depression has been even more challenging for me. Depression can hit anyone at any time but, because autistic people are 'wired' differently, we feel it hits us more often because of the feeling of being different. I was diagnosed with autism more than ten years ago now, and I was also diagnosed with anxiety issues and depression. For me, both anxiety and depression go hand-in-hand.*
>
> *By nature, people with autism are anxious about a lot of things (e.g., what clothes to wear, the bus/train schedule, if places to shop will be noisy). A few of them include "what will people think of me if I open up?", "will people accept me for being Autistic?", "will people believe that I am Autistic if I act the same as them?" With all of these thoughts, for each response I think up that is positive, two are created that lead to depression. I can manage my anxiety better now compared to the early days of being diagnosed, but I still feel depression over the littlest of things. Be it at work or at home, I always have depressing thoughts.*
>
> *An example of depression hitting me is with work. Information Technology (IT) is a really accepting environment to be in, as people know what they need to do and have a routine around it, and Autistic people really like routine. A couple of years ago while working, someone came to my desk and asked to talk to me regarding work. I didn't know if I did something wrong or if it was something that impressed people, so I assumed that it was because I did something*

wrong. During the talk, I learnt that it was because I impressed another team with the work I did, but the person also suggested a few ways to improve the work I had completed. I thought that my work was actually well-done because of what the person told me, but after listening to the suggestions I started to feel as if it wasn't as good as I thought, and the depression hit. I couldn't do much work for a good hour because of the suggestions and went into fight-or-flight mode, and after a while chose flight. Yes, I left work for the day and had the next day off because of it. All because my depression was saying that my work wasn't good enough.

To help manage times like these I would normally listen to music during work times, since it helps me handle my anxieties and depression. I was also able to negotiate a forty-five/fifteen (45/15) minute work schedule, this is where I work for forty-five minutes then have a fifteen-minute break to do personal training, go for a walk, go get coffee etc. These strategies have helped me manage my anxiety, depression, workload and meetings for work.

Psychosocial and Environmental Job Stressors

Although pre-existing mental health challenges can spill over into work, psychosocial job stressors within the workplace can affect pre-existing mental health and well-being and may also precipitate the development of mental health challenges. Indeed, excessive or prolonged exposure to a stressor has long been associated with increases in mental health disorders in the general population (American Psychiatric Association, 2013). There is limited knowledge on how organisations can effectively support well-being amongst autistic employees. We propose that JD-R theory (Bakker & Demerouti, 2017; Schaufeli & Taris, 2014), which is a conceptual model of job stress that accounts for the complex interaction between features of the workplace and employees' mental health, offers a conceptual framework for better understanding the complex interplay between mental health challenges and the work environment. The theory posits a range of negative factors that may undermine performance and well-being at work while also emphasizing positive factors that can encourage employees to flourish. The original JD-R model (Demerouti et al., 2001) was proposed to identify job stressors and explain high levels of burnout across a range of occupations. We build on this model to propose a new Job Demands-Resources for Autism (JD-R-A, see Figure 1) that we believe better captures the experience of autistic employees.

Job Demands. Within the JD-R model, job *demands* are any aspect of the job (physical, psychological, social, or organisational) that require sustained effort and

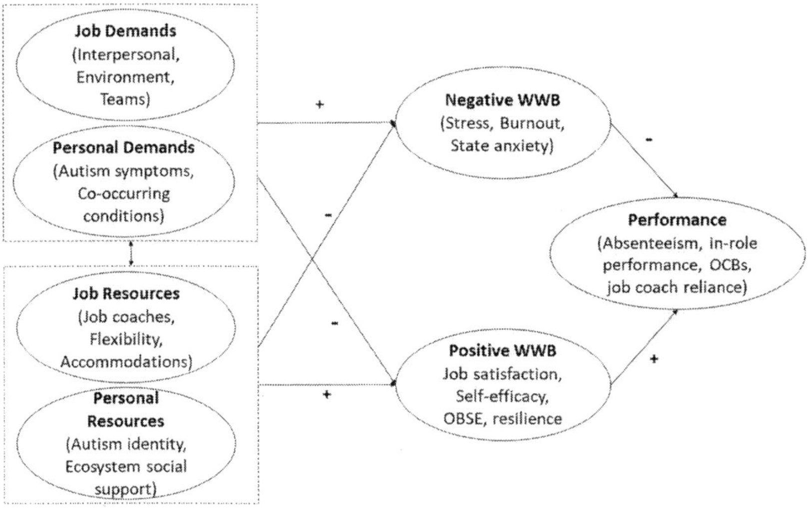

FIGURE 10.1 Conceptual JD-R-A Model

Note: Co-occurring conditions include anxiety, depression, sleep disorder. Ecosystem social supports include family and community supports. WWB = Work well-being. OBSE = Organisational-based self-esteem. OCB = Organisational citizenship behaviour. Model adapted from Bakker and Demerouti (2017).

impact physiological or psychological outcomes (Bakker & Demerouti, 2017). Job demands negatively influence performance via increased strain, which is reflected in exhaustion, anxiety, and negative health. Thus, demands have a negative impact on mental health and well-being in the workplace. Typical job demands include physical demands, risks and hazards, role ambiguity, time pressure, workload, and performance and emotional demands (Schaufeli & Taris, 2014), as well as workplace bullying, sexual harassment, and job insecurity (Harvey et al., 2017; LaMontagne et al., 2010). Due to the core symptoms of autism, certain features of employment (e.g., social interactions, sensory environment) may be more challenging and have greater impact as job demands for autistic employees than their non-autistic peers (Hayward et al., 2020). Based on the prior literature on autism and employment, we propose autism-specific job demands in our JD-R-A. First, autistic employees may experience heightened environmental demands compared to non-autistic employees. Autistic adults who are employed are often working in roles that are a poor fit to their skills, education, and expertise (Cimera & Cowan, 2009; Hedley, Uljarević, Cameron, et al., 2017; Holwerda et al., 2012; Müller et al., 2003; Shattuck et al., 2012). Poor person–job fit and inadequate compensation may also contribute to sporadic work history and high unemployment experienced by many autistic adults.

Differences in social communication and interaction are a defining feature of an autism diagnosis (American Psychiatric Association, 2013) and may mean that interpersonal job demands related to managing interpersonal relationships, communication, conflict, and team-based work may impose a stronger demand on autistic employees (Hayward et al., 2020). Moreover, autistic employees may have more difficulty with ambiguous or unstructured tasks or understanding the unwritten social protocols of employment (Baldwin & Costley, 2016; Bury, Flower, et al., 2020; Hayward et al., 2018, 2020), and the COVID-19 pandemic has resulted in heightened uncertainty and radical change in most workplaces, with a disproportionate effect on workers who were already disadvantaged (Shaw et al., 2020). Furthermore, when social challenges and conflict do arise in employment, they are more commonly attributed to the autistic employee than to the environment or workplace (Bury, Flower, et al., 2020). This could lead to the potential of real or perceived workplace bullying (Baldwin & Costley, 2016; Hayward et al., 2018; Wilczynski et al., 2013). Therefore, job demands relating to social interaction in the workplace come at a greater psychological cost or are more demanding for autistic people (Hayward et al., 2020).

Personal Demands

Recent reviews of JD-R theory have suggested that *personal* demands (Bakker & Demerouti, 2017), which represent individual and non-work factors, may also contribute to negative mental health effects at work. In our model, personal demands can reflect autism symptomology or the co-occurring mental health conditions we discussed earlier in this chapter. Restricted and repetitive behaviours and interests, which are part of the diagnostic criteria in autism (American Psychiatric Association, 2013), could present as cognitive rigidity or difficulties planning and managing workloads (Hillier et al., 2007; Müller et al., 2003). This cognitive rigidity may be mechanistically underpinned by executive dysfunction (South et al., 2007), and so training and strategies (e.g., breaking work tasks into small components, using work planners and other assistive technology, helping individuals to structure their work flow) aimed at supporting executive function could help diminish the impact of this demand. Finally, many autistic adults experience sensory hypersensitivity (Kirchner & Dziobek, 2014; Pfeiffer et al., 2017); thus, the physical work environment (e.g., open-plan office spaces, bright lighting) may impose a significant job demand.

Job and personal demands are cumulative, which can mean that seemingly mundane job tasks may become more difficult to manage, thus increasing negative impacts on workplace well-being (Bakker & Demerouti, 2017). In the general population, job demands have been identified as an "upstream determinant" of mental health disorders (Harvey et al., 2017; LaMontagne et al., 2010, p. 17), such as depression (Theorell et al., 2015), anxiety (Wieclaw et al., 2008), disturbed sleep (Linton et al., 2015), emotional exhaustion/burnout (Seidler et al., 2014; Ståhl et al., 2018), and suicide (Milner et al., 2018). It has also been associated with increased maladaptive behaviours (e.g., increased smoking and alcohol consumption; Kouvonen et al., 2005, 2008), poor physical health, such as coronary heart disease (Aboa-Éboulé et al., 2007; Eller et al., 2009; Rugulies et al., 2020) or disrupted immune response (Nakata, 2012), and even death (e.g., cardiovascular mortality, Kivimäki et al., 2002).

Job Resources

Job resources refer to any aspect of the job (physical, psychological, social, or organisational) that facilitate individuals' personal growth and development (Bakker & Costa, 2014; Bakker & Demerouti, 2017). Resources can positively influence job performance through increased motivation, which is reflected in improved job attitudes (i.e., satisfaction and commitment) and engagement (i.e., energy, enthusiasm). Examples of job resources in the general population include greater autonomy, goal clarity, job challenge, positive feedback, good-quality relationships with supervisor or coworkers, and trust in management (Schaufeli & Taris, 2014). Early research suggests that autistic employees may not benefit from these job resources to the same extent (Hayward et al., 2020). For example, although social support is associated with greater well-being for autistic people (Bishop-Fitzpatrick et al., 2018), the preference for and timing of social support as a resource for autistic employees may differ compared to non-autistic employees (Hayward et al., 2020). Job resources could also include employer resources, strategies or policy initiatives (ILO, 2017), or workplace mental health services (e.g., employment assistance programs), mental health training, workplace well-being programs, the nature of which and their limitations for autistic populations are discussed further in what follows. Autism-specific job resources may include access to an autism consultant or job coach who provides work and interpersonal support (Hayward et al., 2020; Hedley, Cai, et al., 2018; Rashid et al., 2017), and workplace accommodations tailored to the individual's specific needs (e.g., ability to wear hearing protection; Bury et al., 2019, 2020; Hayward et al., 2020).

Personal Resources

In our JD-R-A model we also suggest that personal resources may play a significant role in supporting workplace well-being. Autism-specific personal resources may include an autistic social identity (Cooper et al., 2017) and support from the broader employment ecosystem (i.e., family, community, mental health professionals) (Hedley, Uljarević, Cameron, et al., 2017; Nicholas et al., 2018). Moreover, supports from the broader employment ecosystem (e.g., capacity building for employers, supervisors, and coworkers), independent of family support, may be important for developing autonomy (Nicholas & Klag, 2020).

For autistic employees, personal demands could also undermine their access to standard workplace resources. For example, difficulties identifying and expressing emotions (Poquérusse et al., 2018) and difficulty asking for help can manifest in difficulties related to not knowing when to engage resources (Hayward et al., 2020). Conversely, differences in facial expression and vocal quality (American Psychiatric Association, 2013) and atypical mental health symptomology (e.g., Halim et al., 2018) could mean workplace resources (e.g., managers) are less equipped to know when to provide support.

The JD-R-A Model in Autism Employment Programs

Our JD-R-A model suggests that supporting autistic employees to more effectively manage demands and increase resources could be instrumental in supporting their mental health and well-being, thus contributing to improved employment outcomes. Although not framed in terms of demands and resources, some autism-specific employment support programs have effectively countered some of the negative impact of autism-specific demands. For example, autism employment programs that reduce emphasis on prior work experience or use job coaches to increase person–job fit (Hedley, Uljarević, Cameron, et al., 2017) can help to reduce the environment and interpersonal job demands. Other programs may provide skills training focused on autism symptomology (e.g., social skills training; Smith et al., 2014) or vocational training focused on specific work or technical skills (Flower et al., 2019; Seaman & Cannella-Malone, 2016). Some programs effectively increase job resources through educating colleagues and supervisors in autism for a better-informed support network (Flower et al., 2019) or providing job coaches throughout employment (Hedley, Uljarević, Cameron, et al., 2017; Hedley, Uljarević, & Hedley, 2017).

Case Study: The DXC Dandelion Program

An example of an autism employment program that provides substantial support to autistic employees is the DXC Dandelion Program, which, at the time of writing, has employed more than 120 autistic individuals in the Australian information communication technology (ICT) sector since 2015. Traditional recruitment methods, such as face-to-face interviews, disadvantage autistic people (Flower et al., 2019). Instead, the DXC program utilises an initial information and introduction day, followed by an extended (2- to 3-week) paid training and assessment program. Successful candidates enter a three-year paid program and work in teams of 10 to 13 individuals. Teams are supported by dedicated and experienced DXC and client ICT staff, who train, manage the workload, and provide technical support to the new autistic team members. Team members are also supported by onsite and full-time autism spectrum consultants (ASC), specialist support workers who manage related support needs of autistic candidates and colleagues, provide organisational autism training and other operational roles, and advise on suitable workplace adjustments and arrangements.

The DXC Dandelion Program has demonstrated a high rate of retention of autistic employees (89% retention, Hedley, Spoor, et al., 2018), possibly reflecting successful reduction in demands and an increase in resources. However, longitudinal research has also shown limited improvement in positive mental well-being or negative mental health over the first 12 months of employment (Hedley et al., 2019), suggesting there may not be flow-on effects to these areas. Indeed, within the program co-occurring mental health challenges (e.g., anxiety, depression, sleep disorders) were recognised as complex factors that needed to be supported to maintain the sustainability of the program (Fieldhouse, 2017). Moreover, Fieldhouse (2017) acknowledges that in implementing a neurodiversity program within DXC Technology, sustainability involves "managing autism but other mental health disorders at the same time" (p. 8). Correspondence with support staff in this program highlighted that tools and training specific to autistic employees were not available, which prompted the development of specific tools for this population (Bury et al., 2020).

Case Example: DG

This case study aims to highlight an example of the impact of co-occurring mental health conditions on individuals working to maintain employment and a meaningful career. DG is a man in his mid-thirties, who was recently diagnosed with autism and co-occurring ADHD. This case study is written by DG's autism spectrum consultant (ASC). DG describes his life as very challenging prior to his diagnosis – always wondering why he did not fit in. DG had sought psychological services for anxiety and, by luck, saw a therapist who had expertise in autistic adults who quickly suggested an assessment for autism. DG describes this as being the most profound experience, as he was finally able to understand why life had been so challenging.

It was at this time that DG saw the DXC Dandelion Program advertised. After applying he completed the assessment and was offered a role in one of the teams. DG feels he fits in the ICT industry and has indeed flourished in the role. However, the anxiety DG has experienced all his life was still a concern. With the mentorship of an ASC, DG identified that his anxiety was impacting him both inside and outside of work. Together with the ASC, DG identified several triggers in the work environment and came up with some strategies to manage those.

At work, DG's anxiety was primarily related to sensory processing – he is particularly sensitive to smells and noise. He was also extremely focused on his work and found sudden, unpredictable interruptions extremely 'frightful'. This was manifest in several scenarios:

- Interruptions triggered a fight-or-flight response, typically him shutting down, impacting his ability to focus for hours, which he found embarrassing and upsetting.
- Due to difficulties filtering out the noise of people talking close by he became so anxious he became quite direct and loud in telling people to move away, which caused additional problems.
- Anxiety from his home life made him extremely tired and overly focused on his work and unable to interact with others in his usual friendly way.

While DG was extremely self-aware and normally able to advocate for himself, it was often the ASC who was able to notice the difference in his behaviour. Strategies to manage these issues for DG were negotiated, trialled, and documented on a work profile, which DG has been keen to share with his managers. They included:

- Letting a trusted person (in this case, the ASC) know they are not doing well
- If signs of anxiety were noted by the ASC, a message is sent to DG 'checking in'
- Having an opportunity to 'vent' in a quiet, private space with a trusted person has been a most effective strategy
- Offering the opportunity of flexible work hours and splitting his work week between home and office
- Referral to appropriate professionals
- Support for communication strategies during times of conflict

DG continues to flourish in his work. He has an ongoing partnership with a trusted mental health professional and has independently found trusted colleagues who are now friends with whom who he can share his life.

Supporting Mental Health and Well-Being in the Workplace: Current Initiatives and Future Directions

Although highly supportive autism employment programs can contribute to improved employment outcomes for autistic people (Hedley, Uljarević, Cameron, et al., 2017), there is little focus on supporting their workplace mental health and well-being. Mental health is a workplace demand that is not unique to autistic employees. In this section we discuss current initiatives and interventions aiming to support mental health in the general workforce. Health and well-being initiatives and interventions broadly focus on the primary level (e.g., promoting good health and eliminating the cause of illness), secondary level (e.g., changing how people respond to or perceive illness), and tertiary level (e.g., treat, compensate, or rehabilitate after illness). Moreover, workplace interventions can focus on the individual, the organisation, or the individual/organisation interface (Cooper & Cartwright, 1994; DeFrank & Cooper, 1987). Included in this space are bespoke mental health policies and initiatives launched in individual organisations that have had reported success in reducing absenteeism and turnover due to illness and improving employee satisfaction (ILO, 2017), as well as more broadly accessible initiatives employed across workplaces. We discuss two formal forms of mental health and well-being support that are common in workplaces – employee assistance programs (Attridge, 2019) and mental health first aid (Kitchener & Jorm, 2002) – and discuss their potential role in supporting the mental health of autistic employees.

Employee Assistance Programs

Employee assistance programs (EAPs) are employer-sponsored programs designed to help employees identify and resolve acute personal and behavioural issues that may actually or potentially impact work performance (Attridge, 2019; Joseph et al., 2018). EAPs are widely available to employees in most private and public organisations throughout North America and Australia (Attridge, 2019). EAPs can be administered by external providers or internal staff (Attridge, 2019; Kirk & Brown, 2003). Many EAPs use short-term counselling to address a specific stressor or situation (Attridge, 2019) and tend to be under-utilised and provide limited value to the organisation (Attridge, 2019). More comprehensive and integrated programs provide broader support, training, and resources for both teams and managers, with some EAPs actively involved in health-promotion activities. However, the value of these more comprehensive EAPs is unclear, as research tends to focus on the counselling service (Joseph et al., 2018).

Managers perceive EAPs to be a low-cost risk-mitigation measure that is almost a minimum requirement for an organisation to provide (Joseph & Walker, 2017). Although several studies claim that EAPs have a strong return on investment, the quality and rigor of existing evaluation studies has been criticised

(Cooper & Cartwright, 1994; Joseph et al., 2018; Kirk & Brown, 2003). Based on a recent systematic review, Joseph et al. (2018) concluded that EAP users did experience an improvement in overall functioning and decreased presenteeism. Despite programs' widespread availability in workplaces, autistic employees may find limited value in EAPs. Autistic people report difficulties accessing general and allied health professionals who are willing and able to work with autistic clients (Camm-Crosbie et al., 2019). This knowledge and experience gap likely extends to EAP counsellors, whose opportunities for ongoing professional development related to autism are highly limited. Further, given the limited number of sessions provided by most EAPs (4 to 5 sessions; Roche et al., 2018) and the inherent communication difficulties in autism, the service may struggle to adequately meet the needs of autistic people.

Mental Health First Aid

Mental health first aid (MHFA) was developed in 2000 in Australia to address public understanding of mental health (Kitchener & Jorm, 2002) and has since been adopted in at least 21 countries with several international evaluative studies (e.g., Sweden, Canada; Hadlaczky et al., 2014; Kitchener & Jorm, 2008). MHFA follows a physical first aid model, whereby members of the public are trained to provide initial support to someone developing a mental health issue or experiencing a mental health crisis, until appropriate professional help is available. MHFA follows a five-component action plan: (1) approach and assess risk of harm; (2) listen non-judgementally; (3) give resources and information; (4) encourage person to seek appropriate professional help; (5) encourage self-help and other supports (Kitchener & Jorm, 2002; Morgan et al., 2018). Standard MHFA training and guidelines are regularly revised based on current mental health research (Bovopoulos, Jorm, et al., 2016; Morgan et al., 2018). MHFA training covers common mental health issues and crisis situations including depression, anxiety disorders, psychosis, substance use disorders, suicidal behaviours, panic attacks, traumatic events, drug overdose, and aggressive behaviour (Hadlaczky et al., 2014; Morgan et al., 2018). Specialised courses focusing on help for young people, older adults, and Aboriginal or Torres Strait Islander people are also available (Morgan et al., 2018).

MHFA was originally developed as an intervention for the general public, but it is increasingly used as a workplace intervention (Bovopoulos, Jorm, et al., 2016; Bovopoulos, LaMontagne, et al., 2016). It has been identified as an effective and evidence-based intervention for reducing the stigma of mental illness in the workplace (Hanisch et al., 2016; Szeto & Dobson, 2010). Bovopoulos, Jorm, et al. (2016) recently developed specific guidelines for providing MHFA in a workplace setting, with additional recommendations for first aiders who are also managers. These guidelines help to delineate role clarity between when the person is acting in a MHFA role versus their normal organisation role, as well as issues related to privacy and confidentiality. A growing trend in Australian businesses is to appoint MHFA officers, who are similar to physical first aid officers (Bovopoulos et al., 2018). Qualitative research in organisations with MHFA officers suggests that having these roles and MHFA training more broadly available in the organisation provides mutual benefits to the organisation and individual employees by addressing mental health concerns earlier and before they escalate, as well as leading to a broader knowledge and understanding of mental health throughout the organisation.

Like EAPs, autistic employees may find access to MHFA less beneficial compared to non-autistic employees. MHFA training does not cover autism specifically, and individuals who have received this training may not recognise how common mental health disorders such as depression and anxiety may manifest differently in autistic people. Moreover, even where MHFA officers and other MHFA-trained staff are readily identifiable, engagement with these individuals is likely to depend on the quality of relationship and trust that other employees have with this person (Bovopoulos et al., 2018).

The organisation mental health and well-being interventions discussed in this section are principally focused on tertiary prevention (although comprehensive EAPs may have a health promotion component), and they give less consideration to how mental health concerns could be mitigated or eliminated in the first place (i.e., primary prevention). Moreover, these interventions largely target the individual without addressing issues in the workplace itself or the individual/organisation interface. The lack of autism-specific resources and training within these interventions suggests that they may be inappropriate or inadequate for supporting mental health and well-being among autistic staff. There is a clear need to develop workplace well-being initiatives and supports that specifically consider the needs and experiences of autistic individuals. It may also be important to embed well-being supports within the broader employment ecosystem (Nicholas et al., 2018). Given the limitations identified, new approaches are needed.

New Initiatives to Support the Well-Being and Mental Health of Autistic Employees

Given the limitations of the mental health strategies and resources identified in the previous section with regard to autistic employees, this section briefly details two new initiatives to assist in addressing the gap in supporting the mental health and well-being of autistic and neurodiverse people.

The first initiative recognised a significant gap in support options for addressing mental health challenges identified by the DXC Dandelion Program. DXC Technology, in partnership with Australia and New Zealand Banking Group (ANZ), commissioned research into developing an autism-specific mental health training package, the *Supporting a neurodiverse workforce: A mental health and well-being resource and training package* (Bury, Hayward, et al., 2020), developed further with Untapped Holdings into online training (see Bury et al., 2022). This training package follows a similar model to the mental health first aid training detailed earlier; however, it builds on this approach by providing specific content suitable for recognising and supporting the unique presentation of mental health within autistic employees. With strategies and resources designed specifically for supervisors, colleagues/mentors, and autistic employees themselves, this package aims to develop an employment ecosystem that is better suited to supporting autistic employees and their mental health and well-being.

The second approach that is utilised by DXC Technology is Life Sherpa (3R Behavioral Solutions). This mobile platform provides general behavioural supports that are beneficial to many employees, including neurodiverse employees, that can be linked with supervisors or job-coaches so that they receive updates about their employees. This platform includes apps that can assist in supporting executive functioning such as creating routines in the workplace and managing workloads (e.g., diary tools), thereby reducing job demands and increasing job resources and assisting autistic employees to become more self-reliant in the workplace. It also includes tools to help with daily functioning (e.g., daily routine, shopping, travel), difficulties that can add additional demands for some employees before the workday has commenced. The platform also includes ad-hoc tools that may be beneficial for supporting the mental health of autistic employees (e.g., mood reviews, well-being plan, identifying stressors). One example that may support the communication difficulties is the Status Change for Well-Being activity, which represents an indirect outreach mechanism, whereby changing one's status in the app (e.g., from happy to sad) initiates a message to support staff to alert them that support may be needed.

While these two initiatives are a good first step, there is a paucity of research examining the efficacy of autism-specific mental health and well-being programs. Although the interventions and training programs identified in this chapter were informed by research in autism and mental health, the extent to which these interventions are effective has not yet been tested. This provides the opportunity for research to examine mental health and well-being outcomes amongst autistic staff utilising these tools compared to standard workplace practices.

Future Directions and Conclusion

This chapter examined the complex interplay between the workplace and the mental health challenges of autistic employees. Primarily we argue that poor mental health presents an additional workplace demand for many employees on the autism spectrum. While employment programs and interventions that reduce job demands and increase job resources by managing support needs associated with autism traits do exist, we identified significant limitations in the resources available to support the mental health and well-being of autistic employees. Given the high rates of co-occurring mental health challenges outlined at the beginning of this chapter (e.g., Hollocks et al., 2019), as well as the greater potential for increased demands and reduced resources of autistic employees (Hayward et al., 2020), improving mental health and well-being outcomes has significant implications for the sustainability of autism employment programs and autism employment more broadly. While programs to support mental health and well-being in the workplace, either established programs or bespoke corporate systems, may have some utility in supporting autistic employees and their mental health, experience from community settings suggests that this support may not be sufficient or accessible to employees on the autism spectrum (Camm-Crosbie et al., 2019). Given the complexity of the interplay between autism, mental health and well-being, and the workplace, we believe that the novel application of the JD-R model to this population provides an innovative way to contextualise the interaction of these separate factors.

With the increased interest in neurodiversity, especially in autism employment, we would argue that specific training and tools to better support workplace mental health and well-being should be incorporated as standard organisational policy and practice. With that in mind, we recommend that managers and workplaces increase their own understanding of autism and mental health even if they do not have staff who have disclosed their diagnosis. Mental health training targeted at supervisors has reduced stigma, absenteeism, and presenteeism (Gayed et al., 2018; Milligan-Saville et al., 2017), and extending this to autism-specific mental health and well-being will broaden these benefits. This is also important because not all individuals feel comfortable disclosing a diagnosed condition in the workplace (Johnson & Joshi, 2016; Ohl et al., 2017). While some may manage their work life without revealing their diagnosis, for many masking or hiding symptoms of a diagnosis represents a serious demand and cost and is linked with mental health challenges (Cage et al., 2018). Research in other minority-group employees demonstrated that masking or hiding their minority-group status in the workplace negatively impacts work performance, social inclusion and well-being (Ellemers & Barreto, 2006). Furthermore, management practices that support autistic employees (e.g., direct communication) are often effective with other staff (Hagner & Cooney, 2005), and as neurodiversity presents as a broader spectrum of abilities, specific tools and resources for autistic people may benefit the workforce more broadly.

Despite difficulties accessing and maintaining employment, autistic people want to work (Flower et al., 2019) and achieve greater autonomy (Hedley, Uljarević, et al., 2017). While there has been success in managing the additional demands that may arise for employees on the autism spectrum (Hedley, Uljarević, Cameron, et al., 2017), there are few autism-specific evidence-based interventions to support the mental health and well-being of these employees. Providing skills and support to manage well-being will support their success, and benefits may extend beyond the workplace. Moreover, the resources provided to coworkers and managers will contribute to a workplace culture that supports diversity (Martins & Terblanche, 2003), enhancing inclusion and mental well-being of the workforce more broadly.

Conflict of Interest Statement

S.M.B. declares he has received research funding from DXC Technology, ANZ Bank and Untapped Holdings. D.H. declares research funding from DXC Technology, Untapped Holdings, ANZ Bank, Australian Government Department of Human Services, and Australian Government Department of Defence. D.H. is currently supported by a Suicide Prevention Australia National Suicide Prevention Research fellowship.

Acknowledgments

We would like to thank and recognise Jackson 'Jacky' Shin and Karen Tytler for their excellent contribution of case studies in this book chapter and Michelle Hardingham for her support.

Notes

1. There is significant variability in the preference for how to describe autism (Bury et al., 2020). In line with the *Publication Manual of the American Psychological Association* 7th edition, we use a combination of person-first (i.e., person on the autism spectrum) and identity-first (i.e., autistic person) language to reflect the diverse views of people with an autism diagnosis.
2. Although anxiety features in obsessive compulsive disorder, it is no longer classified under Anxiety Disorders in the most recent iteration of the *Diagnostic and Statistical manual of Mental Disorders* (DSM-5; American Psychiatric Association, 2013).

References

Aboa-Éboulé, C., Brisson, C., Maunsell, E., Mâsse, B., Bourbonnais, R., Vézina, M., . . . Dagenais, G. R. (2007). Job strain and risk of acute recurrent coronary heart disease events. *Journal of the American Medical Association, 298*(14), 1652–1660. https://doi.org/10.1001/jama.298.14.1652

American Psychiatric Association. (2013). *Diagnostic and statistical manual of mental disorders (DSM-5®).* Washington, DC: Author.

Attridge, M. (2019). A global perspective on promoting workplace mental health and the role of employee assistance programs. *American Journal of Health Promotion, 33*(4), 622–629. https://doi.org/10.1177/0890117119838101c

Attwood, T., & Garnett, M. (2016). *Exploring depression, and beating the blues: A CBT self-help guide to understanding and coping with depression in Asperger's syndrome [ASD-Level 1].* London: Jessica Kingsley Publishers.

Australian Bureau of Statistics. (2019). *44300DO060_2018 survey of disability, ageing and carers: Autism in Australia.* Retrieved from www.abs.gov.au/AUSSTATS/abs@.nsf/DetailsPage/4430.02018?OpenDocument

Baker, E. K., & Richdale, A. L. (2015). Sleep patterns in adults with a diagnosis of high-functioning autism spectrum disorder. *Sleep, 38*(11), 1765–1774. https://doi.org/10.5665/sleep.5160

Baker, E. K., & Richdale, A. L. (2017). Examining the behavioural sleep-wake rhythm in adults with autism spectrum disorder and no comorbid intellectual disability. *Journal of Autism and Developmental Disorders, 47*(4), 1207–1222. https://doi.org/10.1007/s10803-017-3042-3

Baker, E. K., Richdale, A. L., & Hazi, A. (2019). Employment status is related to sleep problems in adults with autism spectrum disorder and no comorbid intellectual impairment. *Autism, 23*(2), 531–536. https://doi.org/10.1177/1362361317745857

Bakker, A. B., & Costa, P. L. (2014). Chronic job burnout and daily functioning: A theoretical analysis. *Burnout Research, 1*(3), 112–119. https://doi.org/10.1016/j.burn.2014.04.003

Bakker, A. B., & Demerouti, E. (2017). Job demands – resources theory: Taking stock and looking forward. *Journal of Occupational Health Psychology, 22*(3), 273–285. https://doi.org/10.1037/ocp0000056

Baldwin, S., & Costley, D. (2016). The experiences and needs of female adults with high-functioning autism spectrum disorder. *Autism, 20*(4), 483–495. https://doi.org/10.1177/1362361315590805

Bishop-Fitzpatrick, L., Mazefsky, C. A., & Eack, S. M. (2018). The combined impact of social support and perceived stress on quality of life in adults with autism spectrum disorder and without intellectual disability. *Autism, 22*(6), 703–711. https://doi.org/10.1177/1362361317703090

Boardman, A. P., Grimbaldeston, A., Handley, C., Jones, P., & Willmott, S. (1999). The North Staffordshire suicide study: A case – control study of suicide in one health district. *Psychological Medicine, 29*(1), 27–33. https://doi.org/10.1017/s0033291798007430

Bovopoulos, N., Jorm, A. F., Bond, K. S., LaMontagne, A. D., Reavley, N. J., Kelly, C. M., . . . Martin, A. (2016). Providing mental health first aid in the workplace: A Delphi consensus study. *BMC Psychology, 4*(1), Article 41. https://doi.org/10.1186/s40359-016-0148-x

Bovopoulos, N., LaMontagne, A. D., Martin, A., & Jorm, A. (2016). Delivering mental health first aid training in Australian workplaces: Exploring instructors' experiences. *International Journal of Mental Health Promotion, 18*(2), 65–82. https://doi.org/10.1080/14623730.2015.1122658

Bovopoulos, N., LaMontagne, A. D., Martin, A., & Jorm, A. (2018). Exploring the role of mental health first aid officers in workplaces. *International Journal of Workplace Health Management, 11*(6), 366–381. https://doi.org/10.1108/Ijwhm-06-2018-0082

Buck, T. R., Viskochil, J., Farley, M., Coon, H., McMahon, W. M., Morgan, J., & Bilder, D. A. (2014). Psychiatric comorbidity and medication use in adults with autism spectrum disorder. *Journal of Autism and Developmental Disorders, 44*(12), 3063–3071. https://doi.org/10.1007/s10803-014-2170-2

Bury, S. M., Flower, R. L., Zulla, R., Nicholas, D., & Hedley, D. (2020). Workplace social challenges experienced by employees on the autism spectrum: Perspectives of employees and supervisors. *Journal of Autism and Developmental Disorders, 51*, 1614–1627. https://doi.org/10.1007/s10803-020-04662-6

Bury, S. M., Hayward, S. M., Dissanayake, C., & Hedley, D. (2020). *Supporting a neurodiverse workforce: A mental health and well-being resource and training package*. Bundoora, Australia: La Trobe University.

Bury, S. M., Hayward, S. M., Dissanayake, C., & Hedley, D. (2022). *Supporting a neurodiverse workforce: A mental health and well-being online training course*. Learn OTARC. https://learn.otarc.com.au/

Bury, S. M., Hedley, D., Uljarevic, M., Dissanayake, C., & Gal, E. (2019). If you've employed one person with autism. . .: An individual difference approach to the autism advantage at work. *Autism, 23*(6), 1607–1608. https://doi.org/10.1177/1362361318794937

Bury, S. M., Hedley, D., Uljarević, M., & Gal, E. (2020). The autism advantage at work: A critical and systematic review of current evidence. *Research in Developmental Disabilities, 105*, 103750. https://doi.org/10.1016/j.ridd.2020.103750

Bury, S. M., Jellett, R., Spoor, J. R., & Hedley, D. (2020). "It's something I have" or "it defines who I am": What language do (autistic) Australian adults (on the autism spectrum) prefer? *Journal of Autism and Developmental Disorders*, 1–11. https://doi.org/10.1007/s10803-020-04425-3

Cage, E., Di Monaco, J., & Newell, V. (2018). Experiences of autism acceptance and mental health in autistic adults. *Journal of Autism and Developmental Disorders, 48*(2), 473–484. https://doi.org/10.1007/s10803-017-3342-7

Camm-Crosbie, L., Bradley, L., Shaw, R., Baron-Cohen, S., & Cassidy, S. (2019). 'People like me don't get support': Autistic adults' experiences of support and treatment for mental health difficulties, self-injury and suicidality. *Autism, 23*(6), 1431–1441. https://doi.org/10.1177/1362361318816053

Carmassi, C., Palagini, L., Caruso, D., Masci, I., Nobili, L., Vita, A., & Dell'Osso, L. (2019). Systematic review of sleep disturbances and circadian sleep desynchronization in autism spectrum disorder: Toward an integrative model of a self-reinforcing loop. *Frontiers in Psychiatry, 10*, 366. https://doi.org/10.3389/fpsyt.2019.00366

Cimera, R. E., & Cowan, R. J. (2009). The costs of services and employment outcomes achieved by adults with autism in the US. *Autism, 13*(3), 285–302. https://doi.org/10.1177/1362361309103791

Claussen, B., Bjørndal, A., & Hjort, P. F. (1993). Health and re-employment in a two year follow up of long term unemployed. *Journal of Epidemiology & Community Health, 47*(1), 14–18. https://doi.org/10.1136/jech.47.1.14

Cooper, C. L., & Cartwright, S. (1994). Healthy mind; healthy organization – A proactive approach to occupational stress. *Human Relations, 47*(4), 455–471. https://doi.org/10.1177/001872679404700405

Cooper, K., Smith, L. G. E., & Russell, A. (2017). Social identity, self-esteem, and mental health in autism. *European Journal of Social Psychology, 47*(7), 844–854. https://doi.org/10.1002/ejsp.2297

Croen, L. A., Zerbo, O., Qian, Y., Massolo, M. L., Rich, S., Sidney, S., & Kripke, C. (2015). The health status of adults on the autism spectrum. *Autism, 19*(7), 814–823. https://doi.org/10.1177/1362361315577517

de Lange, A. H., Taris, T. W., Kompier, M. A., Houtman, I. L., & Bongers, P. M. (2005). Different mechanisms to explain the reversed effects of mental health on work characteristics. *Scandinavian Journal of Work, Environment & Health, 31*(1), 3–14. https://doi.org/10.5271/sjweh.843

DeFrank, R. S., & Cooper, C. L. (1987). Worksite stress management interventions: Their effectiveness and conceptualisation. *Journal of Managerial Psychology, 2*(1), 4–10. https://doi.org/10.1108/eb043385

Dell'Osso, L., Carpita, B., Muti, D., Morelli, V., Salarpi, G., Salerni, A., . . . Ballerio, M. (2019). Mood symptoms and suicidality across the autism spectrum. *Comprehensive Psychiatry, 91*, 34–38. https://doi.org/10.1016/j.comppsych.2019.03.004

Demerouti, E., Bakker, A. B., Nachreiner, F., & Schaufeli, W. B. (2001). The job demands-resources model of burnout. *Journal of Applied Psychology, 86*(3), 499–512. https://doi.org/10.1037/0021-9010.86.3.499

Ellemers, N., & Barreto, M. (2006). Social identity and self-presentation at work: How attempts to hide a stigmatised identity affect emotional well-being, social inclusion and performance. *Netherlands Journal of Psychology*, *62*(1), 51–57. https://doi.org/10.1007/BF03061051

Eller, N. H., Netterstrøm, B., Gyntelberg, F., Kristensen, T. S., Nielsen, F., Steptoe, A., & Theorell, T. (2009). Work-related psychosocial factors and the development of ischemic heart disease: A systematic review. *Cardiology in Review*, *17*(2), 83–97. https://doi.org/10.1097/CRD.0b013e318198c8e9

Fieldhouse, M. (2017). *Implementing a neurodiversity program*. Retrieved from https://digitalcommons.ilr.cornell.edu/cgi/viewcontent.cgi?article=1025&context=dandelionprogram

Flower, R. L., Hedley, D., Spoor, J. R., & Dissanayake, C. (2019). An alternative pathway to employment for autistic job-seekers: A case study of a training and assessment program targeted to autistic job candidates. *Journal of Vocational Education & Training*, *71*(3), 407–428. https://doi.org/10.1080/13636820.2019.1636846

Ford, M. T., Cerasoli, C. P., Higgins, J. A., & Decesare, A. L. (2011). Relationships between psychological, physical, and behavioural health and work performance: A review and meta-analysis. *Work & Stress*, *25*(3), 185–204. https://doi.org/10.1080/02678373.2011.609035

Gayed, A., Milligan-Saville, J. S., Nicholas, J., Bryan, B. T., LaMontagne, A. D., Milner, A., . . . Mykletun, A. (2018). Effectiveness of training workplace managers to understand and support the mental health needs of employees: A systematic review and meta-analysis. *Occupational and Environmental Medicine*, *75*(6), 462–470. https://doi.org/10.1136/oemed-2017-104789

Greenlee, J. L., Mosley, A. S., Shui, A. M., Veenstra-VanderWeele, J., & Gotham, K. O. (2016). Medical and behavioral correlates of depression history in children and adolescents with autism spectrum disorder. *Pediatrics*, *137*(Suppl. 2), S105–S114. https://doi.org/10.1542/peds.2015-2851I

Hadlaczky, G., Hökby, S., Mkrtchian, A., Carli, V., & Wasserman, D. (2014). Mental Health First Aid is an effective public health intervention for improving knowledge, attitudes, and behaviour: A meta-analysis. *International Review of Psychiatry*, *26*(4), 467–475. https://doi.org/10.3109/09540261.2014.924910

Hagner, D., & Cooney, B. F. (2005). "I do that for everybody": Supervising employees with autism. *Focus on Autism and Other Developmental Disabilities*, *20*(2), 91–97. https://doi.org/10.1177/10883576050200020501

Halim, A. T., Richdale, A. L., & Uljarević, M. (2018). Exploring the nature of anxiety in young adults on the autism spectrum: A qualitative study. *Research in Autism Spectrum Disorders*, *55*, 25–37. https://doi.org/10.1016/j.rasd.2018.07.006

Hanisch, S. E., Twomey, C. D., Szeto, A. C., Birner, U. W., Nowak, D., & Sabariego, C. (2016). The effectiveness of interventions targeting the stigma of mental illness at the workplace: A systematic review. *BMC Psychiatry*, *16*(1), 1–11. https://doi.org/10.1186/s12888-015-0706-4

Harvey, S. B., Modini, M., Joyce, S., Milligan-Saville, J. S., Tan, L., Mykletun, A., . . . Mitchell, P. B. (2017). Can work make you mentally ill? A systematic meta-review of work-related risk factors for common mental health problems. *Occupational and Environmental Medicine*, *74*(4), 301–310. https://doi.org/10.1136/oemed-2016-104015

Hayward, S. M., McVilly, K. R., & Stokes, M. A. (2018). Challenges for females with high functioning autism in the workplace: A systematic review. *Disability and Rehabilitation*, *40*(3), 249–258. https://doi.org/10.1080/09638288.2016.1254284

Hayward, S. M., McVilly, K. R., & Stokes, M. A. (2020). Sources and impact of occupational demands for autistic employees. *Research in Autism Spectrum Disorders*, *76*, 101571. https://doi.org/10.1016/j.rasd.2020.101571

Hedley, D., Cai, R., Uljarevic, M., Wilmot, M., Spoor, J. R., Richdale, A., & Dissanayake, C. (2018). Transition to work: Perspectives from the autism spectrum. *Autism*, *22*(5), 528–541. https://doi.org/10.1177/1362361316687697

Hedley, D., Spoor, J., Bury, S., & Dissanayake, C. (2018). *The dandelion employment program: Longitudinal findings*. Retrieved from https://digitalcommons.ilr.cornell.edu/dandelionprogram/37/

Hedley, D., & Uljarević, M. (2018). Systematic review of suicide in autism spectrum disorder: Current trends and implications. *Current Developmental Disorders Reports*, *5*(1), 65–76. https://doi.org/10.1007/s40474-018-0133-6

Hedley, D., Uljarevic, M., Bury, S. M., & Dissanayake, C. (2019). Predictors of mental health and well-being in employed adults with autism spectrum disorder at 12-month follow-up. *Autism Research*, *12*(3), 482–494. https://doi.org/10.1002/aur.2064

Hedley, D., Uljarević, M., Cameron, L., Halder, S., Richdale, A., & Dissanayake, C. (2017). Employment programmes and interventions targeting adults with autism spectrum disorder: A systematic review of the literature. *Autism*, *21*(8), 929–941. https://doi.org/10.1177/1362361316661855

Hedley, D., Uljarević, M., Foley, K. R., Richdale, A., & Trollor, J. (2018). Risk and protective factors underlying depression and suicidal ideation in autism spectrum disorder. *Depression and Anxiety*, *35*(7), 648–657. https://doi.org/10.1002/da.22759

Hedley, D., Uljarević, M., & Hedley, D. F. (2017). Employment and living with Autism: Personal, social and economic impact. In S. Halder & L Assaf (Eds.), *Inclusion, disability and culture* (pp. 295–311). Springer. https://doi.org/10.1016/B978-0-12-814715-3.00008-4

Hillier, A., Campbell, H., Mastriani, K., Izzo, M.V., Kool-Tucker, A. K., Cherry, L., & Beversdorf, D. Q. (2007). Two-year evaluation of a vocational support program for adults on the autism spectrum. *Career Development for Exceptional Individuals*, *30*(1), 35–47. https://doi.org/10.1177/08857288070300010501

Hollocks, M. J., Lerh, J. W., Magiati, I., Meiser-Stedman, R., & Brugha, T. S. (2019). Anxiety and depression in adults with autism spectrum disorder: A systematic review and meta-analysis. *Psychological Medicine*, *49*(4), 559–572. https://doi.org/10.1017/S0033291718002283

Holwerda, A., van der Klink, J. J., Groothoff, J. W., & Brouwer, S. (2012). Predictors for work participation in individuals with an autism spectrum disorder: A systematic review. *Journal of Occupational Rehabilitation*, *22*(3), 333–352. https://doi.org/10.1007/s10926-011-9347-8

Hudson, C. C., Hall, L., & Harkness, K. L. (2018). Prevalence of depressive disorders in individuals with Autism Spectrum Disorder: A meta-analysis. *Journal of Abnormal Child Psychology*, *47*, 165–175. https://doi.org/10.1007/s10802-018-0402-1

Hui, S.-K. A., & Grandner, M. A. (2015). Trouble sleeping associated with lower work performance and greater healthcare costs: Longitudinal data from Kansas state employee wellness program. *Journal of Occupational and Environmental Medicine*, *57*(10), 1031–1038. https://doi.org/10.1097/JOM.0000000000000534

ILO. (2017). *Mental health in the workplace: Key issues and good company practices*. Retrieved from www.businessanddisability.org/wp-content/uploads/2018/07/ILO-mental-health-background-report_2017.pdf

Johnson, T. D., & Joshi, A. (2016). Dark clouds or silver linings? A stigma threat perspective on the implications of an autism diagnosis for workplace well-being. *Journal of Applied Psychology, 101*(3), 430–449. https://doi.org/10.1037/apl0000058

Joseph, B., & Walker, A. (2017). Employee assistance programs in Australia: The perspectives of organisational leaders across sectors. *Asia Pacific Journal of Human Resources, 55*(2), 177–191. https://doi.org/10.1111/1744-7941.12124

Joseph, B., Walker, A., & Fuller-Tyszkiewicz, M. (2018). Evaluating the effectiveness of employee assistance programmes: A systematic review. *European Journal of Work and Organizational Psychology, 27*(1), 1–15. https://doi.org/10.1080/1359432x.2017.1374245

Kerns, C. M., Kendall, P. C., Berry, L., Souders, M. C., Franklin, M. E., Schultz, R. T., . . . Herrington, J. (2014). Traditional and atypical presentations of anxiety in youth with autism spectrum disorder. *Journal of Autism Developmental Disorders, 44*(11), 2851–2861. https://doi.org/10.1007/s10803-014-2141-7

Keyes, C. L., Shmotkin, D., & Ryff, C. D. (2002). Optimizing well-being: The empirical encounter of two traditions. *Journal of Personality and Social Psychology, 82*, 1007–1022. https://doi.org/10.1037/0022-3514.82.6.1007

Kirchner, J. C., & Dziobek, I. (2014). Towards successful employment of adults with autism: A first analysis of special interests and factors deemed important for vocational performance. *Scandinavian Journal of Child and Adolescent Psychiatry and Psychology, 2*(2), 77–85. https://doi.org/10.21307/sjcapp-2014-011

Kirk, A. K., & Brown, D. F. (2003). Employee assistance programs: A review of the management of stress and wellbeing through workplace counselling and consulting. *Australian Psychologist, 38*(2), 138–143. https://doi.org/10.1080/00050060310001707137

Kitchener, B. A., & Jorm, A. F. (2002). Mental health first aid training for the public: Evaluation of effects on knowledge, attitudes and helping behavior. *BMC Psychiatry, 2*(1), 1–6. https://doi.org/10.1186/1471-244x-2-10

Kitchener, B. A., & Jorm, A. F. (2008). Mental health first aid: An international programme for early intervention. *Early Intervention in Psychiatry, 2*, 55–61. https://doi.org/10.1111/j.1751-7893.2007.00056.x

Kivimäki, M., Leino-Arjas, P., Luukkonen, R., Riihimäi, H., Vahtera, J., & Kirjonen, J. (2002). Work stress and risk of cardiovascular mortality: Prospective cohort study of industrial employees. *BMJ, 325*(7369), Article 857. https://doi.org/10.1136/bmj.325.7369.857

Kouvonen, A., Kivimäki, M., Elovainio, M., Väänänen, A., De Vogli, R., Heponiemi, T., . . . Vahtera, J. (2008). Low organisational justice and heavy drinking: A prospective cohort study. *Occupational and Environmental Medicine, 65*(1), 44–50. https://doi.org/10.1136/oem.2007.032755

Kouvonen, A., Kivimäki, M., Virtanen, M., Pentti, J., & Vahtera, J. (2005). Work stress, smoking status, and smoking intensity: An observational study of 46 190 employees. *Journal of Epidemiology & Community Health, 59*(1), 63–69. https://doi.org/10.1136/jech.2004.019752

Lai, M.-C., Kassee, C., Besney, R., Bonato, S., Hull, L., Mandy, W., . . . Ameis, S. H. (2019). Prevalence of co-occurring mental health diagnoses in the autism population: A systematic review and meta-analysis. *The Lancet Psychiatry, 6*(10), 819–829. https://doi.org/10.1016/S2215-0366(19)30289-5

LaMontagne, A. D., Keegel, T., Louie, A. M., & Ostry, A. (2010). Job stress as a preventable upstream determinant of common mental disorders: A review for practitioners and policy-makers. *Advances in Mental Health, 9*(1), 17–35. https://doi.org/10.5172/jamh.9.1.17

Lerner, D., Adler, D. A., Rogers, W. H., Lapitsky, L., McLaughlin, T., & Reed, J. (2010). Work performance of employees with depression: The impact of work stressors. *American Journal of Health Promotion, 24*(3), 205–213. https://doi.org/10.4278/ajhp.090313-QUAN-103

Lever, A. G., & Geurts, H. M. (2016). Psychiatric co-occurring symptoms and disorders in young, middle-aged, and older adults with autism spectrum disorder. *Journal of Autism and Developmental Disorders, 46*(6), 1916–1930. https://doi.org/10.1007/s10803-016-2722-8

Limoges, E., Mottron, L., Bolduc, C., Berthiaume, C., & Godbout, R. (2005). Atypical sleep architecture and the autism phenotype. *Brain, 128*(5), 1049–1061. https://doi.org/10.1093/brain/awh425

Linton, S. J., Kecklund, G., Franklin, K. A., Leissner, L. C., Sivertsen, B., Lindberg, E., . . . Hetta, J. (2015). The effect of the work environment on future sleep disturbances: A systematic review. *Sleep Medicine Reviews, 23*, 10–19. https://doi.org/10.1016/j.smrv.2014.10.010

Martins, E.-C., & Terblanche, F. (2003). Building organisational culture that stimulates creativity and innovation. *European Journal of Innovation Management, 6*, 64–74. https://doi.org/10.1108/14601060310456337

Mayes, S. D., Calhoun, S. L., Aggarwal, R., Baker, C., Mathapati, S., Molitoris, S., & Mayes, R. D. (2013). Unusual fears in children with autism. *Research in Autism Spectrum Disorders*, 7(1), 151–158. https://doi.org/10.1016/j.rasd.2012.08.002

Mazurek, M. O. (2014). Loneliness, friendship, and well-being in adults with autism spectrum disorders. *Autism, 18*(3), 223–232. https://doi.org/10.1177/1362361312474121

McKee-Ryan, F., Song, Z., Wanberg, C. R., & Kinicki, A. J. (2005). Psychological and physical well-being during unemployment: A meta-analytic study. *Journal of Applied Psychology, 90*(1), 53. https://doi.org/10.1037/0021-9010.90.1.53

Merikangas, K. R., He, J.-P., Burstein, M., Swanson, S. A., Avenevoli, S., Cui, L., . . . Swendsen, J. (2010). Lifetime prevalence of mental disorders in US adolescents: Results from the National Comorbidity Survey Replication – Adolescent Supplement (NCS-A). *Journal of the American Academy of Child & Adolescent Psychiatry, 49*(10), 980–989. https://doi.org/10.1016/j.jaac.2010.05.017

Milligan-Saville, J. S., Tan, L., Gayed, A., Barnes, C., Madan, I., Dobson, M., . . . Harvey, S. B. (2017). Workplace mental health training for managers and its effect on sick leave in employees: A cluster randomised controlled trial. *The Lancet Psychiatry, 4*(11), 850–858. https://doi.org/10.1016/S2215-0366(17)30372-3

Milner, A., Witt, K., LaMontagne, A. D., & Niedhammer, I. (2018). Psychosocial job stressors and suicidality: A meta-analysis and systematic review. *Occupational and Environmental Medicine, 75*(4), 245–253. https://doi.org/10.1136/oemed-2017-104531

Modini, M., Joyce, S., Mykletun, A., Christensen, H., Bryant, R. A., Mitchell, P. B., & Harvey, S. B. (2016). The mental health benefits of employment: Results of a systematic meta-review. *Australasian Psychiatry, 24*(4), 331–336. https://doi.org/10.1177/1039856215618523

Morgan, A. J., Ross, A., & Reavley, N. J. (2018). Systematic review and meta-analysis of Mental Health First Aid training: Effects on knowledge, stigma, and helping behaviour. *PLoS One, 13*(5), e0197102. https://doi.org/10.1371/journal.pone.0197102

Müller, E., Schuler, A., Burton, B. A., & Yates, G. B. (2003). Meeting the vocational support needs of individuals with Asperger syndrome and other autism spectrum disabilities. *Journal of Vocational Rehabilitation, 18*(3), 163–175.

Nakata, A. (2012). Psychosocial job stress and immunity: A systematic review. In Q. Yan (Ed.) *Psychoneuroimmunology* (pp. 39–75). Totowa, NJ: Humana Press. https://doi.org/10.1007/978-1-62703-071-7

Nicholas, D. B., & Klag, M. (2020). Critical reflections on employment among autistic adults. *Autism in Adulthood, 2*, 289–295. https://doi.org/10.1089/aut.2020.0006

Nicholas, D. B., Mitchell, W., Dudley, C., Clarke, M., & Zulla, R. (2018). An ecosystem approach to employment and autism spectrum disorder. *Journal of Autism and Developmental Disorders, 48*(1), 264–275. https://doi.org/10.1007/s10803-017-3351-6

Ohl, A., Grice Sheff, M., Small, S., Nguyen, J., Paskor, K., & Zanjirian, A. (2017). Predictors of employment status among adults with Autism Spectrum Disorder. *Work, 56*(2), 345–355. https://doi.org/10.3233/Wor-172492

Paul, K. I., & Moser, K. (2009). Unemployment impairs mental health: Meta-analyses. *Journal of Vocational Behavior, 74*(3), 264–282. https://doi.org/10.1016/j.jvb.2009.01.001

Pfeiffer, B., Braun, K., Kinnealey, M., Derstine Matczak, M., & Polatajko, H. (2017). Environmental factors impacting work satisfaction and performance for adults with autism spectrum disorders. *Journal of Vocational Rehabilitation, 47*(1), 1–12. https://doi.org/10.3233/Jvr-170878

Plaisier, I., Beekman, A., De Graaf, R., Smit, J., Van Dyck, R., & Penninx, B. (2010). Work functioning in persons with depressive and anxiety disorders: The role of specific psychopathological characteristics. *Journal of Affective Disorders, 125*(1–3), 198–206. https://doi.org/10.1016/j.jad.2010.01.072

Poquérusse, J., Pastore, L., Dellantonio, S., & Esposito, G. (2018). Alexithymia and autism spectrum disorder: A complex relationship. *Frontiers in Psychology, 9*, Article 1196. https://doi.org/10.3389/fpsyg.2018.01196

Rai, D., Culpin, I., Heuvelman, H., Magnusson, C. M., Carpenter, P., Jones, H. J., . . . Pearson, R. M. (2018). Association of autistic traits with depression from childhood to age 18 years. *JAMA Psychiatry, 75*(8), 835–843. https://doi.org/10.1001/jamapsychiatry.2018.1323

Rai, D., Heuvelman, H., Dalman, C., Culpin, I., Lundberg, M., Carpenter, P., & Magnusson, C. (2018). Association between autism spectrum disorders with or without intellectual disability and depression in young adulthood. *JAMA Network Open, 1*(4), e181465–e181465. https://doi.org/10.1001/jamanetworkopen.2018.1465

Rashid, M., Hodgetts, S., & Nicholas, D. (2017). Building employers' capacity to support vocational opportunities for adults with developmental disabilities. *Review Journal of Autism and Developmental Disorders, 4*(2), 165–173. https://doi.org/10.1007/s40489-017-0105-5

Roche, A., Kostadinov, V., Cameron, J., Pidd, K., McEntee, A., & Duraisingam, V. (2018). The development and characteristics of Employee Assistance Programs around the globe. *Journal of Workplace Behavioral Health, 33*(3–4), 168–186. https://doi.org/10.1080/15555240.2018.1539642

Roux, A. M., Rast, J. E., Anderson, K. A., & Shattuck, P. T. (2017). *National autism indicators report: Developmental disability services and outcomes in adulthood*. Retrieved from https://drexel.edu/autismoutcomes/publications-and-reports/publications/National-Autism-Indicators-Report-Developmental-Disability-Services-and-Outcomes-in-Adulthood/

Rugulies, R., Framke, E., Sørensen, J. K., Svane-Petersen, A. C., Alexanderson, K., Bonde, J. P., . . . Nyberg, S. T. (2020). Persistent and changing job strain and risk of coronary heart disease. A population-based cohort study of 1.6 million employees in

Denmark. *Scandinavian Journal of Work, Environment & Health, 46*, 498–507. https://doi.org/10.5271/sjweh.3891

Schaufeli, W. B., & Taris, T. W. (2014). A critical review of the job demands-resources model: Implications for improving work and health. In G. F. Bauer & O. Hämmig (Eds.), *Bridging occupational, organizational and public health: A transdisciplinary approach* (pp. 43–68). Dordrecht, The Netherlands: Springer.

Seaman, R. L., & Cannella-Malone, H. I. (2016). Vocational skills interventions for adults with autism spectrum disorder: A review of the literature. *Journal of Developmental and Physical Disabilities, 28*(3), 479–494. https://doi.org/10.1007/s10882-016-9479-z

Seidler, A., Thinschmidt, M., Deckert, S., Then, F., Hegewald, J., Nieuwenhuijsen, K., & Riedel-Heller, S. G. (2014). The role of psychosocial working conditions on burnout and its core component emotional exhaustion – A systematic review. *Journal of Occupational Medicine and Toxicology, 9*(1), 1–10. https://doi.org/10.1186/1745-6673-9-10

Shattuck, P. T., Narendorf, S. C., Cooper, B., Sterzing, P. R., Wagner, M., & Taylor, J. L. (2012). Postsecondary education and employment among youth with an autism spectrum disorder. *Pediatrics, 129*(6), 1042–1049. https://doi.org/10.1542/peds.2011-2864

Shaw, W. S., Main, C. J., Findley, P. A., Collie, A., Kristman, V. L., & Gross, D. P. (2020). Opening the workplace after covid-19: What lessons can be learned from return-to-work research? *Journal of Occupational Rehabilitation, 30*, 299–302. https://doi.org/10.1007/s10926-020-09908-9

Smith, M. J., Ginger, E. J., Wright, K., Wright, M. A., Taylor, J. L., Humm, L. B., . . . Fleming, M. F. (2014). Virtual reality job interview training in adults with autism spectrum disorder. *Journal of Autism and Developmental Disorders, 44*(10), 2450–2463. https://doi.org/10.1007/s10803-014-2113-y

South, M., Ozonoff, S., & Mcmahon, W. M. (2007). The relationship between executive functioning, central coherence, and repetitive behaviors in the high-functioning autism spectrum. *Autism, 11*(5), 437–451. https://doi.org/10.1177/1362361307079606

Ståhl, A.-C. F., Ståhl, C., & Smith, P. (2018). Longitudinal association between psychological demands and burnout for employees experiencing a high versus a low degree of job resources. *BMC Public Health, 18*(1), Article 915. https://doi.org/10.1186/s12889-018-5778-x

Szeto, A. C., & Dobson, K. S. (2010). Reducing the stigma of mental disorders at work: A review of current workplace anti-stigma intervention programs. *Applied and Preventive Psychology, 14*(1–4), 41–56. https://doi.org/10.1016/j.appsy.2011.11.002

Tani, P., Lindberg, N., Nieminen-von Wendt, T., Von Wendt, L., Alanko, L., Appelberg, B., & Porkka-Heiskanen, T. (2003). Insomnia is a frequent finding in adults with Asperger syndrome. *BMC Psychiatry, 3*(1), Article 12. https://doi.org/10.1186/1471-244X-3-12

The National Autistic Society. (2016). *The autism employment gap: Too much information in the workplace*. Retrieved from www.autism.org.uk/~/media/nas/get-involved/tmi/tmi%20employment%20report%2024pp%20web.ashx?la=en-gb

Theorell, T., Hammarström, A., Aronsson, G., Bendz, L. T., Grape, T., Hogstedt, C., . . . Hall, C. (2015). A systematic review including meta-analysis of work environment and depressive symptoms. *BMC Public Health, 15*(1), Article 738. https://doi.org/10.1186/s12889-015-1954-4

Törnroos, M., Hakulinen, C., Hintsanen, M., Puttonen, S., Hintsa, T., Pulkki-Råback, L., . . . Keltikangas-Järvinen, L. (2017). Reciprocal relationships between psychosocial work characteristics and sleep problems: A two-wave study. *Work & Stress, 31*(1), 63–81. https://doi.org/10.1080/02678373.2017.1297968

Uljarević, M., Hedley, D., & Cai, R.-Y. (2020). Anxiety and depression in Autism Spectrum Disorder. In F. R. Volkmar (Ed.), *Encyclopedia of Autism*. New York: Springer.

Uljarević, M., Hedley, D., Rose-Foley, K., Magiati, I., Cai, R. Y., Dissanayake, C., . . . Trollor, J. (2019). Anxiety and depression from adolescence to old age in autism spectrum disorder. *Journal of Autism and Developmental Disorders, 50*, 3155–3165. https://doi.org/10.1007/s10803-019-04084-z

World Health Organization. (2020). *WHO urges more investments, services for mental health*. Retrieved from www.who.int/mental_health/who_urges_investment/en/

Wieclaw, J., Agerbo, E., Mortensen, P. B., Burr, H., Tuchsen, F., & Bonde, J. P. (2008). Psychosocial working conditions and the risk of depression and anxiety disorders in the Danish workforce. *BMC Public Health, 8*(1), Article 280. https://doi.org/10.1186/1471-2458-8-280

Wilczynski, S. M., Trammell, B., & Clarke, L. S. (2013). Improving employment outcomes among adolescents and adults on the autism spectrum. *Psychology in the Schools, 50*(9), 876–887. https://doi.org/10.1002/pits.21718

11

ADAPTING OTHER INTERNAL ORGANIZATIONAL RESOURCES TO A NEURODIVERSE WORKFORCE

Nancy Doyle

Introduction

Neurodiversity has traditionally been thought of through the lens of disability, but the precise meaning and implication of the term can be elusive, and many within the self-advocacy movement would not associate with being disabled, whilst others report significant disablement (Baron-Cohen, 2019). In order to contextualize the advice and recommendations in this chapter, I will first briefly define the disability models and the increasingly popular neurodiversity talent narrative. The medical model of disability refers to physical impairment at the individual level, citing atypical deficits which prevent access to normal life; this might include limited literacy, concentration or fine motor control. The social model of disability proposes that disablement is an act of society, for example educational opportunities that are only accessible through literacy rather than video or spoken word or require seated concentration for hours at a time. These actions unfairly penalize a minority who are physically different from the majority (Charlton, 1998; Riddick, 2001).

Neurodiversity researchers and practitioners have increasingly advocated a paradigm that treats neurodiversity as a difference, not a deficit; a natural variation in strengths and weaknesses that confers talents as well as struggle (Armstrong, 2015; Grant, 2009; Mellifont, 2019). This framing of neurodiversity has clear implications for individuals and organizations, when we consider person–environment fit theories (PE fit; Lewin, 1936), which assert that we can achieve optimum levels of commitment, productivity and performance by matching the appropriate person to the appropriate role. For example, PE fit suggests that we might focus on identifying opportunities for organizations to find ways to match the neurodiverse employee, or "specialist thinker" to the best suited role, as per

DOI: 10.4324/9781003023616-11

positive action programs such as Autism at Work. PE fit can be applied to the individual level of analysis, as per the previous chapter on deploying reasonable accommodations to buffer the difference between an employee's natural ability and the demands of the role. This chapter considers what can be activated at the environment or company level to create the conditions for success within a neurologically diverse-workforce. Neurodiversity is increasingly situated as an element within the broader equality, diversity and inclusion (EDI) framework, wherein we acknowledge that conscious and unconscious biases often result in exclusion, typically the result of the normative manner in which organizational systems are constructed and delivered. Traditionally, I/O psychology interventions such as personnel selection and training have treated the environment as fixed, yet in order to undo implicit bias we must question our traditional institutionalized processes and seek ways to improve access and representation. Therefore, as a supplement to the individual-level accommodation and the positive action programs in operation, this chapter provides review of organizational-level resources that can be optimized to influence work participation and success. The chapter explores physical, social, and attitudinal factors which can contribute to an individual's success in the work environment (de Beer et al., 2014; Schulze et al., 2018; WHO, 2001) and is presented in four sections: (1) the principle and practice of universal design, (2) employee welfare, (3) employee resource and business groups, and finally (4) assessing the effectiveness of such endeavours. I will first provide two brief contextual notes on terminology and legislative frameworks.

Terminology

The neurodiversity movement itself is situated in the social model and asserts that individuals diagnosed with ADHD, autism, dyslexia, etc., are natural variations within the human species who do not expect to be "cured", and thus focusing on the individual level alone offers limited leverage for long-term inclusion (Singer, 1998, 1999). The neurodiversity movement also uses the term "neurodiverse" to refer to the human species rather than individuals, and therefore in this chapter I use the term "neurominorities" (Singer, 1998; Chapman, 2020; Doyle, 2020) to denote those with included conditions, who form a significant minority outside the "neurotypical" normal distribution of ability. "Neurodivergent" is also becoming a more prevalent term for individuals in common parlance and stakeholder-led research (Bottema-Beutel et al., 2020). The full range of included conditions under the neurominority/neurodivergent umbrella is inconsistent but usually includes neurodevelopmental conditions such as ADHD, autism, dyscalculia, dyslexia, dyspraxia and tic disorders; also included might be acquired brain injury and chronic neurological conditions such as multiple sclerosis on the basis that they too create a "spiky profile" of clinically significant disparity between strengths and weaknesses (Doyle, 2017). Mild to moderate mental health needs including anxiety and depression also confer a transient spiky profile; they are sometimes included on the basis that they are so common within our population that we cannot dismiss them as abnormal (Armstrong, 2010).

I/O practitioners should be aware of such language evolution when working with employers initiating neurodiversity-inclusive hiring programs and working with neurominority employees themselves. Failure to acknowledge these subtle distinctions and the preferences of people with lived experience for nomenclature that recognizes their status as part of a diverse range of neurological orientations is a feature of ableism. Ableism refers in this case to the tendency towards assuming a neuronormative position on performance, ability, job design, and resources required (Bottema-Beutel et al., 2020; Hujig, 2020).

Legislation

Disability legislation worldwide is increasingly aligned with the social model (which recognizes that disability is sometimes the result of the design of buildings, workplaces, etc., that restrict the opportunities for neurominorities to enter or participate). This legislation is consistent with the United Nations Convention on the Rights of People with Disabilities of 2006 (United Nations, 2006), in which an organization is required to make reasonable accommodations for 'persons with disabilities'.[1] Author's note on language and terminology. While many disabled people prefer to use 'people first' language (I am a person with a disability), this is interpreted by some as separating the person from their disabling conditions. In some communities, including many autistic communities, 'identity first' language (I am a disabled person, or I am an Autist) is prefers. This is seen to center the neurodifferences at the identity level and also to indicate that disablement happens to someone, rather than being something someone has. The latter point makes identity first language congruent with the social model of disability. There are also many people who prefer to capitalize Autism and Dyslexia, as an acknowledgment of their neurodifference as a culture rather than a medical condition. This also occurs in the Deaf community. This chapter has deferred to publisher guidance, but the authors wishes to acknowledge both that current narratives may be at odds with the current grammar and nomenclature, but also that these change swiftly as part of evolving, self-organizing rights and advocacy. Practitioners should place care upon listening to language changes, educating themselves and adopting terms preferred by their clients without hesitation. The need for accommodations places an onus on an employer to make adjustments to the environment and tools available in a workplace and to be responsively flexible in job design; note there is no legal obligation for the employee to change to fit the role, assuming that the basic qualifications for the position are met (training, prior experience expectations, etc.) (Doyle, 2020). Many disability support programs thus solely address workplace adjustments per person in response to difficulty at the individual level, especially if they are actively pursuing affirmative hiring programs for neurominorities. This can be stigmatizing and relies on disclosure of disability from the employee. Since lack of disclosure may not absolve organizational responsibility for broader affirmative action and a need to demonstrate inclusivity of many protected characteristics (von Schrader et al., 2014), a focus on the general inclusivity of workplace environments is advisable for both risk and performance management. The U.N. Statute also introduces the principle of universal design, which requires that disabilities are considered at the structural design stage rather than an accommodation after the fact.

The practical guidance provided in this chapter is aimed at I/O psychologists so that we may gain an understanding of how to assist employers in becoming more inclusive throughout an organization through effective management practices and human resources infrastructure. Armed with this knowledge, I/O psychologists can support progressive employers seeking to retrofit existing job design and organizational norms, as well as factor in neuroinclusive features when developing new human resources processes aimed at improving performance more generally. In the last 30 years, many organizations have made structural changes to improve physical accessibility (e.g., replacing stairs with ramps or elevators); yet the process of changing jobs, roles and organizations to fit the needs and capabilities of a neurodiverse workforce is likely to be more complex, and it may engender unexpected backlash if some employees are given the opportunity to adjust their jobs to fit their needs and strengths (e.g., giving an autistic employee a quieter place to work while refusing similar options for neurotypical employees). These backlashes are common when adjustments are made at the individual level only and demonstrate the lack of understanding as to the difference between equality (everyone gets the same) and equity (everyone gets what they need to start their job tasks from the same baseline). Just as we wouldn't question prioritizing ramps and elevators for wheelchair users, we shouldn't perceive quiet spaces for autistic people as favors. However, such an approach presupposes a fixed environment of scarcity, in which we have accepted as standard noisy, unproductive workspaces. Applying the principles of universal design, we can improve the accessibility of environments and processes for all employees equally.

Universal Design

In its most straightforward definition, universal design (UD) refers to the notion that by creating infrastructure with all abilities and diversity in mind, we can reduce the need for adaptation or accommodation at the individual level. Often referred to in terms of architectural environments for those with physical disabilities (for example ensuring all buildings have wheelchair access), UD for neurominorities has heretofore focused on assistive technology (AT) (García-Betances et al., 2016; Van Laarhoven et al., 2018). However, infrastructure is more than building accessibility and technology. Everyday interactions among coworkers and with supervisors are influenced by the overarching HR policies and practices, which contain our beliefs and attitudes, create a social infrastructure that may help or hinder employees (de Beer et al., 2014; Schulze et al., 2018), and we can apply UD to these features for neurominority inclusion. I will define each of the seven UD principles in turn, interpreting the descriptions provided by the Center for Universal Design (Rickerson, 2009; The Center for Universal Design, 1997) and applying each to the notion of social infrastructure. I will then present, in Table 11.1, how these can be practically applied across six key elements of I/O psychology consulting: job design, hiring, contracting, training, performance and well-being.

Principle One: "Equitable Use"

The aim of equitable use is to avoid segregation and the need for disabled people to have a "different" service/experience to nondisabled people. The question to ask is whether the adjustments you might be providing at the individual level in job design, hiring, training, etc., could simply be interpreted as best practice and therefore should just be the standard rather than the adjustment. The failure to implement the practice of equitable use can create problems for neurodivergent individuals, even if they manage to find employment in an organization. For example, some organizations have targeted hiring for autistic applicants to serve as technologists, a practice viewed by some as exploitative and segregating, despite initial honorable intentions (Bernick, 2019). Autistic applicants hired under such a program may find that if they attempt a sideways move from technology, they may not be welcomed in sales, finance or HR once their confidential medical status has been made public by virtue of their designation in the program. There is also the problem of access to the programs themselves, which depend on autism diagnosis, but tend to exclude ADHD, dyslexia or other disabilities. Label-based inclusion is further vulnerable to discrimination given that having an autism diagnosis itself tends towards being a white, male, socio-economically determined privilege. Females and individuals from communities marginalized by poverty or race are less likely to receive this diagnosis and have to date been participants in far fewer numbers in existing Autism at Work programs. As a result of disparities in autism diagnoses, they are less likely to have the "magic ticket" in the selection process for program participation (Mandell et al., 2009; Young et al., 2020), and therefore, the programs may exacerbate intersectional inequities. In summary, autism-at-work programs are on the very edge of affirmative action/positive discrimination, and it is recommended that they are used as pilots which go on to inform businesses how to change recruitment and onboarding for *all* applicants rather than remaining a special entry vehicle beyond their first few cohorts. I/O psychologists can be of assistance in raising awareness about how to further expand the inclusiveness of these initial neurodiversity inclusion program efforts. Further discussion about some of these issues is provided in the chapter by Saleh and Bernick in this volume.

Principle Two: "Flexibility in Use"

Flexibility in Use refers to the need to build in accommodation for preferences outside the norm, for example being able to adjust the pace of information or response or approaching a task in an unusual manner, without being penalized. The intent is that not everyone will approach a situation equally and that infrastructure needs to accommodate difference. Neurominorities (NMs) may experience particular barriers in formal situations such as timed tests or timed interviews in which performance may not be a reliable measure of knowledge or performance in role. For example, you could send the following text out with the invitation to participate in selection assessment:

We look forward to welcoming you on XXX date. We are aware that some applicants require reasonable accommodations for disability. Here is a list of the accommodations we have provided previously. If you would like to take any of these adjustments, please let us know:

- Assistive technology (speech to text enabled laptop on which to take the test)
- Group discussion questions submitted in advance (we will submit to your whole group if one person takes this up)
- Opportunity to talk through the layout, noise levels, light levels and general environment with one of our team to allay concerns regarding sensory overwhelm
- Additional time may be permitted on texts X,Y and Z if you have a diagnostic report with which we can cross reference recommended timings
- If you have previously relied upon other accommodations, we would be happy to discuss these further in advance of the day. Please contact us on XXX

Advance offers of procedural flexibility provide an acknowledgement that difference is expected and planned for and therefore potentially welcome; choice on take-up ensures that flexibility does not lead to segregation based on stereotype. It must be noted here that we are sorely lacking in knowledge about how various accommodations in selection procedures can effect validity, and this is one area that I/O psychologists can contribute through their research. For example, we may be erroneously assuming that a timed test is the best way to assess a desired applicant quality when, indeed, other measures less prone to adverse impact are just as suitable. Research to date has paid attention to this in terms of race and intelligence testing but not for other measures and neurodiversity.

Principle Three: "Simple and Intuitive Use"

In the principle of simple and intuitive use, care is taken to avoid unnecessary complexity and repetition, ensuring that information is laid out clearly and intuitively. With the design of many processes and tools, the designers become the experts and many easily forget how someone might misinterpret intention or be confused by the details without an overview, headings, visual signposting and more. Language accessibility can be improved by use of the Flesch-Kincaid scale, a grading system which uses the average word length, sentence length and paragraph length to estimate the reading level required to understand text (Flesch, 1948; Kincaid et al., 1981). The Flesch-Kincaid scale is built into the advanced grammar checks of widely available programs such as Microsoft Word, and therefore, most I/O and HR teams would be able to use it as a readability check before releasing company documents. The Federal Plain Language guide advises ensuring recruitment and HR materials be pitched at a level matching the job role, for example (PLAIN, 2011).

Principle Four: "Perceptible Information"

Perceptual information guides us to consider the sensory modality of communication, for example ensuring that it is compatible with accessibility software such as speech-to-text, text-to-speech and alt-text (alternative text) descriptions of embedded visual images. It also encourages the use of visual diagrams and overviews, tactile presentation and more. Though these considerations may seem to focus on people with hearing or sight loss, they are also useful for neurominorities who may find blocks of written word inaccessible or have a cognitive bias for overviews before detail or who may require the additional information within alt text to comprehend the social context of a pictorial metaphor. HR communication can be very dry and focused on compliance; this principle would encourage a more varied approach to information portrayal (perhaps multiple formats) in the dissemination process.

Principle Five: "Tolerance for Error"

Tolerance for error means allowing mistakes and edits. As a result of a possible working memory deficit associated with some NM conditions, there may be otherwise qualified individuals who are less able to self-regulate for errors (Hofmann et al., 2012), for example in an online application form or while using company software or databases. Tolerance for error is about recognizing that not every individual accommodation can be planned for and that systems needs to allow for us to go back, review and correct. This might include HR practices in recruitment, performance appraisal and training.

Principle Six: "Low Physical Effort"

The principle of low physical effort is targeted at predicting and minimizing physical effort. Many NMs experience a great deal of physical discomfort in a number of ways, for example, (1) the tension created by staying still when they need to move (Robertson, 2006), (2) managing overwhelming sensory information if the environment is busy, which can cause pain (Markram & Markram, 2010; Shulamite et al., 2015), or (3) through required additional physical effort for those with developmental coordination disorder (DCD, also known as dyspraxia) (Blank et al., 2019). These differences might affect employees when commuting, for example, in terms of noise sensitivity, time management, and further, both ADHD and dyspraxia may affect way-finding and driving capacity (Blank et al., 2019; Matza et al., 2005). As such, considering low physical effort is a principle that can be applied to role design and consideration of the possible alternative through the application of remote-working and flextime policies.

Principle Seven: "Size and Space for Approach and Use"

Building on low physical effort, size and space for approach and use focuses on the adaptation of environments and workspace. In relation to physical and sensory impairments this might involve consideration of how one moves and communicates within a space. For NM conditions, we must also consider sensory overwhelm, sedentary dependency, and the need to minimize confusion on way-finding. In particular, research has shown a need to consider noise, temperature, protection of personal space and privacy, visual stimulus and movement, smells and more (Shulamite et al., 2015; Whitby, 2018), indicating that overwhelm may be painful for some rather than simply distracting.

The items presented in Table 11.1 describe examples of good inclusion practice across multiple facets of organizational infrastructure and policy. It is arguable to what extent the activities represent disability inclusion specifically or simply good practice for management in general (Sundar, 2017). By adopting such measures as standard rather than optional, the employer has levelled the playing field as opposed to requiring a stigmatizing special request for such an accommodation or adjustment from a population known to resist disclosure (Gerber et al., 2005; Santuzzi et al., 2014; von Schrader et al., 2014). Interestingly, the items in the table have previously been cited as formal accommodations at the individual level (Corbière et al., 2014; Doyle, 2017; Hayward et al., 2019; Schulze et al., 2018), yet in their embedded form they represent informal accommodations or organizational-level accommodations. Incorporating flexibilities and awareness of differing needs into hiring, contracting, training and performance practices, I/O psychologists will help businesses move towards universal design for neurominorities.

Employee Welfare

In this section, we will explore the three typical workplace well-being resources available to employees: employee assistance programs (EAPs), occupational health (OH) resources and medical health benefits. These are typically more available in

TABLE 11.1 Workplace Universal Design for Neurominorities (reproduced with permission from Doyle & McDowall, 2021)

Universal Design Principle	*Designing: Avoiding structural exclusion by focusing on performance output, not input*	*Hiring: Ensuring all candidates can perform at their best during the process*	*Contracting: Terms and conditions of employment to increase access*	*Training: inclusion in standard*	*Performance Review: Optimizing success with inclusive delivery*	*Well-being: Adapting standard well-being services to support NM needs*
Equitable Use	Job design to avoid social constructs in "essential" criteria, such as "team skills" for jobs where performance will be independent.	Use of work sample tests to measure performance in the actual role rather than social expectation–loaded interviews or proxy measures such as timed intelligence tests.	Provision for: (1) remote working; (2) flexible hours (3) general reduction in commuting obligations as standard in all employment contracts where feasible.	Ensuring access to standard training through best practice in preparation and delivery for all in house provision, details as below.	Provision of personal performance training as standard company offer, e.g., time management, planning, prioritizing and other performance issues common to NM, but also relevant to a wide range of employees and newly promoted.	Ensuring a variety of well-being (WB) initiatives, including physical health as equal to mental health. Build access to WB supports into standard onboarding and reviewing protocols so that it is standard.

(*Continued*)

TABLE 11.1 (Continued)

Universal Design Principle	*Designing: Avoiding structural exclusion by focusing on performance output, not input*	*Hiring: Ensuring all candidates can perform at their best during the process*	*Contracting: Terms and conditions of employment to increase access*	*Training: inclusion in standard*	*Performance Review: Optimizing success with inclusive delivery*	*Well-being: Adapting standard well-being services to support NM needs*
Flexibility in Use	Craft roles for specialists as well as generalists, for example permitting senior roles without supervision responsibilities.	Offer a menu of adjustments as standard, which signals that organizational intentions are welcoming of difference. Invite candidates to contact recruiters if they would require time extensions or location flexibility, for example.	Providing flexible options for standard systems such as frequency of supervision and feedback, which may need to be increased during onboarding for some neurominorities.	Adjustable pace in learning program, allow additional time for preparation and any posttraining testing.	Permit mentors in performance reviews, provide feedback written in advance to allow reflection. Appraisal scoring to avoid penalizing where employees excel in specialist areas but are average in others.	Ensure well-being provision incorporates specialists, as standard advice may not be appropriate for some NMs who have additional cognitive and medical needs.
Simple and Intuitive Use	Over time roles develop "creep" and become overlaid with sometimes inconsistent responsibilities. Regular review of performance output variables.	Clear instructions on how to complete application and what to prepare for assessment using simple bullet points or numbered steps.	Well laid-out terms and conditions, signposting to relevant policies and procedures, covering note, use Flesch-Kincaid score to assess language accessibility.	Consistency of formatting and training scheduling to avoid confusion or absence.	Standard format for assessing and reporting performance that is consistent and clearly communicated in advance.	Well-advertised provision with referral routes clearly presented in simple step-by-step format.

	and team structures helps to ensure that jobs are designed simply and intuitively in line with the business goals					
Perceptible Information	Role descriptions to be accessible in format, e.g., multisensory, adjustable text size/background color, printable, editable. Language to be behavioral and output driven, avoiding nuance and interpretation such as "influencing skills".	Application process in accessible formats, e.g., multisensory, adjustable text size/background color, printable, editable.	Understanding the additional needs for psychological contract – what seems obvious may need to be explicit to avoid misunderstandings. Multisensory options for ensuring policy compliance, e.g., safeguarding videos. Written contract in accessible format.	Materials to include accessible written pack and opportunity for discussion, reflection and action before completion of training.	Feedback to be factual and not interpretative, guidance and training provided to supervisors about reporting performance feedback clearly with examples.	Transparency on purpose of well-being initiative, ensure that it is perceived as optional help rather than mandated acquiescence – many NM people have had negative experiences with mental health practice.

(*Continued*)

TABLE 11.1 (Continued)

Universal Design Principle	*Designing: Avoiding structural exclusion by focusing on performance output, not input*	*Hiring: Ensuring all candidates can perform at their best during the process*	*Contracting: Terms and conditions of employment to increase access*	*Training: inclusion in standard*	*Performance Review: Optimizing success with inclusive delivery*	*Well-being: Adapting standard well-being services to support NM needs*
Tolerance for Error	Ensure that safety, risk and client-facing deliverables have second checks built into the role design to reduce the need for 100% accuracy.	Allow candidates to review and edit application information before online submission. Encourage applicants to pause or take breaks in interviews if required. Giving clear instructions on directions and login details, as many NMs have significant impairments in way finding. Do not penalize this specifically.	Standard contract process to include review verbally as well as written, give opportunity to ask questions.	Set a tone in training for the permission of "silly questions" and create an environment of positive regard. Permit multiple attempts at knowledge tests and allow practice tests.	Allow for appeal or negotiation where performance ratings resulted from misunderstanding.	Create feedback loops for employees to submit their experiences, both negative and positive, to ensure employee voice is captured and acted upon.

Low Physical Effort	Understand the additional burden of commuting and busy workspaces for NMs; for some this causes physical pain and extreme fatigue, leading to poor performance. Design with minimal sensory load and travel requirements in mind.	Provision of assistive technology or materials in formats compatible with AT. Consider timing of interviews and offer flexibility around location and need to commute in rush hour.	Create as much time as possible for reviewing and competing the contracting process to avoid slow processing speed anxiety.	Use of AT and regular comfort breaks.	Breaks provided to accommodate sensory overwhelm and aid slow processing.	Proximity of support to reduce travel, ensuring well-being services also meet multisensory design and AT compatible standards.
Space and Size for Approach	Similarly to the foregoing, seek specialist input into the design of workspaces and, where possible, allow flexibility or compromise (shifts) in attendance on busy work sites.	Match the environment to the job performance so that you can assess in context, with the caveat that there should be a quiet environment for preparation and recruitment tasks, as there is likely to be additional anxiety for NMs.	Defined location of workstation, provision of dual monitors, sit/stand desks, and acoustic barriers as standard options in contracts.	Flexibility around onsite versus remote delivery, group size and familiarity.	Performance reviews to be conducted in friendly location and quiet, calm environment, with sufficient notice of who will be present.	Flexibility of access remote via app, video, phone or face to face. Avoid reliance on single delivery method.

larger companies, many of which successfully co-opt such resources to improve the delivery of individual-level accommodations following referral to these services (Bruyère et al., 2006). EAP or OH may be outsourced or in-house. Typically, EAPs are concerned with mental well-being and provide counselling or cognitive behavioral therapy (CBT) type interventions (Joseph et al., 2018), whereas OH tends to incorporate working conditions and physical health (Randall et al., 2005). Neither EAPs nor OH confer automatic specialism in neurodiversity, though both can be co-opted in support of neurominority inclusion if they aim to do so and undertake appropriate specialist training. Additionally, employers provide recourse to medical health benefits, which may offer referral to specialist medical treatment. However, each of these services presupposes that neurominorities are a problem which lies at the individual level, thus coming into conceptual conflict with the legal remit of the employer if referral is mandated. Further, ethical questions are raised about informed consent when job security is contingent on submission to health practice that might include pharmacological treatment. The pedagogy of many health service providers is frequently incongruent with the neurodiversity movement (medical versus social model), and so caution must be exercised when bringing such resources to bear in NM inclusion. Consultants are advised to consider their remit in recommending medical interventions and to caution employers the same, lest employees misinterpret an attempt to support as an imperative to submit for "treatment" in order to retain employment. To elucidate, for organizations to fulfil their legal accommodation duties, care should be taken to ensure that they are not sending individuals away to be "fixed" by medicine or psychology, but rather they are supporting employees with the additional considerations which may accompany the presentation of neurominority characteristics. Disability accommodation is about work performance, and as such, negative affect is a related variable, possibly intervening, but not a target in and of itself. Such consideration does not negate the potential utility of employee well-being programs, but it should influence the commissioning of services – which provider to use and when to refer an individual. We now look in more detail at three employee well-being resources commonly available.

Counselling, Mindfulness and Cognitive Behavioural Therapy via EAP

Many neurominorities experience a higher prevalence of anxiety and depression than neurotypical peers (Francis et al., 2019; Hollocks et al., 2019; Kessler et al., 2009) and thus are more likely to experience negative consequences, as these impinge on day-to-day functioning and performance. However, the success of traditional psychological therapies with this client group is mixed (Brandeis et al., 2013; Hollocks et al., 2019; Weiss et al., 2012; Weston et al., 2016) and may be inappropriate to a workplace context. For example, mindfulness approaches have received positive initial results and may be supportive of work performance difficulties associated with executive dysfunction (Cassone, 2015; Spijkerman et al., 2016; Zeidan et al., 2010). However, these are likely to act via the intervening variables of reduced stress in general rather than a direct impact on cognitive ability (Chambers et al., 2008; Doyle & McDowall, 2019; Jha et al., 2010; Zeidan et al., 2010). Further, when avoidable, cognitive demands are the cause of stress, and only stress is treated, this is akin to a sticking-plaster approach that will not create sustainable performance improvements. Individuals whose performance has been compromised by a loud open-plan office, or refusal of flex-time request may feel justifiably resistant to therapy aimed at affect, when their difficulties come from a genetic, neurobiological difference in sensory perception (Astle et al., 2019; Engert & Pruessner, 2009; Siegel, 2006) that can be accommodated with environmental flexibility/adaptation.

A worst case is that mental health referral may be viewed as abdication of responsibility and create suspicion in a neurominority population that is increasingly self-aware and politically active with regards to marginalization. Critical review of referral for mental health treatment to address behavioral issues is particularly pertinent for female, indigenous, Black and other employees of color, who have been historically misdiagnosed with anxiety, social anxiety, depression, eating disorders and personality disorders by a psychiatric system that is biased toward white, straight, male presentation of neurominority (CDC, 2009; Green, 2019; Mandell et al., 2009; Quinn, 2014; Young et al., 2018). The bias towards misdiagnosis of mental ill health also exists in the context of high IQ, which can mask sensory and cognitive difficulties (Alvares et al., 2019). As such, employees with new or adult diagnosis may wish to avoid mental health referral. They may find it insulting to be advised that self-determined control of their negative affect will improve their ability, as in the mindfulness paradigm for example, which has been critiqued for overpromising where there are biological and systemic causes of anxiety (Dam et al., 2018; Farias & Wikholm, 2016). On the other hand, providing counselling support for individuals who are coming to terms with an identity-shifting diagnosis or recovering from internalized negativity around capabilities and ambition could be cathartic and empowering.

To make EAP referrals work in practice, employers need to ensure that the EAP provider has a specialist referral service when common approaches fail and awareness of neurominority presentation to successfully navigate contentious issues. In summary, EAP for neurominority inclusion should be considered a secondary support rather than a primary support; initial organizational approaches should focus on ameliorating the structural cognitive and sensory demands of the environment, as outlined in Table 11.1.

Assessment by Occupational Health

OH assessments, provided by OH nurses, physicians or occupational/rehabilitation therapists, tend toward capability assessment on return to work following illness or injury and may be part of a rehabilitation program supported by clinical health care professionals. Such services are frequently available in European businesses but are more likely to be accessed via private health care in US businesses. In order to co-opt this service, the professional providing the assessment needs to have specific knowledge of the strengths associated with neurominorities and the range of adjustments that are possible to implement. Health generalists may be subject to the same outdated and prejudiced stereotypes of NM as the general population (Masuch et al., 2019; Nelissen et al., 2016). For example, they may be coming from the belief that autistic people have no capacity for social skills or people with ADHD only display hyperactivity through large physical display and therefore the person who fiddles quietly can't have ADHD. There is a risk that an uninformed professional may downplay severity of symptom or opportunity for growth and advise management of an unfavorable prognosis. Yet when combined with neurodiversity specialist knowledge, OH professionals come equipped with practical options for adapting roles, tools and environments (Rafnsdottir & Heijstra, 2009). OH uses a systematic process by which the demands of the role are compared to the capabilities of the individual, and this can be co-opted for inclusion, providing a powerful ally and resource within the organization. Encouraging employers and employees to utilize this resource for NM can result in good advice and practical guidance at the individual level when embedded organizational-level inclusion resources are insufficient to optimize performance.

Health Benefits

Assessment, diagnosis and treatment are features of the medical model of disability, and we must consider the ethical bind of informed consent when applied to the intersection of health and employment. Can an employee truly give free consent to a medical intervention when their employment or career progression may depend upon it? Similarly to therapy, submission to health treatment such as medication for ADHD or antidepressants for anxiety and depression must consider the reactive nature of symptoms. If the employment context itself is providing the unhealthy stimulus for the difficulty, it may be unethical to focus solely on treatment for the individual. Conversely, employees with performance difficulties who are realizing for the first time that they may be neurodivergent may welcome the catharsis of diagnosis and treatment. A common issue for adults is the realization of their own condition during diagnosis of their child, resulting in coming to terms with many years of masking symptoms and struggling to live up to social norms (McLoughlin & Leather, 2013). Masking is known to compromise performance and career trajectory (Livingston et al., 2019), whereas understanding one's neurocognitive profile may release employees from self-reproach of the sense that if they just tried harder, all would be well. This may spur the employee to accept help, resources and accommodations, thus improving productivity and engagement.

Neurominority conditions correlate with a higher prevalence of health complaints such as insomnia (Doyle & Cleaver, 2015; Fuller-Thomson et al., 2016; Katz et al., 2015) and may confer higher demands on health benefits over time. Ensuring comprehensive coverage may be vital in improving both presenteeism and absenteeism. Interestingly, despite this additional health burden, research has shown that in general disabled employees take *less* time off work than abled, yet this is at odds with employer perceptions (Graffam et al., 2002). I/O psychologists providing awareness training can address these stereotypes. It is important for human resources professionals and business leaders to avoid discriminatory performance judgments that are inference based (Colella et al., 1998; Colella & Varma, 2001).

Employee Resource/Business Groups

Within many large employers there are employee resource groups (ERGs) such as the "neurodiversity champions" networks within UK public-sector employers (Richards & Sang, 2016) or Ernst and Young's dyslexia network (Addison et al., 2018). These are reported by members to be helpful and increase a sense of feeling "heard" and validated. The neurodiversity community has a well-developed activist network online, in which there is an understandable baseline of mistrust towards professional services and employer initiatives, and these groups go some way to restoring power imbalances (Richards & Sang, 2016). However, without recourse to supervision and a broader, more scientific evidence base such networks may perpetuate conspiracy theories and fringe treatments. Further, a reasonable critique has been levied in the more mature fields of race and gender inclusion about placing undue burden on minority employees to take on additional unpaid duties to improve conditions for others like them (Kandola, 2018) and the failure of ERGs to improve access to employment for minoritized applicants and representation within the staff team more broadly (Roberson, 2018). Exploitation of good will and expectations of internal activism should not be a replacement for professional services or formal programs of accommodation. That said, peer networks very much honour the spirit of the social model, in which there should be "nothing about us without us" (Charlton, 1998). Incorporating lived experience into formal programs has worked well when it is co-produced in multidisciplinary networks and operates with clear terms of reference and remit, such as the example provided by therapeutic communities such as Alcoholic Anonymous and some mental health recovery models (Watson, 2019). Adopting such principles into organizational practice requires a delicate balancing act, accepting that individual voices are essential for inclusion, but for translation into organizational policy, reliability and validity of views must be methodically, objectively established. Clear leadership and commitment to inclusion must be role modelled in the leadership of the organization and communicated as such through allocation of resources to employee groups and including them with strategic priorities. The essential role of good leadership has been demonstrated in other forms of diversity inclusion (Bebbington & Ozgilbin, 2013; Nishii & Mayer, 2009); role modelling from the top is featured in the emerging anecdotal examples of in-house groups for neurodiversity. The following case studies explains some key features of making ERGs work.

Company and Network Support Examples

In the consulting firm Ernst and Young, an internal peer network for dyslexia was established in 2010. The founding senior partner, John Levell (who is of course dyslexic himself), concurs that for success, such a group needs a clear purpose and a senior champion. In an interview with him, conducted for the purpose of this chapter, he advised that "you start with a set of objectives to avoid it becoming a moaning shop. You have to make it relevant to the organization's fundamental purpose and wider resourcing strategy". Levell reports that the internal network would support recruiting teams at EY by explaining to them how some standard processes, like ability testing, can inadvertently exclude talented applicants. The teams then built on this feedback by updating and augmenting standard application protocols to widen the successful applicant pool at the initial stages. Levell recalls, "even with these changes, we once had an applicant from a top University, with outstanding credentials who failed some of the cognitive ability testing baseline scores, as well as arriving late for the assessment center. Members of the group were able to educate the recruiters on how employment practices could be adapted to include a high value employee with unusual and potentially difficult habits". In this way, the organization not only provides a supportive resource for neurominority employees but benefited from that resource directly; the group provides a vehicle for two-way engagement and influence, iteratively improving standards of accessibility companywide.

Alignment of employee groups with organizational goals has been expanded upon and institutionalized at Microsoft, whose accessibility team is led and staffed by people with a wide range of disabilities, including neurominorities. The Microsoft ethos is very much that the design team needs to reflect the customer base and therefore, without inclusion, they risk the ability to provide a comprehensive product (Idea, 2016). Microsoft has instituted a global chief accessibility officer at the highest level of its international operation, who is herself Deaf, and in doing so demonstrate congruence of stated intent and delivering on promises. Microsoft's demonstrable organizational commitment of representation confers relevance to being a neurominority/disabled employee building marginalized voices into an active commercial company strategy. The provision of reactive disability support is replaced with the provision of structures for inclusion; the employee is not "done to" but is empowered to become an agent in the organization according to their strength and experience. This is liberating at the individual level and provides role modeling opportunities to inspire new candidates and career advancement for employees who may have felt excluded.

External groups can also provide a powerful liaison point. Groups and initiatives such as the Global Business and Disability Network provide a shared space for company representatives to access networking, HR toolkits and advice. Taking part in these forums and cross fertilizing back into company networks facilitates the sharing of ideas, best practice and troubleshooting at the organization level. There are also a number of specific neurodiversity sites and groups operating, though these are sometimes associated with lived experience only and therefore may be vulnerable to the same issues as ERGs, namely that governance is lacking and so advice may be unsubstantiated. It is a priority for I/O psychology research to provide evidence that can fill this void, since the risks to social exclusion for individuals and legal exposure for employers are numerous. In the interim, practitioners are encouraged to engage in critical appraisal when assessing recommendations for further employer/employee resources in what is currently an unregulated market.

Assessing the Effectiveness of Various Neurodiversity Programs

For whom are the organizational adaptations to workplace policies, practices and available services working? Extant research evaluating the effectiveness of accommodations for disability tends towards the individual unit of evaluation ("Do you like it?"), and there are fewer assessing benefit for the organization as a whole or employers more broadly ("Does it advance organizational goals?") (Sundar, 2017). There are some evaluations of organizational disability accommodations using standard HR data as dependent variables, such as demographic surveys, turnover and absence reporting, productivity grading and self-report of key stakeholders (Lindsay et al., 2018) but few (at time of writing) that specifically highlight neurominorities (Scott et al., 2017). Benefits to the employer are thus of implied monetary value, the net savings incurred from benefits against costs (Graffam et al., 2002; Lindsay et al., 2018). Qualitative and cross-sectional studies assessing the benefits to the individual are more common yet are weighted towards the soft, social benefits of workforce inclusion such as social belonging and mental well-being (Krieger et al., 2010; Paul & Moser, 2009) as opposed to more objective dependent variables such as career progression or financial and performance improvements resulting from accommodations.

In summary, there is a research bias looking at quantitative measures for assessing organizational impact and qualitative measures for assessing individual impact when, in fact, both are relevant, inter- and intra-dependent at all levels of analysis. The fundamental purpose of inclusion policies in all areas is increased access and success for marginalized people, a removal of the systematic, institutionalized barriers and unconscious biases. This is more than just a numbers game. Just as accommodation design should incorporate multiple levels of analysis, so should design of evaluation approaches. To frame this section, I will outline what I would expect to be working well (i.e., dependent variables) if a systematic program of inclusive workplace policies, practices and services had been successful.

Representation Across the Organization, Not Just in "Pockets"

When systemic inclusion is working well, there are roles available to fit specialist thinkers and specialist thinkers within those roles! So frequently diversity and inclusion programs start with a target number of individuals to bring through the door, and instead I recommend that we flip this to a process by which we reflect regularly on the representation and prevalence at all levels, in all departments, as a longitudinal outcome variable and a way to measure success *after* we have implemented changes. This form of evaluation requires regular, anonymized data capture of individual characteristics to extrapolate organizational norms. Researchers should be aware of language here; many NMs will not tick "yes" to disability. Since they may not accept this label, being specific about neurominorities will improve response reliability.

Reduction in Individual-Level, Compliance-Based Adjustments

Accommodations at the individual level represent a (sometimes reluctant) compliance with the law, whereas willingness to evolve and update standard practices represents systemic inclusion. When an organization is embracing inclusion at the organizational level through universal design that begins to permeate all workplace policies, practices and services/programs, there will be less need for individual accommodation requests. These will tail off over time as the example items in Table 11.1 become more ubiquitous. Such a climate of acceptance will be attractive to a wider range of applicants as well as facilitate the career progression of a wider range of talent within, again taking our attention off the need for disclosure or recruitment and placing it on talent and optimizing performance. Evaluation could involve aggregating individual-level accommodation information, perhaps based on the spending of the department or number of referrals for support, to extrapolate the organizational norm, which we would predict to change over time. Obviously, the prevalence rates of NMs would need to be included as a control variable to ensure accommodations were not decreasing due to lower employment rates.

Friendly and Inclusive Language Around Inclusion

An interesting variable of analysis might be inclusive language and narratives within an organization, presupposing that (in)authenticity is projected in standard policies, procedures and advertisements. Consider the examples highlighted by Lester *et al.* in their discourse analysis of two universities' disability policies (Lester et al., 2013, p. 59–60):

Excerpt 1:

"Welcome to the Office of Accessible Education! Stanford University has a strong commitment to maintain a diverse and stimulating academic community, representing a broad spectrum of talents and experiences."

Excerpt 2:

"MIT Student Disability Services, as required under the ADA of 1990 and Section 504 of the Rehabilitation Act of 1973, makes every reasonable effort to provide appropriate accommodations and assistance to students with disabilities. The objective is to ensure that our students receive equal access to all Institute programs and services. To that end, we seek to balance the student's right to access with our obligation to protect the integrity of Institute programs and services."

The first excerpt represents the language of systemic inclusion, of organizational-level accommodation and invitation, though it could be considered a platitude by a more cynical stakeholder. The second indicates that compliance-based inclusion will be administered, but the last sentence could imply begrudgingly, with a higher value placed on the abled "norm". When organizational accommodation is working well, I would expect to see inclusive language filtered into HR policy and procedure in a widespread fashion, updated regularly and with a learning process for iterative improvement integrated into the system. This could be evaluated as an organizational-level variable, reviewing the language in set exemplar documents for changes over time.

Stakeholder Engagement

Qualitative and relational variables are of interest. Interviews, questionnaires and focus groups involving employees with lived experience specifically will garner rich information about the impact of our efforts, which can be translated into pilots and accommodations at scale. There is evidence to suggest that inclusion policies benefit all employees, not just those who have been targeted, leading to increased engagement, company loyalty and feeling positive about work (Downey et al., 2015). As such, stakeholder input should be considered widely; evaluations of employee experience should be intersectional, considering overlapping areas of marginalization and critical analysis of power and voice, as well as gathering of proxy variables such as engagement and perceived organizational justice to understand the embedded, broader impact that accommodation programs are having on company performance.

Conclusion

Many current intervention activities such as assistive technology, coaching and mentoring have been heretofore pitched at the individual level (Doyle, 2017, 2020) and require the employee to make significant adaptations in order to meet the role demands of their position within the workplace. Further, they are often only dispensed in reaction to a problem emerging with performance, leading to conflict and damage to self-efficacy before an accommodation is made. Current practices may therefore be incongruous with legislative requirements and instead come from a medical model wherein neurominorities are considered disordered and in need of fixing, perhaps only when they are causing concern for the wider team. Given these paradoxes, this chapter has provided guidance on moving beyond reactive compliance at the individual level to consider preemptive, systemic inclusion activities at the organizational level across all workplace policies, practices, services and programs. The goal of organizational accommodations is to change "the way we do things around here", creating a welcoming climate for intersectional diversity and an appreciation of the natural variety in human capabilities. In conclusion, the true marker of success for organizational accommodations is when there is no longer a department or team working on inclusion.

References

Addison, R., Spoors, C., & Cooke, B. (2018). *The value of dyslexia*. London: Made by Dyslexia.

Alvares, G. A., Bebbington, K., Cleary, D., Evans, K., Glasson, E. J., Maybery, M. T., . . . Whitehouse, A. J. O. (2019). The misnomer of 'high functioning autism': Intelligence is an imprecise predictor of functional abilities at diagnosis. *Autism*, 1–12. https://doi.org/10.1177/1362361319852831

Armstrong, T. (2010). *The power of neurodiversity*. Emeryville, CA: De Capo Press. ISBN: 978-0-7382-1553-2

Armstrong, T. (2015). The myth of the normal brain: Embracing neurodiversity. *AMA Journal of Ethics, 17*(4), 348–352. Https://doi.org/10.1001/journalofethics.2015.17.4.msoc1-1504

Astle, D. E., Bathelt, J., & Holmes, J. (2019). Remapping the cognitive and neural profiles of children who struggle at school. *Developmental Science, 22*(1), 1–17. https://doi.org/10.1111/desc.12747

Baron-Cohen, S. (2019). The concept of neurodiversity is dividing the autism community. *The Scientific American*. https://blogs.scientificamerican.com/observations/the-concept-of-neurodiversity-is-dividing-the-autism-community/

Bebbington, D., & Ozgilbin, M. (2013). The paradox of diversity in leadership and leadership for diversity. *Management International/International Management/Gestion Internacional, 17*, 14–24. https://doi.org/https://doi.org/10.7202/1015808ar

Bernick, M. (2019, January). Effective autism (neurodiversity) employment. *Forbes*. www.forbes.com/sites/michaelbernick/2019/01/15/effective-autism-neurodiversity-employment-a-legal-perspective/#586692476c18

Blank, R., Barnett, A. L., Cairney, J., Green, D., Kirby, A., Polatajko, H., . . . Vinc, S. (2019). International clinical practice recommendations on the definition, diagnosis, assessment, intervention, and psychosocial aspects of developmental coordination disorder. *Developmental Medicine and Child Neurology, 61*, 242–285. https://doi.org/10.1111/dmcn.14132

Bottema-Beutel, K., Kapp, S. K., Lester, J. N., Sasson, N. J., Hand, B. N., & Otr, L. (2020). Avoiding ableist language : Suggestions for autism researchers. *Autism in Adulthood, 3*(1), 18–29. https://doi.org/10.1089/aut.2020.0014

Brandeis, D., Cortese, S., Daley, D., Holtmann, M., Stevenson, J., Danckaerts, M., . . . Buitelaar, J. (2013). Nonpharmacological interventions for ADHD: Systematic review and meta-analyses of randomized controlled trials of dietary and psychological treatments. *American Journal of Psychiatry, 170*(3), 275–289.

Bruyère, S. M., Erickson, W. A., & Vanlooy, S. A. (2006). The impact of business size on employer ADA response. *Rehabilitation Counseling Bulletin, 49*(4), 194–206.

Cassone, A. R. (2015). Mindfulness training as an adjunct to evidence-based treatment for ADHD within families. *Journal of Attention Disorders, 19*(2), 147–157. https://doi.org/10.1177/1087054713488438

CDC. (2009). Morbidity and mortality weekly report. *Center for Disease Control, 58*(21), 581–608. Retrieved from www.cdc.gov/mmwr/PDF/wk/mm5821.pdf

Chambers, R., Lo, B. C. Y., & Allen, N. B. (2008). The impact of intensive mindfulness training on attentional control, cognitive style, and affect. *Cognitive Therapy and Research, 32*(3), 303–322. https://doi.org/10.1007/s10608-007-9119-0

Chapman, R. (2020). Defining neurodiversity for research and practice. In H. B. Rosqvist, N. Chown, & A. Stenning (Eds.), *Neurodiversity studies: A new critical paradigm* (pp. 218–220). London: Routledge, Taylor & Francis. https://doi.org/10.4324/9780429322297-21

Charlton, J. (1998). *Nothing about us without us: Disability oppression and empowerment.* University of California Press. Retrieved from www.jstor.org/stable/10.1525/j.ctt1pnqn9

Colella, A., DeNisi, A. S., & Varma, A. (1998). The impact of ratee's disability on performance judgments and choice as partner: The role of disability-job fit stereotypes and interdependence of rewards. *The Journal of Applied Psychology, 83*(1), 102–111. https://doi.org/10.1037/0021-9010.83.1.102

Colella, A., & Varma, A. (2001). The impact of subordinate disability on leader- member exchange relationships. *Academy of Management Journal, 44*(2), 304–315. https://doi.org/10.2307/3069456

Corbière, M., Villotti, P., Lecomte, T., Bond, G. R., Lesage, A., & Goldner, E. M. (2014). Work accommodations and natural supports for maintaining employment. *Psychiatric Rehabilitation Journal, 37*(2), 90–98. https://doi.org/10.1037/prj0000033

de Beer, J., Engels, J., Heerkens, Y., & van der Klink, J. (2014). Factors influencing work participation of adults with developmental dyslexia: A systematic review. *BMC Public Health, 14*, 1–77. https://doi.org/10.1186/1471-2458-14-77

Downey, S. N., van der Werff, L., Thomas, K. M., & Plaut, V. C. (2015). The role of diversity practices and inclusion in promoting trust and employee engagement. *Journal of Applied Social Psychology, 45*(1), 35–44. https://doi.org/10.1111/jasp.12273

Doyle, N. (2017). Neurodiversity at work. In BPS (Ed.), *Psychology at work: Improving wellbeing and productivity in the workplace* (pp. 44–62). British Psychological Society. https://doi.org/ISBN 978-1-85433-754-2

Doyle, N. (2020). Neurodiversity at work: A biopsychosocial model and the impact on working adults. *British Medical Bulletin, 135*, 1–18.

Doyle, N., & Cleaver, S. (2015). *Collaborative research on dyslexia: Incidence, adjustments, and health outcomes*. In Division of occupational psychology annual conference. British Psychological Society, Leicester.

Doyle, N., & McDowall, A. (2019). Context matters: A systematic review of coaching as a disability accommodation. *PLoS ONE, 14*(8), 1–30. https://doi.org/10.1371/journal.pone.0199408

Doyle, N., & McDowall, A. (2021). Diamond in the rough? An 'empty review' of research into 'neurodiversity' and a road map for developing the inclusion agenda. *Equality, Diversity and Inclusion: An International Journal*. https://doi.org/10.1108/EDI-06-2020-0172

Engert, V., & Pruessner, J. (2009). Dopaminergic and noradrenergic contributions to functionality in ADHD: The role of methylphenidate. *Current Neuropharmacology, 6*(4), 322–328. https://doi.org/10.2174/157015908787386069

Farias, M., & Wikholm, C. (2016). Has the science of mindfulness lost its mind ? *British Journal of Psychology Bulletin, 40*, 329–332. https://doi.org/10.1192/pb.bp.116.053686

Flesch, R. (1948). A new readability yardstick. *Journal of Applied Psychology, 32*(3), 221–233. https://doi.org/10.1037/h0057532

Francis, D. A., Carunan, N., Hudson, J. L., & McArthur, G. M. (2019). The association between poor reading and internalising problems: A systematic review and meta-analysis. *Clinical Psychology Review, 67*, 45–60.

Fuller-Thomson, E., Lewis, D. A., & Agbeyaka, S. K. (2016). Attention-deficit/hyperactivity disorder casts a long shadow: Findings from a population-based study of adult women with self-reported ADHD. *Child: Care, Health and Development, 42*(6), 918–927. https://doi.org/10.1111/cch.12380

García-Betances, R. I., Cabrera-Umpiérrez, M. F., Ottaviano, M., Pastorino, M., & Arredondo, M. T. (2016). Parametric cognitive modeling of information and computer technology usage by people with aging-and disability-derived functional impairments. *Sensors (Switzerland), 16*(2). https://doi.org/10.3390/s16020266

Gerber, P. J., Price, L. A., Mulligan, R. A., & Williams, P. (2005). To be or not to be learning disabled? A preliminary report on self-disclosure of adults with learning disabilities. *Thalamus, 23*(2), 18–29.

Graffam, J., Smith, K., Shinkfield, A., & Polzin, U. (2002). Employer benefits and costs of employing a person with a disability. *Journal of Vocational Rehabilitation, 17*, 251–263.

Grant, D. (2009). The psychological assessment of neurodiversity. In D. Pollak (Ed.), *Neurodiversity in higher education* (pp. 33–62). Chichester: Wiley-Blackwell.

Green, R. (2019). Women and autism spectrum disorder: Diagnosis and implications for treatment of adolescents and adults. *Current Psychiatry Reports, 21*(4), 22. https://doi.org/10.1007/s11920-019-1006-3

Hayward, S. M., McVilly, K. R., & Stokes, M. A. (2019). Autism and employment: What works. *Research in Autism Spectrum Disorders, 60*, 48–58. https://doi.org/10.1016/j.rasd.2019.01.006

Hofmann, W., Schmeichel, B. J., & Baddeley, A. D. (2012). Executive functions and self-regulation. *Trends in Cognitive Sciences, 16*(3), 174–180. https://doi.org/10.1016/j.tics.2012.01.006

Hollocks, M. J., Lerh, J. W., Magiati, I., Meiser-Stedman, R., & Brugha, T. S. (2019). Anxiety and depression in adults with autism spectrum disorder: A systematic review and meta-analysis. *Psychological Medicine, 49*(4), 559–572.

Idea. (2016, February). *Microsoft's inclusive design*. Retrieved from https://www.microsoft.com/design/inclusive/

Jha, A. P., Stanley, E. A., Kiyonaga, A., Wong, L., & Gelfand, L. (2010). Examining the protective effects of mindfulness training on working memory capacity and affective experience. *Emotion, 10*(1), 54–64. https://doi.org/10.1037/a0018438

Joseph, B., Walker, A., & Fuller-Tyszkiewicz, M. (2018). Evaluating the effectiveness of employee assistance programmes: A systematic review. *European Journal of Work and Organizational Psychology, 27*(1), 1–15. https://doi.org/10.1080/1359432X.2017.1374245

Kandola, B. (2018). *Racism at work: The danger of indifference*. Birmingham: Pearn Kandola Publishing.

Katz, N., Dejak, I., & Gal, E. (2015). Work performance evaluation and QoL of adults with High Functioning Autism Spectrum Disorders (HFASD). *Work-a Journal of Prevention Assessment & Rehabilitation, 51*(4), 887–892. https://doi.org/10.3233/WOR-152001

Kessler, R. C., Lane, M., Stang, P. E., & van Brunt, D. L. (2009). The prevalence and workplace costs of adult attention deficit hyperactivity disorder in a large manufacturing firm. *Psychological Medicine, 39*(1), 137–147. https://doi.org/10.1017/S0033291708003309

Kincaid, J. P., Aagard, J. A., O'Hara, J. W., & Cottrell, L. K. (1981). Computer readability editing system. *IEEE Transactions on Professional Communication, 24*(1), 38–42. https://doi.org/10.1109/TPC.1981.6447821

Krieger, B., Kinebanian, A., Prodinger, B., & Heigl, F. (2010). Becoming a member of the work force: Perceptions of adults with Asperger syndrome. *Work, 43*(2), 141–157. https://doi.org/10.3233/WOR-2012-139

Lester, J. N., Dostal, H., & Gabriel, R. (2013). Policing neurodiversity in higher education: A discourse analysis of the talk surrounding accommodations for university students. In C. D. Herrera & A. Perry (Eds.), *Ethics and neurodiversity* (pp. 52–66). Cambridge: Cambridge Scholars Publishing.

Lewin, K. (1936). *Principles of topographical psychology*. New York, NY: McGraw-Hill.

Lindsay, S., Cagliostro, E., Albarico, M., Mortaji, N., Karon, L., & Lindsay, S. (2018). A systematic review of the benefits of hiring people with disabilities. *Journal of Occupational Rehabilitation, 28*(4), 634–655. https://doi.org/10.1007/s10926-018-9756-z

Livingston, L. A., Shah, P., & Happé, F. (2019). Compensatory strategies below the behavioural surface in autism: A qualitative study. *Lancet Psychology, 6*, 766–777. https://doi.org/10.1016/S2215-0366(19)30224-X

Mandell, D. S., Wiggins, L. D., Carpenter, L. A., Daniels, J., DiGuiseppi, C., Durkin, M. S., . . . Kirby, R. S. (2009). Racial/ethnic disparities in the identification of children with autism spectrum disorders. *American Journal of Public Health, 99*(3), 493–498. https://doi.org/10.2105/AJPH.2007.131243

Markram, K., & Markram, H. (2010). The intense world theory – A unifying theory of the neurobiology of autism. *Frontiers in Human Neuroscience, 4*, 1–29. https://doi.org/10.3389/fnhum.2010.00224

Masuch, T., Bea, M., Alm, B., Deibler, P., & Sobanski, E. (2019). Internalized stigma, anticipated discrimination and perceived public stigma in adults with ADHD. *Attention Deficit and Hyperactivity Disorders, 11*, 211–220. https://doi.org/10.1007/s12402-018-0274-9

Matza, L. S., Paramore, C., & Prasad, M. (2005). A review of the economic burden of ADHD. *Cost Effectiveness and Resource Allocation: C/E, 3*, 5. https://doi.org/10.1186/1478-7547-3-5

McLoughlin, D., & Leather, C. (2013). *The dyslexic adult*. Chichester: John Wiley & Sons.

Mellifont, D. (2019). Neuro magnifico! An exploratory study critically reviewing news text reporting of anxiety-related work performance strengths, challenges and support measures. *Work, 63*, 435–446. https://doi.org/10.3233/WOR-192950

Nelissen, P. T. J. H., Hülsheger, U. R., van Ruitenbeek, G. M. C., & Zijlstra, F. R. H. (2016). How and when stereotypes relate to inclusive behavior toward people with disabilities. *International Journal of Human Resource Management, 27*(14). https://doi.org/10.1080/09585192.2015.1072105

Nishii, L. H., & Mayer, D. M. (2009). Do inclusive leaders help to reduce turnover in diverse groups? The moderating role of leader-member exchange in the diversity to turnover relationship. *Journal of Applied Psychology, 94*(6), 1412–1426. https://doi.org/10.1037/a0017190

Paul, K. I., & Moser, K. (2009). Unemployment impairs mental health: Meta-analyses. *Journal of Vocational Behavior, 74*, 264–282.

PLAIN. (2011). Federal plain language guidelines. In *Federal plain language guidelines* (Issue May). Retrieved from www.plainlanguage.gov/guidelines/

Quinn, P. (2014). A review of attention-deficit/hyperactivity disorder in women and girls: Uncovering this hidden diagnosis. *The Primary Care Companion for CNS Disorders, 16*(3). https://doi.org/10.4088/PCC.13r01596

Rafnsdottir, G. L., & Heijstra, T. M. (2009). Work-related health: Organizational factors and well-being. In I. Soderback (Ed.), *International handbook of occupational therapy*. Cham: Springer.

Randall, R., Griffiths, A., & Cox, T. (2005). Evaluating organizational stress-management interventions using adapted study designs. *European Journal of Work and Organizational Psychology, 14*(1), 23–41. https://doi.org/10.1080/13594320444000209

Richards, J., & Sang, K. (2016). Trade unions as employment facilitators for disabled employees. *International Journal of Human Resource Management, 27*(14), 1642–1661. https://doi.org/10.1080/09585192.2015.1126334

Rickerson, N. (2009). Universal design. In I. Soderback (Ed.), *International handbook of occupational therapy* (2nd ed.). Heidelberg: Springer.

Riddick, B. (2001). Dyslexia and inclusion: Time for a social model of disability perspective? *International Studies in Sociology of Education, 11*(3), 37–41. https://doi.org/10.1080/09620210100200078

Roberson, Q. M. (2018). Diversity in the workplace: A review, synthesis, and future research agenda. *Annual Review of Organizational Psychology and Organizational Behavior, 6*(1), 69–88. https://doi.org/10.1146/annurev-orgpsych-012218-015243

Robertson, M. M. (2006). Attention deficit hyperactivity disorder, tics and Tourette's syndrome: The relationship and treatment implications. A commentary. *European Child & Adolescent Psychiatry, 15*(1), 1–11. https://doi.org/10.1007/s00787-006-0505-z

Santuzzi, A. M., Waltz, P. R., Finkelstein, L. M., & Rupp, D. E. (2014). Invisible disabilities: Unique challenges for employees and organizations. *Industrial and Organizational Psychology, 7*(2), 204–219. https://doi.org/10.1111/iops.12134

Schulze, C., Jakobs, U., Krieger, B., & Pis, B. (2018). Supporting and hindering environments for participation of adolescents diagnosed with autism spectrum disorder : A scoping review. *PLoS ONE*, 13, e0202071.

Scott, M., Jacob, A., Hendrie, D., Parsons, R., Girdler, S., Falkmer, T., & Falkmer, M. (2017). Employers' perception of the costs and the benefits of hiring individuals with autism spectrum disorder in open employment in Australia. *PLoS ONE, 12*(5), 1–17. https://doi.org/10.1371/journal.pone.0177607

Shulamite, A. G., Hernandez, L., Tottenham, N., Krasileva, K., Bookheimer, S. Y., & Dapretto, M. (2015). Neurobiology of sensory overresponsivity in youth with autism spectrum disorders. *Journal of the American Medical Association Psychiatry, 72*(8), 778–786. https://doi.org/10.1001/jamapsychiatry.2015.0737

Siegel, L. S. (2006). Perspectives on dyslexia. *Paediatrics and Child Health, 11*(9), 581–587. https://doi.org/10.1093/pch/11.9.581

Singer, J. (1998). *Odd people in: The birth of community amongst people on the "autistic spectrum": A personal exploration of a new social movement based on neurological diversity*. Sydney: University of Technology, Sydney.

Singer, J. (1999). "Why can't you be normal for once in your life?" From a problem with no name to the emergence of a new category of difference. In M. Corker & S. French (Eds.), *Disability discourse* (pp. 59–67). Buckingham, UK: Open University Press.

Spijkerman, M. P. J., Pots, W. T. M., & Bohlmeijer, E. T. (2016). Effectiveness of online mindfulness-based interventions in improving mental health: A review and meta-analysis of randomised controlled trials. *Clinical Psychology Review, 45*, 102–114. https://doi.org/10.1016/j.cpr.2016.03.009

Sundar, V. (2017). Operationalizing workplace accommodations for individuals with disabilities: A scoping review. *Work, 56*(1), 135–155. https://doi.org/10.3233/WOR-162472

The Center for Universal Design. (1997). *The principles of universal design, version 2.0*. https://projects.ncsu.edu/ncsu/design/cud/about_ud/udprinciples.htm

United Nations Convention on the Rights of Persons with Disabilities. (2006). www.un.org/disabilities/documents/convention/convention_accessible_pdf.pdf

Van Dam, N. T., van Vugt, M. K., Vago, D. R., Schmalzl, L., Saron, C. D., Olendzki, A., . . . Fox, K. C. R. (2018). Mind the hype : A critical evaluation and prescriptive agenda for research on mindfulness and meditation. *Perspectives on Psychological Science, 13*(1), 36–61. https://doi.org/10.1177/1745691617709589

Van Laarhoven, T., Carreon, A., Bonneau, W., & Lagerhausen, A. (2018). Comparing mobile technologies for teaching vocational skills to individuals with autism spectrum disorders and/or intellectual disabilities using universally-designed prompting systems. *Journal of Autism and Developmental Disorders, 48*(7), 2516–2529. https://doi.org/10.1007/s10803-018-3512-2

von Schrader, S., Malzer, V., & Bruyère, S. (2014). Perspectives on disability disclosure: The importance of employer practices and workplace climate. *Employee Responsibilities and Rights Journal, 26*(4), 237–255. https://doi.org/10.1007/s10672-013-9227-9

Watson, E. (2019). The mechanisms underpinning peer support: A literature review. *Journal of Mental Health, 28*(6), 677–688.

Weiss, M., Murray, C., Wasdell, M., Greenfield, B., Giles, L., & Hechtman, L. (2012). A randomized controlled trial of CBT therapy for adults with ADHD with and without medication. *BMC Psychiatry, 12*(1), Article 30. https://doi.org/10.1186/1471-244X-12-30

Weston, L., Hodgekins, J., & Langdon, P. E. (2016). Effectiveness of cognitive behavioural therapy with people who have autistic spectrum disorders: A systematic review and meta-analysis. *Clinical Psychology Review, 49*, 41–54. https://doi.org/10.1016/j.cpr.2016.08.001

Whitby, M. (2018). Composite mapping for evaluation of usability of targeted affordances 1 breaking down barriers to usability of inclusive affordances for neurodiverse populations. In P. Langdon, H. Dong, J. Lazar, & A. Heylighen (Eds.), *9th Cambridge workshop on universal access and assistive technology*. Cambridge: Cambridge University Press.

World Health Organization. (2001). *ICF. International classification of functioning, disability and health*. Washington, DC: Author.

Young, S., Adamo, N., Ásgeirsdóttir, B. B., Branney, P., Beckett, M., Colley, W., . . . Woodhouse, E. (2020). Females with ADHD: An expert consensus statement taking a lifespan approach providing guidance for the identification and treatment of attention-deficit/

hyperactivity disorder in girls and women. *BMC Psychiatry, 20*(1), Article 404. https://doi.org/10.1186/s12888-020-02707-9

Young, S., González, R. A., Fridman, M., Hodgkins, P., Kim, K., & Gudjonsson, G. H. (2018). The economic consequences of attention-deficit hyperactivity disorder in the Scottish prison system. *BMC Psychiatry, 18*, Article 210. https://doi.org/10.1186/s12888-018-1792-x

Zeidan, F., Johnson, S. K., Diamond, B. J., David, Z., & Goolkasian, P. (2010). Mindfulness meditation improves cognition: Evidence of brief mental training. *Consciousness and Cognition, 19*(2), 597–605. https://doi.org/10.1016/j.concog.2010.03.014

12

AUTISM HIRING PROGRAMS AND INTERFACE WITH THE LEGAL AND REGULATORY ENVIRONMENT

Matthew C. Saleh and Michael Bernick[1]

Introduction

In this chapter, we discuss the relationship of the federal legislative and regulatory requirements (e.g., under the Americans with Disabilities Act and Section 503 of the Rehabilitation Act) to autism hiring initiatives and programs, including (a) compliance with disability disclosure and medical inquiry requirements; (b) provision of reasonable accommodations; (c) structuring autism and, more broadly, neurodiversity hiring processes; (d) integrating job coaches, mentorship opportunities, and other support staff in an equitable fashion; and (e) ensuring equality across the employment process, including performance management, advancement, discipline and termination, and benefits eligibility. Our focus reflects the fact that autism hiring initiatives are rapidly expanding and form the majority of the hiring initiatives for adults with developmental differences. Our focus also reflects autism as a proxy for a range of other developmental differences, so lessons learned from autism employment are applicable to other developmental differences.

This chapter does not cover all the potential federal and state laws that might apply to employees and employers within autism hiring initiatives and programs but instead narrows its focus to the federal requirements related to employment nondiscrimination in the workplace, particularly around hiring, accommodating, advancing, and equal access to the benefits and privileges of employment. Examples of laws that are not discussed but may be applicable to employees within autism hiring programs include the Occupational Safety and Health Act of 1970, the Family Medical Leave Act of 1993, and state workers' compensation. While these important employment laws warrant attention from employers, the considerations implicated by those laws should not be significantly different within

DOI: 10.4324/9781003023616-12

autism hiring programs than they are across all workplace contexts. Therefore, this chapter aims to focus on federal legal frameworks under which unique considerations might arise for employers.

Autism hiring programs are becoming increasingly common, especially among larger employers that have outlined neurodiversity as part of their corporate mission and diversity and inclusion efforts (Austin & Pisano, 2017), as well as a growing number of small and medium-sized employers that are discovering the benefits and strengths of hiring neurodiverse employees (Employer Assistance and Resource Network on Disability Inclusion, n.d.).

While a number of employer-side benefits to disability- and neurodiversity-focused hiring practices have been observed in the management literature (Lindsay et al., 2018; Austin & Pisano, 2017), autism hiring programs also give rise to some novel legal considerations in which employers are attempting to go beyond mere compliance with the federal legal and regulatory landscape but must do so in a manner that ensures equality of opportunity across the employment experience under federal laws covering civil rights in employment for people with disabilities. It should be noted that many states also have civil rights laws pertaining to disability discrimination in the workplace that mirror or even exceed federal requirements, so while there may be state-specific considerations, this chapter is focused on federal law.

The objective of this chapter is to set out processes by which employers can meet their goals of increasing neurodiverse talent pools and employees while also satisfying federal legal requirements for nondiscrimination in opportunity across the work experience (including hiring, advancement, and what are termed the "benefits and privileges" of employment) and even applying what they have learned to more traditional hiring practices within the organization to increase organizational adherence to nondiscrimination requirements across the board. Employment activities that are meant to open doors for some applicants who have traditionally had reduced employment opportunities should be carefully implemented and evaluated to ensure that they do not result in differential treatment.

A key theme throughout this chapter will involve the importance of ensuring that neurodiversity programs do not disproportionately prioritize the "front end" of the employment experience (e.g., recruiting, hiring, and on-board training) at the expense of treating employees, once integrated into the organization, as equal participants in the workforce entitled to the accommodations, job development opportunities, and workplace climate that will allow them to carry out fulfilling work on an equal basis with others.

For employers who are considering developing neurodiversity hiring programs – and the industrial and organizational (I/O) psychologists involved in designing and implementing more neurodiversity-inclusive interview processes – there are important legal and regulatory aspects of piloting and maintaining such programs, and there are some important aspects of such programs that warrant specific attention for their interaction with the federal legal landscape around disability employment.

Threshold Legal Considerations for New or Existing Autism Hiring Programs: What Type of Employer Are You?

When starting or maintaining an autism hiring program, one of the first considerations is the characteristics of the employer and the responsibilities that this can entail. For instance, the number of employees that an organization has, its level of resources, and whether there is existing involvement with government contracts can have important implications for legal and regulatory requirements. Examples of why considerations like these will matter include:

- Under the Americans with Disabilities Act of 1990 (ADA), only private employers with fifteen or more employees are covered by the Act (Americans With Disabilities Act, 1990).
- Private employers that have federal government contracts or subcontracts may have specific reporting requirements demonstrating progress towards setting affirmative action goals and progress towards the 7% utilization goal for employing people with disabilities under the Rehabilitation Act, Section 503 regulations (U.S. Office of Federal Contract Compliance Programs [OFCCP], 2014).
- In determining whether an accommodation would constitute an "undue hardship" for an employer under the ADA, courts will consider the overall financial resources at an employer's disposal, as well as the "type of operation" that the employer is engaged in (e.g., geographic location, structure of the workforce, function of the workforce, and administrative or fiscal relationship to the employee (Americans With Disabilities Act, 1990)).

Because of these and other considerations, any employer should be careful to situate their existing legal requirements within their efforts to develop an autism hiring program and should assess generally whether their organization is currently doing a good job of meeting their legal requirements around providing accommodations, ensuring equal opportunity in career development, and providing inclusive workplace policies, practices, and environments. In other words, an autism hiring program is unlikely to serve as a corrective if an employer is not already exhibiting strong organizational practices in disability inclusion overall, both in line with federal legal requirements for the workplace and more generally. While enhanced hiring opportunities can play an important role in creating more opportunities for recruitment, hiring, and retention of people with autism, the success of these hires may entail activities and changes that go beyond baseline legal requirements.

The goal of an autism hiring initiative should be to enhance diversity and inclusion within an organization rather than to offset substandard practices in the hiring process and employment practices more generally. It is important to remember that a targeted program does not exempt an employer from adhering to ADA nondiscrimination and accommodation requirements throughout the rest of their employment and hiring practices. Nondiscrimination requirements under federal law apply to the entire workforce. Along the same lines, one major consideration is whether a targeted program is supplementing the traditional recruitment process and increasing neurodiversity across organizational roles rather than merely steering neurodiverse candidates into a particularized set of jobs (Bernick, 2019).

What Are the Components of the Autism Hiring Program?

Another threshold factor is the type of neurodiversity hiring program the employer is considering, piloting, or implementing. Some prominent examples of neurodiversity programs have included programmatic elements such as (a) replacing traditional job application and interview processes with month-long training opportunities in which job matching with open positions occurs; (b) internship or apprenticeship programs aimed at young people with autism; (c) work experience, job training, and skills-building opportunities within organizations; (d) assigning an organizational "project team" to work with external resources to source, select, onboard, and support new hires; (e) publicly partnering with autism-focused community organizations for job tailoring, matching, and placement; and (f) modifying traditional application and interview procedures based on consultations with key stakeholders (Employer Assistance and Resource Network on Disability Inclusion, n.d.).

Some companies have combined various elements such as these, and in some cases, there is a risk of blurring the line of when a participant in such a program becomes an applicant or an employee entitled to protections under the ADA. To provide one example, participants in a non-employment training opportunity may well become a target of recruitment efforts by the company – in fact, this is often the goal of such training opportunities – and it is important to have procedures in place for ensuring that when this happens, participants in the program are accommodated and evaluated appropriately as required under the ADA's requirements for job applicants (Americans With Disabilities Act, 1990).

The ADA's central nondiscrimination requirement for covered entities prohibits employers from "limiting, segregating, or classifying a job applicant ... in a way that adversely affects the opportunities or status of such applicant or employee because of the[ir] disability" (Americans With Disabilities Act, 1990). Therefore, if training opportunities are meant to be direct conduits to employment, employers should take care to ensure that they are treated as such, and applicants coming from these talent pools should be offered the same opportunities and accommodations as other applicants.

Following this same line of reasoning, an important initial consideration for employers is whether the program is explicitly a hiring program or initiative, as distinct from a work experience program. While many federal legal requirements protect people with disabilities in the workplace generally, it is important to note that for prospective and current employees with autism, there exists an "expanding legal frontier," both as laws such as the ADA are more-specifically applied through regulatory guidance and enforcement to ensure inclusion of neurodiverse employee groups – who have been substantially underrepresented in the workforce even compared with other disability categories – and as employers take steps to affirmatively cultivate, hire, and accommodate more neurodiverse talent pools (Hensel, 2017, p. 74).

Some threshold questions that employers may ask themselves, which may have legal implications, could include: Is the goal of the program to hire more neurodiverse individuals? Does the program use alternative/separate recruitment and application procedures? Are these alternative procedures scalable, and can they help remove barriers to neurodiverse individuals in the traditional hiring process? Does the program focus on filling specific job types or categories? If so, what types of jobs and job characteristics (e.g., entry-level, pay/salary, benefits, hours, tasks, opportunity for advancement)? What processes and strategies for providing accommodations are in place? What steps are being taken outside the program to ensure a workplace culture of understanding and inclusivity?

Human resources, I/O professionals, and in-house legal staff can ask important early-stage questions that will guide the planning process as they balance their affirmative neurodiversity efforts with fairness to other prospective and current employees (including other employees with disabilities who are not seeking employment through the initiative) and still meeting the company's core operational and human resource needs. Embedded within these considerations are questions about whether and how to fairly incorporate a separate recruiting and hiring process, what issues exist with disclosure and confidentiality, and issues with ensuring that the targeted hiring program does not represent an alternative to fair and equitable hiring practices in the organization overall.

Federal Legislative and Regulatory Landscape

In this section, we provide a more categorical overview of the specific federal legislative and regulatory requirements for employers that are considering, preparing, or implementing autism hiring programs. As mentioned above, two federal statutes are most relevant to outlining the employment rights of individuals with Autism in the workplace: the Rehabilitation Act of 1973 (29 U.S.C. § 794 *et seq.*) and the Americans with Disabilities Act of 1990 (ADA; 42 U.S.C. § 12101 *et seq.*), as amended by the Americans with Disabilities Amendments Act of 2008 (ADAAA; Pub. L. 110–325).

The ADA will be most relevant to the present discussions, because it covers all private employers with fifteen or more employees. Title I of the ADA prohibits covered employers from discriminating against qualified individuals on the basis of disability, with respect to applications, hiring, firing, advancement, compensation, training, or the privileges and benefits of employment (Americans with Disabilities Act, 1990). While most neurodiversity hiring programs (branded as such) are currently happening in the private sector, it is worth noting that Rehabilitation Act requirements, which apply to federal-sector employment, are likely to apply to the large number of private organizations that receive government contracts over a certain threshold level. For this reason, considerations pertaining to the Rehabilitation Act (and regulations) are also included in this discussion.

In what follows, we begin with considerations pertaining to structuring the hiring process within, or connected to, an autism hiring program. As noted, one key consideration is whether and how the program develops talent pipelines of potential applicants and ensuring that those applicants are equitably evaluated.

Structuring the Hiring Process

One growing consideration involves acknowledgement of the ways that certain existing interview and hiring processes affect the employment outcomes of individuals with autism. These include such things as normative assumptions regarding the background, behaviors, nonverbal social cues, and self-presentation strategies exhibited by "ideal" candidates that have the effect of weeding out qualified candidates who do not exhibit normatively "neurotypical" physical and social traits, as well as some disadvantageous aspects of the interview environment (e.g., high sensory stimulus load) and design (e.g., day-long, multiperson interview process) itself. The chapter by Saleh, Chang, Bruyère, and Vogus in this volume discusses barriers in the recruitment, selection, and interview processes that might create barriers to becoming employed for individuals with autism and provides examples of ways that recruitment, screening, and hiring practices can be modified to be more inclusive of people with autism.

While this is a relatively evolving area of law (Hensel, 2017), the ADA prohibits employer selection procedures that have a discriminatory impact and may be required to eliminate procedures that disproportionately exclude certain disability types for reasons not related to job qualifications of business necessity (U.S. Equal Employment Opportunity Commission [EEOC], 2007). Even where – or especially where – an employer is engaging in neurodiversity efforts, it is essential that they audit their hiring practices to consider the reasons neurodiverse applicants may not have been successful in the past and consider modifications to those processes that may represent barriers to people with autism being hired.

Many neurodiversity hiring programs focus on specific job paths and roles within organizations, as well as utilizing apprenticeships or internships as a gateway to employment. It is worth noting that the very basis of disparate impact theory in U.S. law is derived from precedent in which promotion decisions for current employees, based on seemingly neutral criteria that were not appropriately tailored to employees' ability to perform the job, led to the *effect* of steering of a protected group into lower-paying work (*Griggs v. Duke Power Co.*, 1971).

This points to the importance of ensuring that neurodiversity hiring programs, even with good intentions, do not result in steering qualified candidates with autism into particular job types, especially job types that may be lower paying, have fewer benefits and job securities, or offer less-desirable working conditions. This is also mirrored by the statutory requirement in the ADA that discrimination against an applicant can include "limiting, segregating, or classifying" a job applicant on the basis of their disability (Americans With Disabilities Act, 1990).

For example, according to the EEOC, compensation discrimination can occur where an employer pays employees with disabilities less than similarly situated employees without disabilities, sets the pay for jobs predominantly held by people with disabilities at a lower level in a manner that can't be effectively rationalized (e.g., through a job evaluation study), or steers employees with disabilities to lower-paid jobs than persons outside the class (U.S. Equal Employment Opportunity Commission [EEOC], 2000). Government attention to the issue of steering has particularly focused on entry-level jobs with different pay or career advancement prospects (see, e.g., U.S. Department of Labor, 2013).

In the spirit of enhancing organizational inclusion while also adhering to federal legal requirements, autism hiring programs should be structured to include aspects of career development, opportunities for promotion, and the availability of "lateral moves" to different job types. Similarly, the construction of recruitment pipelines in autism hiring programs (e.g., through training-as-recruitment efforts or through targeted recruitment and outreach through external partners) should not automatically steer applications to entry-level jobs or particular skill areas if other job openings exist and the applicant has the skills and experience to perform the essential job duties.

Autism hiring programs that operate on baseline assumptions about skill and ability may themselves run afoul of disability nondiscrimination requirements, as one of the original goals of the ADA, for instance, was to address employer "myths" and "unfounded beliefs" about various disabilities (Regulations to Implement the Equal Employment Provisions of the Americans with Disabilities Act, 2012). Even well-intentioned efforts that lean heavily on myths or assumptions about autism in job placement efforts rather than on individualized assessments of candidates' skills and abilities are not in line with the intent of the ADA.

Disclosure and Confidentiality

The issues of disclosure and confidentiality are inextricably linked within affirmative recruitment programs. Often, affirmative hiring programs will seek to *know* that their program is having the desired effect or impact, which can be difficult without directly asking employees to disclose their disability. However, there are limitations to inquiries of this nature placed on employers by federal law, as well as confidentiality requirements that are triggered in cases in which disability or medical information is disclosed.

Therefore, when implementing a successful neurodiversity hiring program, an employer is bound to confront the issue of applicant disability disclosure, both to ensure that they are recruiting from neurodiverse candidate pools and to evaluate the success of their affirmative recruitment and hiring efforts. Title I of the ADA places limitations on the type and use of medical inquiries that are permitted by employers, particularly in the preemployment phase before a conditional offer of employment has been made (42 U.S.C. § 12112(d)(2)), which, for obvious reasons, is an important phase in the development of neurodiversity hiring initiatives (Americans with Disabilities Act, 1990).

Medical inquiries and examinations can constitute a type of discrimination under the ADA (42 U.S.C. § 12112(d)), and the general rule is that such inquiries can only be made after a conditional offer of employment exists if all entering employees in the job category – regardless of disability – are subjected to such an examination and if it is job related and consistent with business necessity (42 U.S.C. § 12112(d)(3)-(4)) (Americans with Disabilities Act, 1990). The standards are more or less the same for organizations who are federal contractors, but to aid in affirmative action, Section 503 of the Rehabilitation Act regulations require contractors to invite applicants to self-identify during the pre- and post-offer phases, using a standardized U.S. Department of Labor (DOL), Office of Federal Contract Compliance Programs (U.S. Office of Federal Contract Compliance Programs [OFCCP], 2016) "invitation to self-identify" form, although this form is optional and some applicants will still choose not to self-identify.

Because of the limitations on medical inquiries, neurodiversity programs will usually rely on voluntary disclosure by applicants. This presents its own set of challenges, as disability self-identification, and voluntary disability disclosure more generally, remains a complex issue for employers and employees alike. Since many neurodiversity hiring programs are affirmatively seeking candidates with disabilities, there may be more openness about disability during the hiring process than is the norm, but it is important that employers and hiring professionals respect candidates' agency in discussing their disability, focus on candidate abilities generally and not on the limitations (real or unreal) caused by their disability, and adhere to ADA unlawful medical inquiry requirements.

Additionally, it must be acknowledged that for prospective and current employees, some known barriers to employee self-identification include a perceived risk of bias in the employment process, limitations on promotion opportunities, unsupportive management, and differential treatment by coworkers and supervisors (von Schrader et al., 2013). As such, simply offering an opportunity to self-disclose may not be enough to attract neurodiverse candidates. Further discussion about self-identification is included in the chapter by Santuzzi and Keating in this volume.

Employers may want to focus on outreaching through community organizations – with access to talent pools and experience navigating employment processes for their clients – to help identify and recommend potential candidates. Developing new partnerships is one way to encourage disclosure without missing the mark on ADA requirements. Collaborations with community service providers (e.g., job placement specialists) have proven to be an effective and feasible means for improving hiring of people with disabilities, but empirical research shows that it is underused by organizations (Phillips et al., 2019).

The issue of applicant and employee confidentiality bears a close relationship with the issue of disclosure discussed earlier. The ADA provides that employers must keep any employee medical information or medical histories that it receives, including such information that is voluntarily disclosed by an employee, in separate medical files and treat all such information as a confidential medical record (42 U.S.C. § 12112(d)(3)(B) & (4)(C)(1994); 29 C.F.R. §1630.14(b)(1)) (Americans with Disabilities Act, 1990; Regulations to Implement the Equal Employment Provisions of the Americans with Disabilities Act, 2012). This includes sharing information regarding an employee's medical or disability history with coworkers, including mentioning that they are providing an employee with a reasonable accommodation (U.S. Equal Employment Opportunity Commission [EEOC], 1997).

Therefore, within autism hiring programs, an employer must maintain the confidentiality of disclosure information except in certain narrowly defined exceptions, such as implementing an agreed-upon accommodation, in the provision of emergency medical treatment by first aid and safety personnel, and to government officials investigating compliance with the ADA (42 U.S.C. § 12112(b)(3)(B)) (Americans With Disabilities Act, 1990). However, it is important not to apply these exceptions too broadly, because while there are some cases in which supervisors may need to know the specific disability so accommodations can be effectively implemented – and in such cases the employer should still check with the employee before sharing information with the supervisor and explain their reason for doing so – there are also many cases in which the supervisor does not need to know the specific disability in order to implement an accommodation (Job Accommodation Network, n.d. [a]).

In many cases, it might be reasonable and/or required for an employer to accommodate in individual with autism by providing or allowing/facilitating interpersonal assistance through coaching or mentoring, which will be necessarily "visible" or observable to other coworkers in the workplace, but there are important steps that can be taken to avoid violations of confidentiality while also helping to facilitate alternative modes of communication that make workplaces more inclusive. One way to facilitate this without unlawful breaches of confidentiality is to provide training and awareness-building opportunities on disability and neurodiversity to employees throughout the organization or in supervisory roles, helping to create an accommodating workplace without violating confidentiality (Hensel, 2017).

Providing Reasonable Accommodations

Some employees and applicants with autism will not need any accommodations at all to thrive in the workplace, and generalizations about the diverse experiences and skills of individuals with autism are cautioned against, especially insofar as they sometimes fall into assumptions about difficulties communicating or socializing in the workplace (Bury et al., 2019). The provision of reasonable accommodations to neurodiverse employees and applicants is likely to be a key feature of any autism hiring program, although the ADA reasonable accommodation requirements apply to all individuals with disabilities regardless of their participation in such a program or initiative (42 U.S.C. § 12112) (Americans with Disabilities Act, 1990).

What constitutes a reasonable accommodation requires an individualized determination and an interactive process of determining what the best accommodation is, and the ADA does not require accommodations that present an undue hardship for employers (29 C.F.R. § 1630.2(o)(3)-(4)) (Regulations to Implement the Equal Employment Provisions of the Americans With Disabilities Act, 2012). Part of the ADA definition of a "qualified" individual is whether they can perform the essential job functions, with or without reasonable accommodation (29 C.F.R. § 1630.2(m) Regulations to Implement the Equal Employment Provisions of the Americans with Disabilities Act, 2012).

A reasonable accommodation is any modification or adjustment to a job, employment practice, or work environment that makes it possible for a qualified individual with a disability to participate in the job application process, perform the essential functions of a job, and/or enjoy benefits and privileges of employment equal to those enjoyed by employees without disabilities (U.S. Equal Employment Opportunity Commission [EEOC], 1992).

The reasonable accommodation requirement is central to the mandate of non-discrimination against people with disabilities. Under the ADA, discrimination includes a failure to make necessary reasonable accommodations to a qualified individual with a disability, absent an "undue hardship" on the organization (29 C.F.R. § 1630.2(o)(4)), including denying opportunities to job applicants and current employees that result from a failure to accommodate (29 C.F.R. § 1630.2(o)(1)(i)-(ii)) (Regulations to Implement the Equal Employment Provisions of the Americans with Disabilities Act, 2012).

The ADA provides the following examples of reasonable accommodations: job restructuring; part-time or modified work hours; reassignment to a vacant position; acquisition or modification of equipment or services; appropriate adjustment or modifications of examinations, training materials, or policies; and provision of qualified readers or interpreters (29 C.F.R. § 1630.2(o)(2)(ii)) (Regulations to Implement the Equal Employment Provisions of the Americans with Disabilities Act, 2012). Examples of accommodations that have been used in neurodiversity initiatives have included things like headphones for employees with noise sensitivity, dimmer rooms for employees with light sensitivity, flexible online and hybrid work opportunities, and messaging apps for those who prefer to communicate nonverbally (Employer Assistance and Resource Network on Disability Inclusion, n.d.).

Additionally, some employees recruited through such a program may require job coaches, mentors, or other support staff to ensure full participation, and some autism hiring programs may even offer increased opportunities/facilitation of this type of support to increase workplace success. Research with providers serving working-age people with autism shows the importance of flexibility and individualization in job structuring and allowing for job coaching and mentor support in the workplace (Seitz & Smith, 2016).

Yet despite general knowledge of ADA requirements among larger employers, providers noted that there is an overall lack of guidance and education about organizational compliance specifically for individuals with autism, where unemployment levels are especially high, and regarding the facilitation of support staff in work settings (Seitz & Smith, 2016). One specific legal challenge involves the fact that U.S. courts have not clearly outlined the types of reasonable accommodations that may be required to increase interpersonal relations between individuals with disabilities and their coworkers and/or supervisors, which can sometimes be a relevant factor in hiring and employment success for neurodiverse individuals. Further discussion about the role of coworkers in creating a climate for neurodiversity inclusion is provided in this volume in the chapter by Longmire and Taylor.

For instance, the 11th federal circuit has held that "[a]n employee's ability to handle reasonably necessary stress and work reasonably well with others are essential functions of any position" (*Williams v. Motorola, Inc.*, 2002, p. 1290). But, as Hensel (2017, 96) notes, "this type of categorical approach is simply inconsistent with the ADA's requirement of an individualized inquiry . . . [c]contrary to conventional wisdom, many jobs exist which do not require refined social skills, even if they may be desirable." Therefore, careful consideration of what the true "essential" features of different job types within an organization may help clarify the types of accommodations that may be appropriate or required under the ADA, within an autism hiring program, as well as accommodations that can help facilitate successful social interactions (whether they are required by law or go "beyond compliance"). Employers should differentiate essential requirements (job duties that an employee must be able to perform, with or without accommodations) from desired attributes (marginal aspects of a job that can be adjusted or removed).

Equitably Integrating Support Staff

A job coach is a person who provides specialized on-site training to an employee with a disability. A job coach's typical role is to provide one-on-one assistance to an employee with a disability as they learn and perform a job, including helping the employee acclimatize to the work environment through individualized coaching tailored to specific individual and disability attributes and driven by the goal of self-sufficiency (Job Accommodation Network, n.d. [b]). Employers with and without neurodiversity hiring initiatives must be prepared to allow job coaches and other types of support roles in the workplace while also carefully ensuring that confidentiality is not broached and ensuring that the presence of such support does not negatively impact workplace experiences and integration for individuals with autism.

Job coaches are specifically mentioned in EEOC ADA guidance about accommodating individuals with intellectual disabilities in the workplace (U.S. Equal Employment Opportunity Commission [EEOC], 2013), and the EEOC has also outlined that "an employer may be required to allow a job coach paid by a public or private social service agency to accompany the employee at the job site as a reasonable accommodation" (U.S. Equal Employment Opportunity Commission [EEOC], 2010). However, as with all accommodation issues, the "reasonableness" of any one accommodation is often highly individuated and fact driven, and the ways that courts have interpreted the difference between temporary versus full-time job coaches has varied (see, e.g., *Miller v. Santa Clara County Library*, 9th Cir., 2001; *Roberts v. Progressive Independence, Inc.*, 10th Cir., 1999). Typically, job coaching that involves training for employees during onboarding or to navigate role change will be covered by the ADA, but the reasonable accommodation requirement does not apply to personal assistance that results in a coach or additional personnel performing essential job functions for the employee with a disability (see, e.g., *Miller v. Santa Clara County Library*, 9th Cir., 2001). For example, in *Sieberns v. Wal-Mart Stores, Inc.* (7th Cir. 1997, p. 1022) the Court noted that, for a clerk/sales associate position that required the employee to flag, stock, and price many types of highly expensive merchandise, to accommodate the plaintiff, a blind individual, "they would have to hire someone else to help perform some duties . . . [t]hat clearly was beyond a reasonable accommodation."

As with many of the conversations throughout this chapter, however, while not necessarily required by law, there is no reason an employer cannot thoughtfully integrate support staff, like job coaches, into their workforce as an accommodation measure and in a manner that goes beyond compliance. Some neurodiversity-focused employers have, in fact, taken the step of internally hiring one or more full-time job coaches to help facilitate training and onboarding efforts as well as continued job success (National Association of Colleges and Employers, 2018).

In one example, the EEOC filed a disability discrimination lawsuit, and later settled, with an employer in the hospitality industry on the basis of failing to reasonably accommodate – and ultimately terminating – a front-desk employee by denying them a state-funded job coach whose role would have been to help the newly onboarded employee master job skills through autism-specific training techniques (*EEOC v. Tarsadia Hotels d.b.a. Comfort Suites*, 2010; see also U.S. Equal Employment Opportunity Commission [EEOC], 2011). The employer initially hired the front-desk clerk in 2008. The employee, an individual with autism, had prior hotel experience in a similar position which earned him a positive recommendation.

The EEOC contended that upon hire, the employee was belittled by his supervisor, denied access to a state-funded job coach, disciplined, and ultimately discharged within four months of hire. The EEOC charged that the employee was not only denied access to his job coach but that the job coach was made to leave the premises even though she requested only to observe the employee working. The job coach would have provided services free of any charge to the hotel. Arbitrarily denying or limiting job coaches as an accommodation – especially where this runs through state vocational rehabilitation funding mechanisms and therefore has little or no cost to the employer – may well lead to a violation of the ADA. At the same time, job coaches can play an important role in onboarding and integration efforts within autism hiring programs, with long-term benefits that outweigh any temporary costs.

Progressive Discipline and Performance Management

Under the ADA, employers can maintain performance standards that apply to individuals with and without disabilities, and this can include the maintenance of job-related and necessary conduct standards, as well as equitably applied discipline for employees who violate those standards (even when the conduct is related to a disability) (U.S. Equal Employment Opportunity Commission [EEOC], 1992; Regulations to Implement the Equal Employment Provisions of the Americans with Disabilities Act, 2012; Americans with Disabilities Act, 1990). As discussed elsewhere, these legal requirements apply equally to all employees, whether or not they are participating in an autism hiring program.

Maintaining performance and conduct standards that comply with the ADA requires consistency in the enforcement of companywide policies (i.e., discipline policies cannot be disproportionately applied to employees with disabilities in a manner that indicates a disparate impact) and must avoid allowing stereotypes about behavior and ability to drive performance evaluations or discipline decisions (U.S. Equal Employment Opportunity Commission [EEOC], 1992). (Further discussion on performance management and career development for employees with autism is provided in the chapter by Hunter and Hunter in this volume.)

Employers who are engaged in autism hiring programs should be prepared to utilize progressive discipline policies, preferably on an organizationwide level rather than specifying unique policies towards individuals hired through a targeted hiring program. Again, this is because it is important to, wherever possible, modernize organizational practices and culture to provide equitable employment practices to all individuals with disabilities within the company. Progressive discipline is a process for providing counseling and interventions where workplace behavior by an employee does not meet communicated performance standards (Heathfield, 2020).

The key principle underlying progressive discipline focuses on replacing punishment with consultation and collaborative efforts to identify opportunities for improvement or compliance with performance standards (Heathfield, 2020). Regarding neurodiversity hiring initiatives, it is important also to reframe organizational policies and practices so that standards of discipline to not disproportionately punish employees with disabilities. One common example is managing absenteeism: employers must be cognizant of whether an employee's disability requires a scheduling or remote-work accommodation that would allow them to perform the essential functions of the job while still being absent from the work setting at times that would otherwise trigger structured attendance-management policies.

Regarding neurodiverse individuals more specifically, it might be important not to arbitrarily impose standards for communication, teamwork, or customer service that rely on normative standards of neurotypical behavior in workplace interactions that are not meaningfully related to job performance or essential functions of the position. Pence and Svyantek (2016) note that termination decisions are often based on the concept of person–organization fit and the ways that social interactions by employees are interpreted as underperformance. (Further discussion about person–organization fit for neurodiverse individuals is provided in the chapter by co-authors Giannantonio and Hurley-Hanson in this volume.)

Within autism hiring programs, such decisions must follow the ADA's legal procedures for reasonable accommodation and assessment of whether the individual is qualified to perform the essential functions of the position; that is to say that any job analysis of organizational fit must be tied to specific characteristics needed to perform the job, must be linked to some type of performance criteria for the essential functions of the position, and must be made on an individualized basis and with consideration of accommodations and modifications that might be needed (Pence & Svyantek, 2016).

Jones and Saundry (2011) note that progressive discipline and performance evaluation frameworks for many employers – especially larger employers in which operational management and human resources (HR) management delegate disciplinary responsibilities – will also entail a focus on intramanagement relations rather than solely focusing on management–labor relations. This is because, at many organizations, the operationalization of disciplinary decision-making often falls on operational managers, while HR managers retain important roles in providing expertise and advice to operational managers about compliance with internal procedures and external legal requirements (Jones & Saundry, 2011).

With regard to autism hiring and employment programs, this points to the need for targeted sensitivity training at both the operational and HR management levels, so that informal, individualized, and flexible decision-making in performance management (that is often the purview of the operational manager) can be supplemented by HR expertise about the technical, regulatory, and more formalized interventions that may be needed in ensuring that the employee is being appropriately assessed, accommodated, and disciplined within the requirements of the ADA.

It is particularly important to ensure synergies across these manager roles, because when responding to and investigating performance or misconduct issues, employers are required under the ADA to take steps to ensure that an employee is receiving the appropriate reasonable accommodations, both to allow their participation in the investigation and also to ensure that the interactive process has been appropriately adhered to in providing accommodations to the employee so that they can meet their essential job functions and the company's performance and conduct standards.

Targeted hiring programs should not limit employer flexibility in administering progressive discipline or lead to increased liability if the company's internal processes were already complying with federal law, and in fact a well-structured autism hiring program might well lead to improvements to these processes that extend companywide to all employees with disabilities, perhaps even increasing adherence to the ADA and decreasing the risk of liability.

Workplace Culture

Research has shown that organizational culture constitutes an integral dimension of employees' willingness to request assistance, guidance, and accommodations from supervisors; the perception of a supportive work environment that values the integration of people with disabilities has been shown to have importance for employees as they pursue workplace accommodations and modifications (Baldridge & Veiga, 2001).

While the ADA's objective is to reduce workplace discrimination, there are potential barriers to workplace integration that exist at the level of organizational culture, for instance, when a company has a culture of treating accommodations as special treatment rather than everyday practices or when an organization is resistant to flexible work responsibilities (or fails to review job requirements at intervals to determine whether job descriptions are necessarily inclusive and refined), flexible scheduling, or shared responsibilities of work tasks (ADA National Network, n.d.).

Research indicates that, at the organizational level, experience with disability alone does not always lead to a better understanding of the ADA or to improved implementation, and staff, supervisors, and executives may need to be educated about what inclusive workplaces look like in practice (through training opportunities, collaborations with disability community organizations, and sharing of success stories from other companies) (Gould et al., 2018). (Further discussion about building a neurodiversity-inclusive workplace across the employment process is presented in the chapter in this volume by Volpone, Avery, and Wayne.)

A content analysis of patterns and trends of litigation in all reported U.S. Appellate Court ADA cases charged under the theory of disparate impact (unintentional discrimination, 1992–2012) found that barriers resulting from workplace culture are a persistent theme in ADA litigation for disparate impact litigation despite not being a type of violation, per se, under the Act, indicating the importance of factors that include attitudes (latent and expressed), company-specific policies and procedures, contractual agreements pertaining to job qualifications and requirements, the materials companies use to hire, train, promote, discipline, and discharge employees (e.g., written and unwritten policies on absenteeism, tardiness, and sick leave; job and position descriptions; and retirement and health care policies); and the tension between legal compliance and maximizing employee potential (Johnston, 2013). While there are not legal requirements for organizations to adjust their cultures, specific organizational practices that contribute to "workplace culture" (for example, treating accommodations as special treatment rather than everyday practices, supervisor and human resources sensitivities and practices) might have legal implications; culture is one of the "gray areas" where an employer may or may not run afoul of the law but where there might be a major impact on the long-term success of efforts to provide opportunities for neurodiverse applicants.

Advancement and Access to Privileges and Benefits of Employment

The ADA prohibits covered employers from discriminating against people with disabilities in the full range of employment-related activities, from recruitment to advancement to pay and benefits (42 U.S.C. § 12112) (Americans with Disabilities Act, 1990). For this reason, employers engaged in autism hiring programs must be careful not to initiate programs that focus only on entry-level roles and offer few opportunities for advancement. The EEOC's Enforcement Guidance on the ADA provides one example in which an employee wrongly denies a screen reader accommodation to an employee with a visual impairment that would allow the individual to perform reading functions at the same speed as their peers without disabilities, thus denying the employee the ability to achieve the same level of performance and hence denying them an equal opportunity to compete for promotions (U.S. Equal Employment Opportunity Commission [EEOC], 2002).

Absent an undue hardship, the EEOC describes this scenario as an ADA violation, both as a failure to accommodate and denying equal opportunity in competing for promotions (U.S. Equal Employment Opportunity Commission [EEOC], 2002). Elsewhere, the U.S. EEOC (2008a) guidance provides the example of a long-term employee in good standing whom coworkers observe talking to himself in a quiet, nonthreatening manner that does not affect their job performance; upon learning that the observed instances stem from a psychiatric disability, a manager nevertheless transfers the employee to a night-shift position where they will work in relative isolation and have fewer opportunities for advancement. The EEOC advises that under these circumstances, the discipline (a transfer that will affect promotion consideration) would constitute a violation of the ADA (U.S. Equal Employment Opportunity Commission [EEOC], 2008a).

Another important factor is that the ADA requires equal opportunity to access the benefits and privileges of employment for employees with disabilities (42 U.S.C. § 12112(a)) (Americans with Disabilities Act, 1990). For example, the ADA reasonable accommodations requirement may include "modifications or adjustments that enable a covered entity's employee with a disability to enjoy equal benefits and privileges of employment as are enjoyed by its other similarly situated employees without disabilities" (29 C.F.R. § 1630.2(o)(1)(i-iii)) (Regulations to Implement the Equal Employment Provisions of the Americans with Disabilities Act, 2012). Benefits and privileges of employment include but are not limited to offerings like employer-sponsored training, services (e.g., employee assistance programs, credit unions, cafeterias, lounges, gymnasiums, auditoriums, transportation, as well as things like parties or other social functions (e.g., retirement and birthday celebrations and company outings) (29 C.F.R. pt. 1630 app. § 1630.9) (Regulations to Implement the Equal Employment Provisions of the Americans with Disabilities Act, 2012).

Benefits of employment will also include common employer-offered examples like life insurance, health insurance, long-term and short-term disability benefits, disability retirement benefits, severance benefits, service retirement benefits, and early-retirement incentives (U.S. Equal Employment Opportunity Commission [EEOC], 2000). Privileges of employment also extends to the facilities that house those offerings. For instance, the duty to accommodate applies to all nonwork facilities provided or maintained by employers for employees, including cafeterias, lounges, auditoriums, company-provided transportation, health and wellness offerings, and counseling services (U.S. Equal Employment Opportunity Commission [EEOC], 2008b). The general takeaway is that employers who are planning, preparing, or currently implementing autism hiring programs must take care to ensure that employees in the program are not excluded from the wide array of offerings that may be considered "benefits and privileges" of employment.

One potential unique issue may involve the provision of increased accommodation and services offerings for autism hiring initiatives. Employees with disabilities who are part of the general workforce at a company may seek access to such accommodations as well, and while the duty to accommodate is an individualized standard with minimum requirements for legal compliance, the ADA reasonable accommodations standard *will* consider available resources and offerings within an organization, as well as the "costs" of such accommodations and financial resources of the organization, which may be altered if the company develops new offerings connected to an autism hiring program.

To provide pertinent examples, if an organization creates new counseling, professional development, and training modules embedded within the organization for participants in autism hiring programs, it is conceivable that employees with disabilities who are not part of that program should be provided access to those offerings as well if they fall under the privileges and benefits of employment or if they constitute an accommodation that did not exist prior to the development of the program and could help an employee – maybe even an employee who had not previously disclosed their disability – perform the essential functions of their position. As such, when developing more robust frameworks for accommodations, professional development, counseling, and flexibility connected to autism hiring programs, employers should be prepared to extend those offerings to employees with disabilities in the general workforce, including those who may not have disclosed their disability until recently (42 U.S.C. § 12111(10)) (Americans with Disabilities Act, 1990). As possible, employers who integrate enhanced accommodations, services, and support offerings connected to autism hiring programs should make those same accommodations available to the rest of their workforce, acknowledging that issues of disclosure and workplace culture may have prevented employees elsewhere in the company from requesting similar accommodations in the past.

Conclusion

Autism hiring programs are becoming increasingly popular, both among larger employers that have outlined neurodiversity as part of their corporate mission and larger diversity and inclusion efforts – including prominent examples like Microsoft, Ford, Ernst & Young (EY), and JPMorgan Chase & Co. – as well as several small and medium-sized employers that are also discovering the benefits and strengths of hiring neurodiverse employees (Employer Assistance and Resource Network on Disability Inclusion, n.d.). A number of employer-side benefits to disability and neurodiversity-focused hiring practices have been observed in the management literature (Lindsay et al., 2018; Austin & Pisano, 2017) and give rise to some novel legal considerations in which employers are attempting to go beyond mere compliance with the federal legal and regulatory landscape but must do so in a manner that nevertheless ensures equality of opportunity across the employment experience under federal laws covering civil rights in employment for people with disabilities.

As more organizations undertake the development of neurodiversity hiring programs, human resources, I/O professionals, and in-house legal staff can ask important threshold questions that will guide the planning process as they balance their affirmative neurodiversity efforts with fairness to other prospective and current employees (including other employees with disabilities who are not seeking employment through the initiative) and while still meeting the company's core operational and human resource needs. Embedded within these considerations are questions about whether and how to fairly incorporate a separate recruiting and hiring process, what issues exist with disclosure and confidentiality, and issues with ensuring that the targeted hiring program does not represent an alternative to fair and equitable hiring practices in the organization overall.

This chapter provided an overview of some of the key legal issues that may underlie a new or existing program focused on increasing neurodiversity within an organization. It is important to remember that a targeted program does not exempt an employer from adhering to ADA nondiscrimination and accommodations requirements throughout the rest of their employment and hiring practices. Employers, with the guidance of I/O professionals, HR leadership, and in-house legal staff, can use the opportunities arising from a new autism hiring program to review their existing practices as an organization more broadly and holistically. The best way to ensure that an autism hiring program will be a success is to make sure organizational culture and practices are already compliant. This sets the foundation for an employer to move beyond compliance through developing new talent pipelines and ensuring equality throughout the employment process.

Note

1. The authors would like the thank Anjuli M. Cargain, Esq. for providing legal expertise and feedback to this chapter.

References

ADA National Network. (n.d.). *Workplace culture and the ADA*. Chicago, IL: Department of Disability and Human Development, ADA National Network, University of Illinois at Chicago. Retrieved from https://adata.org/research_brief/workplace-culture-and-ada

Americans with Disabilities Act of 1990, 42 U.S.C. § 12101 *et seq*. (1990). Retrieved from www.ada.gov/pubs/adastatute08.htm

Austin, R. D., & Pisano, G. P. (2017). Neurodiversity as a competitive advantage. *Harvard Business Review, 95*(3), 96–103.

Baldridge, D. C., & Veiga, J. F. (2001). Toward a greater understanding of the willingness to request an accommodation: Can requesters' beliefs disable the Americans with Disabilities Act? *The Academy of Management Review, 26*(1), 85–99. https://doi.org/10.5465/amr.2001.4011956

Bernick, M. (2019, January 15). Effective autism (neurodiversity) employment: A legal perspective. *Forbes*. Retrieved from www.forbes.com/sites/michaelbernick/2019/01/15/effective-autism-neurodiversity-employment-a-legal-perspective/?sh=741018cd76c1

Bury, S. M., Hedley, D., Uljarević, M., Dissanayake, C., & Gal, E. (2019). If you've employed one person with autism: An individual difference approach to the autism advantage at work. *Autism, 23*(6), 1607–1608.

Employer Assistance and Resource Network on Disability Inclusion. (n.d.). *Neurodiversity hiring initiatives and partnerships*. Retrieved from https://askearn.org/topics/neurodiversity-in-the-workplace/neurodiversity-hiring-initiatives-partnerships/

Gould, R., Harris, S. P., & Caldwell, K. (2018). *Research brief: Workplace culture and the ADA*. Chicago, IL: Department of Disability and Human Development, ADA National Network, University of Illinois at Chicago. Retrieved from https://adata.org/research_brief/research-brief-workplace-culture-and-ada

Griggs v. Duke Power Company. (1971). 401 U.S. 424.

Heathfield, S. M. (2020, August 2). Progressive discipline in the workplace. *The Balance Careers*. Retrieved from www.thebalancecareers.com/what-progressive-discipline-1918092

Hensel, W. F. (2017). People with autism spectrum disorder in the workplace: An expanding legal frontier. *Harvard Civil Rights-Civil Liberties Law Review, 52*(1), 73–102.

Job Accommodation Network. (n.d.-a). Confidentiality of medical information under the ADA. *Consultants' Corner, 11*(1). Retrieved from https://askjan.org/publications/consultants-corner/vol11iss01.cfm

Job Accommodation Network. (n.d.-b). *Job coaches*. Retrieved from https://askjan.org/topics/Job-Coaches.cfm

Johnston, S. P. (2013). *Unequal treatment or uneven consequence: A content analysis of Americans with Disabilities Act Title I disparate impact cases from 1992–2012* (ProQuest Dissertations Publishing. 3595112). The University of Iowa. Retrieved from https://search.proquest.com/docview/1443861344?pq-origsite=gscholar&fromopenview=true

Jones, C., & Saundry, R. (2011). The practice of discipline: Evaluating the roles and relationship between managers and HR professionals. *Human Resource Management Journal, 22*(2), 252–266. https://doi.org/10.1111/j.1748-8583.2011.00175.x

Lindsay, S., Cagliostro, E., Albarico, M., Mortaji, N., & Karon, L. (2018). A systematic review of the benefits of hiring people with disabilities. *Journal of Occupational Rehabilitation, 28*(4), 634–655.

Miller v. Santa Clara County Library, 2001 U.S. App. LEXIS 26639, 9th Cir. 2001.

National Association of Colleges and Employers. (2018, September 23). *Considerations for starting a neurodiverse hiring program*. Retrieved from www.naceweb.org/diversity-equity-and-inclusion/best-practices/considerations-for-starting-a-neurodiverse-hiring-program/

Pence, S., & Svyantek, D. J. (2016). Person-organization fit and autism in the workplace. *Journal of Business Management, 22*(1), 117–133. https://doi.org/10.6347/JBM.201601_22(1).0007

Phillips, K. G., Houtenville, A. J., O'Neill, J., & Katz, E. (2019). The effectiveness of employer practices to recruit, hire, and retain employees with disabilities: Supervisor perspectives. *Journal of Vocational Rehabilitation, 51*(3), 339–353. https://doi.org/10.3233/JVR-191050

Regulations to Implement the Equal Employment Provisions of the Americans with Disabilities Act, 2012 29 C.F.R. app., pt. 1630. (2012). Retrieved from www.govinfo.gov/app/details/CFR-2012-title29-vol4/CFR-2012-title29-vol4-part1630-app-id989

Rehabilitation Act of 1973, 87 Stat. 355, 29 U.S.C. Sec 794 *et seq.*

Roberts v. Progressive Independence, Inc., 183 F.3d 1215, 10th Cir. 1999.

Seitz, S. R., & Smith, S. A. (2016). Working toward neurodiversity: How organizations and leaders can accommodate for Autism Spectrum Disorder. *Journal of Business Management, 22*(1), 135–152. https://doi.org/10.6347/JBM.201601_22(1).0008

Sieberns v. Wal-Mart Stores, Inc., 125 F.3d 1019, 7th Cir. 1997.

U.S. Department of Labor. (2013, November 4). *News release: G&K services Co. settles claims of pay and hiring discrimination with the U.S. Labor Department*. Retrieved from www.dol.gov/newsroom/releases/ofccp/ofccp20131104

U.S. Equal Employment Opportunity Commission. (1992). *A technical assistance manual on the employment provisions (Title I) of the Americans with Disabilities Act*. Washington, DC: EEOC.

U.S. Equal Employment Opportunity Commission. (1997, March 25). *Enforcement guidance on the Americans with Disabilities Act and psychiatric disabilities* (No. 915.002). Washington, DC: EEOC.

U.S. Equal Employment Opportunity Commission. (2000). *EEOC compliance manual.* Washington, DC: EEOC. Retrieved from www.eeoc.gov/laws/guidance/section-10-compensation-discrimination

U.S. Equal Employment Opportunity Commission. (2002). *Enforcement guidance on reasonable accommodation and undue hardship under the ADA.* Washington, DC: EEOC. Retrieved from www.eeoc.gov/laws/guidance/enforcement-guidance-reasonable-accommodation-and-undue-hardship-under-ada

U.S. Equal Employment Opportunity Commission. (2007). *Employment tests and selection procedures.* Washington, DC: EEOC. Retrieved from www.eeoc.gov/laws/guidance/employment-tests-and-selection-procedures

U.S. Equal Employment Opportunity Commission. (2008a). *Applying performance and conduct standards to employees with disabilities.* Washington, DC: EEOC. Retrieved from www.eeoc.gov/laws/guidance/applying-performance-and-conduct-standards-employees-disabilities

U.S. Equal Employment Opportunity Commission. (2008b). *The ADA: Your responsibilities as an employer.* Washington, DC: EEOC. Retrieved from www.eeoc.gov/publications/ada-your-responsibilities-employer

U.S. Equal Employment Opportunity Commission. (2010, September 16). *EEOC sues comfort suites for disability discrimination.* Washington, DC: EEOC. Retrieved from www.eeoc.gov/newsroom/eeoc-sues-comfort-suites-disability-discrimination

U.S. Equal Employment Opportunity Commission v. Tarsadia Hotels dba Comfort Suites. (2010). Case No. 10-CV-1921-DMS-BGS). Filed in in U.S. District Court for the Southern District of California.

U.S. Equal Employment Opportunity Commission, Department of Labor. (2011, Nov. 16). Comfort Suites to pay $132,500 for disability discrimination against clerk with Autism. Retrieved from www.eeoc.gov/es/node/21915

U.S. Equal Employment Opportunity Commission, Department of Labor. (2013). *Questions & answers about persons with intellectual disabilities in the workplace and the Americans with Disabilities Act (ADA).* Retrieved from www.eeoc.gov/laws/guidance/persons-intellectual-disabilities-workplace-and-ada

U.S. Office of Federal Contract Compliance Programs, Department of Labor. (2014). *Section 503 regulations frequently asked questions.* Retrieved from www.dol.gov/agencies/ofccp/faqs/section-503

U.S. Office of Federal Contract Compliance Programs, Department of Labor. (2016). *The ADA Amendments Act of 2008: Frequently asked questions.* Retrieved from www.dol.gov/agencies/ofccp/faqs/americans-with-disabilities-act-amendments

von Schrader, S., Malzer, V., & Bruyère, S. M. (2013). Perspectives on disability disclosure: The importance of employer practices and workplace climate. *Employee Responsibilities and Rights Journal, 26*(4), 237–255. https://doi.org/10.1007/s10672-013-9227-9

Williams v. Motorola, Inc., 303 F.3d 1284, 1290 (11th Cir. 2002).

13

IMPLICATIONS AND NEEDED NEXT STEPS

Adrienne Colella and Susanne M. Bruyère

As has been made clear in every chapter in this book, the topic of neurodiversity in organizations is quite new outside of the education, advocacy, and supported employment realms. The I/O psychology literature has had relatively little to say about this topic in terms of understanding the experiences of neurodivergent people at work or of addressing how organizations can best operate to create an inclusive environment for this population, which has a record of vast employment inequities in terms of hiring, compensation, meaningful employment, and promotion within one's field. Yet the field has provided a great deal of knowledge about workplace discrimination (c.f., Colella et al., 2017) and diversity and inclusion (c.f., Roberson et al., 2017); however, this work to date has not extended to a conversation about how this research and knowledge may apply to fostering neurodiversity and a neurodiverse workforce. This is despite some organizations taking a well-publicized, proactive approach to the hiring and inclusion of neurodivergent individuals and statistics demonstrating that the population of people diagnosed as neurodivergent is growing. Thus, the chapters in this book provide an excellent topic for a SIOP Frontiers volume in that they all address some aspect of the organizational experience (e.g., recruiting, selection, leadership) and the legal and cultural landscape that can lead to new I/O research on this very important issue that integrates science and practice. Our aim for this volume was to bring the topic of neurodiversity into the realm of I/O psychology research. To that end, we will close this volume by noting and discussing some fertile avenues for future research and important questions that are woven through the chapters in this volume. Each chapter in this volume provides a great deal of material for furthering research in this area. Our discussion is divided into four areas addressing some general issues which cut across chapters: generalizing from research on other traditionally disadvantaged groups to neurodivergent people, reconsidering the role of social skill in

DOI: 10.4324/9781003023616-13

the assessment of job applicants and employees, borrowing from other disciplines and practices, and focusing on the role of leaders and coworkers in the inclusion of neurodivergent individuals. We then also discuss the implications of this work in the context of the rapidly changing workplace. However, before moving on to next steps, we strongly encourage that research on neurodiversity in the workplace include neurodivergent individuals in all aspects of the research process, from problem identification, through analysis of the results, and dissemination to the intended stakeholders. Only by so doing, will we truly be as useful as possible in contributing to improving employment outcomes for neurodivergent individuals.

Generalizing from Research on Other Traditionally Disadvantaged Groups – Disability, Sex, Race – to Neurodivergent People

Neurodivergent individuals are rarely considered specifically in organizations' diversity, equity, and inclusion statements and policies (see Volpone et al. Chapter 2), and if they are, it is often under the category of people with disabilities. As mentioned frequently throughout these chapters (e.g., Doyle, Chapter 11), the neurodiversity movement does not consider neurodivergent conditions (e.g., autism) disabilities but rather considers differences in cognitive function a normal dimension of diversity (Doyle, 2020; Kapp et al., 2013; Krzeminska et al., 2019; Singer, 1999). The movement eschews the medical model of neurodiversity and treats neurodiversity as a source of positive self-identity rather than a deficit (Armstrong, 2015; Grant, 2009; Kapp et al., 2013; Mellifont, 2019). On the other hand, from a legal perspective, neurodivergent conditions (e.g., autism, ADHD, etc.) are covered under the Americans with Disabilities Act (see Saleh & Bernick, Chapter 12) and thus are accorded the same protections as those with disabilities who qualify under the ADA. From a psychological medical perspective, according to the DSM-5 (American Psychiatric Association, 2013), most neurodivergent conditions are treated as neurological disorders or developmental disabilities. Despite this classification, there is still a great deal of ambiguity over whether neurodivergent conditions should be treated as mental illnesses (Emens, 2005; O'Reilly et al., 2015).

This issue goes beyond a labeling issue because it has implications for what types of challenges and barriers neurodivergent individuals may face in the workplace compared to other disadvantaged groups. Several chapters in this volume discuss how social processes or practices that may benefit other groups may be problematic for neurodivergent individuals. Santuzzi and Keating (Chapter 5) point out that neurodivergent individuals may have specific difficulties in disclosing their condition due to communication challenges. Bury et al. (Chapter 10) discuss how well-being programs developed for other groups of employees may not be successful for neurodivergent employees.

There are also conceptual reasons one may question whether research and theory developed for other groups may generalize to neurodivergent people. For example, in a recent conceptual paper on the barriers facing people with mental illnesses in the workplace, Colella and Santuzzi (in press) did not treat neurological and developmental conditions as a category of mental illness because (among other reasons) the extent and content of stigmatization is likely to differ. While we know quite a bit about the content of stereotypes held toward women, African Americans, those with mental illness, and other groups, we know significantly less about the stereotypes held about people with autism. One recent study (Wood & Freeth, 2016) found that 8 out of the 10 most common stereotypes held toward autistic people were negative (poor communication skills, introverted/withdrawn, poor social skills, difficult personality, poor emotional intelligence, awkward, obsessive, low intelligence), and 2 were positive (special abilities and high intelligence). However, the stereotypes held about people with general disabilities were more negative than those held toward Autistic people. Whereas the negative stereotypes towards autistic people focused mainly on traits likely to lead to social avoidance and exclusion, those associated with disability mainly focused on incompetence and helplessness (e.g., dependent, incompetent, lazy, homeless, inferior, weak, and passive). These differing sets of stereotypes are quite likely to lead to different sets of barriers for these two groups. It is also interesting to note that stereotypes of Autistic individuals contain opposing traits, i.e. both high and low intelligence (Wood & Freeth, 2016). This is not surprising because as recently as the 1990s, Autistic people were believed to be on average of low intelligence (Skuse, 2018). However, more recent research has revealed that most Autistic individuals possess average verbal and nonverbal intelligence and that more than two-thirds of newly diagnosed individuals have intelligence quotients in the normal range (Skuse, 2018; Wingate et al., 2012). Furthermore, due to the relatively recent neurodiversity movement and a flux of media (e.g., Temple Grandin, *The Good Doctor*, *Love on the Spectrum*, *Atypical*) showing autistic people in a more realistic light, stereotypes may become more malleable over time.

Another reason it is difficult to generalize from research on other groups to a neurodivergent population is that there is a great deal of variance in how people with neurological conditions present themselves. Thus, while some individuals may have a unique identity as a neurodivergent person, neurotypical individuals may not experience neurodivergent individuals as one particular group. In Chapter 1, we defined neurodiversity as "the diversity of ways in which human brains think, learn, relate to others and interpret the world" (Honeybourne, 2020). Neurodivergent conditions include a variety of diagnoses such as dyslexia, attention deficit hyperactivity disorder, and autism spectrum disorder, among others. Neurological conditions are invisible to others unless they are disclosed or they result in behavior which violates neurotypical norms. This behavior, if present, can vary a great deal in severity and content from one neurodivergent individual to another (see Condo, 2020). For example, the core symptoms of autism are the social and communication challenges and repetitive and restrictive behaviors (Autism Speaks, 2021). Social and communication challenges can include but are not limited to recognizing emotions and intentions in others, difficulties in speech, recognizing one's own emotions, seeking emotional comfort from others, feeling overwhelmed in social situations, and taking turns in conversation. An Autistic person may exhibit none of these symptoms or behaviors, whereas another may exhibit all of them and to a severe extent. Clearly, these two individuals will have different experiences at work and different interactions with their colleagues. Autism and other neurological conditions fall on a spectrum (Patton, 2019; Rothstein, 2012), unlike other group identities. Furthermore, there is evidence that neurological conditions may covary with other behavioral and mental issues such as depression and anxiety (Bury, Spoor, Hayward & Hedley, Chapter 10), further complicating the situation. Thus, future research needs to take this complexity into account.

Finally, since neurological conditions can lead to behavior that goes against neurotypical norms and scripts, future research needs to consider the impact of that behavior on the reactions to and experiences of the person in question rather than just considering that one has been labeled or diagnosed as neurodivergent. Much has been written on what happens when women behave in a manner that is incongruent with traditional sex-role stereotypes (e.g., Amanatullah & Tinsley, 2013; Eagly & Karau, 2002) and the ensuing backlash that can occur. It would seem that this type of framework would be useful for examining the treatment of neurodivergent individuals at work. However, we know a lot more about sex-role stereotypes and scripts for how men and women are expected to behave than we do about neurotypical norms for interaction in the workplace, and these norms can vary from one environment to another (Longmire et al., 2021). In Chapter 2, Volpone, Avery, and Wayne get at this indirectly by examining how an organization's climates for diversity, inclusion, and justice (which would encompass norms for relationships and interactions among organizational members) can influence the treatment and specifically the inclusion of neurodivergent individuals. Other authors in this volume also addressed the notion of person–organization fit, which is usually conceptualized as fit in terms of values; however, the fit between one's behavior and local norms for behavior would also be relevant.

Reconsidering the Role of Social Skill in the Assessment of Job Applicants and Employees

One theme that ran through almost every chapter in this volume is that there may be an overreliance on the assessment of social skills in evaluating job applicants and incumbents, which could lead to adverse impact against those with neurological conditions, particularly when those social skills are not related to job performance. Volpone et al. (Chapter 2), Giannantonio and Hurley-Hanson (Chapter 3), and Saleh, Chang, Bruyère, and Vogus (Chapter 4) all point out how this is particularly problematic in the interview situation and discuss how organizations that are proactive in creating a neurodiverse workforce employ alternatives to the interview when hiring. Seitz (Chapter 6) points out that social skill, such as self-promotion, can influence the relationship one builds with his or her supervisor, and that may disadvantage neurodivergent individuals who do have relationship or communication challenges. Volpone et al. (Chapter 2) also discuss how lack of self-promotion may adversely impact the advancement opportunities of neurodivergent employees. Giannantonio and Hurley-Hansen (Chapter 3) also point out how differences in one's ability to market oneself may disadvantage neurodivergent individuals during recruitment or that using terms in job descriptions such as "team player" or "good communication skills" may discourage neurodivergent people from applying for a job.

A major problem with overcoming the overreliance on social skill in assessment is that often, the influence of social skill on evaluations, whether the assessments are used to hire or promote, are covert and not explicit (Johnson, 2001; Srivastava & Shree, 2019; Van Scotter & Motowidlo, 2000). Thus, organizations cannot just decide not to use assessments of social skills, as would be the case with deciding not to use cognitive ability tests, because they result in adverse impact. Research clearly needs to be done which views the potentially contaminating effects of social skill judgements on evaluations as a form of adverse impact against those with conditions which may impact social skills. This would include analyzing jobs in terms of the extent to which various social skills are a necessary requirement (see Chapter 12 by Saleh & Bernick), comparing the differential validity of various assessment methods for those who are neurotypical and those who are neuroatypical, and, finally, developing alternative assessment methods and measures which do not discriminate based on social skill. All of these issues are fertile grounds for research by I/O psychologists.

In addition to social skills unfairly influencing the personnel evaluations of neurodivergent individuals, social skill challenges can negatively impact actual, in-role job performance. One way this can happen is through creating stress as one tries to deal with situations which neurotypical people would not usually find stressful. Bury et al. (Chapter 10) adapt the job demands-resources (JD-R) theory (Bakker & Demerouti, 2017; Schaufeli & Taris, 2014) to demonstrate how neurodivergent employees may experience more stress, less well-being, and impacted performance compared to others because they experience more job and personal demands (sensory sensitivity, interpersonal challenges) and fewer job and personal resources to meet those demands. Longmire and Taylor (Chapter 7) discuss how challenges and stress from interpersonal interactions with coworkers can influence performance in a variety of ways. Hunter and Hunter (Chapter 9) liken the concept of extra-role work behavior to the hidden curricula in educational settings and borrow from the educational literature to illustrate why those who are neurodivergent may be challenged by this part of their total performance unless otherwise accommodated.

The issue of how symptomology is related to actual performance needs much more study, along with those organizational policies, practices, and accommodations that may ameliorate any negative effects. This would be in conjunction with any practices aimed at creating an inclusive environment for neurodivergent employees (cf. Volpone et al. Chapter 2). In other words, in addition to barriers to inclusion and fair treatment, we must also be concerned with barriers to optimal performance so that organizations can fully benefit from the talents of their neurodivergent employees and those employees can fully benefit from working to their full potential. Considering the issue of how certain social and communication challenges may influence performance can lead to an expansion of how we think about accommodation for neurodivergent conditions (see Patton, Chapter 8). Most suggested accommodations for neurodivergent individuals focus on accommodations to address sensory challenges, such as alternative lighting, sound machines, and periodic rest breaks (see The Job Accommodation Network (n.d.) for an extensive list). Many other suggested accommodations involve assisted employment practices (e.g., job coaches, mentors) or teleworking. There is very little discussion about the role that coworkers and supervisors may play in providing reasonable accommodation. We say more about this later in this chapter.

Borrowing From Other Disciplines and Practices

The inclusion of neurodivergent people in contexts other than work has received more in-depth attention in other fields than ours. Borrowing theory and practice from these fields to apply in a work context can move the field forward not only on the topic of neurodiversity but in the general area of diversity, equity, and inclusion for all. Two chapters in this volume borrowed heavily from those literatures and practices to make suggestions on what organizations could specifically do to be more inclusive and supportive of neurodivergent individuals. Hunter and Hunter (Chapter 9) provide an illustrative example of how the performance management processes can be adapted based on applied behavior analysis, which "focuses on solving problems of social importance using the principles and procedures of behavior analysis" (Fisher et al., 2013, p. 3). An example of one prescription that runs through this work suggests that there is a need for clarity and specificity in goal setting, feedback, and performance–outcome linkages.

Boyle (Chapter 11) discusses universal design, which is the design of an environment, product, or service so that it can be accessed, understood and used to the greatest extent possible by all people regardless of their age, size, ability, or disability. The universal design movement stems from the field of architecture and the barrier-free disability movement and has become important in educational literature and practice (McGuire et al., 2006). Despite the popularity of universal design in the design of physical environments and pedological methodology, the concept is not addressed in the field of I/O psychology. Doyle provides suggestions for how the seven principles of universal design (Goldsmith, 2007; Rickerson, 2009) can be integrated into several personnel activities such as hiring, performance review, and training, thus providing a framework for future research in this area.

Finally, throughout the chapters in this volume, case studies and examples are provided from companies that are proactively encouraging neurodiversity and from assisted-employment programs. However, these practices have not been addressed in the I/O literature from either an organizational-level conceptual perspective or from an evaluation research perspective. The following are several questions which would benefit from attention from the field of I/O psychology.

To what extent will certain practices developed in one company generalize to others? The companies that are proactive in considering neurodiversity (e.g., SAP, JPMorgan Chase, Ernst & Young, Microsoft, DXC Technology) tend to be clustered in the technology, financial, and professional services industries. Will these programs generalize to other industries and organizations that are smaller in size? What motivates certain companies to proactively encourage neurodiversity inclusion, and how can we motivate other companies to do so?

Another important question concerns the criteria we should we be considering to assess the success of neurodiversity practices. Saleh and Bernick (Chapter 12) warn about only focusing on entry criteria (e.g., number of people hired) and to consider what happens over the course of neurodivergent individuals' careers. Very little research exists on issues such as compensation inequities, leadership development (see Seitz, Chapter 6), or even performance management (see Hunter & Hunter, Chapter 9). This is particularly important on the issue of disclosing one's neurodivergent condition (see Santuzzi, Chapter 5) at work. Research on this topic often only considers short-term or self-report outcomes and rarely examines long term consequences of disclosing or not disclosing one's condition.

Focusing on the Role of Leaders and Coworkers in the Inclusion of Neurodivergent Individuals

The neurodiversity movement often criticizes practices that serve to extinguish behavioral differences between neurodivergent and neurotypical individuals (Kapp et al., 2013). Yet many practices aimed at creating a more positive environment for neurodivergent persons put the onus on the individual to change rather than changing the practice or the behavior of others, such as training neurodivergent people to take interviews rather than finding a replacement for interviews. It was evident from Seitz's chapter on leadership and Longmire and Taylor's chapter on relationships with coworkers that the people working with neurodivergent individuals play a very important part in the success of any inclusion effort. Yet there is very little research on how the behavior of coworkers and leaders influences neurodivergent individuals and what specific policies and practices can be put into place so that their behavior enables the success of their neurodivergent colleagues.

Seitz (Chapter 6) provides a very interesting conceptual framework for answering the question of how leaders' behavior influences the inclusion of neurodivergent employees. She reexamines the efficacy of different types of leadership in terms of what effect it may have on their relationships with neurodivergent individuals. Research along these lines moves away from solely focusing on the challenges facing neurodivergent individuals because of their condition to examine interpersonal interactions as an interaction between various individuals, where both persons' behavior plays a role in the social dynamic. Ironically, neurotypical people also vary to a great extent in which they are empathetic, able to read social situations, and communicate effectively (e.g., see the literature on emotional intelligence; Salovey & Mayer, 1990). Neurotypical people also vary a great deal in the extent to which they are able to function according to cultural scripts different from their own (see literature on cultural intelligence; Earley & Mosakowski, 2004; Triandis, 2006). Thus, some coworkers and supervisors are going to be better equipped to be empathetic and create meaningful relationships with those who are different from them, including those who are neurodivergent. Perhaps training all employees in skills associated with emotional intelligence and cultural intelligence would have the benefit of creating a more inclusive environment for those who are neurodivergent, as well as many other benefits to all involved. Along these lines, Longmire and Taylor recommend empathy training as a practice to create more inclusive environments.

Woven throughout other chapters in this volume are other suggestions on the training and behavioral guidance to be given to coworkers and supervisors (see Volpone et al., Chapter 2, for a discussion of climate). One particular recommendation given by both Hunter and Hunter (Chapter 9) and Doyle (Chapter 11) is the need to provide clear and concise feedback. Hunter and Hunter came to this recommendation through an applied behavioral analysis framework, and Doyle derived this suggestion from a universal design framework. What if employees were taught the principles of universal design and how to apply them in everyday activities and communication?

It would also be useful to examine how neurotypical individuals can learn from neurodivergent individuals – a topic which is rarely addressed in the literature. The recommendations given focusing on social skill training and the application of universal design principles to everyday interactions would create employee skill sets which would help maintain a climate of inclusion as well as have interpersonal benefits for the employees themselves. This expands the issue of coworker training from just "awareness training" to developing skill sets that allow them to effectively function in a neurodiverse environment. Thus, a neurodiverse environment can create the need for development on the part of everyone as well as expose neurotypical employees to new ways of thinking. We know of no research that examines these issues; however, it is a fruitful area for future research.

Neurodiversity Workplace Inclusion and the Future Workplace

Several most significant events have occurred over the past months during which this SIOP Frontiers volume was being developed, events that will likely change the nature of the workplace and the workforce indelibly. These events include the pandemic and its resultant impact on forced remote work and also on the mental health of the American people and the increasing tension around social justice and diversity, equity, and inclusion issues. We would be remiss if we didn't close this volume with some due reference to the relevance of these significant events and trends and the implications for the workplace neurodiversity inclusion focus that we have been discussing.

During the most recent recession, commonly called the Great Recession, the effects of the economic downturn were disproportionately felt by working-age people with disabilities, including a steeper decline in employment and higher increases in poverty rates than for people without disabilities (Livermore & Honeycutt, 2015). In the labor market generally, people with disabilities are more likely to experience precarious employment circumstances, less likely to report having job security, and are often the last workers to be hired and first to be fired (Sheldon, 2009; Kaye, 2010). Research shows that business cycles amplify negative employment trends for people with disabilities, who are often "the first to be laid off in a recession and the last to be hired when conditions improve" (Kruse & Schur, 2003, p. 31; Kaye, 2010).

These historical trends were no less true in the economic downturn starting in March 2020 imposed by the pandemic. The Society for Human Resource Management (SHRM) reported that approximately 1 million U.S. workers with disabilities lost their jobs; citing the U.S. Bureau of Labor Statistics, this amounted to 1 in 5 workers, compared with 1 in 7 in the general U.S. population (Smith, 2020). Since people with disabilities are often disproportionately engaged in short-term seasonal or part-time employment, in such jobs as restaurants and hospitality, they were also significantly impacted by the lay-offs occurring in these industries. In addition, individuals with disabilities with the intersectional identities of being female and/or being racial/ethnic minorities experience even greater socioeconomic disparities, even preceding the pandemic. The intersectionality of poverty, disabilities, and multiple minoritized identities (e.g., gender, race, and ethnicity) is well documented (McAlpine & Alang, 2021). For example, the poverty rates for white Americans without a disability from 2021 U.S. Census data is 9%, while the poverty rate for white Americans is 24%, and for Black Americans with a disability, 36% (Erickson, 2021). Since a disproportionate number of participants in the autism-at-work programs seem to still be white, male, and college educated, these statistics highlight the need to address the employment needs of Autistic women and ethnic-racial minorities, a need that companies are already increasingly aware of (Molko, 2021).

Despite these statistics about the disproportionate negative impact of the pandemic on the socioeconomic status of Americans with disabilities, some positive effects were identified for neurodiverse individuals who were seeking employment or employed during this time. Although we do not have specific data about the employment rates for neurodiverse people, anecdotal reporting by companies with autism-at-work programs demonstrates ingenuity in continuing programs for new recruits despite needed health risk mitigation requirements. Microsoft, for example, went from its already-existing four-day in-person interviews and screening processes for its Autism at Work Program to an online interview process using *Minecraft*. The Microsoft Inclusive Hiring team, responding to the prompt of the COVID-19 pandemic and the need to mitigate the health risks of in-person activities, designed a set of online challenges that can be utilized by the groups of Autistic job seekers selected by Microsoft to be participants in the program; this approach afford participants an opportunity to demonstrate their skills in competency areas such as teamwork, creative problem solving, leadership, and communication (Minecraft, 2021). This approach reportedly also addresses some of the difficulties that Autistic people have faced in the traditional interview process, as discussed by Saleh et al. in this volume (Chapter 3).

Other potential benefits introduced by the pandemic and the need for many workers to work remotely for these extended periods of time now were also reportedly experienced by Autistic individuals. Many people with disabilities, including neurodiverse or Autistic individuals, were requesting remote work prior to the pandemic but finding employers previously hesitant to provide it as an accommodation (Lashbrook, 2021). Since workplaces can be difficult to navigate for some individuals with autism due to environmental sensitivities (e.g., heat, light, smells, sounds, etc.), and social anxiety, the ability to work remotely has been reportedly helpful (Ardil, 2020; Samuel, 2021). Because remote work appears to be an increasingly possible future alternative for many people in the longer term, as the pandemic continues and we learn about the benefits of this alternative, this may be a desired possible future choice for neurodivergent individuals who find being in the workplace difficult. Research will be needed to study the impact and possible benefits of these workplace and workforce alternatives for neurodivergent individuals, and we may learn from this research about transferable benefits for the general U.S. workforce in this process.

Conclusion

Our hope is that this SIOP Frontiers volume will spark much-needed research on the area of neurodiversity in organizations. As is evident from the volume's chapters, our field has not been active in conducting research in this area despite the natural association of this issue with well-studied topics such as diversity, inclusion, and equity issues, employee well-being, performance management issues, leadership, employment law, and employee assessment and recruiting issues. While creating an understanding of how organizations can create more inclusive neurodiverse environments, research on this topic also expands our thinking about some more traditional lines of research such as leadership and brings in relevant thought typically outside the area of I/O psychology, such as universal design. Furthermore, to really understand the issue of neurodiversity in organizations, it takes a multidisciplinary effort. This is evidenced by the diversity of our authors' backgrounds, which range from traditional I/O psychology, clinical psychology, organizational behavior, law, political science, and rehabilitation psychology to founding a social enterprise focused on the rights of neurominorities. We thank all of our authors for helping to create such an important volume.

References

Amanatullah, E. T., & Tinsley, C. H. (2013). Punishing female negotiators for asserting too much . . . or not enough: Exploring why advocacy moderates backlash against assertive female negotiators. *Organizational Behavior and Human Decision Processes, 120*(1), 110–122.

American Psychiatric Association. (2013). *Diagnostic and statistical manual of mental disorders* (5th ed.). Washington, DC: Author.

Ardill, L. (2020, September 4). Working from home: An autistic person's perspective. *Siliconrepublic*. Retrieved from www.siliconrepublic.com/people/working-from-home-autistic-perspective

Armstrong, T. (2015). The myth of the normal brain: Embracing neurodiversity. *AMA Journal of Ethics, 17*(4), 348–352. https://doi.org/10.1001/journalofethics.2015.17.4.msoc1-1504

Autism Speaks. (2021). Retrieved from www.autismspeaks.org/what-are-symptoms-autism

Bakker, A. B., & Demerouti, E. (2017). Job demands-resources theory: Taking stock and looking forward. *Journal of Occupational Health Psychology, 22*(3), 273–285.

Colella, A., Hebl, M., & King, E. (2017). One hundred years of discrimination research in the Journal of Applied Psychology: A sobering synopsis. *Journal of Applied Psychology, 102*(3), 500–513.

Colella, A. & Santuzzi, A. (in press). Known and unknown mental illness: Uncovering the multiple routes to workplace inequities. *Journal of Management*.

Condo, C. (2020, March 3). 'You don't look autistic': The reality of high-functioning autism. *The Washington Post*. Retrieved from www.washingtonpost.com/lifestyle/2020/03/03/you-dont-look-autistic-reality-high-functioning-autism/

Doyle, N. (2020). Neurodiversity at work: A biopsychosocial model and the impact on working adults. *British Medical Bulletin, 135*(1), 108.

Eagly, A. H., & Karau, S. J. (2002). Role congruity theory of prejudice toward female leaders. *Psychological Review, 109*(3), 573.

Earley, P. C., & Mosakowski, E. (2004). Cultural intelligence. *Harvard Business Review, 82*(10), 139–146.

Emens, E. F. (2005). The sympathetic discriminator: Mental illness, hedonic costs, and the ADA. *The Georgetown Law Journal, 94*(2), 399–487.

Erickson, W. (personal communication, May 20, 2021, based on analysis of 2018 American Community Survey (ACS) Public Use Microdata Sample (PUMS) data).

Fisher, W. W., Piazza, C. C., & Roane, H. S. (Eds.). (2013). *Handbook of applied behavior analysis*. New York: Guilford Press.

Goldsmith, S. (2007). *Universal design*. Abingdon: Routledge.

Grant, D. (2009). The psychological assessment of neurodiversity. In D. Pollak (Ed.), *Neurodiversity in higher education* (pp. 33–62). Hoboken, NJ: Wiley-Blackwell.

Honeybourne, V. (2020). *The neurodiverse workplace: An employer's guide to managing and working with neurodivergent employees, clients, and customers*. London: Jessica Kingsley Publishers.

Job Accommodation Network. (n.d.). Retrieved from https://askjan.org/disabilities/Autism-Spectrum.cfm?cssearch=3797654_1

Johnson, J. W. (2001). The relative importance of task and contextual performance dimensions to supervisor judgments of overall performance. *Journal of Applied Psychology, 86*(5), 984–996.

Kapp, S. K., Gillespie-Lynch, K., Sherman, L. E., & Hutman, T. (2013). Deficit, difference, or both? Autism and neurodiversity. *Developmental Psychology, 49*(1), 59.

Kaye, H. S. (2010, October). The impact of the 2007–09 recession on workers with disabilities. *Monthly Labor Review*, pp. 19–30. Retrieved from www.bls.gov/opub/mlr/2010/10/art2full.pdf

Kruse, D., & Schur, L. (2003). Employment of people with disabilities following the ADA. *Industrial Relations, 42*(1), 31–66. https://doi.org/10.1111/1468-232X.00275

Krzeminska, A., Austin, R. D., Bruyère, S. M., & Hedley, D. (2019). The advantages and challenges of neurodiversity employment in organizations. *Journal of Management & Organization, 25*(4), 453–463.

Lashbrook, A. (2021, July 25). I struggled with office life. Now others are alive to benefits of remote working. *The Guardian*. Retrieved from www.theguardian.com/world/2021/jul/25/working-from-home-mental-health

Livermore, G. A., & Honeycutt, T. C. (2015). Employment and economic well-being of people with and without disabilities before and after the great recession. *Journal of Disability Policy Studies, 26*(2), 70–79. http://doi.org/10.1177/1044207315583875

Longmire, N. H., Vogus, T. A., & Colella, A. (2021, August). *Causes and consequences of experiencing relational misfit at work*. Presented virtually at the Annual Meeting of the Academy of Management.

McAlpine, D. D., & Alang, S. M. (2021). Employment and economic outcomes of persons with mental illness and disability: The impact of the great recession in the United States. *Psychiatric Rehabilitation Journal, 44*(2), 132–141. https://doi.org/10.1037/prj0000458

Mcguire, J. M., Scott, S. S., & Shaw, S. F. (2006). Universal design and its applications in educational environments. *Remedial and Special Education, 27*(3), 166–175.

Mellifont, D. (2019). Neuro magnifico! An exploratory study critically reviewing news text reporting of anxiety-related work performance strengths, challenges and support measures. *Work, 63*, 435–446. https://doi.org/10.3233/WOR-192950

Minecraft. (2021, October 1). How Microsoft is making hiring more inclusive with Minecraft. Minecraft Education Edition. Retrieved from https://education.minecraft.net/en-us/blog/inclusive-hiring-programs-minecraft

Molko, R. (2021, June 25). How race and ethnicity affect diagnosis, treatment and support for Autistic children and adults. Forbes. Retrieved from www.forbes.com/sites/forbesbooksauthors/2020/06/25/how-race-and-ethnicity-affect-diagnosis-treatment-and-support-for-autistic-children-and-adults/?sh=2bf079ce7f8b

O'Reilly, M., Karim, K., & Lester, J. N. (2015). Should autism be classified as a mental illness/disability? Evidence from empirical work. In *The Palgrave handbook of child mental health* (pp. 252–271). London: Palgrave Macmillan.

Patton, E. (2019). Autism, attributions and accommodations: Overcoming barriers and integrating a neurodiverse workforce. *Personnel Review, 48*, 915–934. https://doi.org/10.1108/PR-04-2018-0116

Rickerson, N. (2009). Universal design. In I. Soderback (Ed.), *International handbook of occupational therapy*. Springer.

Roberson, Q., Ryan, A. M., & Ragins, B. R. (2017). The evolution and future of diversity at work. *Journal of Applied Psychology, 102*(3), 483–499.

Rothstein, A. (2012). Mental disorder or neurodiversity? *The New Atlantis, 36*, 99–115.

Salovey, P., & Mayer, J. D. (1990). Emotional intelligence. *Imagination, Cognition and Personality, 9*(3), 185–211.

Samuel, A. (2021, March 8). Vast new possibilities open for Autistic people. *The Wall Street Journal*. Retrieved from www.wsj.com/articles/as-remote-work-becomes-the-norm-vast-new-possibilities-open-for-people-with-autism-11615222804

Schaufeli, W. B., & Taris, T. W. (2014). A critical review of the Job Demands-Resources Model: Implications for improving work and health. In G. Bauer & O. Hämmig (Eds.), Bridging occupational, organizational and public health (pp. 43–68). Dordrecht, the Netherlands: Springer. http://dx.doi.org/10.1007/978-94-007-5640-3_4

Sheldon, A. (2009). Recession, radicalism and the road to recovery? *Disability & Society, 24*(5), 667–671. https://doi.org/10.1080/09687590903011139

Skuse, D. (May 9, 2018). *Few people mourn Asperger syndrome's loss from diagnostic manuals*. Retrieved from https://www.spectrumnews.org/

Singer, J. (1999). Why can't you be normal for once in your life? From a problem with no name to the emergence of a new category of difference. In M. Corker & S. French (Eds.), *Disability discourse* (pp. 59–67). Buckingham, UK: Open University Press.

Smith, A. (2020, August 29). A million people with disabilities have lost jobs during the pandemic. *SHRM Employment Law*. Retrieved from www.shrm.org/resourcesandtools/legal-and-compliance/employment-law/pages/coronavirus-unemployment-people-with-disabilities.aspx

Srivastava, A. P., & Shree, S. (2019). A review of extra role behavior as an organizational asset. *SAMVAD, 18*, 39–46.

Triandis, H. C. (2006). Cultural intelligence in organizations. *Group & Organization Management, 31*(1), 20–26.

Van Scotter, J., Motowidlo, S. J., & Cross, T. C. (2000). Effects of task performance and contextual performance on systemic rewards. *Journal of Applied Psychology, 85*(4), 526–535.

Wingate, M., Mulvihill, B., Kirby, R. S., Pettygrove, S., Cunniff, C., Meaney, F., . . . Yeargin-Allsopp, M. A. (2012). Prevalence of autism spectrum disorders – autism and developmental disabilities monitoring network, 14 sites, United States, 2008. *MMWR Surveillance Summary, 61*(3), 1–19.

Wood, C., & Freeth, M. (2016). Students' stereotypes of autism. *Journal of Educational Issues, 2*(2), 131–140.

INDEX

Note: Page numbers in **bold** indicate a table on the corresponding page.